CREAM

The World's First Supergroup

CREAM

The World's First Supergroup

by Dave Thompson

First published in Great Britain in 2005 by
Virgin Books Ltd
Thames Wharf Studios
Rainville Road
London
W6 9HA

ISBN 1 85227 286 4

Typeset by Phoenix Photosetting, Chatham, Kent
Printed and bound in Great Britain by C.P.D. Wales

CONTENTS

Introduction   1
Further Reading   9

1. Beginnings: The Devil Came from Richmond   11
2. A Solid Bond in The Blues   23
3. Five Live Yardbirds   33
4. The Organiser   47
5. The Blues and Those Who Broke Them   59
6. And They Shall Be Called . . .   69
7. . . . The Cream   85
8. How Does a Hat Stand Feel?   95
9. A Spoonful of Wrapping Paper   107
10. Muddy Waters on Mars   119
11. The Sunshine of Your Blues   129
12. Music in The Fifth Dimension   139
13. My Aunt Jemima's Christening Dress   147
14. Hey, Hey, We're The Creamies   165
15. The Most Incredible Performing Band I've Ever Seen 173
16. All Hail The Blues Messiahs   185
17. Seven Minutes to Midnight   197
18. The Elephants Are Dancing   211
19. Fare Thee Well   223

Epilogue Buried by the Machine   237
Appendix Where Next, Young Man?   242
Discography   259
Index   273

INTRODUCTION

'I said all along that, if England won the World Cup, we'd be alright. They did and we will be.'

Ginger Baker, autumn 1966

On 30 July 1966, a packed Wembley Stadium watched in wonder as eleven men, representing the best of English football, swept to a 4–2 victory in the World Cup final. Almost exactly 24 hours later, a somewhat smaller but no less enthralled audience gathered on the other side of the city, in Windsor, to witness a coronation of no less significance, as three men representing the best of British rock music took the stage for their official public debut, and were carried to a glory of their own.

It was, the trio admitted afterwards, a fraught occasion. Unlike the Wembley battle, there were no dramatic last-minute equalisers, exhausting slabs of extra time, or hotly disputed third goals to contend with. But there was plenty of cause for concern regardless, as the musicians took the stage with more nerves than songs and, though they were convinced that their music was worth playing, they really didn't know whether anyone wanted to listen.

Only when it was all over, and their 45-minute set was answered by the loudest roar of the afternoon . . . as loud as that which greeted the final whistle at Wembley the previous day . . . could they finally relax and enjoy what they'd wrought, absorb all the plaudits that now fell like rain, and revel in the knowledge that the sum of their endeavours was truly the equal of its parts: the country's greatest guitar player, Eric Clapton; its most brilliant bassist, Jack Bruce; and its finest drummer, Ginger Baker; together in the best band the world had ever seen. They were called the Cream, and so richly did they deserve that name that, within days, the definitive article had been dropped from their name. Now they were simply Cream.

Nigh on forty years removed, they still are. So much water has passed beneath the rock'n'roll bridge since then; so many other bands that have, for however long, grasped the mantle that was Cream's by default. But still Clapton, Bruce and Baker – like Charlton, Banks and Hurst (et al.) – remain the yardstick by which true brilliance is measured; still they occupy the loftiest peaks in any sensibly surveyed 'best-ever' line-up.

There are, should one choose to pursue them, other parallels between the Kings of Football who were crowned in July 1966, and the Rulers of Rock who were elevated alongside them. Like the footballers, the three members of Cream have never shaken off the memories of the events that were ignited by that summer; like the footballers, their deeds were so heroic that they now border on the mythological; and, like the footballers, their reign was cut brutally short.

For England, the title of World Champions was snatched away on a sweltering Mexican afternoon in June 1970, when the West German side they'd defeated four summers earlier exacted the best possible revenge in the World Cup quarter-final. For Cream, their own throne was lost a full two years earlier, with the news that they were to break up. And that was the difference. England had their status taken from them. Cream voluntarily abdicated theirs, stepping away at the brilliantine peak of their all-conquering success, with the tacit acknowledgement that such success was never a part of their plan. They formed a band, it became a circus; they dreamed of freedom, they were enslaved by routine; they hoped they'd be liked, they wound up being worshipped. And somewhere in the midst of all that, the music simply got lost.

There was one night from the memory of which Jack Bruce still recoils, the evening when they walked on stage into a hail of deafening feedback. The audience was still applauding as the band began their first number, each of them lost in wonder. How could they ever follow *that*?

How indeed.

Rock'n'roll supergroups had always existed on paper, and a handful of combos even stepped beyond that. What was the so-called Million Dollar Quartet, the ad hoc studio jam that linked the youthful Elvis Presley, Jerry Lee Lewis, Johnny Cash and Carl Perkins at Sun Studios, if not a supergroup – albeit one whose true 'superbness' had yet to be recognised by the world outside? Or the legendary jams in the jazz clubs of London, where passing musicians simply dropped by to play, and Alexis Korner's Blues Incorporated became the breeding ground for an entire generation of fervent young British blues acolytes? Or the mix'n'match studio jam sessions that the young Jimmy Page convened, as he was cutting his teeth in the mid-60s' studio?

All were supergroups in the true meaning of the word, but none were more than passing fancies, brought together as much by chance and happenstance as any deliberate notions. Cream were different. The three players knew their abilities, and knew their reputations; they knew, therefore, precisely what their union portended. Or, at least, they thought they did.

Three momentous talents, three momentous egos, and three musicians who rarely saw eye-to-eye on anything could never have existed in the same room for long; and, listening to the words of both the players and their pals, it sometimes seems astonishing that Cream survived for as long as they did; that they didn't simply self-destruct at the first opportunity they had. In the end, Jack Bruce said, the band existed for as long as it needed to.

'We did what we set out to do, and I don't think we could have done any more,' he reflected in 2004. 'I think it lasted just the right amount of time to make the little statement it did.' In fact, rumours that Cream were to disband were common currency long before the band members themselves acceded to the inevitable, and all three members have also admitted that, though Cream survived, it was not necessarily because they wanted to, or even needed to.

They survived because it was easier to do so, because the alternative was even more uncertain than the reality, and because management – as aware as anybody else of the tensions and struggles that comprised the band – made sure of it, keeping the group so busy that there was barely time for a shit and a shave, let alone a reflective exploration of the Story So Far. That became history's task: to dissect all that went into the creation of Cream; and all that went into its destruction as well.

Many bands are credited with 'kicking down the doors' through which others subsequently waltzed, igniting through circumstance a need within an audience that others then filled deliberately. The Beatles 'kicked down the doors' that let the Beat Boom into the room; Marc Bolan 'kicked down the doors' that released the hordes of Glam Rock; Suede 'kicked down the doors' to allow Brit Pop to flourish. Cream, however, did not kick down any doors. They built the doorway in the first place.

Little of what Cream actually accomplished was entirely without precedent. It was the manner in which they accomplished it that mattered: the ease with which the smallest possible combination of instruments mutated into the largest possible sound; the stealth with which they crept from unknowns at the foot of a New York bill to become the biggest concert draw in America; and the manner in which they totally realigned an entire generation's listening habits, luring them away from the structure and songs of the past, into a world of free-form improvisation wherein even a drum solo became a potential hit record.

Before Cream, Procol Harum's Gary Brooker once marvelled, 'nobody would have sat down and listened ten minutes to a guitar solo. Nobody would even have *thought* of playing one.' Now Clapton was unleashing at least one every set, and the bass and drums were not far behind.

Other bands – the Beatles, Dylan, Hendrix, the Airplane – pushed the concept of the song into new limitless arenas. Cream pushed the concept of the *musician* just as far, and then kept on pushing, until only the realisation that they'd travelled too far for even the most sophisticated audience harshly dragged them back to earth. The hordes that offered an ovation to the feedback was not applauding out of ignorance. It was applauding out of awe, and the belief that anything that the three gods before them enacted on stage was a piece of immaculate genius.

Of course it wasn't. As Jack Bruce once said, 'sometimes we played like crap. And we still got an encore.' But what audiences demanded, musicians had to provide, and the ensuing decade's worth of increasingly (over-) ambitious virtuosity that poured out of the Heavy Metal and Progressive Rock marketplaces not only learned their life's lessons at Cream's knee, they were happy to admit it. When Led Zeppelin signed to Atlantic Records, Robert Plant declared it was an honour to sign to the same label as Cream.

Cream cannot be blamed for all the musical indignities that would be wrought in their memory, for all the nights an audience sat through a twenty-minute solo by a drummer who could barely keep time, or a bowel-baking showcase by a bassist with less soul than strings. Cream encouraged virtuosity because they were virtuosos. Most of those that followed their example simply *hoped* they were.

And besides, to dwell upon all that Cream created for the future is to overlook all that they accomplished throughout their lifetime, and that is the purpose of this book, to trace the mercurial months in which Cream played together as they unfolded *at the time*, as opposed to the lashings of hindsight that have flavoured other accounts.

Hindsight, of course, can offer fresh insights, but it can also steer the historian very much in the wrong direction. No musician is blessed with second sight, few have unerring powers of prophecy, and, while we can look back now and hypothesise how, say, a broken string in 1967 might be umbilically linked to a broken heart in 1993, at the time it was simply a broken string.

Similarly, one might seize upon Eric Clapton's explanation for Jimi Hendrix's success in Britain ('everybody . . . thinks spades have big dicks'), and draw a straight line to remarks he made eight years later, inciting his audience to vote for Enoch Powell – the right-wing politician whose platform on race relations many believe was the source for so much suffering in the 70s.

But to condemn the common vernacular of one time as a blood relative to the drunken venom of another is to perform a gross disservice, not only to Clapton and to history, but also to the reader. It is the writer's duty to tell the story; it is the reader's right to draw his or her own conclusions, without being steered into what might well be the shark-strewn waters of conjecture and assumption. The thinker alone knows what he is thinking. Everyone else is merely guessing and, most times, they guess wrong.

Of course, some revisionism is inevitable. Any interview or conversation conducted once an event has been consigned to memory is certain to distort the details to some extent, and the more years that have elapsed since the moment in question, the more pronounced that distortion will be. Similarly, the simple repetition of the same tales – for, in Cream's case, we are talking of little more than a two-year span, experienced close to four decades ago – can easily lead to forgetfulness and muddle.

Early on in my own researches, I received a charming email from one potential interviewee, turning down my request with the plaintive confession that 'the only new stories I could tell you would be ones I've just made up' before documenting the appearance, backstage at a London pub, of the glamorous Siamese triplets (*triplets*!) who wanted to bed the entire band at once. 'But I'm afraid you can't use that because I just invented it.'

Even those people who were willing to talk at length cautioned, 'it was all a very long time ago', and it was surprising (or maybe not) how frequently, as I checked their recollections against the press of the day, 'key' events in their own lives were skewed by the passing of time – and how often a return call to recheck some simple fact elicited another tale entirely.

I quickly learned not to take such things personally. Other books bear the same misremembrances (to pick upon one of the most egregious, the long-held belief that Cream's management was responsible for the band not appearing at the Monterey Pop Festival – it wasn't); others perpetrate the same distortions. Musicians would not be human if they didn't have flawed memories, but this book would not have been worth writing if it didn't attempt to correct them, by returning to the day in question and allowing the future to unfold as it wished.

No band exists in a vacuum, not even one that formed to fill one; and, while history is often content to allow Cream's story to zip off into a stratosphere of its own, the actions and reactions of the artists they themselves describe as their contemporaries – the Jimi Hendrix Experience, the Jeff Beck Group and the Who in particular – could not fail to impact upon both Cream's music and their accomplishments, particularly during the group's first year of life, as they ground around the UK concert circuit. The ultimately baleful influence of Bob Dylan and the Band, too, indicated the extent to which Cream were affected by outside forces, and so each of those performers took their own vital station in the unfolding story.

Crucial, too, were the opposing worlds into which Cream found themselves flung as their career progressed: the greasy spoonfed grind of their life on the road in mid-60s Britain; the psychedelic fog of Swinging London '67; the reactionary brutality of America '68. Cream's swing across the college campuses of the United States through the first half of that latter year exposed them to a world of seething discontent and rebellion that, itself, could not help but flare responses within the band members. The volatility that was intrinsic to Cream's own make-up found any number of flashpoints as it travelled that circuit.

Within those parameters, loose though they are, the story of Cream unfolds not as the genesis and revelation of some Biblical superpower, but as the life and death of a group that placed itself precisely upon the dividing line of two very separate universes: the isolated Britain that the members knew as they served their apprenticeship on the blues and jazz circuit of the early-mid 1960s, and the global market into which the end of the decade poured its rock heroes.

From the Moist Hoist to Madison Square, from the Blue Boar to Berkeley, the last of the 60s beat groups were also the first of the 70s rock monsters, and the only people who seemed unaware of that fact were Cream themselves. They could have conquered the planet. Instead, they left it for others.

Yet what could be a sad story, or at least an extraordinarily salutary one, nevertheless remains one of the most glorious interludes in rock history, a parallel to the famous tale of *The Little Engine That Could*. 'When we first started,' Jack Bruce has admitted, 'we didn't know if anybody would like us.' Almost forty years on, it is difficult to find many people who don't, with Cream's reputation now vast enough that, even today, the emergence of a new rock trio will instantly bring comparisons to one of the oldest of them all; and so all-pervading that, if one were to excise Cream's lifetime from the historical record, the ramifications would be heard (or, rather, *not* heard) across the entire musical spectrum.

From Miles Davis (*Bitch's Brew* was cut firmly in the thrall of Cream) to Rory Gallagher (the three-piece Taste was conceived in deliberate emulation); from Led Zeppelin, who stepped directly into Cream's concert-cramming shoes, to every young percussionist who was sent on his path by the extravagance of 'Toad', Cream's impact is as profound as it is, seemingly, permanent.

Their music has sold cars and computers; has bolstered modern movie soundtracks and nostalgic compilation albums. Their songs have launched entire careers – when Ian Mitchell left the Bay City Rollers in 1976, his first act was to record a cover of 'Sunshine of Your Love'; when Hugh Cornwell stepped out of the Stranglers for a solo moment, his first single was a version of 'White Room'.

'I Feel Free' has drawn covers from as far afield as Belinda Carlisle and David Bowie; 'Badge' by Fanny and the Jeff Healey Band; and even Cream's cast-offs have a life of their own. 'Theme From an Imaginary Western', a song that the group themselves never took past Jack Bruce's demo stage, was covered by Mountain and Colosseum, while the blues that they resuscitated as part of their early live set were promptly reborn as staples of the age.

The late Mick Ronson recalled covering Willie Dixon's 'Spoonful' with his 60s band The Rats, 'because we were all such huge fans of Cream' (it was Ronson that prompted Bowie to start playing 'I Feel Free' as well), while the fledgling Jethro Tull cut 'Cat's Squirrel' in devoted tribute to Cream's first B-side. Neither was Cream's reputation the only beneficiary of such attention. Shortly after the death of bluesman Skip James, all three band members received letters from his widow informing them that royalties from their recording of his 'I'm So Glad' both paid for his medical treatment through the last years of his life, and covered the cost of his funeral, too.

That – all of that – is the legacy of Cream; is the fruit of the music they created across the 27 months, four LPs and the 300-or-so gigs that they played together, an entire career fitted into less time than a modern band makes its fans wait for a new album. Everything else, the doors that they opened, the future iniquities that they unwittingly ignited, the entire circus of gross exaggeration that rock became in the decade that followed, is an irrelevance at best, an irritant at worst. Cream may have curdled at the end. But their milkshakes were delicious, and now is the time to thank everybody who shared them with me.

For interviews and conversations conducted in person, by phone or, latterly, via email over the course of the past decade and more, all awaiting the day when they could fall into this framework, my thanks to Jack Bruce, Ginger Baker, Jeff Beck, John Mayall, Dick Heckstall-Smith, Tony Palmer, Jim McCarty, Peter Green, Peter Frampton, John Entwistle, Noel Redding, Long John Baldry, Mike Vernon, Mick Farren, Dave Walker, Bill Levenson, Dave Brock, Doug Yule, Kathy Etchingham, Danny Adler, John Fiddler, Tony Calder, Brian Auger, Graham Gouldman, Pete York, Bernie Tormé, Chas Chandler, Tony Secunda, Ivan Kral and Alan Merrill, together with everybody who agreed to speak with me, but asked that they not be identified ... as one helpful soul so modestly put it, 'really, who wants to hear me rehashing my misspent youth one more time?'

Grateful acknowledgements also go out to Stuart Slater and all at Virgin Books, my agent Sherrill Chidiac; to Amy Hanson, Jo-Ann Greene, John Donovan, Veronique Cordier, Mary-Lu Farrell, Dave Makin, Steve Peasant, Jorgen Angel, Kevin Michaels, Holm Kogel, Brian Paige, Wayne, Cathy and Greg at *Goldmine* magazine and, finally, everybody else who helped bring the beast to life: Anchorite Man, Bateerz and family, Blind Pew, Mrs B East, Ella and Sprocket, Gaye and Tim, Gef the Talking Mongoose, the Gremlins who live in the furnace, K-Mart and Snarleyyowl, Geoff Monmouth, Naughty Miranda, Nutkin, Pointy Ghost Face, Sonny, a lot of Thompsons and Neville Viking.

FURTHER READING

My own researches were largely spent within the yellowing remains of period music papers: *Melody Maker, New Musical Express, Disc & Music Echo, Rolling Stone, Hit Parader* and *Crawdaddy*, surfacing occasionally to seek out clarification from such modern-day bibles as *Goldmine, Mojo, Uncut, Classic Rock* and *Record Collector*. These archives, whether begged, borrowed or buried in my basement, proved priceless as I wove between memories and the actual moments.

From the realms of more contemporary writings on the subject of Cream and its components, Chris Welch's *Cream: The Legendary Sixties Supergroup* (Miller Freeman Books revised edition, 2000), Dick Heckstall-Smith & Peter Grant's *The Safest Place in the World – Blowing the Blues* (Clear Books revised edition, 2004) and Ray Coleman's *Clapton! An Authorised Biography* (Warner Books, 1985) were especially valuable. I also found myself regularly referring to the following:

Bob Brunning: *Blues: The British Connection* (Helter Skelter revised edition, 2002)

Mark Cunningham: *Good Vibrations: A History of Record Production* (Sanctuary revised edition, 1998)

Bill Graham & Robert Greenfield: *Bill Graham Presents* (Doubleday, 1992)

Andy Neill & Matt Kent: *Anyway Anyhow Anywhere: The Complete Chronicle of the Who* (Friedman & Fairfax, 2002)

Don Paulsen: *Cream – First US Tour* (interview CD) (Acadia Records, 2004)

John Pidgeon: *Eric Clapton: A Biography* (Vermillion revised edition, 1985)

John Platt, Chris Dreja & Jim McCarty: *Yardbirds* (Sidgwick & Jackson, 1983)

John Platt: *Classic Rock Albums: Disraeli Gears* (Schirmer Books, 1998)

Noel Redding & Carol Appleby: *Are You Experienced?* (Da Capo, 1996)

Marc Roberty: *Eric Clapton: The Complete Recording Sessions* (Blandford Press, 1993)

Greg Russo: *The Five Phases of Manfred Mann* (Crossfire Publications, 1995)

Greg Russo: *Yardbirds: The Ultimate Rave-Up* (Crossfire Publications, 1997)

Michael Schumacher: *Crossroads: The Life & Music of Eric Clapton* (Hyperion, 1995)

Harry Shapiro: *Alexis Korner: The Biography* (Bloomsbury, 1996)

Harry Shapiro: *Graham Bond: The Mighty Shadow* (Guinness Publishing, 1992)

Harry Shapiro & Caesar Glebbeek: *Hendrix: Electric Gypsy* (St Martin's Press, 1995)

Jeff Tamarkin: *Got a Revolution: The Turbulent Flight of Jefferson Airplane* (Atria, 2003)

Leslie West & Corky Laing: *Nantucket Sleighride* (SAF, 2003)

Numerous reference books detail different aspects of Cream's career. Those consulted most frequently include: *Rock Family Trees* by Pete Frame (Omnibus Books, various editions); *The Great Rock ... and Psychedelic Discography* by Martin Strong (Canongate Books, various editions); *Guinness Book of British Hit Singles ... Albums* (Guinness World Records, various editions); *Top Pop Singles ... Albums* by Joel Whitburn (Record Research, various editions); *In Session Tonight* by Ken Garner (BBC Books, 1992); *The Top 20 Book* by Tony Jasper (Blandford Books, various editions).

1. BEGINNINGS: THE DEVIL CAME FROM RICHMOND

The British blues scene of the late 1950s and early 1960s, the years before the Stones, the Yardbirds and the rest of that gang came pumping through, was fierce, dedicated, and ruthlessly self-contained.

It was a world in which fans patiently queued all night outside a handful of specialist record stores, to be first to get their hands on the latest American import.

It was one in which a young Tom McGuinness once walked three miles to catch a glimpse of a John Lee Hooker album cover. He didn't know the record's owner, and he didn't hear the record. 'I knocked on his door and said I hear you've got . . . and he brought it to his door to show me.'

And it was a place where friendships, families and, indeed, entire lifetimes hinged upon the chance meeting of two like-minded youths, drawn to one another because one happened to be walking past clutching the latest Muddy Waters album – Mick Jagger and Keith Richard connected on the train between London Bridge and Dartford, when one saw the records that the other was cradling.

The first bands developed along similar lines, devotees getting together to play – not extemporise, not ad lib and certainly not improvise around – the music they loved, as Sidcup Art College student Phil May asserted, nearly forty years on. 'People didn't have big record collections. . . big R&B record collections. You'd have a handful of albums and a few reel-to-reel tapes; someone else would have a handful more. The trick was never to buy a record that someone else had, because it wasn't about owning as many different records as you could, it was about *hearing* as many. So these records and tapes would just be passed around and, if you wanted to hear something that someone else had, but they weren't sitting in the room with you with the record, you tried to play it yourself, as close as you could get to the original.'

At first, these human jukeboxes simply performed for themselves. Then a few friends dropped by, to play along or listen. They'd bring other friends. Soon, college common rooms and inner-city bedsits alike were transforming into impromptu concert halls, as the best musicians in the area came together to play their best approximations of the music they loved, while others sat around to listen, applaud and comment.

Few of these players called themselves 'groups'; few went on to form one. Even after the audiences expanded beyond the confines of those earliest gatherings, and local pubs began staging blues nights, even those musicians who went on to greater things – McGuinness with Manfred Mann, Jagger and Richard with the Stones, May amid the Pretty Things – were little more than half-familiar faces within a vast floating aggregation that faded in and out of focus as the demands of their day-to-day life required.

There were, however, a handful of players for whom the blues did represent a viable musical direction. And to them fell the onerous duty of educating the world.

A panel-beater by day, but a walking encyclopaedia of blues by vocation, harmonica wizard Cyril Davies and guitarist Alexis Korner both drifted out of the jazz scene that was then the beating heart of the British underground, expanding other combos' token dips into sundry blues catalogues until they filled an entire set.

Back in 1949, guitarist Korner himself was a near-founder member of the legendary Chris Barber's Jazz Band. But, as early as 1953, he and Davies were playing in a blues duo together; and, when Korner rejoined Barber in 1956, Davies accompanied him, developing a blues routine in the midst of Barber's more traditional outfit.

The following year, the pair opened their own club, the Blues and Barrelhouse, in the Roundhouse pub on London's Wardour Street. 'It started as a folky club,' singer Long John Baldry remembered. 'Cyril played twelve-string guitar in those days, but he and Alexis used to bring in a lot of guest artists, including a huge number of bluesmen: Speckled Red, Roosevelt Sykes, Champion Jack Dupree, people like that. Muddy Waters was there in 1958, with Otis Spann.'

By the end of the decade, Korner was hosting his own blues programme on the BBC World Service and, in early 1962, emboldened by the ever-growing success of the Barrelhouse, he and Davies quit Barber's unit to form a group of their own, Blues

Incorporated. Built loosely around a shifting clutch of Barrelhouse regulars, the new act debuted on 17 March 1962, in the basement beneath the ABC tearoom on Ealing Broadway, a drinking dive by day, a jazz club by night.

In terms of hygiene, it was a sordid pit. The condensation that oozed from every available surface had long since seen the venue nicknamed the Moist Hoist. But, while the conditions never changed, the club's name did. As Blues Incorporated drew ever-larger crowds to their regular performances, the Moist Hoist became the Ealing R&B Club, the pulsating heart of the blues revolution that the musicians were set to ignite.

That opening evening, Blues Incorporated included Korner and Davies, guitarist Art Wood (brother of future Rolling Stone Ronnie) and drummer Charlie Watts, vocalist Keith Scott and stand-up bassist Andy Hoogenboom. As time passed, however, Blues Incorporated accepted into its ranks any number of would-be suburban bluesmen. Baldry, who was as close to being a regular as any preternaturally tall sixteen-year-old could be, continued, 'this was the period when Paul Jones, Mick Jagger, John McLaughlin, Big Jim Sullivan, Spike Heatley, Dick Heckstall-Smith, everybody was just passing through the band.'

Blues Incorporated's reputation started to grow and, with it, their workload. And with that came an audience. Articles began appearing in both the regular music press and the specialist jazz papers, detailing the Korner group's almost obsessive urge to get the blues right and, slowly, acolytes emerged from the darkest corners of suburbia-and-beyond to check it out. Eric Burdon hitchhiked down from Newcastle, just to breathe the Ealing Club air, Lewis 'Brian' Hopkin-Jones was lured to London from his home town of Cheltenham by the allure of Blues Incorporated, while his travelling companion, Paul Jones (no relation) recalled 'meeting people from all over Britain at the Ealing Club', all drawn to the Big Bang that reshaped their entire universe.

When Blues Incorporated first came together, they played just one gig a week, at the Ealing Club. In early May, they took on a second, at the Marquee Club, a jazz-blues haunt on the corner of Oxford Street and Poland Street. And, though their initial appearance drew a curious audience of just 127 people, still it was the launch pad for a Thursday night residency that is now as legendary as the band itself.

The group's renown was not slow in percolating elsewhere into the music industry. Korner was already recording regularly at this point, for a succession of specialist blues, jazz and folk labels. Now he was leading Blues Incorporated, with Baldry, Heatley and Heckstall-Smith on board, into Decca's West Hampstead studios, not merely to record their own first album, but also to cut the first blues album ever made in Britain, the seminal *R&B From the*

Marquee. But, even as the group revelled in its new-found celebrity, even as the members awaited their album's release, Korner's relentless pursuit of perfection continued unabated. The line-up that cut the LP was great. But there were even greater players out there, and Korner wanted to play with them.

It was Dick Heckstall-Smith who stumbled upon the first piece of the jigsaw that Korner was envisioning. In early June, taking advantage of a rare night off from Blues Incorporated, the saxophonist agreed to put together a one-off line-up of jobbing jazzers, to entertain the oiks at a Cambridge University student May Ball. They were just approaching the conclusion of their first set when Heckstall-Smith espied 'this little bloke', as fresh-facedly youthful-looking as any of the watching students, make his way up to the stage – 'and, in a powerful Scottish accent, ask if he could play with us'.

Heckstall-Smith detailed the remainder of the encounter in his autobiography, *The Safest Place in the World*.

'"What do you play?" I asked.

'"Ah plee be-ass," he replied.'

Heckstall-Smith hesitated; the set was almost over and, besides, he knew what his drummer, Peter Baker – known as Ginger, for his blazing red hair – thought about unannounced sit-ins. But the newcomer was persistent and Heckstall-Smith was at least impressed by that. The group's next set was taking place in a cellar elsewhere in town, later in the evening, and he invited the lad along, merely reminding him to bring his own instrument. 'And lo!' Heckstall-Smith reported, just a few numbers into the second show, the top end of a stand-up bass could be seen bobbing through the revellers and heading determinedly stagewards. 'Ginger and I exchanged a look. Tactic 17b was indicated.'

In the world of late 50s jazzers, unwritten (and, in truth, unnumbered) contingency plans existed for every kind of situation. Tactic 17b, in this case, involved frightening away the interloper by unveiling the most complicated number in the team's entire repertoire, and demanding he play along with it. 'Twelve bar in beef,' announced Heckstall-Smith, and he counted in 'Blue'n'Boogie', an already frenetic number that tonight raced past at supersonic speed. 'And, holy shit, the little guy stormed into it like there was no tomorrow. It was demonic.'

Unable to believe what he'd witnessed, and with Baker's mouth, too, hanging open in amazement, Heckstall-Smith introduced a second number, 'Lover Man'. 'And you,' he instructed the stranger, 'play the tune. And by God he did. Beautifully, faultlessly, vibrato, in tune, the lot.'

As they came off stage, the stranger introduced himself: Jack Bruce. Heckstall-Smith wrote the name down, and took his phone number as well. Days after, he dialled it, to invite the lad down to meet Blues Incorporated at the Ealing Club on Sunday. One swinging jam session later, Bruce was asked to join the group full time. Much to his own surprise, he agreed.

'I didn't know anything about blues really, at that time,' Bruce has since confessed. 'It sounded to me like rock'n'roll' – and his career, such as it was, had thus far studiously avoided any hint of that particular diabolical beat. Born in Bishopbriggs, near Glasgow, on 14 May 1943, John Simon Asher 'Jack' Bruce's earliest musical training was in piano and singing – a fine soprano soloist, he was a regular competitor in music competitions around Scotland and, joining his parents in their travels around the US and Canada, abroad as well.

'My home was very musical. My mother sang Scottish folk songs and my father was a huge traditional-jazz fan of people like Fats Waller and Louis Armstrong. But my older brother loved modern jazz. There'd be, literally, physical fights in my house between my father and brother, arguing about the role of the saxophone in jazz or something, real punch-ups. Music is a valid part of my background. I didn't adopt music, music adopted me.'

Bruce's early gifts were amplified when he won a scholarship to the Royal Scottish Academy of Music in 1960, to study cello and composition. It was not an altogether joyous experience. Music, he was convinced, was not a discipline that one could be taught. Either you felt it or you didn't, and – if you did feel it – then your own soul alone knew the directions you should take. 'I really feel strongly that they teach the wrong things,' he condemned. 'They teach everybody the same things, regardless of what their individual capabilities are. They don't seem to take the trouble to find out people's individual characteristics.'

One day, when he was fourteen or so, Bruce handed a teacher a self-composed cello concerto he'd just completed. She handed it back smothered in red ink corrections, accompanied by a terse note informing him that he couldn't write music, and he shouldn't waste his time trying. 'It took me about a year to get over that,' he reflected – and most of the 1960s to get over the rest of his schooling.

He quit the Academy, then abandoned the cello. 'The first thing that really gathered me up was Bach, because ... believe it or not ... he was the guv'nor of all bass players.' Acquiring his own first stand-up bass, Bruce knew exactly where his future lay.

Every week, he picked up the latest edition of *Melody Maker* and scoured the Musicians Wanted ads, desperate to take his next step – getting the hell out of Scotland. Finally, spring 1961 introduced him to his escape route, taking the train down to Coventry to meet the showmen of the Murray Campbell Big Band. Fellow Scots, Campbell and co. were bowled over by the youngster; no more than seventeen, he could sight-read music with the best of 'em, while his musical party piece, the Dizzy Gillespie Orchestra's 'One Bass Hit', was at least the equal of any older player's fanciest trick.

Life with the Big Band was to be a short-lived experience. The group's first booking was an Italian tour, clad in kilts and playing up their Scottishness for all they were worth. But, as if that was not humiliating enough, one of the promoters then did a runner with the band's money, leaving the broke musicians stranded in Milan for a month and a half.

Back in London, and with another Italian jaunt (as roadie for a showband touring the American airbases) behind him, Bruce next found himself joining the Jim McHarg Scotsville Jazz Band as the replacement for the recently sacked McHarg.

The Scotsville Jazz Band was very much a part of the British trad-jazz boom, albeit one of the last flickering embers of a movement whose decade-long lifespan was now coming to an end. Long-accustomed to acting as a staging post for other musical flavours (the skiffle craze of five years before was derived wholly from banjo-player Lonnie Donegan's starring role within jazzman Chris Barber's band), trad had most recently been beset by the rising tide of dedicated bluesmen; most notably, Alexis Korner and Cyril Davies' departure from, again, Barber's group.

Unfortunately, those performers that maintained their jazz bearings while all around them turned to the blues were scarcely rewarded for their persistence. Audiences sagged, record sales declined, record contracts dried up. By the time Mr Acker Bilk scored one of the biggest British hit singles ever, with 'Stranger on the Shore' in January 1962, his clarinet might as well have been blowing the Last Post, so far as the trad scene was concerned, and Bruce knew it.

Still Bruce remained with the Scotsville Jazz Band, until spring brought that fateful encounter with Dick Heckstall-Smith and Blues Incorporated. He resigned from the jazz world immediately and, on 12 July 1962, Bruce found himself making his debut as a member of Blues Incorporated, when the group made its own debut appearance on BBC radio's *Jazz Club*.

It was an exhilarating turn of events for the bassist, although history remembers that same night for another event entirely. For the last couple of months, one Mike (as he liked to be called) Jagger was sitting in as a more-or-less regular vocalist with Blues Incorporated. But though he was enthusiastic, he was scarcely the most experienced frontman in Korner's arsenal and, for the group's own maiden journey into the bowels of the Beeb, it was experience that Korner preferred to bank on. Informing Jagger that his services were not required that evening, Korner instead called in Art Wood, prompting the jilted Jagger to decide, there and then, to throw his full attention into his own blues project, the newly named Rollin' Stones.

With drummer Charlie Watts and pianist Dave Stevens joining Korner, Davies, Bruce and Heckstall-Smith, the BBC session version of 'Hoochie Coochie Man' is the only recorded evidence of this particular incarnation of Blues Incorporated. Just weeks after that, Watts announced that he, too, was departing because he, alone of the Blues Incorporated gang, didn't want to turn professional; it was too insecure a lifestyle for a young, responsible, married man. Finally bowing out after another BBC date demanded that Korner bring along a paid-up Musicians Union member, as opposed to the proudly freelance Watts, the drummer followed Jagger into the still-part-time Rollin' Stones. Ginger Baker replaced him.

Fiery, irascible, temperamental, obnoxious ... Ginger Baker has been described as each of these things. He is a man who not only knows the value of the money in his pocket, he retains that value, so that decades removed, he can still recall, to the last penny, the injustice of a payment here, an unpaid debt there, a bar tab somewhere else.

He has also been called the greatest rock drummer there has ever been, a player whose abilities not only transcend the limitations of his instrument, they transcend its possibilities as well. Into the 1970s, when drum solos became *de rigueur* for any player who believed his kit had something to say (even if it was the thunder of diarrhoea) it became very fashionable to blame the influence of Baker's own percussive extravaganzas for every hammering indignity ever inflicted upon the attention spans of the average rock audience.

The difference was, when Baker solo-ed, you listened; not because you'd paid ten bob for your ticket and intended wringing every halfpenny's-worth of enjoyment out of it, but because you weren't listening to a mere drum solo. You were listening to a concerto, a symphony, a succession of sounds that were as melodic in their own way as anything any other player on the stage could muster; as thoughtful as any lyric, as lasting as any tune. 'There aren't many drummers who can do a drum solo and excite the audience,' Baker reasoned. 'When I do a solo, I'm very conscious of the audience. At some point or other the audience turn me on. Eventually the audience plays the drums through me. What the audience wants comes out.'

He was great, and he knew it. 'I haven't ever heard anybody who'd cause me any worry,' he only half-jested to *Beat Instrumental* magazine in 1972. 'The only time I did begin to worry was when I walked into a club and heard an album playing with a drummer who I thought was incredible. Then I found out it was me.'

Baker, like Bruce, cut his musical teeth in a trad act. Born in Lewisham, south London, on 19 August 1939, Baker was an untried eighteen-year-old, a juvenile racing bike champion, when he blagged his way into Bob Wallis's Storeyville Jazzmen, playing alongside Heckstall-Smith, and proving that some musicians don't need 'prior experience' before they start paying their way. Some are born with it, and need only to be pointed in the right direction. So it was with Baker, and Wallis knew it. Taking the youth under his wing, Wallis provided Baker with a second-to-none education in early jazz, an experience that not only shaped Baker's future career, it also provided him with his first musical role model, Baby Dobbs, drummer with Louis Armstrong's band. 'I fell in love with what he was playing. Baby Dobbs was the link between western military drum techniques and African drummers. He was the man who first successfully married the two. He was the first jazz drummer.'

Within a year, Baker had graduated to Terry Lightfoot's often-scintillating combo, infuriating his bandleader with his restless drive to try out fresh ideas. A new-found infatuation with be-bop drummer Max Roach saw Baker begin incorporating his style into the Lightfoot set, an act of musical insubordination that Lightfoot simply could not countenance. Finally, Lightfoot snapped, wheeling round and demanding Baker play four to the bar on the bass drum, 'and nothing else'. Baker's reply saw him thrown out of the band on the spot. 'You can stick your band up your arse.'

Baker moved on to a succession of other, generally lesser bands, but few of these gigs lasted long. Baker's talents were enormous; aside from being a prodigious player, he had taught himself to sight-read music, and even hand built his own drum kits. But he was also possessed of a volcanic temper and such firmly held musical ideas that almost all of his engagements ended with the order of the boot – including once, touring Europe with jazzman Dis Disley, when he was unceremoniously cast adrift, penniless and starving, in Germany.

Other groups evicted him because of the sheer, uncontainable noise he made – more than one exasperated bandmate turned and accused him of being a rock'n'roller in disguise, one of the direst insults that could be thrown at any jazz man, but such was Baker's musical reputation that he was seldom out of work for long. Though he was occasionally forced to make ends meet with a spot of manual labour, by 1960 Baker was gigging regularly with the Ken Oldham Showband, hanging out with jazz drummer Phil Seaman, and guesting across both the trad and the modern jazz spectrums.

Of all the drummers Baker admired or with whom he associated, Seaman (more precisely his presence) hung heavy over much of what he was destined to achieve, at least in the years prior to the formation of Cream, and the development of Baker's own unique and influential style of playing; famously, the drum pattern that he grafted onto the Graham Bond Organisation's 'Train Time' was based almost wholly on a drum exercise that Seaman taught him, while Baker's long-held love of African drumming and culture was another of Seaman's gifts to him. But Seaman also possessed a dark side, the life-long dalliances with alcohol and heroin that finally killed him in 1972.

By the time he linked up with Blues Incorporated, Baker was already regarded among the most troubled, and troublesome, characters on the entire circuit, but balanced that reputation with his undisputed status among the most brilliant drummers in the country. 'With the advent of Ginger, *the* classic Blues Incorporated line-up, one which I think could not be bettered, was set,' Heckstall-Smith reminisced, and Charlie Watts agreed with his summary. 'Ginger had this incredible sound and you could hear this thing that Jack and Ginger had between them. I didn't want to get in the way of that.' But the convolutions had not ended.

For weeks, the jazz press was speculating that Korner was preparing to broaden Blues Incorporated's horizons even further, by luring away the Don Rendell Jazz Band's brilliant young saxophonist/organist, the eighteen-stone gangster-faced Graham Bond. It was a move that Bruce, Baker and Heckstall-Smith were thoroughly in favour of; throughout the summer, all three had played alongside Bond in an almost wholly improvisatory octet led by another Rendell band member, Johnny Burch. (A horn section of Glen Hughes, Nigerian trumpeter Mike Falana and John Mumford completed the group.)

Never describing their peregrinations as anything more than 'a mutually instructive blow', as Burch put it, the Octet nevertheless made a splash. Regular appearances at Klook's Kleek, upstairs at the Railway Hotel in West Hampstead, and the Plough pub in Ilford were supplemented by a handful of shows at the Marquee and, across a few memorable days, a tour of Wales.

For the most part, though, the Octet was content to jam together in empty basements, which is where *Jazz News* caught them, in September 1962, banging away a Tuesday afternoon at the Partisan Club in Carlisle Street. Then, when the session was over, writer John Merrydowns came away raving at the prowess of this 'unlikely mix of fugitives from the Don Rendell and Alexis Korner groups . . . a swinging little band [that] has been meeting whenever and wherever it can over the past three months just for kicks.'

Those kicks were fine at a distance, but even the possibility that they might start swinging within Blues Incorporated was enough for Cyril Davies. He had joined Blues Incorporated to play the blues. Already, the arrival of Heckstall-Smith, a move that the horn-hating Davies had furiously opposed, had sent the music veering off in an entirely different direction. Bond's arrival could not help but skew things even further.

Further insult accumulated around the knowledge that, after almost six months of waiting, *R&B From the Marquee* was finally on the eve of release. Yet the line-up . . . the very sound . . . that was preserved in those grooves was so far removed from the Blues

Incorporated that now existed, that it could have been another group entirely. To the record-buying public, *R&B From the Marquee* was a brand new record. In fact, as *Jazz News & Review*'s reviewer remarked, it was already 'practically a historic document'.

Even before Korner invited Graham Bond down for an exploratory jam, Davies had made up his mind. In November 1962, he announced he was quitting to form his own new group, the Cyril Davies All Stars.

It was a blow that could have scuppered any lesser band. Davies, as everyone who ever worked with him is quick to point out, was a musical genius, a skilled player but, more than that, a man whose very presence on stage breathed bluesy authenticity. 'It was,' Heckstall-Smith mused with massive understatement, 'a major upheaval.' Korner, however, was not perturbed, as he promptly swooped for Bond, in the knowledge that wherever Blues Incorporated went now, it was not any place its audience recognised.

Baker and Bruce were thrilled and fascinated by the musical shift with which Bond's arrival infected Blues Incorporated, with the arrival of the Hammond organ, in particular, opening up fabulous new avenues of musical daredevilry. Long before the likes of the Nice and Atomic Rooster hit the road with their own three-piece, organ–bass–drums, assaults on the conventions of musicality, Baker, Bruce and Bond were playing their own occasional shows together, and astonishing audiences with the sheer immensity of the ensuing sound.

'I was the first one to be taking the Hammond around the country, except for people like Harold Smart,' Bond told *Beat Instrumental*; he was also the first gigging musician to realise that the Hammond could be cut in half, to make it easier to transport. 'It was necessary to do [that] to get around in those days.'

The trio, named for Bond himself, gigged whenever the members had a free night – and sometimes when they didn't. Twice during December, the Graham Bond Trio opened for Blues Incorporated at the Marquee. On other occasions, with both Blues Incorporated and the still-vibrant Johnny Burch Octet having already booked shows of their own, Baker, Bond and Bruce found themselves having to juggle three separate engagements, all on the same evening and, at every one, serving up a propulsive fusion of twisted blues and modern jazz that could stray as close to Charles Mingus as it might, nudge Muddy Waters, and challenge its listeners at every turn.

It was a contentious hybrid, and the musicians knew it. Modern rock fans are well accustomed to the divisions that arise between pop and rock, punk and prog, Mods and Rockers. But even the most fervent of these disputes pales into insignificance alongside the vast gulfs that rent the scene of the early 1960s, as folkies lined up against bluesers, trad jazzers aligned against modernists, and each of them warred against all of the others. It was not even a matter of differing tastes, it was an ideological divide, one that could – and frequently did – provoke grown men to fisticuffs in the fight to uphold their chosen flavour's honour.

'There was an incredible amount of snobbery going down at this time,' organist Brian Auger recalled. Barely out of his teens, Auger was already a staple on the jazz scene, a regular performer at almost every significant niterie in London, and he explained, 'we jazz buffs really looked down on rock'n'roll and the blues. When the Gunnell brothers [promoters John and Rik] took over the All-Nighter at the Flamingo, and started putting on people like Georgie Fame, Alexis Korner and Zoot Money, there was an incredible amount of resistance from within the jazz community. To admit you liked what these people were doing amounted to heresy.'

Blues Incorporated was dedicated to promulgating that heresy. Korner himself first met Heckstall-Smith when he sat in, on deeply bluesy guitar, at a jazz jam at the Troubadour in Earl's Court; among the band's own favourite shows were the folk clubs where they could send half the audience screaming for the exits. Now Korner had set his sights on re-educating the blues mob itself, and Bond was an integral part of the ensuing vision.

'Notice how the wheel has turned full circle in the R&B world?' asked *Jazz News* in its report on this latest upheaval. 'Alexis used to threaten to write a number called "What Will the Boys Down Ronnie's [jazzman Ronnie Scott's eponymous club] Think?" If he goes on [like this], there won't be any of them left down there to think anything.'

On 3 January 1963, the newly aligned Blues Incorporated were back at the Decca studios, to record half an album's worth of material: Bond's Hammond showcase 'The Organiser', BB King's breast-beating 'Everyday I Have the Blues', a heart-rending 'Lonely Am I', an ode to an imaginary breakfast cereal called 'Philboyd Sturge', and two songs that remained in the various players' repertoire for the remainder of the decade, a frantic 'Night Time Is the Right Time', and the American slavery-era work song 'Early in the Morning'. (Baker's solo Airforce unveiled a fabulous version of the latter on German television's *Beat Club* in 1970.)

Three weeks later, Blues Incorporated were back at *Jazz Club*; and, in between times, they were gigging constantly. It was an exhausting routine, and clearly the players – Bruce, Baker and Bond in particular – knew they could not keep it up indefinitely. The question was, which of their projects should they give up? All had something to recommend them, after all, be it the sheer exuberance of jamming with the Octet, or the more tangible joys of Blues Incorporated's hectic go-round of BBC broadcasts, sold-out concerts and, fleetingly, the promise of another record release.

But there was something about the Graham Bond Trio that transcended any of those attractions, all the more so after Decca rejected the January tapes on account (they said) of Bond's unconventional sax playing. Neither was the new venture's appeal purely musical. In late February 1963, the Trio played a show in Manchester and found themselves earning almost four times as much money – £70, compared with the usual £15–£20 – from the one performance than they ever had with the seven-piece Blues Incorporated, or the eight-piece Octet.

Thoughtfully, the threesome returned to London, arranging to meet up at the Flamingo, where Blues Incorporated were now rehearsing. They felt, Bruce says, laughing, 'like we'd just won the pools', but Bond was adamant that their windfall was not to be a one-off. Talking with journalist Harry Shapiro, biographer for both Korner and Bond, Baker recalled emerging from the lavatory to see Bond and Korner in deep conversation on the stage. 'And then he came up to me and Jack and said, "We've left the band."'

Baker was stunned. So far as he was aware, they had never even discussed the possibility of quitting Blues Incorporated. But, before he and Bruce could even react, Korner had walked over and bid his farewells. Baker continued, 'he said "it's really good you're doing this thing with Graham, and I wish you the best of luck" and all that. And it was a bit difficult to turn round and say, "Well, I don't really want to leave the band, you know. "'

2. A SOLID BOND IN THE BLUES

Of all the cities that so warmly welcomed Blues Incorporated on their journeys away from the faithful womb of the capital, none was quite so hospitable as Manchester, both to the band and to the music they played. The £70 that the Graham Bond Trio earned there was predicated almost wholly on their renown as members of Blues Incorporated, while Korner himself played the city so frequently that he wound up renting a flat for the band in Cheetham Hill.

Among Blues Incorporated's closest friends in the city was a young couple, John and Pamela Mayall, whose own house became a virtual second home for the group. There they unwound after gigs, either sitting around listening to John's prodigious collection of blues records and tapes, or holding marathon singalongs while their host accompanied them on the organ. And there, Korner first became aware of the behemothic talent that was John Mayall.

Like Korner and Davies, Mayall was devoted to the blues in their most authentic form. On the eve of his thirtieth birthday in 1963, five years younger than Korner, but just a year or so Davies' junior, a Korean War veteran and father of three young children – the willowy, gently spoken, and so intense-looking Mayall should already have settled down into life as art director at a local graphic design studio. But though he worked for a living, he lived for music. A brilliant guitarist and self-taught boogie-woogie pianist, he had amassed one of the most amazing libraries of American blues records that Korner and Davies had ever seen. Ever.

'Through my father, I had been exposed to a great many styles of music,' Mayall related. 'Primarily it was all early jazz, people like Louis Armstrong, Django Reinhardt and Eddie Lang. From there, the dividing line between my interest in jazz and blues was very fine. [But] when I was about thirteen, I started to get into blues and boogie-woogie, having heard records by people like Meade Lux Lewis, Albert Ammons and Pete Johnson.'

He began collecting blues records in 1949, writing away to America for copies of albums that didn't stand a snowball's chance of finding a British release. Soon, every spare penny was going on additions to his collection, while his nights were spent recording the output of the American-backed radio stations that beamed across the North Sea from the continent. American DJ Willis Connover's late, late jazz programme, broadcast on Voice of America, was a particular favourite for Mayall and every other connoisseur of the age, but locating it could often prove an all-night chore. The broadcasts were specifically targeted at the then-Communist states of Eastern Europe, where jazz was regarded as particularly subversive, and irate local governments frequently jammed the station.

On the occasions that it did come through, Mayall painstakingly taped and catalogued every new record he heard and, by the time he met Korner and Davies at the Bodega Jazz Club in 1962, he was hosting regular Saturday night open houses at his home, inviting the entire local blues scene, it seemed, back to listen to music. Other nights, he could be found playing his own shows at the Bodega and elsewhere, sometimes unaccompanied, but more frequently with his own ever-changing band, the Powerhouse Four.

The heart of the band, Mayall aside, was drummer Peter Ward, whom Mayall met at Manchester Art College, following his return from Korea. 'Peter was my friend at college, one of the people who got together with me to play at lunch times. He had his drum kit, I'd play piano, and we'd get these lunchtime jam sessions together.' The Powerhouse Four was never a permanent arrangement; rather, explained Mayall, 'that was the name we gave it if there was a school dance or something. It was usually Peter and I and whoever else was around at the time; Peter and I plus a bass player and a guitar player, a saxophone player, whoever.'

Mayall's repertoire was solidly blues-based, naturally. Rock'n'roll was certainly making inroads into the local psyche, either in the form of imported American sensations, or the homegrown thumping of the British aspirants, but Mayall remained stubbornly unconvinced by its virtues. 'The first rock records I heard all seemed like a reworking of the music I had already been exposed to,' he explained. And he wanted to go beyond that.

As his local reputation spread, Mayall found himself giving music lessons to a city's worth of would-be bluesmen in the form of free-for-all jam sessions at a youth club in Wythenshawe. It was there that he met another young drummer who would play a major part in his future, Hughie Flint. But Mayall's first taste of anything approaching fame came when the Manchester *Evening News* set out to write a short story on his musical aspirations, and instead found itself fascinated by his living arrangements. At a time when students, automatically synonymous with beatniks and bohemians, were renowned for living in squalor, filth and an alcoholic stupor, the Manchester paper found one newly engaged couple that lived thirty feet up a tree, and drank only milk and vegetable juice.

'Actually, it was a tree house,' the teetotal Mayall commented, correcting the popular misconception. 'The tree house was basically my room in my grandfather's house (on Acre Lane, Cheadle Hulme), where I didn't have much space. It was at the bottom of the garden, away from the house, but near enough that I could run electricity up there.' That was where he kept his record player and his guitar; that was where he and Ward talked and played music.

He and his fast-growing family had long since moved on from there by 1962, and were soon moving further still, as Korner and Davies first suggested to him, then began cajoling him, to get himself down to London, to work the burgeoning blues scene. Early in the spring of 1963, he finally did so.

The emergence of the blues as a major musical force in Britain, Mayall remembered, 'was very sudden. Everything had been Kenny Ball and Chris Barber; trad jazz ruled the clubs throughout the country. And then one day the *Melody Maker* had a blaring double page about how the Marquee Club was turning people away from this brand-new phenomenon. Alexis Korner and Cyril Davies were bringing amplifiers into the clubs, which was considered heresy – they were playing *electric blues music* ... the music I had been playing all these years.' Perhaps now, he hoped, 'people would know what I was on about'.

With the loyal Ward alongside him, Mayall made his London debut at the Ricky Tick Club in Windsor's Star & Garter pub, enticingly billed as 'The Blues Syndicate, London's newest raving R&B sensation, the Roland Kirk of the R&B world, playing three instruments.' Things started moving immediately. 'Alexis was very instrumental in bringing me to London, and encouraging me to make a start down there,' Mayall confirmed; and, once he was in the city, Korner continued to influence Mayall, introducing him to promoters Rik and John Gunnell, and 'the nucleus of musicians I would need to get me started'.

Philip Hayward, booking agent at the Ricky Tick Club, described his own introduction to Mayall. Korner called him up one day to announce, 'He's a nice fellow, he makes his own musical instruments ... give him twenty quid and he'll play.' And sure enough, he would.

With new venues opening, or reopening all the time, and Korner cheerleading at every opportunity, Mayall was perfectly positioned to take advantage of the city's hunger for blues. 'We were playing Klook's Kleek, Eel Pie Island, the same circuit as everybody else. But the foundation of it all for me was the Flamingo, which was run by Rik Gunnell, because that was open seven nights a week, and used to hold these sessions, these all-night sessions.'

It was there that Mayall sweated into the wee hours, jamming with whichever musicians happened by the club. Insisting that 'we never rehearsed, so the gigs became the auditions', Mayall and Ward slowly pieced together the first line-up of the soon-to-be-legendary Bluesbreakers; anxious to work in as many different settings as he could, however, Mayall also struck up a partnership with folk veteran Davy Graham, unwittingly initiating what became a personal tradition of working with the hottest guitarists around.

Korner, once again, provided the introduction. He and Graham had cut an album together in 1961, the *Three Quarters AD* fusion of both their own styles, and the host of African and eastern themes that Graham picked up as an itinerant musician travelling the world through the 1950s. Now Korner was suggesting that Mayall, too, could learn something from Graham's eclecticism.

'Alexis considered him to be a pretty original player; he was an acoustic player, and at that time I didn't have any preconceived ideas of what it should sound like. So Davy and I did a lot of gigs, we roomed together. We got a flat together near Baker Street, and we conferred musically quite a bit, and we did the gigs together.' Their sets were a magical hybrid of what Mayall summed up as 'Chicago blues standards, Muddy Waters stuff, and Davy's own originals'.

As strong-willed as Mayall, but nowhere near as single-mindedly devoted to one style of music, Graham, inevitably, did not remain by the bluesman's side for long. Other players stuck around longer.

Early summer, 1963, brought bassist John McVie into Mayall's orbit. Now a member of Fleetwood Mac, McVie remembered, 'the first gig I did with [Mayall] was at the White Hart in Acton. I had been playing in a Shadows-style group and I knew nothing at all about blues music. Mayall just gave me a stack of records and asked me to listen to them, to see if I could grasp the style and feeling.'

Guitarist Bernie Watson, a former member of Screaming Lord Sutch's Savages, underwent a similar baptism. Mayall recalled, 'When the group settled down after a lot of chopping and changing, Bernie came in on guitar and, by that time, I had John McVie, and Peter [Ward] was able to take time off his day job, so that was really the foundation of the Bluesbreakers.'

Gigs were coming fast and furious. The Bluesbreakers seemed to play every night, sometimes long into the night and, after a time, their itinerary blurred into one long, solid blob of shows, under-pinned by a repertoire that, according to Mayall, 'was basically Chicago-type songs, original songs, and Bernie could play just about anything, lesser-known Chuck Berry instrumentals, whatever. We had a really good set list together for the first year.'

Mayall's record collection remained the jealously guarded source for much of this material, and one of which he is, understandably, both proud and, perhaps, a little smug. He reflected:

There's always much talk about this shortage or difficulty in hearing American blues music around this time. But I'd been collecting blues records since 1949, so there was no shortage as far as I was concerned. The only ones that were coming in the early 1960s that were hard to find were the 45s: John Lee Hooker, Freddie King, Bo Diddley. But those things came out at pretty much the same time on LP, so it wasn't really very difficult. As far as I was concerned, these were the albums you had to get; all the Chicago players were very well represented on LP, and there were specialised shops in London that carried the singles.

Just because you could find the records, however, did not mean you could afford them, which meant that, for many fans – aspiring players as well as admiring listeners – a John Mayall gig was the closest you might come to hearing some of the greatest blues ever made.

Playing around the same circuit of clubs with his own band, the Yardbirds, Eric Clapton was a firm convert to the Bluesbreakers; and, in London in 1964, Eric Clapton was God. It said so in spray-paint on walls across the city and, though the conventional Church might have had something to say about that, remember this: Clapton did not start taking the Eucharist regularly, but Church Youth Leaders did begin playing the guitar.

The writing on the wall notwithstanding, not everybody believed in Clapton's deification, not even when he had a guitar in his hand. 'When I first heard Eric with the Yardbirds, he didn't sound all that impressive,' Mayall mused, although he also admitted that, within the Yardbirds' own frame of local reference, the presence of the seventeen-year-old Clapton was a major attribute, if only because nobody knew quite what to make of him.

The rest of the band neither looked nor behaved much different to any other musicians on the circuit. Vocalist Keith Relf had a smouldering blond good-looks thing going, albeit one that the Stones' Brian Jones had already patented, but guitarist Chris Dreja, bassist Paul Samwell-Smith and drummer Jim McCarty could have been any players, any place. And then there was Clapton, who stood out simply because he stood *there*. In any other band, the lead guitarist slashed and posed and made shapes for the chicks in the audience. Clapton, on the other hand, sometimes didn't even seem aware that there *was* an audience, staring fixedly into a private void, while his fretboard and plectrum all but played themselves. The kids called him 'Slowhand', and the name fitted him like a comfortable suit.

If he seemed distanced on stage, off it he was even more reserved, an attribute that he was subsequently to transform into an artform, and which has sent a lifetime's worth of biographers delving into the deepest recesses of his upbringing, in search of clues to his legendary detachment.

That may or may not be a worthwhile pursuit; Clapton himself has rarely spoken of his upbringing, much less blamed (or credited) it for any subsequent development in his life, beyond proudly pointing out that he was born into a very musical family. Both his mother, Patricia, and his grandmother, Rose, were pianists, and one of Clapton's own earliest memories involves standing in the bay window in the living room, singing 'I Belong to Glasgow' to the family.

Patricia Clapton, was just sixteen when her son was born in Ripley, Surrey, on 30 March 1945; the father was a Canadian airman named Edward Fryer, stationed in southern England during the last years of the Second World War, but with his own family back across the ocean. He returned to Canada once his military duties were complete, leaving Patricia behind with their child.

She was not to remain there for long. Patricia herself moved away when her son was two, first to Germany and then to Canada, where she married a soldier, and had two more children. The boy remained in Ripley with her parents; all concerned agreed that he was better off there, in an environment and family that he already knew, a belief that was confirmed when Patricia and the eldest of her Canadian children returned for a visit when Clapton was nine. He already understood that his family background was somehow 'different' to that of his schoolfriends, but the reappearance of his mother and a half brother still came as a shock. The moodiness and solitariness that characterised his teens now came bubbling to the surface, transforming a once well-balanced boy into what the terminology of the times could have described as a 'problem child'.

'I was the one that used to get stones thrown at me because I was so thin and couldn't do physical training very well,' Clapton reported years later. 'I was always the seven-stone weakling. I used to hang out with three or four other kids who were all in that same kind of predicament. The outcasts. They used to call us the loonies.'

As his schoolwork plummeted, his love of music strengthened, only now, instead of 'I Belong to Glasgow', the pre-adolescent Clapton was more likely to be caught singing songs by the American bluesmen whose music was an occasional highlight of one of BBC Radio's most fondly remembered children's programmes, hosted by Derek 'Uncle Mac' McCulloch.

Already an established broadcaster and author (he wrote a number of early volumes within the long-lived *Ladybird* series of children's books), Uncle Mac was 57 when he took over the BBC's *Children's Hour* in 1954; 'a very old man', as a young Clapton put it, 'with one leg'. His show was largely dominated by children's music: 'Nellie the Elephant', 'The Laughing Policeman' and 'Gilly Gilly Ossenfeffer Katzenellen Bogen By The Sea' were all Uncle Mac favourites. But, as Clapton continued, 'he'd play things like [Frankie Laine's] "Mule Train", and then every week he'd slip in something like a Buddy Holly record, or a Chuck Berry record'. And one week, he 'slipped in' a song by Sonny Terry and Brownie McGhee, 'with Sonny Terry howling and playing the harmonica. It blew me away.'

Clapton was no more than eleven or twelve at the time, but he immediately began seeking out more music that sounded the same, disavowing the rising tides of rock'n'roll and skiffle that transfixed his schoolfriends, in favour of what he considered a more authentic, more emotional, sound.

For his thirteenth birthday, Clapton's grandparents handed him his first guitar, a £14 Spanish acoustic, and that isolated him even further from his peers, as he retreated to his bedroom night after night, trying to master the instrument. He had neither tutor nor tutelage; rather, he listened to music and then tried to replicate what he heard. On more than one occasion, frustrated by his snail-like progress, he came close to giving up.

But another birthday brought him a Grundig reel-to-reel tape recorder, on which he preserved his practice sessions and, by the time Clapton moved on to Kingston Art College in 1961, aged sixteen, his guitar playing had advanced so far that, in his own words, people were starting to notice him. Fully aware of his failure to 'fit in' with the other kids, he discovered that 'guitar playing . . . [is] like a bluff. Covers up all your wimp things. The first recognition I ever got amongst the crowd I used to hang out with was for my guitar playing.'

For that crowd, the centre of the world lay in the then-vibrant culture that congregated around the coffee bars, darkened and decidedly un-*Starbucks*-ian dens where bohemians, beatniks, folkies and freaks congregated to whisper conspiratorially about whichever revolution they believed was due to come. It was within the coffee bars that Britain's first rock'n'roll bands cut their performing teeth; there that Aldermaston anti-nuke marches were born; there that the entire shape of the British 1960s was first blueprinted by earnest young dreamers. And there that Clapton had his destiny confirmed.

'From hanging around in coffee bars and so on, I met a certain crowd of people, some of whom played guitar' – Long John Baldry was one of the young Clapton's earliest acquaintances and, given his towering height, one of the most memorable, sitting in a corner with his frame wrapped round a twelve-string guitar, picking folk and blues.

'Every night there would be a meeting at someone's house, and people would turn up with the latest imported records from the States,' Clapton continued. One week 'someone showed up with that Chess album, *The Best of Muddy Waters*, and something by Howlin' Wolf. Then I sort of took a step back, discovered Robert Johnson and made the connection to Muddy. And that was it for me.'

For Clapton, the blues represented more than a musical passion. They offered a way of life to a young man who was seriously struggling to understand himself. 'I felt, through my youth, that my back was against the wall and that the only way to survive was with dignity, pride and courage. I heard that in certain forms of music, and I heard it most of all in the blues, because it was always an individual.'

He studied the blues, and extrapolated the lives of the music's makers from the handful of resources that were available then; a few lines of text on the back of a record sleeve, a footnote or two in some dusty tome on Prohibition-era America; a paragraph, maybe, in the pages of *Melody Maker* and *Down Beat,* and the over-amplified sensationalism of urban myth.

He learned of Robert Johnson selling his soul to the devil at the crossroads, and of the night the devil returned to collect it. He heard about Blind Willie Reynolds, who could see as well as you and I, until he fell into a fight with a man armed with a shotgun; and he read, with horrified fascination, about Bessie Smith, the Empress of the Blues, who was already lying, dying, by the side of a car wreck when a passing truck raced past her outstretched body, and severed her right arm. According to American folklorist Alan Lomax, she might still have lived, had she only received immediate hospital treatment. Unfortunately, the closest hospital, in nearby Clarksville, only admitted whites.

Blues was not only a way of life, then, it was a way of death as well, that most irreversibly intimate of all human experiences, and Clapton was spellbound by that realisation. 'It was one man and his guitar versus the world. When it came down to it, it was one guy who was completely alone and had no options, no alternatives other than just to sing and play to ease his pains. And that echoed what I felt.'

He read the music papers and discovered Blues Incorporated. Sometimes he'd take his guitar along, and sit in on whichever jams were taking place; 'I was just a blues aficionado with a guitar attempting to sing. When Mick [Jagger] got a sore throat, I used to get up and deputise for him at the Ealing club.' On other occasions, Clapton and a friend, Dave Brock, visited local folk clubs, and ran through their blues repertoire there. (Brock subsequently re-emerged as the mainstay behind space rockers Hawkwind.) Slowly ambition began to coalesce.

Clapton and art college parted ways in spring 1962; he was dismissed when it became apparent that art was one of the last things on his mind. Instead, he went to work as an assistant to his bricklayer grandfather, and ploughed his wages into buying his first electric guitar, the same cutaway Kay that Alexis Korner was then playing. No more than a few weeks later, Clapton was joining his first band, Rhode Island Red and the Roosters.

According to one legend, Clapton met fellow guitarist Tom McGuinness at a Rollin' Stones show at the Crawdaddy in early 1963; according to another, McGuinness's girlfriend of the time knew Clapton from college and set up the meeting when she heard that his band, the Roosters, were seeking a lead guitarist.

Either way, the pair hit it off, and the Roosters were soon at work, trundling around the pubs and clubs of south-west London, but learning the hard way that they were just one more bunch of blues-mongers amid the myriad that were now howling the odds around the home counties, and no more proficient than any of them. Although Clapton, McGuinness and pianist Ben Palmer each remained intent on making careers in music, and were willing to put up with the long hours and lousy pay, bandmates Terry Brennan and Robin Mason were less obsessed. By the end of summer, the group had splintered although Clapton and McGuinness were not idle for long, as they linked up with Casey Jones & the Engineers, Liverpudlian Jones's attempt to shrug off the Merseybeat image that the Beatles' recent breakthrough conferred upon every musician in that city, by abandoning beat and playing the blues.

Clapton and McGuinness played their first show as Engineers in September 1963, in John Mayall's old stomping ground of Macclesfield; other gigs took them round Liverpool, Manchester and as far south as Reading, before Clapton quit after just seven shows (McGuinness, bound now for Manfred Mann, left after eight).

Such short-lived enterprises notwithstanding, still Clapton was developing a reputation as a damned useful blues guitarist, a lot more confident than his reticent appearance let on, and a lot more developed than many guitarists two or three years his senior. Certainly when another local band, the Yardbirds, lost their own guitarist, Tony 'Top' Topham, in October 1963, both rhythm guitarist Chris Dreja (who knew Clapton from school), and vocalist Keith Relf (who'd attended Kingston alongside him) were adamant that Clapton was the player who would push the Yardbirds' ambitions to the next level.

With a repertoire built around Topham's father's collection of blues records, the Yardbirds themselves were just months old at the time, but already they'd garnered a loyal following around west

London. Rehearsing at the South Western hotel, just across the road from the Station hotel in Richmond, the group had an unobstructed view of the local landscape in all its musical glory; and, though nobody has ever been able to explain how and why this particular corner of the capital was to become as significant to British blues as the Mississippi Delta was to American, it was clear that the neighbourhood was hopping.

The Rollin' Stones had had a residency in the basement of the Station, in what the venue's promoter, the bearlike Russian émigré Giorgio Gomelsky dubbed the Crawdaddy Club. It was there, in April 1963, that aspiring entrepreneur Andrew Loog Oldham first spotted the Stones and set about grooming them for infamy. (He also reinstated the errant 'g' halfway through the band's name.) Cyril Davies and his All Stars were similarly stationed at Eel Pie Island ... an island indeed, in the Thames at Twickenham. You made your way across a little wooden bridge to reach it, and even that was a relatively new installation; a decade earlier, only a rickety old chain ferry ... literally, a small ferry boat that was pulled to and forth across the water on chains ... was the only means of access.

The Downliner Sect were Thames Valley natives, the young Ian Gillan lived in Hounslow, Nick Simper was born in Southall, Micky Waller was from Greenford. Jimmy Page and Ritchie Blackmore both hailed from Heston, Jeff Beck from Wallington. You could fill a small telephone directory with the local faces and names that would some day headline the music papers, but who, for now, were merely reading them, scouring the gig guide for the next night's blues-wailin' excitement. And, so far as they were concerned, nothing was as exciting as the news that the Yardbirds had recruited Eric Clapton.

Under Topham's calm tutelage, the Yardbirds had already started moving up the local pecking order. When the Stones scored their first hit single, and swam off for a nationwide tour, it was the Yardbirds who took over their Crawdaddy residency in Richmond; they maintained that position when Gomelsky relocated the club to the Star hotel in Broad Green, near Croydon, in October 1963. But Clapton was to take them even higher. Vocalist Relf made the call that brought the guitarist down to a Yardbirds rehearsal; according to Dreja, 'he turned up and immediately fitted in. He was obviously so much more talented as a guitarist, knew a lot more numbers. The whole thing went straight into another dimension.'

3. FIVE LIVE YARDBIRDS

With Clapton watching critically from the dance floor, Topham's final show with the Yardbirds took place at the Crawdaddy on 19 October, 24 hours after the entire audience was granted a first-hand glimpse of what this blues business was really all about, at the opening night of the 1963 American Folk Blues Festival.

At a time when few American bluesmen had visited Europe (one reason why so many young white suburbanites took to playing the music themselves), a time, in fact, when there were few outlets for them in their homeland, either, German promoters Horst Lippman and Fritz Rau hit upon the idea of importing an entire evening's worth of authentic performers, not only to tour a curious Europe, but to headline their own television broadcast as well. Lippman was also the director of the German Südwestfunk network's *Jazz Gehört und Gehesen* (*Jazz Heard and Seen*), and arranged for one entire show to be given over to the visiting bluesmen. (Filmed at the network's Baden-Baden studio, this broadcast, and those that followed in later years, were the sources for the series of *American Folk Blues Festival* DVDs released during 2003–2004.)

With bluesman Willie Dixon, at the Chess Studios in Chicago, pulling together the attractions and organising the band that would back them (Dixon himself was the bassist), Memphis Slim, T-Bone Walker, John Lee Hooker and Sonny Terry and Brownie McGhee were booked into shows in Scandinavia, Germany, France, Austria and Switzerland. Lippman's attempts to secure some British dates for the package, however, were doomed to failure. Well aware of the grassroots support in that country, Lippman was staggered to discover that few promoters were even halfway interested.

Just one venue was willing to take a chance on the show, the Free Hall in John Mayall's Manchester home town, but if Lippman feared that distance might deter an audience from attending, he reckoned without the fierce devotion of the London crowd. Jimmy Page still recalls piling into a rental truck alongside fellow enthusiasts Brian Jones, Keith Richards, Mick Jagger and Dave Williams, to drive the three hundred miles for the concert and, once there, the travellers recognised any number of other familiar faces from the London circuit ('The bush telegraph was pretty serious,' another trekker, Paul Jones, remembered). And, back in London, they regaled all the stay-at-homes with their vivid song-by-song accounts of this first sighting of the musical Gods. By the time Lippman was ready to plan a second festival tour, in October 1963, British promoters were queuing up to stage concerts.

The British dates were ultimately arranged by Giorgio Gomelsky and Harold Pendleton, one of the organisers of the annual National Jazz Festival, and stretched across a week of shows, kicking off at Croydon's Fairfield Hall with a bill littered with legends. Muddy Waters, Willie Dixon, Memphis Slim, Victoria Spivey, Lonnie Johnson and Sonny Boy Williamson II were all booked to appear, and Long John Baldry spoke for an entire theatre full of onlookers when he averred, 'It was an enormous, great thrill. They all seemed so much larger in life than just a disembodied voice on a record groove.'

Of course the Yardbirds were in attendance that night; the following evening, they were astonished to discover that two of the stars of the Festival show, Sonny Boy Williamson and Lonnie Johnson, were repaying the favour at the Crawdaddy. But Gomelsky had an even greater thrill in store for the group. When the festival outing ended in November, Williamson would be returning to the UK to tour in his own right. And the Yardbirds were one of the bands he had selected to accompany him.

Eric Clapton's own first date with the Yardbirds came at Studio 51, on Great Newport Street, the evening after the Crawdaddy show; that same weekend, he moved into the communal flat that the entire group, bar drummer Jim McCarty, shared in Kew, and quickly revealed that his much-vaunted shyness was equally much in the eye of the beholder. Visiting the chaotic pad on an almost daily basis, McCarty was especially struck by Clapton's penchant for slapstick comedy, his love of custard-pie jokes, and the arsenal of comical faces and voices that he could summon up at a moment's notice, each of whom had its own readily definable personality. 'He reckoned he'd go home one day and they'd all be waiting for him.'

The sudden success that awaited him as a member of the Yardbirds played its own part in Clapton's awakening. His past outfits were content to play around the tiniest of local circuits, knocking out their earnest approximations of 'Boom Boom', 'Hideaway' and the occasional Larry Williams number ('because you had to have the odd rock'n'roll number in there'). The Yardbirds' following, on the other hand, was growing at such a pace that Gomelsky – now installed as the band's own manager – was regularly compensating the fans who were locked out of one gig, by giving them free tickets for another. And so the word spread. No matter where the Yardbirds played, they brought their own devoted audience with them. And the audience brought the excitement.

Among the Yardbirds' earliest faithful acolytes were the brothers Mike and Richard Vernon, and their friend Neil Slaven, devout blues lovers whose enthusiasm had prompted them to launch their own fanzine, the now-legendary *R&B Monthly*. (Future Yardbirds manager Simon Napier Bell co-published another, *Blues Unlimited*.) Wherever there was an R&B club, the Vernons could be found selling their magazine on the street outside, but their favourite pitches were outside the Crawdaddy and the Star in Richmond. And their favourite events were Yardbirds gigs.

'Both places were very strong Yardbirds territory,' Mike Vernon explained, 'so I got to know the band initially through going there.' In fact, he was one of the many bystanders who sat in with the group on those all-too-common evenings when the asthmatic Keith Relf's health prevented him from playing a full set. 'There were a lot of people who used to do that,' Vernon recalled. 'Gary Farr, Rod Stewart, Ronnie Jones . . . Mick Jagger used to sit in sometimes, as well. And one guy who had the most ridiculous name of Hogsnort Rupert.'

Named for what Long John Baldry described as his 'quite big nose', Hogsnort was 'one of the many people who did it all for fun, for a couple of pints on a Friday night'. Baldry continued, 'he never went into it thinking of a career in music, but then, how many of us did?' (In fact, Hogsnort's own, eponymous Good Good Band did step out of the shadows occasionally, regulars at the Ricky Tick and even opening for Manfred Mann at the Marquee. Hogsnort himself subsequently re-emerged as Genesis/Van Der Graaf Generator producer John Anthony.)

Vernon usually performed one or two songs an evening, an event that Clapton quickly came to look forward to. 'We'd do "Stormy Monday" and "Goin' Down Slow", good old security blanket blues. Eric always used to complain that the Yardbirds never played any slow numbers in their set, which is why we chose those.' Clapton still relished his nickname of 'Slowhand', but as the Yardbirds' renown grew, and musicianship blurred into a sprint for the finishing line, he was rarely granted the opportunity to justify it. Vernon's occasional guest appearances gave him the chance to show what he was *really* capable of.

In terms of their repertoire, the group's set included as many R&B favourites as any other acolytes of the age: Chuck Berry's 'Too Much Monkey Business', Howlin' Wolf's 'Smokestack Lightning', Slim Harpo's 'Got Love if You Want It'. But no one played them like the Yardbirds, a blur of glorious noise that reverberated off the most unforgiving walls, and echoed through the most resilient stomach.

The Yardbirds' *tour de force* was the Rave Up, a slice of sheer aural assault that saw them remorselessly raise the tempo of the performance by whipping up a frenzy that could not help but communicate itself to the audience. Bassist Paul Samwell-Smith kicked it off – lifting the idea from Ricky Brown, bassist in Cyril Davies' band, he started moving up the fretboard, cueing the rest of the pack to lock into the same dizzying sequence, until each had climbed as high as they could. Then they'd come back down again, and start again even faster.

'The fans evolved this strange dance,' recalled McCarty. '[They] would take their shirts off, get on each other's backs and just rave. It started at the Crawdaddy, but [soon began] happening everywhere we played. People had simply never heard music that would let them rip like that.' Neither did the Yardbirds' audience allow circumstance to diminish their brutal commitment to the rave, as Sonny Boy Williamson was soon to discover.

Born in Glendora, Mississippi, in 1899, Williamson (as the oft-appended designation of 'the second' implies) was actually the second bluesman to ply his trade under that name; indeed, the first, John Lee Williamson, was still active in the Chicago area when Howlin' Wolf's brother-in-law, Aleck 'Rice' Miller, first adopted his name in the early 1940s, and began touring around the Mississippi Delta, insisting that *he*, and not the Chicago-based artist, was the real thing. It was an audacious feat to say the least, although the only people who appear to have been confused by it were British blues fans. Both men were active songwriters and, for many years, songs composed by the original Williamson were routinely attributed to the second, including one of the all-time classic blues numbers, 'Good Morning Little Schoolgirl'.

By the late 1940s, Williamson II was a regular on local radio, and an advertising icon for King Biscuit Flour, the public face of the company's Sonny Boy brand of white corn meal. He kicked off his recording career in 1951, with the classic 'Eyesight to the Blind'; 'Don't Start Me Talkin'', 'Bring It on Home', 'Nine Below Zero' and more followed and, as the decade progressed, Williamson established himself among America's greatest living bluesmen, at least so far as European audiences were concerned.

According to future Savoy Brown and Fleetwood Mac frontman Dave Walker, who recorded his own album-length tribute to Williamson in 2004 (*Mostly Sonny*), 'there was a simplicity to Sonny Boy ... the same as Jimmy Reed, it was just a shuffle, but it was a beautiful shuffle. Some of those old guys, you listen to the records and they're out of tune, or you can't understand them. But Sonny Boy's records were so warm, and so exciting.'

Reviews of the 1963 American Folk Blues festival gigs unanimously singled out Williamson, whose three-song set closed the first half of the show, as the runaway star of the evening. With that renown still ringing, Gomelsky had little difficulty in booking him a seemingly endless succession of dates around the country, with every halt offering up a new clutch of backing musicians who might ordinarily have expected to sell their souls before they could share a stage with such a legend.

In Newcastle on New Year's Eve, Williamson was accompanied by the still-unknown Animals, the Geordie aggregation whose fire utterly consumes the live recording that Gomelsky made of the proceedings (*The Animals with Sonny Boy Williamson*). Other shows saw Williamson team up with the Brian Auger Trinity, to cement a relationship which grew so strong that finally, shortly before Williamson's return to the US, Gomelsky put the team (plus guitarist Jimmy Page) in the studio together, to cut what became the *Don't Send No Flowers* album.

Williamson's best-known partnership, however, was with the Yardbirds, thanks largely to American Folk Blues Festival promoter Horst Lippman arranging to record a couple of their earliest shows (at the Crawdaddy over 8/9 December), for release on his own L&R label. The result is one of the most atmospheric of all British blues recordings, not to mention one of the precious few Yardbirds recordings that actually permits Clapton to show off everything he had learned throughout his years of practice and listening. Embellishing the gaps around Williamson's vocals and harp, his playing on numbers like 'My Little Cabin' and 'Mister Downchild' prefigures any of his subsequent accomplishments on his own solo blues recordings.

Despite their obvious compatibility, however, the Yardbirds' relationship with Williamson did not get off to the best start: 'These British want to play the blues so bad,' Williamson once remarked, 'and they play the blues so bad!'

'He wasn't very tolerant,' Clapton revealed to *Rolling Stone* twenty years on. 'He put us through some bloody hard paces. In the first place, he expected us to know his tunes. He'd say "we're gonna do ... 'Fattening Frogs for Snakes'", and then he'd kick it off and, of course, some of the members of ... the band had never heard these songs.'

Slowly, Williamson warmed to the youngsters' obvious enthusiasm and respect for him; 'He did take a shine to us after a while,' Clapton said with a smile. But Williamson's own aficionados continued to disparage the pairing. Kevin Nolan, a schoolteacher who caught the team at the Birmingham R&B Festival on 28

February 1964, long remembered the fury he felt when, midway through one of the blues giant's most exquisite numbers ('it may even have been "My Little Cabin"'), half the Town Hall audience suddenly clambered onto the other half's back, and began waving its arms and legs in the air. Raving.

Sonny Boy, accustomed now to such raucous applause, was not perplexed, and the band didn't seem to notice. But, if there was any moment, Nolan said, when it became apparent that the British blues were breaking apart, splitting down lines that were dedicatedly purist on the one hand, and heretically hybrid on the other, that was it. The blues were a music you treated with respect. You did not . . . repeat *not* . . . take your shirt off and start acting like an idiot.

But the polarisation from which Nolan recoiled was not confined to the behaviour of a few hundred Yardbirds fans. For three years or more, any advances made on the British blues scene, commercial, musical or otherwise, were enacted more or less of the scene's own volition. Now, outside forces were moving in, outside musicians, outside businessmen, outside influences.

Record companies were swooping down on any even halfway competent band and, if they couldn't find one, then they were creating their own. Halfwit harmonica players hung on every street corner, honking discordant approximations of their favourite Jagger, Relf or Cyril Davies riffs, and destroying them in the process. High street clothes stores were peddling specially tailored 'blues' caps and jackets. From every direction, a cosy movement was collapsing in on itself – more than that, it was devouring itself, and the only question that remained was, what could the future possibly hold for a music whose most faithful adherents demanded it remained locked almost cerebrally into the past?

Nolan's thoughts found a pensive echo in Eric Clapton's own. Even as the Yardbirds' own renown on the circuit rocketed ever higher, borne on the wildness of a stage act that made even the soaraway Stones seem sometimes staid, he itched to return to basics, and watched enviously as John Mayall's Bluesbreakers poured all their energies into their music alone, virtuosity and sincerity oozing from every pore.

There was little opportunity, however, for him to do anything about that. True, he could always rely on Mike Vernon to climb up onstage when he, Clapton, truly felt the need to play a song that didn't race by at Mach 2. But the Yardbirds' career was now barrelling along with a will of its own, with Gomelsky determined not simply to lock the group into a position of power, but to knock the Stones off their own pedestal in the process. Before Andrew Loog Oldham came along, after all, Gomelsky was the nearest thing the Stones had to a manager and, though he had only himself to blame for letting them slip away, still the alacrity with which Oldham transformed the group from the raunchiest thing in

Richmond to the biggest thing since sliced Beatles bothered him. He was not going to make the same mistakes again.

In February 1964, Gomelsky booked the Yardbirds into RG Jones recording studio in Morden, south London – the same cheap, but nevertheless utterly reliable set-up that virtually every young band of the day turned to in their hour of fulfilment. With them went Mike Vernon, stepping away from both the microphone and the typewriter to take his first steps towards fulfilling another of his ambitions, to become a record producer.

The session succeeded on both counts. Three songs long (Sonny Boy Williamson II's 'Baby What's Wrong', John Lee Hooker's 'Boom Boom' and Relf's own 'Honey in Your Hips'), the ensuing demo was more than sufficient to land the Yardbirds a deal with Columbia, at exactly the same time as Vernon's own enthusiasm and knowledge brought him a job at Decca, as an in-house producer at their West Hampstead studios.

Naturally, the move shifted Vernon out of the Yardbirds' own orbit; instead, Gomelsky shouldered the production duties himself and, by early summer, Columbia was gearing up to issue the Yardbirds' debut single, 'A Certain Girl'. The only problem was the record didn't actually sound anything like the Yardbirds. Live, the band was raw, rough and ready; in the studio, they were clean, bright and sparkling.

No matter that all but the last ten minutes of the recording session were spent twitching 'A Certain Girl' to perfection; when it came to actually releasing the record, even Columbia agreed that it was the B-side, the product of those final ten minutes, which came the closest to capturing the Yardbirds they'd signed. A wiry cover of Billy Boy Arnold's 'I Wish You Would' was released in June 1964 and, though it never threatened to storm the chart, it at least landed the group some national attention – an appearance on television's newly born *Ready Steady Go* included.

Though they remained sanguine about it, the failure of the Yardbirds' first single came as something of a surprise. Even as it hit the stores, the Animals were topping the chart with 'The House of the Rising Sun'. The Stones were riding the Top Ten seemingly at will, and behind them, Manfred Mann, the Mojos, the Swinging Blue Jeans, the Moody Blues, Lulu and the Luvvers and the Kinks were all jostling for hits.

The mania for the music had even reached backwards into its own prehistory, to present Chuck Berry with his first run of major hits since the mid-1950s: 'Go Go Go', 'Let It Rock', 'Memphis Tennessee', 'Run Rudolph Run', 'Nadine', 'No Particular Place to Go', 'You Never Can Tell', 'The Promised Land'. Every one of them could be heard being ground out on some provincial stage or another, every night of the week, courtesy of the latest bunch of fresh-faced blues aficionados. But Berry brought the originals to bear, and it became a badge of honour to buy them. So why weren't the Yardbirds selling?

Squeezing in another session between the gig list that was now dragging them up and down the country, the Yardbirds tried again. Released in October 1964, Sonny Boy Williamson (the first!)'s 'Good Morning Little Schoolgirl' was a Clapton favourite – onstage, he even sang it – but again it was too clean, again it sounded too polished. And when it, too, fell short of success, it was clear that the Yardbirds had only one alternative. Their next recording session, aimed this time at an album, pulled them back to the one arena where they could never fail.

Every Friday night, the Yardbirds took over the Marquee Club in London for a wild celebration of the Rave Up. Now they moved a mini-studio in as well; and, leaving the bells and whistles in the deft hands of engineer Philip 'the Spaniel' Wood, they played as loud and fast as they could, for as long as the tape kept rolling. Weeks later, *Five Live Yardbirds* was in the stores, an adrenalined blast which made up in excitement for all that it lost in fidelity, a brutal snapshot of the Yardbirds at their frenetic best, and Clapton at his most unrestrained.

John Mayall hated it. 'If you listen to the *Five Live Yardbirds* album, there are a couple of tracks where Eric takes a guitar solo, and it's pretty wild. But it doesn't have the technique or the finesse or whatever you want to call it. It's pretty ordinary.' He acknowledged, however, that the fact he was even listening to the record indicated that he had heard the rush of acclaim that now accompanied every mention of Eric Clapton's name, and was curious to find out more.

Mayall's own recording career was off the ground by now. Immediately after Mike Vernon joined Decca, and proved his worth by producing Curtis Jones's *In London* album, the Bluesbreakers became his maiden signing to the label and, on 20 April 1964, the pair entered the studio to cut the 'Crawling Up a Hill' single.

'Mike Vernon was the blues A&R man if you want to put a title to him,' Mayall explained. 'He was a big blues fan, he used to go round all the clubs and he selected the bands which he thought Decca ought to record. He produced them, and they seemed to sell OK. Decca didn't pretend to understand what it was all about, [but] the sales sheets were fine so they just left Mike to it, which was very good from Mike's point of view, and very good from ours.' Or, at least, it would be eventually.

'Crawling Up a Hill' was not what Mayall would describe as an auspicious debut, as he recalled how this 'clumsy, half-witted attempt at autobiographical comment' sold a pitiful 500 copies, and was swiftly deleted. In fact, if he has any affection whatsoever for the record, it is for its status as Bernie Watson's first and only recording with the Bluesbreakers:

That was the only record Bernie was on, and then he gave up playing ... although he was barely there when we were playing anyway, because he'd sit on a chair in a corner with his back to the audience. You look at publicity photos from that era, and that's all you'll see, Bernie's back. I don't know how he ever got on with Screaming Lord Sutch, but I guess he didn't want any more of it after that. It was very difficult, because when he played, he was beautiful; when he was on, and he really wanted to play, he was great. But he was very moody, and if he didn't feel like putting out, you wouldn't get much out of him.

Watson's replacement in the Bluesbreakers was one Roger Dean (no relation to the similarly named artist who rose to fame with the floating islands and whatnot of Yes).
Mayall continued:

Bernie left because he wanted to go back to studying classical guitar music, which is where he started, but it did leave a hole. There might have been a few auditions ... I did try a few different people until Roger came along. But Roger was the one I stuck with.
   Roger was a very competent technician. He didn't truly have the background knowledge of what the blues was really all about, but at that time not many people did. But he was a great technician, a great guy to get along with, with a very positive attitude, and he became the guitar player for about eighteen months.

There was also a change at the back of the stage, as Peter Ward announced that he was coming to the end of his days as a musician.
Mayall recalled:

We were both in commercial art and advertising, so for the first year, Peter did the drumming. But, when I turned professional, because there was more work coming in, he opted to continue with his job in advertising, so he dropped out. So there was a lot of chopping and changing, and in the meantime there were a lot of gigs.

All that finally ended in late 1964, when Mayall received a call from that keen young drum student from his days as a Wythenshawe youth club instructor, Hughie Flint. He was moving to London and looking for work. Mayall took him on board immediately.
It is one of history's great injustices that it is the constantly shifting line-up that characterised the Bluesbreakers for which the group is best remembered. Terms such as 'ruthlessly restless' and 'a gifted

bandleader who demanded total dedication' are applied to Mayall with numbing regularity, with the string of albums he released during the 1960s relegated almost to the status of sideshows, whose only purpose was to spotlight the latest instrumental prodigy to wander into the Bluesbreakers' latest vacancy.

What is not discussed is the sheer innovation for which Mayall himself was responsible. Unquestionably it is true that *certain* of his records are flavoured by the presence of *certain* of his musicians, but the overall feel of the albums was Mayall's, and Mayall's alone. He was a great songwriter and a well-tuned instrumental virtuoso whose own, personal direction dictated the course of the Bluesbreakers, as he confirmed in 1991:

> I maintain such a strong identity in my music and playing that, when musicians join, their sole responsibility is to be creative in that context. The mood of the music has already been set. So much importance seems to be attached to these [line-up] changes, [but] at that time, it didn't seem important. If you're a band leader, your main focus is to play your own music. Invariably, over time, you'll find that some players aren't on the same wavelength any more ... or perhaps they wanted to use my band as a stepping stone for their own music and career. For me, it was business as usual.

And business as usual, in December 1964, meant recording the group's first album, as the Bluesbreakers and Mike Vernon followed the Yardbirds' yardstick and set up the mikes around Klook's Kleek, to record the in-concert *John Mayall Plays John Mayall*. The venue itself was a Decca favourite, situated just yards away from the label's West Hampstead studio base, and the resultant record does indeed boast all the benefits of having been recorded so close to a state of the art facility.

John Mayall Plays John Mayall receives few warm words from its maker: '... lots of "yeas" and "alrights"... terrible!' Hughie Flint has been kinder. 'It was a very bright, interesting album. It was indicative of what John was doing at the time, very rough and ready blues.' Furthermore, it was astonishingly well-recorded for the time (compare it with *Five Live Yardbirds*) and comprised, almost exclusively, Mayall's own, original compositions (the sole exception is the 'R&B Time' medley of 'Night Train' and Little Richard's 'Lucille').

Alexis Korner, too, had nothing but praise for the album. Penning liner notes that introduced Mayall as 'one of the country's finest R&B artists, recorded at one of London's top R&B clubs', he continued, 'All the feeling, all the life, all the personality came through in a way which is often alien to the recording studio.' Alluding to the slightly stinted nature of that earlier Mayall 45, Korner enthused, 'this is what [he] really needed. Here he was, with the support of a truly enthusiastic audience, and the knowledge that no one was going to worry about times or anything else. So he moves his head around and shouts encouragement, he pushes along on organ, pulls strange sounds out of his harmonica, plays his nine-string guitar. It all comes over in the way it should.'

It was, in short, an excellent album – and it was completely ignored by the public. 'It didn't sell at all well,' Mayall recalled, flinching. 'It did about five hundred copies in the first six months, and an equal amount in the second six months.' And when the Bluesbreakers' second single, the rambunctiously punchy 'Crocodile Walk', met with much the same fate, 'Decca dropped us.'

However, momentous events were afoot elsewhere, events which not only led to Mayall's triumphant return to Decca, but which also paved the way for the full-fledged emergence of one of the greatest guitarists of all time. In March 1965, the same month as the Klook's Kleek album was released, Eric Clapton quit the Yardbirds. Mayall was on the scent immediately.

The year's end release of *Five Live Yardbirds* had coincided with the Yardbirds' most prestigious outing yet. Earlier in 1964, the group toured as support to Billy J Kramer and the Dakotas, one of the other Liverpudlian lights in Beatles manager Brian Epstein's NEMS stable. Epstein caught several of the shows, and pronounced himself utterly bowled over by the opening act – so much so that, as he set about organising the Beatles' Christmas concerts at the Hammersmith Odeon, he personally invited the Yardbirds onto the bill.

The shows themselves passed off as well as they could under the circumstances – a hall full of screaming kids at the height of Beatlemania, each of them keening their Fab fave's name, was scarcely conducive to any musicians who actually wanted to play a strong show. Backstage, however, a degree of peace reigned, and it was there that the Yardbirds came face to face with their immediate future, in the form of a quietly spoken young Mancunian named Graham Gouldman, who had written a song he thought they might like.

Though they probably weren't aware of the fact, Gouldman was actually a labelmate of the Yardbirds – his own group, the Mockingbirds, were newly signed to Columbia, and had already decided that their debut single would be 'For Your Love', a song Gouldman wrote in the changing-room of the men's clothing shop where he worked. Columbia, incredibly, had other ideas; they rejected 'For Your Love' in favour of another Gouldman original, taped on the same day, 'That's How It's Gonna Stay'.

But Gouldman and Mockingbirds manager Harvey Lisburg retained their faith in the earlier song, as Gouldman detailed. 'Harvey said, "this is such a great song, let's play it to the Beatles", to which I replied, "I think they're doing alright in the songwriting department, actually.'" But Lisburg still mentioned the idea to a publisher friend, Ronnie Beck, who suggested that they should offer the song to the Yardbirds instead.

Gouldman was already a confirmed Yardbirds fan – 'The first time I saw them [with Eric Clapton], they blew my head off.' Now he was making his way backstage, so nervous that he handed his demo tape (the Mockingbirds' own scrapped version of the song) to the first Londoner he met.

As luck would have it, he'd found Yardbirds bassist Paul Samwell-Smith, and the rest of the tale is history. Samwell-Smith played the tape that same evening, and fell hopelessly in love with the song, then confirmed his own talents as an arranger by introducing the bongos, harpsichord (from a guesting Brian Auger) and bowed bass that gave the Yardbirds' performance its unique flavour. Gomelsky, too, was stunned; abandoning the Otis Redding cover that Clapton was determined should be the Yardbirds' next single, he presented Columbia with 'For Your Love', and the record gave the band their first Top Three hit.

Looking back on a record that the *New Musical Express* accurately described as 'unusual, it makes you sit up and take notice', Graham Gouldman admitted, 'their version took me by surprise, because I thought it was so weird. Ours used an acoustic guitar instead of a harpsichord, which was what really made their version work. It was amazing. It was fantastic having such an entry into the Yardbirds; they did try things and, even though they sort of failed, they did stick with it.' (Gouldman went on to write several other numbers for the group, alongside smashes for the Hollies and Herman's Hermits.)

'"For Your Love" really suited the band's personality,' Chris Dreja agreed. 'Or most of the band's personality. Unfortunately, it didn't fit Eric's. He was a purist, he wanted a purist sound, and the idea of bringing in a harpsichord and congas and things like that just weren't in his parameters.'

Aghast at Samwell-Smith's arrangement, and Gomelsky's immediate decision to elect him the Yardbirds' full-time musical director; horrified by the gimmick-strewn pop turn that events had suddenly taken, Clapton announced that he was leaving the group, seven days before 'For Your Love' was released.

He had felt himself losing interest in the Yardbirds for a few months now, ever since the Stones broke out of the Crawdaddy scene and, as he liked to say, 'sparked ambition in some members of the [Yardbirds]. The Stones were getting on big package tours, they were on TV, they got a Chuck Berry song ["Come On"] onto the chart, and some of the Yardbirds and Giorgio began to see a future in being internationally famous.' Clapton, on the other hand, 'couldn't see what was so wonderful' about that; was still in thrall to the internal purist who insisted 'music is this, it's not that'.

The Yardbirds would not suffer from his departure. They replaced the single-minded Clapton with the decidedly less finicky (but equally monumental) Jeff Beck, and continued on their merry way. Within a year, the Yardbirds were die-hard chart regulars, and they scarcely remembered the days of Slowhand.

Clapton, however, didn't have a clue what he intended to do next, and might have remained lost in indecision for months to come. But the moment the news of his departure from the Yardbirds hit the grapevine, John Mayall leaped into action.

His earlier reservations about Clapton had finally been swept away – dismissed, ironically enough, by the B-side of the record that got the guitarist so flustered in the first place. 'For Your Love' was an unadulterated pop song, anathema to the puritan bluesman. The instrumental 'Got to Hurry', on the other hand, was classic Yardbirds, classic Clapton, and Mayall was adamant, 'by the time he got to the end of the Yardbirds, which was only about six months after [*Five Live Yardbirds*], the changes were remarkable. The first time I heard "Got to Hurry", it just turned me around how much he'd improved.

'It was an amazing piece of blues. I got that record and I played it over and over again, and [that] did it for me. I couldn't think of any other way to go, apart from having Eric with me. Which was very, very bad news for Roger [Dean], who would probably have stayed in the band a lot longer if it was not for the emergence of Eric. But, from my point of view, the music had to come first.'

4. THE ORGANISER

John Mayall was Mike Vernon's first recruit to Decca. His second, again in the run-up to Christmas 1963, was Graham Bond.

Vernon's enthusiasm for Bond was boundless. 'Exciting, full of ideas and expression,' the producer proclaimed, 'he has the gift of being able to improvise freely ... and, still more importantly, he retains the necessary swing.' The group's version of the standard 'Hoochie Coochie Man', a song that every band of the age, it seemed, had sunk their teeth into, was one of the wildest Vernon had ever heard, and, as Decca's chief blues A&R man, charged with checking out every blueswailer that looked as though it could even *spell* 'Wang Dang Doodle', he'd heard a lot.

He also knew that he was picking up one of the hardest-working combos on the circuit; indeed, the year since Bond, Baker and Bruce departed Blues Incorporated had raced past in a blur of one-night stands. An audience, after all, was not the only thing the Graham Bond Trio inherited from Blues Incorporated; manager Ronan O'Rahilly, the Irish-born owner of Studio 51, also came aboard, bringing with him his own vast network of contacts and club-owners.

Few of the group's early engagements were quite as lucrative as the Manchester concert that inspired them to step out on their own in the first place, and Bond confessed that, at first, it was difficult pushing the band forward. 'Things were very hard because our sound was too way out at that time,' he told *Melody Maker*, a burden that the group went some way towards alleviating in April 1963, with the arrival of 21-year-old guitarist John McLaughlin.

Fresh from organist Georgie Fame's Blue Flames, McLaughlin made his live debut at the Marquee that same month; days afterwards, he joined his new bandmates in the studio, as EMI recruited them to back veteran rock'n'roller Duffy Power on his latest comeback single, an insidiously funky rendition of the Beatles' 'I Saw Her Standing There'.

The label had spent a few months keeping tabs on the Bond Trio (or Quartet, as it was now known); back around the time of Blues Incorporated's abortive attempt at recording a second Decca album, EMI had commissioned their own demo from the group. The powers that be eventually passed on the tape, but a few ears remained open to Bond's own activities and, when Power requested a powerful R&B act to back him, the call went out to Bond – and, with it, the offer of a five-year contract with the Parlophone label for the Quartet itself. The group signed.

Marred only by Power's apparent insistence on slurring half his lyrics, 'I Saw Her Standing There' was an incredibly punchy release, while the mere mention of its composers was sufficient to induce a storm of applause as the same team toured the UK that spring, as part of a package with Joe Brown and Marty Wilde. But any fears that exposure to the teen-scream audience might in some way derail the Quartet's own musical direction was firmly disavowed once they returned to their own itinerary; in June, the Quartet was recorded live at Klook's Kleek, with the resultant tapes (three tracks included within Bond's *Solid Bond* compilation in 1970) emphasising precisely how removed from the rest of British R&B the band actually was.

Sonny Rollins's 'Doxy', the Bond/McLaughlin co-write 'The Grass Is Greener' and an eight-minute improvisation around Jack Bruce's 'Ho Ho Country Kicking Blues' (which is neither country nor blues, ho ho) were far closer to free-form jazz than anything the Stones, the Yardbirds or John Mayall were pitching onto the scene. But they do indicate the freedom that the group held so dear, with all four members given their own time in which to shine, and Bond's saxophone punctuation almost negating the absence of any words or lyrics. Unfortunately, though the potential of the line-up was vibrant, this particular incarnation of the Quartet was never allowed the opportunity to truly shine.

According to Baker, McLaughlin was one of those people who could always find the downside to any development, a pessimism that quickly came to infect the entire band. The guitarist also had a disconcerting habit of speeding up on stage, playing faster and faster while his colleagues struggled to keep up with him. Just six months after McLaughlin's arrival in the band, he was fired – but not by Bond. It was Baker, settling into a role he enjoyed (or, at least, aspired towards) in so many of the groups he played in, who delivered the killing stroke. Bond, ostensibly the band's leader, remained on the sidelines and silently watched.

The group did not revert to its Trio status for long. Around the same time as McLaughlin was fired from the Bond group, Dick Heckstall-Smith found his tenure with Blues Incorporated coming to an end – and, ironically, for many of the same reasons that Cyril Davies' did; that is, the realisation that Korner's music was fast approaching the same heights of jazziness that he, Heckstall-Smith, had joined a blues band to escape from.

Bond had already tried to lure Heckstall-Smith into his own band on several occasions, beginning the very day that the Trio walked out on Blues Incorporated. This time, he accepted and, with his arrival permitting Bond to lay down his own sax to concentrate on keyboards, the Quartet underwent its final name-change ... the Graham Bond Organisation was chosen partly because it emphasised the band's lead instrument and partly because Bond's dapper young gangster look had now communicated itself to his bandmates as well.

Bond was not losing his taste for jazzier elements – as he told *Melody Maker*, 'the Organisation is a co-operative group in that there is no star and everybody is indispensable. I think the visual thing is extremely important, but the point about both our musical policy and presentation is that at least ninety per cent is completely improvised.' But the rapid popularisation of so many R&B bands had, he continued, 'made young people able to appreciate the sort of blues and gospel things we do', and the band was determined to at least meet the audience halfway, as Mike Vernon discovered when he auditioned the Organisation at Decca's West Hampstead studios towards the end of the year.

The group was still officially contracted to Parlophone, but that label's interest in the band had never taken off after the Duffy Power single failed to take off. Vernon and fellow producer Richard Lloyd, on the other hand, felt strongly enough about the group that such details were, according to which source one chooses to believe, either sorted out via some kind of sub-licensing deal, or ignored altogether. Bond biographer Harry Shapiro considers it quite conceivable that 'Graham "omitted" to mention they already had a deal.'

Either way, and Vernon's enthusiasm notwithstanding, the deal with Decca was itself to be very short-lived, amounting to just one three-hour session, during which the Organisation recorded six songs: a dramatically shaking version of 'Long Tall Shorty', which became their debut single in May 1964, 'Long-Legged Baby', 'Little Girl', 'Strut Around', a brittle cover of the standard 'Hi-Heeled Sneakers', and the take on 'Hoochie Coochie Man' that so overwhelmed Mike Vernon. Spread across the single, an eponymous EP and Decca's year's end *Decca Rhythm & Blues* compilation album, all evidenced just how much the group had changed in the year since the Klook's Kleek tape, and displayed a versatility that remained one of the Organisation's most in-demand attributes.

Certainly, Island Records chief Chris Blackwell was sufficiently impressed to recruit the Organisation to accompany Jamaican guitarist Ernest Ranglin on an EP of instrumental cocktail-jazz numbers; while the band was also called upon to back Motown star Marvin Gaye on a television show during his first UK visit in November 1964. Accompanied by Long John Baldry's Hoochie Coochie Men, the Organisation brought an entire new dimension to televised performances of 'How Sweet It Is (To Be Loved by You)' and 'Baby Don't You Do It', prompting Gaye's brother Frankie, some three decades later, to recall Marvin returning to the States positively raving about the fresh energies and ideas he had picked up from the Bond group's performance.

Gaye was especially taken with Jack Bruce. '[Marvin] really flipped about my bass playing. He told me there was nobody in the States playing bass like me, and he said he wanted me in his band.' Bruce thanked him, but declined. It was a massive honour, and it probably paid more per night than the Organisation earned in a month. But he also believed that there was a lot more to making music than simply making money, and churning out Motown hits every night of the year was never going to fulfil those urges.

The Organisation remained busy. Heckstall-Smith looked back upon 1964 and calculated that they were working almost every day of the year – one particularly intensive spell, between 12 May and 4 July, saw them play 50 shows in 54 days, 'and three of the four days off were consecutive'. A nationwide tour alongside Memphis Slim and, again, Long John Baldry, played its own part in this hectic itinerary, while Duffy Power resurfaced once more to lead the band through his next single, a positively scorching take on Mose Allison's ode to the Mississippi State Penitentiary, 'Parchman Farm'.

There was even a role for the group in the movies, as they were recruited to the musical cast of the comedy/sci-fi/pop-spoliation movie *Gonks Go Beat*. Only marginally relevant to a plot that involved aliens from the planet Gonk (named for the popular fluffy toys of the day) battling to prevent war breaking out between the neighbouring states of Beatland and Ballad Isle, the Organisation were joined by fellow Decca acts Lulu and the Luvvers, the Nashville Teens, the Long and the Short and Ray Lewis and the Trekkers and, like them, their role was fairly minimal.

Donning matching turtle necks and sunglasses, the group was filmed wildly raving to just one number, a live recording of a Bruce composition, 'Harmonica'. But, while it soon became awfully fashionable to describe that as the highlight of the film, most people who knock *Gonks Go Beat* probably haven't even seen it – or weren't paying attention when they did. In a moviemaking field that was giving a celluloid break to almost any act that looked like it could grow its hair past its shoulders, *Gonks Go Beat* was actually an extraordinarily enjoyable romp.

At the end of July, the Organisation launched a twice-weekly residency at the Marquee; from there, the group's next major engagement took them to Richmond, for that year's Fourth National Jazz Festival – or Jazz & Blues as it was, for the first time, now termed. Having spent two years firmly in the thrall of the jazzers, the 1963 festival saw the bill open up to include the blues of the Rolling Stones and Cyril Davies, the first step towards the event's eventual consolidation as the Reading Rock Festival. Nineteen sixty-four was to be even broader, as the Stones returned to headline the opening, Friday, night; Long John Baldry and Manfred Mann joined American bluesmen Jimmy Witherspoon and Memphis Slim on the Saturday bill; and Sunday night exploded out with Mose Allison, Georgie Fame, the Yardbirds and the Organisation.

It was an astonishing weekend, a veritable coming out party for the blues scene in general. The BBC were on hand to film a handful of sets on the Saturday and Sunday evenings, but for at least a handful of the participants, the highlight of the event came at the end of the festival.

There are, perhaps surprisingly, several eminently listenable documents capturing the sound of the Yardbirds in concert. The Sonny Boy Williamson live recordings, though they essentially preserve the group as backing musicians only, nevertheless capture a brutal energy, while tapes of the Birmingham R&B Festival and the Marquee (*Five Live Yardbirds*) both flash with a rare fire.

The finest recording of all, however, is a tape that did not come to light until a full 39 years after it was recorded, capturing the Yardbirds in concert in July 1964, just weeks – maybe even days – before the Richmond festival.

Just eight songs, little more than half the set, long, much of the tape reprises *Five Live Yardbirds*, topped and tailed by a crudely curtailed 'Someone to Love Me' (somebody's string broke) and the newly adopted Clapton showcase 'The Sky Is Crying', the stately Elmore James blues that the guitarist revisited a decade later, on his album *There's One in Every Crowd*.

But the differences in the performance are evident from the outset, as the Yardbirds lay the hands of experience upon what had hitherto been raw exuberance alone, and propel themselves through a set that is as well-balanced and paced as any great rock show should be. Much the same set rang out over Richmond that Sunday night, and the audience was still howling its approval as the Yardbirds wrapped things up by inviting a clutch of friends onstage with them . . . Georgie Fame, Mike Vernon, Graham Bond, Ginger Baker and Jack Bruce.

Vernon still laughs to recall just how 'unnerved' he was: 'I remember I was drunk, but I had to be. The most people I'd ever sung in front of was 300 at the Crawdaddy. At the festival, I sang "Stormy Monday" in front of 15,000.' For Bruce and Baker, however, the jam was soon taking on an even greater historical resonance. 'That was the first time I ever met Eric,' said Bruce. 'I was playing there with Graham and he was playing there with the Yardbirds, and we had a kind of jam session afterwards.'

A mild friendship – more a friendly acquaintanceship – was inaugurated; 'He used to come down to some of Graham's gigs,' Bruce continued. It was pure coincidence, then, that just weeks later, he and Baker found themselves cementing another alliance that, though they could never have known it, was to prove equally significant to their future endeavours.

Although Ronan O'Rahilly continued working hard for the Organisation, his attentions had recently become engrossed elsewhere, as he threw himself into launching (in March 1964) and establishing Britain's first-ever pirate radio station, Caroline, from aboard a ship moored just outside territorial waters in the North Sea.

For any performer, having a manager who also owned a radio station could not help but be an advantage, and Caroline's daily programming was certainly geared towards much the same audience as frequented an Organisation gig; Ray Charles, Etta James and Cy Coleman were all station favourites, together with a smattering of pop and light orchestral music. But the rigours of actually running the station were time-consuming, even with a growing staff and, as the year wore on, the group began looking further afield for representation. Enter, then, Robert Stigwood.

Born in Adelaide, Australia, Robert Stigwood arrived in London in 1955, a 21-year-old graduate of his home town's Sacred Heart College, with a stint working as a copywriter for a local advertising agency behind him. He hitchhiked his way to England, a months-long journey that saw him undertaking any occupations he could, to raise money for the next leg of his voyage.

Finally arriving in Britain, Stigwood worked for a short time as a housemaster at an establishment devoted to 'backward' teenaged boys; but moved on soon after becoming friends with Stephen Komlosy, a young man with serious aspirations towards a showbusiness career. With a £5,000 loan from Komlosy's mother, the pair established their own theatrical agency, Robert Stigwood Associates, at 41 Charing Cross Road, and hit early pay-dirt when a young actor named John Leyton, 'Ginger' in the on-going *Biggles* television series, fell onto their books.

With Leyton proving an aspiring vocalist as well as a thespian, Stigwood set about breaking his young charge into the music industry, arranging for auditions with both EMI and Pye. Neither was successful, but an introduction to producer Joe Meek proved more valuable. Just setting out at the helm of his own Triumph label, positively the first independent British record label of the rock'n'roll era, Meek was hungry for fresh talent. Leyton, already a household name (albeit a minor one), was ideal for his purposes.

Though Leyton himself admitted that he could barely 'sing a note', Meek and his arranger Charles Blackwell saw only challenges where other ears had heard obstacles. In August 1960, the team celebrated their first hit single, as Leyton's spectral lament for a dead girlfriend, the effects-heavy 'Johnny Remember Me' marched to the top of the chart, crushing the opposition of the day and dismissing, too, the popularly held belief that, in order to taste success in the music industry, you were first required to abide by the industry's rules and take your appointed place within that nicely regulated world in which managers managed, publishers published and record companies recorded.

The idea that an independent operator could simply step into this highly stratified universe and so indiscriminately scrap the system was anathema to the power brokers of the age. But even though some of the cream was scraped off the Leyton pie when the actual mechanics of manufacturing and distributing a major hit single forced Meek to license the recording out to the established Top Rank label, rather than release it on Triumph, still 'Johnny Remember Me' represented a significant milestone – one which Stigwood kept in mind as he formulated his own brilliantly reactionary Reaction label deeper into the decade.

Prior to that, however, he busied himself making further, equally lasting incursions into the British music scene, both alongside Meek (Leyton was quickly joined by another Stigwood discovery, Mike Berry) and then, following their falling out in mid-1962, under his own banner.

The Australian's influence grew even stronger after he concluded an arrangement with EMI, guaranteeing the label first option on any other records he made, then rewarding them with further hits by Leyton, Berry and, later, Mike Sarne, the archetypically sounding Cockney comedian who was, in fact, a German. Sarne scored a quartet of hits under Stigwood's aegis during 1962–63, including one, 'Come Outside', which simultaneously made a star of Stigwood's own secretary, fifteen-year-old Wendy Richards, more familiar in future years as Miss Brahms in *Are You Being Served?*, and, in *EastEnders*, as Pauline Fowler.

Not all of his ventures were gold-plated. Stigwood invested – and lost – heavily from an ill-fated attempt to convert Anglo-Indian singer Simon Scott into a major star; overlooking the requirements of any potential audience, he instead went for the media jugular, subjecting the hapless Scott to such a degree of hype that, even today, the singer is best remembered not for his one lower-Top Forty hit ('Move It Baby', in summer 1964), but rather for the plaster head-and-shoulders busts with which Stigwood deluged journalists, DJs and television producers.

Stigwood struck out, too, with Billie Davis, an astonishingly photogenic singer who, having first shone for Meek, was then recruited to Stigwood's side, groomed to near-perfection, and relaunched as the female antagonist on Mike Sarne's 'Will I What?' Months later, Davis's cover of the Exciters' Stateside hit 'Tell Him' reached the Top Ten, but a broken jaw, sustained in a car accident while returning home from a concert in Worcester, effectively slammed her career to a halt. A follow-up single, 'He's the One', flickered out at number forty due to Davis's inability to promote it, and, by the time she was able to work again, her early momentum had long since dissipated.

But still future Yardbirds manager Simon Napier Bell was moved to describe Stigwood as, 'in every way, the first British music business tycoon, involved in every aspect of the music scene, and setting a precedent that was to become the blueprint of success for all future pop entrepreneurs'.

Stigwood's acquisition of the Graham Bond Organisation seemed primed to prove the wisdom of those words. Audiences adored the band, the music papers respected them, and their peers applauded them. Only their record sales were at all disappointing. Bruce confessed, 'We tried our damnedest to have hits, but because of the way we looked, there was no way we were ever going to.'

Stigwood disagreed. All the Organisation needed was a push in the right direction and, having reinflated the group's moribund relationship with EMI, Stigwood had already given that a lot of thought.

At his prompting, the Organisation's first single for the company, for release on the Columbia imprint, was a cover of the 1957 Debbie Reynolds' hit 'Tammy', rhythm'n'bloozified sufficiently to engrain it with some grit, but moody, some might say mawkish, enough to infiltrate the most strait-laced appreciation of modern pop. In other words, it was ghastly, and, though it did inch to the lowest echelons of the chart (number 81 can scarcely be called a hit), it was clear that the experiment had failed. Stigwood remained the band's producer, but he never interfered with their choice of music again.

More rewarding, for musicians and fans alike, was the Organisation's inclusion in another Stigwood venture, as he organised and promoted Chuck Berry's latest British tour, a multi-act package that travelled through January and February 1965. Appearing alongside the Five Dimensions, the Moody Blues and another of Stigwood's managerial clients, singer Winston G (Long John Baldry was originally scheduled to appear, but fell ill on the eve of the tour), the Organisation frequently found themselves receiving the best reviews of the tour, and with good reason.

Berry openly performed on auto-pilot, with eyes only for the cheques he demanded Stigwood hand over before each performance; while the Moodies openly chafed at the injustice of playing second fiddle to Berry, at the same time as their latest single, Bessie Smith's 'Go Now', was topping the UK chart. Finally, as the package pulled into Manchester at the end of January, Moodies' manager Tony Secunda announced that they were leaving the tour, to launch their own headlining outing.

Horrified at the prospect of losing what was, for obvious reasons, the single greatest attraction on the entire tour, Stigwood was able to pull the group back on board by raising their fee. But still the Moodies' less-than-sparkling performances made it obvious that they continued to resent their position on the bill, while Stigwood quickly discovered that, in his haste to mollify the artful Secunda, he had lost sight of his own bottom line. The tour had just hit its halfway point when, with debts of £40,000, Stigwood was forced to call in the receivers.

The tour struggled on, but all concerned breathed a sigh of relief as it finally reached its end, and they could return to their own routines – which, for the Organisation, involved going back out onto the road, this time in support of *The Sound Of '65*, the band's debut album.

Recorded in three hours, for release in February 1965, *The Sound Of '65* was an eclectic mix, but one that was greeted by the *New Musical Express* as 'way-out blues sounds, weird at times, but always fascinating'. There was, the review continued, 'plenty of wailing harmonica and raving vocalistics', as the Organisation first breathed fresh life into such hoary old standards such as Muddy Waters' 'Got My Mojo Working' (surely the best version ever committed to Beat-Boom-era vinyl), and then forged ahead into absolutely uncharted musical territory.

Bond was naturally at the fore, proving why the sound of the Hammond organ was rapidly taking over from even the harmonica and the guitar on the club scene; Brian Auger, Georgie Fame and the Spencer Davis Group's Steve Winwood were all pushing the instrument towards new heights; within months, Auger confirmed its ascendancy with his own sparkling rendition of Booker T's 'Green Onions', pointedly retitled 'Green Onions 65'.

But it was *The Sound Of '65* that truly captured the past, present and future of the Hammond organ as a rock instrument. Bond's playing through a frenetic 'Wade in the Water' was nothing if not a portent of all that the Nice and Deep Purple were to accomplish throughout their earliest years, while Baker's drum showcase, 'Oh Baby', itself prefigured not only his own subsequent work-outs but, again, those of a horde of subsequent hard rockers. There was a remarkable, and remarkably eerie reprise for the old Blues Incorporated staple 'Early in the Morning'; and then there was 'Train Time', Bruce's brilliantly phrased answer to that long-ago schoolteacher who told him not to waste his time trying to write, and one of the finest locomotive blues ever written.

Based on a Forest City Joe song that Bruce encountered on one of American folklorist Alan Lomax's collections of blues recordings, 'Train Time' marked a very rare vocal excursion for its composer. 'When I became a jazzer,' the former soprano confessed, 'singers were seen as second rate and frowned on. It was very much a snob thing.'

Slowly he was breaking away from that conditioning, just as he was snapping away from another phobia, by breaking out a burst of breathless harmonica. For a long time, Bruce just hadn't seen any point in playing the instrument, regarding Cyril Davies as so far ahead of every other player that even the best shot could only wind up sounding like a pale imitation. But Davies was dead now, stricken by leukaemia in early 1964, and Bruce finally picked up the instrument in anger. 'Harmonica', the punching blues that was the Organisation's contribution to *Gonks Go Beat*, was Bruce's own tribute to the fallen king; 'Train Time' was the sound of him jousting for the now-vacant throne.

Both by name and nature, then, *The Sound Of '65* represented one of the most courageously forward-looking albums of the year, as remarkable in its own sonic caste as any of the purported 'classics' of the same spell – the Beatles' *Rubber Soul*, of course, tops *that* roll call. Yet by the time it appeared in the stores its creators were already looking even further ahead, as Bond prepared to take delivery of an instrument that changed the sound of the year, the band, and rock and pop music in general, forever.

The origins of the Mellotron date back to 1946, when Californian organist Harry Chamberlin first began experimenting with a tape recorder, pre-programming a series of drum loops that could be activated through a specially adapted organ. Aimed at the light pop market and a favourite toy for trendy television organists and seaside entertainers, Chamberlin's Model 100 Rhythmate debuted towards the end of the decade and, over the next ten years, expanded into the monster Music Master, with 35 keys, a ⅜-inch tape, and a secondary keyboard filled with rhythm tapes and sound effects.

Yet for all the technical wizardry that was stuffed inside its mighty cabinet, still the device was prone to any number of annoying problems, not least of all an alarming habit of playing one rhythm when another was demanded – as anyone who tried to Charleston while the organ Bossa Nova'd will recall. One of Chamberlin's salesmen, however, was convinced that these difficulties could be ironed out, if not by Chamberlin, then by the Bradley brothers' Bradmatic Ltd, an engineering company he knew of in Birmingham, England.

They indeed proved up to the task; they also, eventually, wound up purchasing Chamberlin's entire interest in the Music Master for £30,000 and, in partnership with orchestra leader Eric Robinson and magician David Nixon, formed a new company, Mellotronics, to sell and distribute what they now called the Mellotron. In the meantime, the first examples of their handiwork were made available for road-testing. Bond was only too happy to become the Bradleys' guinea pig.

April 1965 had already brought a new single, 'Tell Me (I'm Gonna Love Again)' – welcomed by *Disc Weekly* as 'a real swinger from this very good group . . . far more commercial than anything they've done before, yet they still retain that gravelly quality'; while Bond and Baker alone could also be heard on 'Please Don't Say', the first

45 by their Chuck Berry tour mate, Winston G. The Mellotron arrived a few weeks after that, making its bow as an unfamiliar monster looming over the stage at the Marquee on 8 July, reappearing on *Ready Steady Go* a couple of weeks later, and finally chewing up vinyl on the Organisation's next single, 'Lease On Love'.

Bond was absolutely enamoured with his new toy, even offering *Melody Maker* readers a crash course in its basic operation. 'The Mellotron uses pre-recorded tapes of other instruments. For example, every note in the register of the trumpet is recorded, and I can play it on the organ keyboard, getting the real sound.' He was less impressed, however, with the instrument's temperament, as Heckstall-Smith mourned in the pages of *Blues-Rock Explosion*. 'It went out of tune the whole bloody time. It was also very big.'

The Organisation made their second appearance at the National Jazz & Blues Festival that summer, with their live work again alternating with studio sessions, as they worked towards their second album, *There's a Bond Between Us*, a rip-snorting leviathan that pulled from influences that ranged from Booker T to Ray Charles, romped through the Blues Incorporated favourite 'Night Time Is the Right Time', and positively peaked with two songs whose own classic status has long since become established, Bond's 'Walking in the Park' (later to be immortalised by Colosseum), and Billy Myles's 'Have You Ever Loved a Woman' (a future staple of Eric Clapton's repertoire).

However, where *The Sound Of '65* concentrated on capturing the mood of the Organisation's live performances, this latest set was more experimental, with the novelty of the Mellotron riding roughshod over everything. Even as it conjured up what hindsight describes as an almost perfect proto-prog mood (Baker's closing 'Camels and Elephants' is positively prescient in that respect), the instrument was horribly overworked, with even a generally positive *NME* review cautioning, 'here's a restless, wailing rhythmic and sometimes overpowering sound'. *Record Mirror*, meanwhile, could not get over the absence of the 'live . . . atmosphere', while it was also becoming apparent that the group's musical advances could not paper over the cracks that were beginning to appear in the line-up.

The most ominous problems were those that divided Bruce and Baker. As Harry Shapiro pointed out in his biography of Bond, 'Ginger thought Jack too fussy, Jack thought Ginger too loud.' Bruce himself confirmed this, when he explained, '[Ginger] thought I was too busy on the bass. When we first started working together, I was playing stand-up acoustic bass. But, once I got an electric bass, I could be heard, which took away some of his thunder.'

Pete Brown, a jazz poet who had known Baker since the drummer's earliest days on the jazz scene, and who occasionally borrowed the Organisation en masse to accompany him at his own live performances, watched the ensuing ballet with horrified fascination. 'They were doing musical things to each other . . . Ginger would go, "Right try this, I'm gonna really drop you in it now. . . I'm gonna drop three beats just as I go into that break, and you're really gonna have to do something there, or you're really in the shit."' Then Bruce would do something similar back, until entire shows could be broken down into two halves – the booby-traps that Baker set for Bruce; the landmines that Bruce left lying around for Baker.

Baker tried various ways of persuading Bruce to turn down, some politic, others decidedly not. All, however, were to no avail, so he adopted another approach. 'Ginger really got through to me psychologically, that I was no good as a bass player,' Bruce mourned.

Taking solace in other people's opinion of his playing, Bruce tried to put Baker's spitefulness out of his mind, but it was difficult. 'I looked upon Ginger as my big brother, because he's three years older than me, which is quite a gap when you're seventeen or eighteen. He was very experienced, he was married, and he knew all the African stuff. He was definitely a mentor, and I looked up to him a lot. But he can be a little fiery at times.'

The rows continued: on the road, where fights between the pair came close, on at least a couple of occasions, to involving the entire band in a road accident; onstage, where the pair constantly appeared to be playing against the other – a fatal state of affairs for a rhythm section; and, ultimately, at a gig at the Golders Green Refectory, just days after the Windsor Festival, where Baker whiled away one of Bruce's bass solos by throwing drumsticks at his head.

Finally Bruce had had enough. Whipping around, he hurled his own instrument at Baker, demolishing the drum kit and then fearlessly coming to blows with a drummer several times his size. A couple of fast-moving bouncers broke up the battle, but Bruce's time with the Organisation was up – even though Bruce himself was not yet ready to concede defeat. Baker sacked him from the band that night, but Bruce refused to heed his self-proclaimed master's voice. So far as he was concerned, the Organisation was a four-man democracy, and Baker could huff and puff all he wanted to. Until Bond and Heckstall-Smith placed their own weight behind a decision, Bruce was staying put.

At first, his stubbornness appeared to be paying off. The first time Bruce showed up at a gig, Baker glared, but otherwise ignored him, offstage and on. The second time, too. But, finally, the drummer decided that enough was enough. Leaping to his feet as Bruce walked into the club, Baker pulled out the knife he had obviously brought along specifically for the occasion, and let Bruce know precisely where he stood in relation to the Graham Bond Organisation.

'If you show up at one more gig, this is going in you.'

Bruce never went back again.

5. THE BLUES AND THOSE WHO BROKE THEM

John Mayall dropped the axe on Roger Dean following a Bluesbreakers show in Nottingham, in April 1965, although Dean himself wasn't actually in the room when the blade fell. According to Hughie Flint, 'John gathered us round the jukebox and said to me and John McVie, "listen to this guitar player and tell me what you think?"' He punched in the Yardbirds' 'Got To Hurry'. 'So we listened to it, and the solo was pure Chicago blues. So we said "yes, that sounds very good, John", and he said "well, that's Eric Clapton and he's just left the Yardbirds, so shall we ask him to join?" So we said "yeah".'

The invitation went out immediately the group returned to London, but Clapton wasn't sure whether he wanted to leap from the frying pan of the Yardbirds' commerciality, into the fire of the Mayall's foreboding reputation. They never actually argued about it, but Mayall was certainly losing patience with the guitarist's reticence when he finally decided to lay it on the line: 'Look, we're a blues band, you're a blues guitarist. What do you have to lose?'

Clapton considered for a moment, couldn't think of a single thing, and agreed to at least give the offer a try. By the end of the day, he had even moved into Mayall's house on Southbrook Road in Croydon. 'When Eric left the Yardbirds... he didn't really live anywhere,' Mayall recalled. 'But I had a spare room [actually, it was a large cupboard] at my house, and that enabled him to have free access to my huge, at that time, record collection, which was a pretty hefty blues archive. [The collection was destroyed during the firestorm that swept Laurel Canyon, where Mayall was then living, in 1979.] So he felt right at home, and we did listen to so many records, and get excited about them, and they found their way into the repertoire.'

'He had a great collection of records, just everything,' Clapton confirmed. 'And a lot of it was unlisted, just a reel-to-reel machine with compilation stuff', the fruits of the many nights Mayall spent grappling with Voice Of America. But he listened, he absorbed, and a decade on, Mayall's record collection lived on in his mind as he pieced together his comeback *461 Ocean Boulevard* album, and settled on recording one of the blues he'd first discovered on one of Mayall's tapes, 'Give Me Strength'. 'I picked up on that song, never found out who it was by, [but] it was a great song, because it was exactly what I was thinking about and feeling at that time, and it came off straight away. It was obviously the key song to the album.'

Clapton was introduced to his new colleagues in the van on the way to the Bluesbreakers' next gig, on 6 April 1965. It was not a comfortable journey. 'Mayall was amazing,' Clapton reflected. 'He had his own bunk in the van. You had to sit upright, while he got into his bunk and went to sleep.'

In fact, the van had three bunks, with the rest of the group taking turns either to sleep, or to sit in the front seat with the driver. Neither was there any point in complaining. 'We never stay overnight anywhere,' Flint warned Clapton as they set out. 'We drive back from Newcastle, get home at four in the morning, and the next day we're leaving at noon for Birmingham.'

In the van, Clapton wondered what on earth he'd let himself in for. On stage, however, he realised that every sacrifice was going to be worthwhile. 'The Bluesbreakers had become pretty established on the scene,' Mayall mused. 'But I always felt that I was the only member of the band . . . who really understood what the blues were all about. Everyone else on the scene seemed to have just come into it, picking up Muddy Waters and Little Walter records and so forth.' With Clapton on stage beside him, however, 'it was a revelation, it was unbelievable to play with him for the first time, because we were on the same page, so to speak. It was "Yes! This is it!"'

Clapton was equally impressed by the chemistry. Mayall continued, 'so that was it. Once he got in the Bluesbreakers, and was playing the kind of material he wanted to play, that he hadn't been able to play with the Yardbirds, he just went from strength to strength. He was with me for a year and, in that time, his playing was unbelievable, it really was. It was like he was on another planet. It gave you thrills at four in the morning down at the Flamingo.'

Clapton was with the Bluesbreakers for less than a month when he first realised just how vast his new bandleader's reputation was. Bob Dylan had just arrived in London, at the outset of his 1965

British tour, and the first person he wanted to meet was John Mayall, the author of 'Crawling Up a Hill'.

Mayall himself was flabbergasted by the request: 'this stupid first single of mine! So the word went out, and I went over to the Savoy Hotel, which was a total circus. He had a suite of rooms, and all these Americans and Donovan was up there. He was requesting the presence of all these people, Marianne Faithfull, everybody. After he left London to go up to Birmingham or some place like that, he had a limo and I travelled up with him and Joan Baez in the back seat, while Pennebaker was doing his film *Don't Look Back*. Dylan would go off at tangents; he'd be talking, then he'd go off into a corner and write something down. But he was so surrounded by his entourage that it was hard to get more than five minutes with him.'

Dylan did make time, however, for Mayall and the Bluesbreakers to join him and producer Tom Wilson at Levy's Recording Studio on 12 May, for what Clapton described as 'just a jam session. We did a lot of his blues songs. He was making it up. We played for about two hours.'

Yet for all their renown, the Bluesbreakers remained exactly where they were after Decca dropped them, with their chances of landing a new record deal seemingly less than zero as label after label turned down the opportunity to sign them. Shortly after the Dylan session, however, manager Rik Gunnell finally caught a break.

Another of his clients, blues belter Chris Farlowe, was newly signed to Rolling Stones manager Andrew Loog Oldham's fledgling Immediate label; with the Animals' Eric Burdon producing, his first single, 'The Fool', was being readied for release. Mick Jagger was keen to work with him as well, and the label was understandably entertaining high hopes for the singer.

If lightning could strike once . . . Gunnell contacted label manager Tony Calder to offer the Bluesbreakers' services and remind him, if necessary, of one of Immediate's own founding maxims. The label may have been aiming for the sweet smell of success with the majority of its releases, but Oldham and Calder also nurtured the belief that certain artists should be presented to the public, even if the company lost money. The Bluesbreakers, coming off two flop singles and a zero-selling album, doubtless fell into that latter category, but Calder agreed to release a new single regardless.

Deciding upon a coupling of 'I'm Your Witchdoctor' and 'Telephone Man', Mayall and Clapton alone cut both sides during one frenetic recording session in early summer, 1965, under the watchful eye of Jimmy Page, the 21-year-old prodigy who was carving his initials into the London session circuit since he first left school, and who was now being schooled by Oldham in the finest arts of record production. (Mayall, too, knew Page's renown; had, in fact, once considered him as a potential Bluesbreaker. 'He turned me down,' Mayall said with a shrug. 'He said he was too busy with his session work.')

Page had produced a mere handful of records at this time, and the Mayall–Clapton coupling was without doubt the biggest name he had ever been offered. But the greatest challenge of the day, he revealed, lay in convincing the engineer not to shut up shop the moment Clapton started to play. Deafeningly loud, an impenetrable growl, Clapton seemed to be purposefully decrying every studio convention, never content until every needle was peaking in the red zone. Finally, Page revealed, laughing, 'the engineer, who was used to doing big bands and orchestras, suddenly turned off the machine and said "This guitarist is unrecordable!" I told him just to record it, and I'd take full responsibility. The guy couldn't believe that someone was getting that kind of sound out of a guitar on purpose.'

Page also took advantage of Clapton's proximity to record some extracurricular performances, inviting him down to his own house, and suggesting they jam together in the living room. According to Tony Calder, a tape recorder tucked away in the bathroom did the rest. 'Then Jimmy came in [to Olympic Studio, with bassist Bill Wyman, pianist Ian Stewart and drummer Chris Winters] and did some overdubbing, and that was the material we put on *Blues Anytime*' – an excellent series of Immediate label compilations that pursued the British blues scene through rare and unreleased material by the Savoy Brown Blues Band; Dave and Jo-Ann Kelly, future Groundhog TS McPhee, and the grandiosely named Santa Barbara Machine Head.

Page's own liner notes to the third *Blues Anytime* volume, released in 1968, attempted to justify the release of the Clapton jams by insisting, 'As precious little exists of his ability on record between The Yardbirds and the first John Mayall and Eric Clapton albums, I thought it essential to make these tapes available to the serious collector to illustrate the transitional period which helped to build Eric's fantastic reputation.' In fact, with the exception of the super-slinky 'Snake Drive', they do nothing of the sort, despite having now been repackaged across so many different collections and albums that even Clapton's most rabid collecting acolytes quickly grew tired of seeing them.

The Immediate single was still awaiting release when Mayall swung the axe once again, this time cutting John McVie out of the band, following one drunken binge too many from the bass player. As Mayall recalled with a shudder:

John was impossible sometimes, so drunk that he was completely unable to hold his instrument. When he joined me initially, he was an eighteen-year-old schoolboy, very straight, but being in the music business and around enough people who drank . . . I didn't, I used to do these all-nighters with a pint of milk. But there were enough other people around who did drink, and John got addicted to alcohol rather quickly. And, in the end, it got the better of him.

He was a marvellous blues bass player, and that's the thing that I remember always about John, how good he was. The drinking thing was just something we had to put up with.

Until he decided not to. McVie was sent on his way in late August 1965; in his place came Jack Bruce, fresh and still smarting from his exit, just days earlier, from the Organisation.

Clapton was thrilled. From the first night they played together in the Bluesbreakers, he swore, 'Jack . . . drove that band. McVie was a great bass player, but he didn't have the same fire as Jack.' Mayall, too, has acknowledged that he had very high hopes for this latest incarnation of the Bluesbreakers; that he would never, in fact, have dismissed McVie if Bruce had not so suddenly become available.

No sooner had Bruce settled in, however, than Clapton announced that he was heading out. At the end of August, he declared that he was leaving the Bluesbreakers . . . leaving the country, in fact . . . to embark upon what was grandly described as a world tour, but which ultimately got no further than a few tense days busking in a restaurant in Greece with the Roosters' Ben Palmer, and a handful of other friends. He played his final show with the band at Bexley's Black Prince pub on 30 August.

'He wanted to get away from the commerciality, to team up with a bunch of friends and just go off somewhere,' Mayall explained, but still the Bluesbreakers found themselves in an awkward position. After all, while Clapton was off sunning himself on some faraway beach, his erstwhile bandmates were left to flog themselves up and down the motorway in a van, looking for someone to take God's place.

Mayall continued, 'We held one or two auditions at gigs, John Gilbey played for a while, and Jeff Kribbett.' And then, one night at the Zodiac Club in Putney, a mutton-chop-sideburn bedecked young man, who claimed to be the answer to all the group's problems, approached Mayall. 'He kept coming down to all the gigs and saying, "Hey, what are you doing with him?" – referring to whichever guitarist was onstage that night – "I'm much better than he is. Why don't you let me play guitar for you?" He got really quite nasty about it, so finally, I let him sit in. And he was brilliant.'

'It was always difficult when somebody left the band, because I had a full calendar of gigs, so any changes in the line-up, I couldn't stop to cancel gigs and get in new musicians. So auditions were gigs, they came to the gig to try out, and that was it. There wasn't any rehearsal or anything.' Peter Green, then leaped in at the deep end, and he was a revelation.

Green himself confessed that he barely understood the sheer magnitude of his task; admitted, too, that he'd only fallen into the blues because 'I couldn't see anything else around at the time with any sort of soul in it, from the white guys. There seemed to be not much around at all. I looked ... well, I didn't really look hard, but I just got that message, and that's what inspired me.

'I got a feeling from Eric [Clapton], I guess, that there really wasn't anything else around. I mean, I'd never heard anything. I'd heard all the music and all the Liverpool groups. There was a leaning towards the blues with Keith Richard and the Stones, Brian Jones, the way the Stones played harmonica, they were the nearest. But they were an attempt to make an English kind of music. It seemed to be a style of clothing, and we had to have freedom of dress before anything could happen. Then Eric happened, and he had freedom of dress.'

But, if Clapton really did inspire Green to play the blues with such wild ingenuity, he also encouraged him to develop his own style, a gift that proved of unimagined importance when Green first stepped into his shoes that late summer of 1965. 'I was very naive. I didn't understand the prestige of playing with Mayall, or the pressure of replacing Eric Clapton.' Neither, he said, was he at all bothered by it. 'I didn't care about it. I just enjoyed the chance to play the way I wanted.'

Unfortunately for him, he was not to enjoy the chance for long. Green played no more than seven shows before Clapton returned to London, and Mayall welcomed him home with open arms. 'I'd promised him the job back when he got through with his roaming around, which was unfortunate for Peter, who was just getting into it. He'd got the gig, and he had to stand down to let Eric back in.'

Once again, the savage union between Clapton and Bruce could be resumed; but, once again, the alliance was doomed from the outset. Mayall continued: 'Jack only stayed in the Bluesbreakers for a few months because, being a Scotsman with an eye for some extra money, he got an offer from Manfred Mann, who were really doing rather well at that time. So he went off with them, and at that point John McVie, who promised to behave himself in future, came back in.'

Brief though it was, the Clapton–Bruce line-up of the Bluesbreakers did not go unrecorded. Mayall himself was regularly taping the Bluesbreakers' shows and when, in 1977, he compiled a selection of his personal favourite moments for the *Primal Solos* retrospective, he included five tracks recorded live at the Flamingo. (A sixth subsequently appeared on another compilation, *Looking Back*.)

The recording quality is rough enough to almost negate Bruce's contributions to the performances, but Clapton's guitar and the ghost of Mayall's organ glow through a magnificent 'Stormy

Monday' with such assurance that it is clear there was more going on than meets the ear. 'Have You Ever Loved a Woman', the Billy Myles number that Bruce brought over from the Graham Bond Organisation, Sonny Boy Williamson's 'Bye Bye Birdie' and a flaming excerpt from the ever-ubiquitous 'Hoochie Coochie Man' further distinguish the tape, and Mayall is happy, today, to admit that Bruce's recruitment to the Bluesbreakers was an inspired, and a prescient move. 'The fact of Eric and Jack meeting each other on stage set up the alliance which became Cream.'

At the time, however, Bruce's departure for the hit-making pastures of the Manfreds, left Mayall seething. Immediately, even before Bruce had finished serving out his mandatory one-month's notice, through November 1965 (his final gig was at the Flamingo on 28 November), Mayall put pen to paper to exorcise the bitter betrayal of 'Double Crossing Time', and make no secret of the fact that it was dedicated to Bruce. Further salt was rubbed into the wound when Mayall announced that, together with the hyperactive 'On Top of the World', the song would be his next single, again for Immediate.

At the same time, however, Mayall felt distinctly uncomfortable about continuing to record for the label. He couldn't put his finger on the precise problem. It may have been something as simple as the fact that he never met Andrew Loog Oldham in all the time he was with Immediate. But, even before the Bluesbreakers went into the studio with Mike Vernon, Mayall was asking whether there was any chance of Decca taking another look at the group.

Vernon thought there was, particularly given the extra incentive of Clapton's presence, and, promising to push Decca to give the Bluesbreakers another chance, he suggested they prepare the ground by recording another single entirely, a one-off, no pressure 45 for the producer's own independent label, Purdah. Cancelling the release of the Immediate single ('On Top of the World' subsequently became another staple of the Immediate blues compilation catalogue; 'Double Crossing Time' was held over for the Bluesbreakers' own future use), Mayall agreed.

Purdah was one of three labels that Vernon had launched over the past year, to spotlight those corners of the blues that the major labels, Decca included, could not reach. The first, which was destined to become the most successful, was Blue Horizon: launched with a single by Howlin' Wolf's regular guitarist, Hubert Sumlin, sold through *R&B Monthly* number 12 in January 1965, Blue Horizon had gone to release red hot waxings by boxer-turned-bluesman Champion Jack Dupree, Eddie Boyd, Little George Smith and more, and was soon to be turning out major UK hit singles as well.

A second label, Outa-Site, was launched in September 1965, to handle what Vernon described as 'the more commercial R&B

material': Larry Williams, Johnny 'Guitar' Watson and Jimmy McCracklin. Purdah then followed, with its eye set firmly on home-grown talent (a fourth label, the gospel-oriented Wheel, was planned, but never got rolling).

A single by Tony 'TS' McPhee marked Purdah's entry into the marketplace; Jo-Ann Kelly's version of Memphis Minnie's 'Ain't Nothin' in Ramblin'' was next on the schedule, but it was cancelled before release – 'My vague recollections are that neither the quality of performance nor recording were good enough,' mused Vernon, and he started casting around for a replacement.

For a time, he hoped that two of the tracks he co-produced with Giorgio Gomelsky for the Yardbirds back in February 1964 might fill the gap. Purdah, like Blue Horizon and Outa-Site, was a strictly collectors-only operation, specialising in extremely limited edition releases and, to avoid being hit with the then-pernicious Purchase Tax, singles were pressed in quantities of just 99 copies (the cut-off point for tax exemption). As he reminded Gomelsky, not only was there no danger of his release competing with anything that the Yardbirds themselves might issue at the same time, there was also little chance of any but the most devoted Yardbirds fan even hearing the group's most primitive rumblings.

Gomelsky refused to authorise the release (the tracks appeared, instead, on a Dutch label later in 1966), but Vernon remained adamant that Purdah's next release should retain at least some flavour of the Yardbirds. 'Both John and Eric had embraced our dream of a small independent UK blues label,' he explained, 'so studio time was booked at Wessex Sound and, within three hours of our arrival, the job had been completed.'

As with the Immediate single, Clapton and Mayall alone appeared on the two numbers they recorded that day, the piano–guitar instrumental 'Bernard Jenkins' and the harp-driven 'Lonely Years' – most of the studio time, according to Vernon, was spent 'repositioning the one microphone in use, searching for that sonic picture which created the illusion of a Chicago recording studio from the early 1950s. That we at least came near in achieving this aim is borne out by the critical acclaim of the many ensuing reviews.'

Released in early 1966, 'Bernard Jenkins' became the biggest seller yet in Vernon's independent catalogue, not only selling out its original pressing in record time, but actually forcing Purdah back to the pressing plant, to push the (admittedly still-limited) edition up to a record 500 copies, Purchase Tax be damned. And, all the while, Vernon kept on hammering away at Decca.

'We were really packing them in, in the clubs,' said Mayall, 'so Mike went back to Decca, and said you really ought to have another look. So, just on Mike's word, they did that and, of course, when sales went through the roof, they were very, very pleased, and that led to them giving him total freedom to do all the other albums.'

Mayall's return to Decca was inaugurated with a session backing American bluesman Champion Jack Dupree on his *From New Orleans to Chicago* album. 'Mike was always doing these things, whenever an American bluesman came over,' said Mayall. 'We also did one with Eddie Boyd. Mike obviously picked the cream of the British crop to back them. You didn't need any rehearsal for that. As far as I can remember, Mike used different groups and combinations of musicians as the backing band.' Drummer Keef Hartley, bassist Malcolm Pool and Tony McPhee joined Mayall and Clapton on the Dupree sessions.

The Clapton-era Bluesbreakers, however, are undoubtedly most lionised for recording what is, alongside Blues Incorporated's *R&B at the Marquee*, the best-known and best-loved record of the entire British blues era, the utterly seminal and oft-repackaged *Bluesbreakers with Eric Clapton* – *The Beano Album* to aficionados, so titled for the comic within which Clapton has his head buried on the so-casually posed front cover.

Mayall's biggest-selling album ever, *Bluesbreakers with Eric Clapton* is a truly remarkable record, one of those precious few albums that really do live up to all the hype that the years have lavished upon them. Like the Klook's Kleek concert set, it is very rough and simple (it was, in fact, recorded live in the studio for the most part) and, in terms of sheer musicality, *A Hard Road*, its Clapton-less successor, is a far more satisfying experience. But the relentless energy of *Bluesbreakers with Eric Clapton* cannot be denied, with Clapton's guitar a major force in creating, and perpetuating, those energies.

More than three decades later, talking with *Mojo* magazine's Paul Trynka, Clapton summed up his playing as 'a combination of real anger and frustration and arrogance. I was convinced I was the only person who knew what was going on.' He was fortunate, however, that in Mayall, he had a bandmate who was prepared to let him get on with proving it.

Clapton continued, 'I think I would have been so intimidated if I hadn't had some kind of advocate.' Instead, with Mayall quietly egging him on, Clapton walked into the studio as though he owned it, and literally dictated the set-up he wanted. 'When they tried to set up the recording, I wouldn't let them put the microphone anywhere near my amplifier. And there was some real "who do you think you are, telling me how to record an album?" going on. But I intuitively knew it wasn't going to sound good, miked close.'

His conviction prevailed. No matter what else is going on elsewhere in a track, Clapton's guitar screams out, a barrage of beautiful noise more shattering than any which had ever been preserved on a British blues record. *Melody Maker*'s review cautioned, 'there isn't a spark of humour in anyone's playing . . . it's joyless and savage and gives grim satisfaction'. But an admiring

Hughie Flint marvelled, 'Eric played through his Marshall exactly as he would on stage.'

Feedback, leakage, distortion, Clapton didn't care what he wrought on the hapless recording equipment, just so long as it felt right, until even Vernon was taken aback, seated with engineer Gus Dudgeon, desperately trying to figure out how they could capture the sound of the master in full flight. 'We didn't know how to deal with the volume that Eric was playing at, so we had to find a way ... and that was an exciting thing, it was almost as exciting as the music itself.'

The result was a violent statement of intent, a defiant roar that not only confirmed Clapton and Mayall's supremacy within their own time and space, it also provided both musicians with the blueprint that sustained them throughout the remainder of the decade: Clapton with Cream, whose debt to the Bluesbreakers album was seldom disguised; Mayall with the succession of future line-ups that followed.

Indeed, had Clapton not been lured away by a sudden dream, there is no saying what a second Bluesbreakers album might have been capable of, and responsible for. Unfortunately, it was not to be. For, even as he let rip with the guitar that was to confirm for the world all of his youthful brilliance, Clapton was already secretly celebrating his own next move.

6. AND THEY SHALL BE CALLED . . .

It was Graham Bond who first suggested that Jack Bruce might be the right man for Manfred Mann and, whereas much of the rest of Bond's life was going wrong at every turn, on this occasion, he was spot on. Neither, as so many rock histories insinuate, was Bruce merely passing through the group. The seven months that he spent as a member saw Manfred Mann record some of their most adventurous music yet, not to mention one of their biggest hits ever.

Since forming (as the Mann-Hugg Blues Brothers) in the early 1960s, and briefly sharing the Organisation's roost at the jazzier end of the R&B spectrum, Manfred Mann had developed into one of the country's most reliable hit-making acts, honing a succession of deceptively progressive concepts into ready-to-wear hit singles – the anthemic stompers '5-4-3-2-1' and 'Doo Wah Diddy Diddy'; the more refined 'Come Tomorrow' and 'Oh No, Not My Baby'; a genre-bending revision of Bob Dylan's 'If You Gotta Go, Go Now', released a full two years before the writer's own version saw even a limited release on an obscure Dutch 45; and so on.

Dig deeper into their output, and the group was even more adventurous. It was not their numerical strength alone that convinced the quintet to title their debut album *The Five Faces of Manfred Mann*; it was the spectrum-stripping dexterity with which they could turn their hand to anything they chose, be it a groundbreaking stomp through 'Smokestack Lightning' or a freakish reinvention of Herbie Hancock's 'Watermelon Man'.

With such virtuosity, however, there came problems. The group's greatest recordings, as Mann himself once complained, were on their albums and EPs; the hit singles, on the other hand, were little more than pop-fodder by comparison, but that was what they were known for – that, it seemed, was *all* they would ever be known for. Anger set in, a bilious, schizophrenic anger that threatened to shatter the group altogether. Paul Jones, their so-charismatic vocalist, was on the verge of departing. He agreed to stay on only for as long as it took the Manfreds to find a replacement, and they knew they could not stall forever. Guitarist Mike Vickers, on the other hand, did not even permit the group that luxury. In October 1965, he walked out, never to return.

Melody Maker heralded the split with banner headlines – MANFRED WANTS MORE MENN; and the shocked musicians shuffled. Bassist Tom McGuinness, Eric Clapton's old bandmate from the days of the Roosters, took over Vickers's duties, which at least spared the Manfreds the bother of trying to find a new lead guitarist. Settling upon a new bassist, too, was easy, for Graham Bond was not the only person who was pushing Jack Bruce's name forward. Manfred Mann's colleagues were, as well. Only he was less than convinced of the wisdom of the move.

McGuinness explained, 'we all said [to Manfred], "we want Jack Bruce, he's the best bass player around." And Manfred was, "I can't ask him, John Mayall's my neighbour." But we kept badgering him, saying, "he's the one we want, we've got to get him"', until finally, Mann made the call. For all his reluctance to rock the neighbourial boat, he knew it was the right decision, even before he picked up the phone.

So did Bruce, the moment he answered it. He accepted Mann's offer, although he was not available immediately, as the disgruntled Mayall demanded he first work out that month's notice. A couple of interim players, Pete Burford and David Hyde, flitted through Manfred Mann's ranks as they waited but, finally, the end of November 1965 saw Bruce take his place in the band, alongside two further newcomers, a horn section of Henry Lowther and Lyn Dobson. Thrown into the closing phases of the Manfreds' latest tour, a sixteen-date UK outing that paired them with the Jeff Beck-fired Yardbirds, Bruce made his debut onstage at Northampton's ABC Cinema on 29 November, the night after his final show with Mayall. He did not even have time to rehearse with his new bandmates.

'I came in at the last minute and I learned the whole set. I mean, I played the whole set without rehearsal and I think that impressed them . . . I played "Do Wah Diddy Diddy" right off – do you know what I mean? No probs!'

Manfred Mann himself left nobody in any doubt over the newcomer's importance to the band. 'Jack is an invaluable asset,' he told *Melody Maker* shortly after Bruce's arrival. 'He plays wonderful bass guitar and has a ridiculous sense of time.' Bruce was also 'the most forceful personality among the new guys, he's got a great wariness against being had'. In fact, Mann still has just one misgiving about the entire affair. 'Jack was miscast, poor sod,' he confessed. 'Because he was in a band ... some of us had jazz backgrounds, and we were edging that way again. But Jack was a great bass player, and his abilities were irrelevant to what we were doing.'

Tom McGuinness agreed, telling the BBC's *Rock Family Trees* documentary, 'he was so good that he was quite impossible to play with at times, and we often quite literally couldn't follow him. We'd just be looking at each other, going "where is 'one', where is 'one'?"... as in "one-two-three-four". He was completely wasted, playing [with us.]'

Bruce, however, had no complaints; in fact, he suddenly discovered that he had double cause for celebration. Throughout Bruce's time with the Graham Bond Organisation, Robert Stigwood had regularly encouraged him in his songwriting, regardless of whether or not his efforts actually wound up in the recording studio with the group. Finally, towards the end of his time with Mayall, 'Stigwood was kind of pottering about and he said to me, "You should make a single." So I wrote a couple of songs, or I tried to, then went into Abbey Road, I think it was, and recorded them with a bunch of jazz musicians, because I didn't know anybody else, any rockers. John Stevens was playing drums.'

Bruce today is almost gleefully disparaging of the resultant record, adamantly describing it as '... not my finest work. It was a very adolescent attempt at trying to write something and it didn't work.' Still, the boozily good-time 'Drinkin' and Gamblin', backed by the marvellously wordy, and almost tongue-twistingly contagious 'Rootin' Tootin'', was released in December 1965 on Polydor, the release cunningly timed to within days of Bruce's official arrival in Manfred Mann.

The record did not sell, but still the extra few lines of column space that it garnered was certainly worth the effort of the exercise. Manfred Mann's core audience, after all, was scarcely likely to be *au fait* with past line-ups of the Organisation or the Bluesbreakers and, to them, Bruce would have seemed a total unknown. But at least he was an unknown with his own single in the shops.

The potential of this new line-up was immense, a promise that was first fulfilled when the new-look Manfreds cut a BBC session in early December, and then by the string of Abbey Road recordings that filtered out over a slew of subsequent releases, each one testifying to the group's new-found confidence, as they discovered what they could do with a 'real' bass player on board (McGuinness never claimed to be anything but a guitarist doing someone else's job). There was also a wild performance at the Marquee on 28 December, where Eric Burdon leaped onstage with the band, to propel them through a dynamic encore. But it took misfortune to truly wring the best out of the band.

Just weeks after Bruce's arrival, travelling back to London from a gig in early January, the Manfreds' van was involved in a collision. Mann sustained several bruised ribs, but vocalist Jones broke his collarbone, not only forcing him off the road, but keeping him out of the studio as well.

As if they were deliberately attempting to raise the standard of their game to match their bassist's undoubted abilities, the remainder of the group promptly threw themselves into an era of dedicated experimentation. January 1966 saw the group record the series of instrumentals that, combined across the *Instrumental Asylum* EP that summer, gave pop fans the opportunity to hear precisely what a rocking jazz band was capable of doing to the Stones' 'Satisfaction', the Yardbirds' 'Still I'm Sad', the Who's 'My Generation' and Sonny and Cher's 'I Got You Babe'. Hits of the past twelve months, all four had all but defined 1965. How appropriate, therefore, that Manfred Mann's own next move, following the recuperated Jones's return to action, was among the records that similarly defined 1966.

'Pretty Flamingo' was an almost infuriatingly catchy love song, to which the Manfreds grafted strumming acoustic guitars, a haunting keyboard wash, delicate harmonies and even a sweetly clumsy recorder. The overall combination could have been cloying; instead, it was devastating. The moment, just after the one-minute mark, when Jones announces for the first time, 'some sweet day, I'll make her mine', is positively heart-stopping, while the stark guitar that launches the number quickly located a willing echo in the Kinks' 'Autumn Almanac' – like 'Pretty Flamingo', one of that handful of records that will forever epitomise the English summers of the mid-1960s. Yet, as quickly as Bruce arrived to help Manfred Mann alchemise a moment of magical history, he was being tempted to depart once again.

The last months of the Graham Bond Organisation were akin to being trapped forever in a bitter winter. Bruce's departure should have steadied a rocky ship – that, after all, was Baker's own justification for firing him. Instead, the storms just kept coming.

Bond replaced Bruce with former John Burch Octet trumpeter Mike Falana, while compensating for the absent tones by playing the bass pedals on his organ and, for a few shows, everybody revelled in the new atmosphere. No more heated arguments in the back of the van, as Bruce's liberal politics spilled out in a stream of do-gooder idealism; no more protracted rows over the length of songs and solos; and no more fussy, show-off-y bass lines wandering wherever they jolly well pleased. Even Bond and Heckstall-Smith agreed that there were times in the back of that van when simply being in the band was akin to serving in a war zone. Peace, Baker now assured them, had finally been declared.

But it hadn't. Rather, the fractious friction that Baker had hitherto confined to his relationship with Bruce was now spilling out in other directions, seeking new targets, new whipping posts, new victims. The drummer's drug habit, the heroin addiction that dated back to the days of Blues Incorporated, left him constantly on edge, and in moments of regretful lucidity, during his attempts to clean up, he admitted as much.

The Organisation could carry the weight of one junkie; had spent three years so doing. It could not, however, bear the load of two, particularly once Bond's own growing reliance on smack began tangling with the rest of his personal life.

His home life disintegrated. By early 1966, Bond was entombed within a protracted divorce battle; drifting towards homelessness and such despair that, on one occasion, he was forced to break into his own former home, just to get some blankets. According to biographer Shapiro, Jack Bruce – still a close friend, despite his departure from the band – helped him out on that particular escapade and, when the bassist married Organisation fan club secretary Janet Godfrey later in the year, a still-grateful Bond gave him the blankets as a wedding present but was then forced to ask for them back, as his personal situation continued to deteriorate.

The root of all of these problems, in Baker's mind, was money or, rather, the lack of it. The Bond group was still working hard, but they were making no headway, nor any profit. Drugs were an escape from the grinding monotony of one one-night stand after another, Bond's divorce was a consequence of the same. The Organisation did hold together sufficiently to record one more single, a version of the old blues 'St James' Infirmary' that was both haunting *and* haunted, but the band members themselves had grown so distant that Baker was now missing as many shows as he played. By March 1966, Bond had reluctantly recruited a new part-time drummer, Red Reece, from Georgie Fame's group, and was courting Jon Hiseman away from Mike Taylor's jazz quartet as a full-time replacement. Baker was essentially a free agent once again.

Baker's final recording with the Graham Bond Organisation was, ironically, to become the group's best-selling record yet. 'Waltz For a Pig' was cut in early 1966, after Robert Stigwood found himself faced with an unusual, but seemingly intractable dilemma that threatened not only to drag him into a messy contempt-of-court action, but also to derail the fruition of one of his own fondest dreams, the launch of his own record label.

Searching for a way out from the financial morass of the Chuck Berry tour, Stigwood folded his earlier Robert Stigwood Associates, and launched a new company, the Robert Stigwood Organisation – RSO. He also abandoned his long-time relationship with EMI, and pledged his talents instead to Polydor, the German-based record label that was just making its first serious inroads into the British market.

Part of this latest arrangement echoed Stigwood's arrangement with EMI, in that Stigwood would bring his own discoveries and productions to Polydor, a move facilitated by the appointment of Roland Rennie, Stigwood's closest ally at EMI, as Polydor's new managing director. (Jack Bruce's solo single was one of the earliest fruits of this new relationship.)

Even more important was Polydor's willingness to hand Stigwood his own label. One of his greatest misgivings about his relationship with EMI was that even his most successful productions disappeared into the tangled catalogue of the company's various subsidiaries – a Parlophone 45 here, a Columbia one there. Under the new arrangement, all future Stigwood-related releases would be gathered together on one imprint, the newly founded Reaction label. Now all he needed to do was ensure that the label was launched with a splash.

Although the nature of the company's distribution deal with Polydor insisted that Reaction was little more than another subsidiary of an already sprawling major, Stigwood was adamant that the label should maintain a distinct whiff of independence, well aware that that added a great deal to its charm.

It was, after all, the age of the plucky go-it-alone-r, an era ushered in the previous year by Andrew Loog Oldham's Immediate, and followed through with vibrant alacrity by a host of other producer/manager-owned concerns. American born, London-based producer Shel Talmy's Planet wrestled with Reaction to be the first off the block; Giorgio Gomelsky's Marmalade, Yardbirds manager Simon Napier Bell's SNB, Kinks producer Larry Page's Page One and so many more followed. And, though none – Reaction included – ever proved as successful, or as long-lived, as the set-up they all strove to emulate, still the sheer implausible adventurousness of their existence left a lustrous legacy that enthrals record collectors even today, close to four decades after they closed their doors.

Whereas those other labels looked to either talent or gimmickry to kick them off, however, Stigwood took another tack entirely. Reaction was birthed amid a firestorm of anger, betrayal and controversy.

Late in 1965, for the princely sum of £500, Stigwood had purchased exclusive booking-agency rights for the Who. It was a shrewd move. Just three hit singles into their career, the group had already garnered a reputation that seemed destined to blossom into a major pop sensation. Soon after, the group's management team, Kit Lambert and Chris Stamp, began sub-letting space in Stigwood's office and, when they approached him over a contractual wrangle that had recently blown up with the Who's original mentor, Shel Talmy, Stigwood was swift to come to their – and his own – aid.

Devoted to breaking the Who's contract with Talmy, Lambert and Stamp not only intended the band to record their next single,

'Substitute', under their own steam, they also determined to release it as far from Talmy's grasp as they could, abandoning the Brunswick label to which Talmy tied them, in favour of a deal of their own choosing. As Pete Townshend reflected six years later, 'Shel Talmy had to be got rid of, and the only guy who was really powerful enough, who was connected with the Who in any way whatsoever, and who wouldn't suffer by it was Robert Stigwood.'

In early 1966, Lambert and Stamp signed the Who to Reaction; then selected the Townshend composition 'Circles' for the B-side of this new single, knowing that Talmy had already scheduled an earlier recording of the same number as the group's next Brunswick A-side. The Who's only concession to Talmy's plans was to retitle the song 'Instant Party' and, just a couple of weeks after the Talmy production was released, Reaction unveiled 'Substitute'.

Furious, Talmy promptly applied for a High Court injunction, but cleverly argued not that the Who had broken their contract, which would doubtless embroil everyone in a long-winded legal stalemate, but that they were breaking a copyright that he had established via his own initial recording of 'Circles'/'Instant Party'. The Court agreed and, on 11 March 1966, Polydor – as Reaction's manufacturer and distributor – was barred from continuing to press and sell copies of any record that featured the disputed number. (At the same time, Talmy grasped full advantage of the publicity garnered by the legal affray, by retitling his version of 'Circles' as 'Instant Party' as well.)

The decision rattled Reaction badly. As the follow-up to 'My Generation', not to mention one of the greatest songs the Who ever recorded, 'Substitute' was a sure-fire hit; indeed, the very day that the High Court injunction was issued, the 45 broke into the UK chart at number 33. Hastily, Lambert and Stamp scrambled for a replacement for the injuncted number, only to discover that the Who had nothing else on the shelf, and no time in which to record anything. For a moment, the record's very future hung in doubt; for a moment, too, Reaction's own prospects of hitting the ground running were looking decidedly shaky.

Stigwood was not going to allow that to happen. The Who might not have had any unused material laying around, but the Graham Bond Organisation did, in the form of a funky instrumental, 'Waltz For a Pig'. Smirking, perhaps, at the apparent aptness of its title, he recredited the performance to 'The Who Orchestra' and ushered that into production as the new B-side to 'Substitute'. Even more impressively, he did so with such speed that the record's sales performance barely wavered for a moment.

Rising to number eighteen on 19 March, as record shops continued selling their stock of the 'Instant Party' coupling, the following week saw sufficient 'Waltz For a Pig' flips hit the stores to push the record to number fifteen. Then, with production back in full swing, the record continued to rise. By mid-April, 'Substitute' stood at number five and, with every copy sold, the Graham Bond Organisation received a new (if, perhaps, unaware) listener.

Sadly, it was too late to do the group any good. Although the sudden influx of money did permit Baker to buy his first ever motor car, negotiating an advance on the royalties to come, he picked up a yellow Rover 2000; it could neither paper over the divisions that rent the Organisation, nor still Baker's excitement at the thought of the untrammelled future that now lay ahead of him. The only question in his mind was, what form would that future take, and he already had a good idea of the answer to that one. He would form his own band, comprising only those players whose skill on their instrument was as great as his – a supergroup of superb players. Eric Clapton was the first name that came to mind.

Strangely enough, the concept of rock supergroups seemed to be on a lot of people's minds during early 1966. Interviewed 33 years later, the Who's own John Entwistle detailed how 'one of the papers . . . I think it was probably *Melody Maker*, because they liked doing things like that . . . ran a poll, "who would be in the ultimate pop supergroup?" They were asking all manner of people – Pete and Keith (Who bandmates Townshend and Moon), Paul Jones, and so on. And it ended up with me on bass, Eric Clapton on guitar and Ginger Baker on drums. I don't remember who else was voted in, but a few months later, the Cream came along, and I did wonder if somebody was maybe believing too much of their own press.'

Neither was he alone in noting the proximity of Baker's resolution to the publication of *Melody Maker*'s supergroup fantasy. Clapton biographer John Pidgeon reached a similar conclusion in his masterful study of the guitarist's career, 1976's *A Biography*. But there were other audacious plans afoot during the first months of 1966 and, hanging around the office that Robert Stigwood still shared with Kit Lambert and Chris Stamp, Baker enjoyed a bird's eye view of the wildest of them all.

After a year in the Yardbirds, during which he had at least equalled, and occasionally eclipsed Eric Clapton's contributions to that band's legend, Jeff Beck was finally nearing the end of his tether. Tired of touring, more tired still of the often absurd double bills that the Yardbirds found themselves booked onto, Beck not only announced he was quitting the group, he, too, was resolved only to play with people whose abilities matched his own.

At the same time as Jimmy Page was recording Eric Clapton jams from his bathroom, he was also supervising a series of sessions that paired Beck with the remnants of Cyril Davies' All Stars, drummer Carlo Little, pianist Nicky Hopkins and bassist Cliff Barton. Neither was the combo a mere pipe-dream. The resultant contributions to the *Blues Anytime* series rate among the most spectacular offerings in the entire series.

Beck himself, however, had even higher hopes for a union with Keith Moon and, for a few weeks, the Who-shattering possibility that this new project might eclipse Moon's ties to Townshend, Daltrey and Entwistle hung very palpably over the Reaction offices. In the event, and one short recording session notwithstanding, the grand scheme came to naught. 'Moonie needed the Who,' Beck sighed. 'He wasn't about to leave on the pretence that we were going to form a band overnight, and become huge and successful. He just had a terrible five minutes with them, then made amends and went back.' Beck, too, would recant, and return to the Yardbirds, albeit for a just few months more. But the possibility of a clutch of masterful musicians combining in one heavy-hitting unit was nevertheless a tantalising one and, once the genie was out of the bottle, it was not easily going to be locked up again.

'I knew I wanted Eric,' Baker recalled, 'so I called up Rik Gunnell, to find out where the Bluesbreakers were playing next. He told me they were in Oxford that night, so I jumped in the car and took off there. I sat in on some numbers, and it just went "whoosh!" The entire gig took off on another level.' It was the first time the pair had played together since that jam at the Richmond Festival two years before, but the flashes of inspiration that both registered that memorable evening had only grown more dazzling with time. If Baker had had any questions in his mind before he motored up to Oxford that March afternoon, not one now remained.

He had still to pop the question, however – that came later in the evening, after Baker offered to drive Clapton back to London in the Rover. 'I was *very* impressed,' Clapton admitted. 'Musicians didn't have cars. You all got in a van. [Ginger] drove me home at eighty mph.'

For a time, the pair merely chatted. But finally, Baker delivered his payload. 'I'm thinking of forming a band. Do you want to be the guitar player?' Clapton thought for a moment, but only a moment, then answered. 'Yes.' 'And then,' Baker shivered, 'he asked "What about a bass player?" Hmmm, I hadn't thought about that yet. And he said, "Well, what about Jack?"'

Now it was Baker's turn to fall silent. Jack ... Jack who? Jack Bruce? You've got to be kidding.

Clapton was stunned. Insulated in the back of the Bluesbreakers' van, or buried away in John Mayall's music room, absorbing that miraculous record collection, Clapton really didn't get out much. His closest friends tended to be those who had only the most tenuous connections to music ... Ben Palmer, pianist in Clapton's long-ago Roosters, and one of his partners in his Greek adventure, was the greatest. He rarely listened to gossip and rumour.

Naturally, he and Bruce had talked a lot during the bassist's three-month stint in the Bluesbreakers; they'd hit it off as comrades just as well as they'd gelled as musicians. But the reasons behind Bruce's departure from the Organisation rarely came up, any more than his reasons for leaving the Bluesbreakers. Musicians moved on, it was the nature of the beast. But they also reunited and, though Clapton personally was never a great fan of the Organisation ('it was too jazzy for me'), he nevertheless assumed that Baker would be thrilled to reunite with his old partner in rhythmic crime. The truth of the matter, as Baker laid it out, left Clapton wondering what on earth he'd so precipitously agreed to. It was time to retrench.

'I withdrew,' Clapton shrugged. If this new band was to be as great as Baker said it should be, then each of its players had to be the best in the business. Baker and Clapton knew they fitted that bill; Bruce, Clapton was adamant, was the only bassist who similarly matched that same lofty criteria. 'I said I would only go on in with Ginger if he would go in with Jack.'

Finally Baker agreed to at least give *rapprochement* a shot. The following day, he drove round to the council flat in St John's Wood that Bruce shared with his new bride and her parents, to try and rebuild the bridges that were so viciously slashed asunder seven months before. And the fact that Bruce even let him into the house surprised him.

Quietly, Bruce listened while Baker outlined his scheme – with Clapton on board, after all, it was no longer a dream. A coming together of the very best musicians in the land ('you didn't take any notice of that thing in *Melody Maker*, did you?'), dedicated to making the greatest music that they could. They would produce themselves, compose their own songs . . . Bruce had already proven himself useful with a pen; his vocal excursions with the Organisation proved that he could sing. This new band would offer him opportunities to perform like he'd never had in his life.

It was, Bruce intuitively knew, the kind of chance that rarely comes along, maybe once in a lifetime; the opportunity, for the first time in his life, to truly become the master of his own musical destiny. 'Ginger drove up in his new Rover, which was very impressive, and asked me – without a knife – whether I wanted to join this band. I said yes. I'd missed playing with Ginger, obviously; but I'd missed his company as well, so it sounded like a good idea.'

There was, however, just one niggling little detail. Everything that Baker laid out before him existed only in some as-yet undefined, and certainly unrealised future. With a young wife to support, a home to buy (Jack and Janet certainly didn't intend staying with the in-laws forever), and dreams of starting a family as soon as they could, Bruce had to keep a close eye on the present as well. And the present, thank you very much, could scarcely be any better.

'Pretty Flamingo', Manfred Mann's latest single, was already destined for the top of the chart, the group's first number one since 'Doo Wah Diddy Diddy' in 1964. The group was recording regularly, and pushing their musical frontiers so dramatically forward that, twice in the last few months, the Manfreds had appeared at the Marquee without a support act, and opted instead to display their entire repertoire: pop, blues, R&B and jazz. He was even beginning to make inroads in the lucrative world of sessions, as he was booked to play on an upcoming Hollies session, recording the theme to the latest Peter Sellers' movie, *After the Fox*.

For the first time in his career so far, Bruce was facing a certain future in a group that was already established among the most successful, and highest-earning acts around. But he also knew that the world Baker offered him packed even more riches than that, a temptation that, for all his practical reservations, he knew was irresistible. That was confirmed to him a few days after Baker's fateful visit, as he sat in the Blue Boar service station, on the way home from another Manfreds gig up the M1 someplace.

He'd already given Baker a tentative 'yes', but he'd yet to speak to Clapton. Now, as he looked up from his pie and chips, who should be walking into the restaurant, but the man himself. The Bluesbreakers, too, were on their way home from a show and had stopped off to grab a quick meal. Bruce laughed, 'suddenly I see Eric coming in, and I got so excited seeing him that I threw this pie and chips at him. He ducked, and it hit this woman right in the face. I'm probably one of the very few people ever to be banned from the Blue Boar. And I still got into the band!'

Bruce, Baker and Clapton came face to face for the first time around the end of March 1966, gathering in the front room of Ginger Baker's maisonette on Braemar Avenue, Neasden; pushing back the G-Plan Scandinavian-style furniture to accommodate Baker's home-made green Perspex drum kit; and, beneath the watchful eye of the drummer's treasured collection of African tribal artefacts, launching into what they assumed to be a tentative jam, an attempt to get the feel of one another's playing, a loose 'pleased to meet you' through the handful of blues that they all knew they knew.

Sun Records bluesman Doctor Ross's 'Cat's Squirrel' was there, a thunderous 'Lawdy Mama'. . . and something else; an indefinable chemistry that all three musicians, quite independently, and unerringly through the four decades since then, have described with just one word: 'magic'.

'It was the combination of Eric's at the time, very pure blues playing, and our kind of pushing him beyond what he thought his limits were,' Bruce explained. Whatever else had sparked between Bruce and Baker through their years with the Organisation, it was clear that the musical chemistry that they had enjoyed was still present; more than that, it was also ready to absorb Clapton's energies. 'It was very exciting. It was one of those rare moments when we started playing, and then we were looking at each other, just grinning. Anything we tried seemed to work.'

Neither were the trio the only people who thought they had something special going on. Glancing out of the window towards the massive Welsh Harp reservoir that sat behind Baker's back garden, the musicians were astonished to see a gaggle of kids pressed up against the fence and on up the hill, dancing to the music that was suddenly blasting out of that unimposing suburban home.

There was an argument at the first meeting, of course, as Baker and Bruce rehashed some old wrong – Clapton recalled overhearing one or other snarl 'there, you've done it again', as though some long-contentious historical failing had just raised its ugly head once more. But he thought little of it; all he could concentrate upon for now was the sheer excitement of playing with two musicians who seemed as dedicated to their music as he was; who saw beyond the loose jamming and reconstituted classics that had consumed his time for so long now, and into a future of untrammelled opportunity.

'We decided we wanted to play with each other more than anyone else in the country,' he confirmed. 'And [we] formed a band. We just did it. It wasn't hard, it was easy. We had no idea what we really wanted to play. We just knew that we wanted to play together.'

So great was his excitement that he even calmed the voices at the back of his head that insisted he might not be any happier in this group than he was in any of his past outfits. Though, at 21, he was by far the youngest member of the group, with Bruce 23 and Baker a positively prehistoric 25, Clapton somehow envisioned himself as the band's 'leader', in terms of musical direction if nothing else, playing a music that was so free and natural, so warm and personal, that even if you didn't know the songs, you knew what they were saying to you.

It could be blues, it could be pop, it could be country, it could be anything and everything. He dreamed of visiting the greatest songbooks in the world, from Bo Diddley to Bob Dylan, from Ledbelly to Lennon, and playing the music as it needed to be played. Neither were his sights set solely on the frontiers of music. 'The initial agenda was that Cream was going to be a dada group,' Clapton told *Uncut* in 2004. 'We were going to have all these weird things happening on stage, and it was going to be experimental and funny and rebellious.' The group's earliest joint purchase, picked up at a London junkstore, was a large stuffed bear that they intended placing to one side of the stage while they played; other mad props, the trio agreed, would be accumulated as they travelled the country.

It was only much later that Clapton realised that, from the outset, these dreams were doomed. 'When we had our first rehearsal, [Jack and Ginger] took over. Jack brought in the songs that he'd written and I just had to go along with it. Because it was very interesting, and because Jack's songs are so good and the combination of the musicians was interesting, I found that I let my idea take a back seat and actually die in the end.'

The group's first rehearsal ended only when Bruce announced he had to go. The Manfreds had a gig that evening, 'and I was already wondering how to tell them that I was going to leave'. It was only a matter of days, however, before the trio was offered its first opportunity to flex its muscle in public, as American producer Joe Boyd, an A&R man at the newly opened London office of Elektra Records, offered Clapton more-or-less unlimited studio time, in return for a clutch of tunes to include on a new blues compilation, *Good Time Music*.

The majority of the album's contributors were American; part of the appeal for Clapton, then, was the opportunity to line his blues up against those of the music's very homeland, as the Lovin' Spoonful, the Paul Butterfield Blues Band, Al Kooper and Tom Rush all offered up their own interpretations of numbers that Clapton himself had all but grown up with – Chuck Berry's 'Almost Grown', Willie Dixon's 'Spoonful'; Butterfield was even serving up his own interpretation of the Sonny Boy Williamson song that the Yardbirds had chosen for their own second single, 'Good Morning Little Schoolgirl'.

Gleefully, Clapton decided to give as good as he got. Memphis Slim's 'Steppin' Out', S Macleod's 'I Want to Know', and a first, seething assault on what became his career-defining reconstruction of Robert Johnson's 'Cross Road Blues' were all lined up to be recorded, together with a hand-picked band comprising the Spencer Davis Group's Steve Winwood, Manfreds' frontman Paul Jones, Clapton's old pal Ben Palmer and, of course, Bruce and Baker.

Baker alone turned him down; apparently he had other plans that day, or maybe he didn't want to show the new group's hand too early. No matter: Winwood promptly offered up his own band's Pete York, in a line-up that Clapton, reanimating the memory of one of John Mayall's old outfits, promptly christened The Powerhouse.

'Joe Boyd was a great enthusiast and had heard all of us in our various bands,' recalled York. 'I don't know how much he influenced Eric in the choice of musicians or vice versa. We all knew each other and jammed together.

'The studio was a very classic building in, I think, the area of Regent's Park. It was named after a famous figure in British music [Cecil Sharp House, the heartbeat of the British trad folk movement], and the session went very quickly and easily; it was all familiar material. Because of contracts with the Spencer Davis record company, Fontana, Steve and I had to use false names. So did Paul Jones. Steve was Steve Anglo, I was Peter Howard and Paul is listed as Jacob Matthews.' In fact, York's only regret is that 'sadly, this hot combination never did anything else'. With Jones still reaching towards his solo career, and the Davis Group now at the height of their commercial pre-eminence, the unions that the Powerhouse portended were not to survive.

Neither would the high hopes that *Good Time Music* (or *What's Shakin'*, as it was titled in the US and on subsequent British reissues) initially engendered, as the Powerhouse tracks proved very much to be the only genuinely *threatening* cuts on an album that otherwise played things very safe.

The American blues scene was undergoing its own renaissance at the time, as though the nation's musicians had suddenly realised that the army of British invaders chewing up the charts of the day were essentially selling back to them a heritage they should never have abandoned in the first place. Unfortunately, in attempting to reclaim their own birthright, the majority of American blues bands first felt they needed to re-create it.

What kept the British blues scene so vibrant was the various participants' refusal to sit still for a moment. You could compile an entire album, for instance, from the multitudinous versions of 'Smokestack Lightning' ... 'Hoochie Coochie Man' ... 'Got My Mojo Working' ... laid down in English studios between 1963 and 1964, but you struggled to find even two that sounded the same. American acts, on the other hand, excelled at achieving an authenticity that made even John Mayall and Cyril Davies look avant-garde by comparison, as Ginger Baker confirmed to *Melody Maker* in 1967.

'There are some very good groups out there – the Electric Flag and the Bloomfield Band are very good indeed. But it's a different scene. They all rehearse all day and work in the evening [which means] they get a very rehearsed sound.' The best British bands prided themselves on getting a different feel every night. And that feel (not to mention that pride) was about to broaden even further.

Bruce, Baker and Clapton continued to meet whenever they could, clandestinely slipping out of sight of their regular bands to play and plot to their hearts' content. Ideas were flowering constantly; some – the music they'd play, the freedom they'd enjoy – were grasped as naturally as breathing. Others, however, required lengthier consideration.

One of the earliest dilemmas the threesome wrestled with was the ultimate shape of the group itself. Somewhere within their fledgling deliberations, the possibility of adding a fourth instrument, keyboards, to the brew was broached. Hardly surprisingly, Graham Bond's name arose as a possible addition to the band.

Clapton scotched that one – 'far too jazzy', the guitarist reflected. Still buoyant from the Powerhouse sessions, his own first (and only) choice was Steve Winwood, although he knew, deep down, that that wouldn't work either. 'If Steve had joined, it would have been more of what I wanted it to be,' he has since remarked. 'But I think there would have been a difficulty there, because Jack was the singer.' It was only much later that Clapton discovered that might not have been too much of an obstacle. As Bruce put it thirty years down the line, 'I became the lead singer in Cream by default. We had a compe-tition as to who didn't want to be the lead singer. I sort of lost.'

Indeed, Bruce also entertained the notion of inviting Winwood into the fold. 'He was the one we were thinking of, but to me, the magic of the thing was the challenge of only having three live instruments, so that's the way it went.' He told the American *Hit Parader* magazine, in 1968, 'we're comfortable with the trio format. If we stop progressing, we might think about other members. [But] if we had another guitar, we'd become very limited because Eric plays so much by himself. [And] if we had an organ, we'd have harmonic things, which is not our music. Our music is lines and counterpoint. Harmonic changes would limit us incredibly.'

Clapton, too, was spellbound by the idea of a simple trio. Modern-day blues legend Buddy Guy had visited Britain as part of the 1965 American Folk Blues festival, playing with that same configuration and, for Clapton, every gig he caught was a revelation. 'It was unbelievable. He was in total command and I thought "this is it!" It seemed to me you could do anything with a trio.' In fact, that was the role that he believed was being mapped out for him by this new combo: 'Buddy Guy with a rhythm section,' as he put it.

There was another advantage to the three-man format, as future Gillan/Ozzy Osbourne guitarist Bernie Tormé explained. 'It is very difficult to do that wild, free-form rock jam if the band is larger than three people, and it also takes a certain kind of bass player and drummer (not just timekeepers), and there are *very* few of those around. Jazz ethic applied to rock. I just love it, but again it takes awesome players to do it well.'

A more troublesome spectre arose when Baker proposed that the Graham Bond Organisation's manager, Robert Stigwood, be invited to take up a similar capacity for the new group. It was not an immediately popular suggestion. Although Clapton did not seem bothered either way, Jack Bruce furiously resisted Stigwood's enlistment, arguing that the very nature of the group, the founding principles that brought the trio together in the first place, demanded that they manage themselves.

It was bad enough that they were going to have to deal with agents, accountants and record company chiefs, but at least that tier of bureaucracy had a function. What did the average rock manager do beyond push his charges to the limits of their endurance, bombard them with demands for 'one more tour', 'one more single', 'one more push', and then stick them on a package tour with Goldie and the Gingerbreads.

Baker disagreed. A good manager – and Stigwood certainly fell into that category – would also ensure that the group got the best treatment, the best deals, the best money. Indeed, barely had Bruce finally succumbed to the drummer's exhortations than Stigwood was deep in discussions with Atlantic Records' Turkish-New Yorker chief Ahmet Ertegun, fixing up the Stateside end of the band's future, and talking virtual telephone numbers by way of an advance.

He was, as he well knew, preaching to the converted. The two men had long been close allies, bound together not only by their mutual friendship, but also for their almost psychic understanding of the music industry's most treasured alchemy, the art of translating base music into gold. It was not by luck alone that Ertegun had transformed Atlantic Records from a tiny independent specialising in scarcely marketable race records in the early 1950s, into one of the most successful, and profitable, record companies the world had ever seen; just as it was not chance that decreed Stigwood now lived in a fifteen-room Tudor mansion, secreted within 37 acres of land, and drove a white Rolls Royce.

The pair also shared a ribald sense of humour; they were, as Warners promo man Stan Cornyn affectionately termed them, 'pranksters'.

Once, sharing a flight to London, Stigwood replaced Ertegun's passport photograph with a picture of a girl with someone's dick in her mouth; in Los Angeles, where Stigwood rented a house flanked by a small army of statues, Ertegun crept out in the middle of the night and spray-painted them all a shocking shade of pink. At times like that, both men joked that they dared not turn their back on the other for a moment. But when it came to business, Ertegun trusted Stigwood's judgement implicitly. Besides, he already knew all he needed to know about this Eric Clapton character.

On 11 March, Ertegun was in London to catch one of his label's biggest hitters, soul giant Wilson Pickett, headlining the Astoria Theatre in Finsbury Park. The concert over, artist, musicians and label bigwigs made their way down to the Scotch of St James in Mayfair, one of the capital's most fashionable niteries, to while away the wee hours.

Ertegun was sitting with Pickett when something from the stage caught his ear. As a massive jam session got under way, Pickett's own band mixing with the Scotch's usual patron, a sharp blues guitar solo drifted out of the melange. Ertegun paused appreciatively in mid-sentence, then turned to Pickett. 'That can only be your guitarist. Man, he can sure play the blues.'

Pickett turned around. 'No, my guitar player is having a drink at the bar.' What Ertegun heard was Eric Clapton, and he never forgot the impact that the young Englishman, 'this beautiful kid with an angelic face, playing the guitar like BB King and Albert King put together', had on him. The moment he heard who was involved in this new Stigwood discovery, Ertegun knew he had to have them.

7. ...THE CREAM

T he headlines that coloured the British press during the middle
weeks of June 1966 were dominated by the up-coming World
Cup, as the game that England invented (in the vernacular of a later
time), came home for its greatest tournament ever. There were,
however, a lot of other attractions at large. On television, Saturday
evening's *Doctor Who* was preparing to undergo one of the most
radical changes any programme had attempted, as the Doctor himself
changed into an entirely different person. 'Regeneration', the show's
makers called it. 'Unbelievable poppycock,' responded its antagonists.
The show, they predicted, would be dead before Christmas.

In Parliament, the Labour Government was steeling itself for the
introduction of legislation that finally outlawed pirate radio, the
offshore transmitters that had spent the last two years blasting a
non-stop pop fusillade through the creaking hull of the BBC's
broadcasting monopoly – the Maritime Offences Bill was to be
published on 2 July.

In America, the Civil Rights movement was simultaneously
traumatised and galvanised by the shooting of James Meredith, the
first black ever to break the colour bar at the University of
Mississippi, less than a week after more than 2,000 people attended
a conference on the issue at the White House. An American
spaceship, *Surveyor I*, had just become the first man-made object to
make a controlled, 'soft' landing on the moon; and the escalating
war in Vietnam was already forcing ever-widening cracks through
the very fabric of the so-called 'home front'.

And the Silly Season was in full swing, as the Who's Roger Daltrey awoke one morning to discover he was dead – or so the French and German press was insisting. Of course he wasn't, but for readers of the music press, such bizarre allegations at least interrupted the constant flow of speculation that otherwise dogged the summer months, as the Beatles worked towards completing the successor to *Rubber Soul* – already the most eagerly awaited album in the history of pop (or, at least, since their last one); as the Rolling Stones strove to prove that the three-headed clout of 'Satisfaction', 'Get Off of My Cloud' and '19th Nervous Breakdown' was not the sum of their abilities; as Bob Dylan strove to demonstrate that electric guitars had a place in his poetry.

Of course, there was also the usual ferment of up-and-comers, gallant survivors and one-hit wonders, to be getting on with, and the tantalising knowledge that any one of them was as capable of mustering a major step forward as of falling far behind – Phil Spector, who'd shrugged away rumours (there were *always* rumours about Phil) of his impending demise by concocting his most dramatic hit yet, Ike and Tina Turner's 'River Deep, Mountain High'; Winwood and York's Spencer Davis group, who'd fused Birmingham blues with a Jamaican songsmith and scored two successive chart-topping hits.

Then there were the ramifications of Indian sitar maestro Ravi Shankar's recent visit to London to be absorbed, together with Beatle George Harrison's unbridled fascination with what he heard at the concert. There was the latest album from the Beach Boys, the super-ambitious *Pet Sounds*, to be dissected, and a fresh masterpiece from the Yardbirds, the demented Cossack rhythms of 'Over Under Sideways Down'. There was a new single from the Hollies, as Graham Gouldman's 'Bus Stop' was proclaimed their greatest offering ever, and the Kinks, whose 'Sunny Afternoon' wasn't far behind it in those stakes. If we all closed our eyes and wished hard enough, one of them, please God, would soon be knocking Frank Sinatra off the top of the charts.

And then there was a story that had little to do with any of the hardest hitters of the pop glitterati; and was probably of little interest to anybody beyond a handful of die-hard blues aficionados. Certainly *Melody Maker*, who published it, seemed uncertain quite what to do with it – journalist Chris Welch's exclusive was boxed up on the news pages, the unpromising headline 'Eric, Jack & Ginger Team Up' balanced midway between a report on Sinatra's joy at his UK chart-topper, and a Musicians Union assault on Radio Caroline.

Tipped off by Baker, Welch himself was very conscious of what the union portended and, if you read on, his excitement was contagious. Having formally introduced the players to his readers and described them, in his opening sentence, as 'a sensational new

"Group's Group"', he continued, 'top groups will be losing star instrumentalists as a result. Manfred Mann will lose bassist, harmonica player, pianist and singer Jack Bruce; John Mayall will lose brilliant blues guitarist Eric Clapton, and Graham Bond's Organisation will lose incredible drummer Ginger Baker. The group say they hope to start playing at clubs, ballrooms and theatres in a month's time.'

Bruce read the *Melody Maker* story and flipped. So far as he was concerned, the new group still had a few kinks to iron out, still needed to test its mettle in more than a handful of friendly get-togethers and jam sessions. It was certainly no time to be blabbing the entire affair to the press, all the more so since neither he nor Clapton had yet told their own respective employers what was going on. Now, it rather looked as though they didn't need to. Bruce lay down the paper and braced himself for the phone to start ringing.

John Mayall, too, was astonished by what he read – astonished and, as Hughie Flint put it, 'very displeased'. They were sitting in Mayall's back garden at the time, enjoying what had started out as a gloriously sunny morning. The clouds that suddenly swept across their idyll were not dispersed for several weeks to come.

'It was very sudden and very quick,' Mayall recalled. '[Eric]'d got together with Ginger and Jack, they'd got Cream together, they'd got management together. To a certain extent, they were scheming and planning because they wanted to keep it secret, so they could just burst onto the scene and surprise everybody. I didn't know about it, nobody knew about it, it was very sudden.'

It was also very hurtful. Not only had Clapton not mentioned anything, he had even encouraged both Baker and Bruce to drop by sundry Bluesbreakers shows, just to sit in and play, at the same time as he was preparing to shaft the rest of the band. Back in March, in fact, Bruce played close to a fortnight's worth of shows with the band during another of John McVie's enforced lay-offs, including the Flamingo concert immortalised on the *Primal Solos* compilation and a BBC session two days later. Neither player breathed a word of their intentions.

Even more infuriatingly, the album Clapton recorded with the Bluesbreakers was still awaiting release. It was on the schedules for September, by which time it wouldn't even be ancient history. It would be utterly irrelevant to anything that either Clapton or the Bluesbreakers were now doing.

Confronted with the evidence of his perfidy, Clapton immediately offered a month's notice. Mayall accepted it, then set about trying to lure Peter Green back into the Bluesbreakers. 'But it was difficult for me to get Peter back, because he was pissed off that he'd been kicked out in the first place, so he really made me wait around for a decision on it.'

Complicating Green's own decision was the fact that he'd since received another offer, this time from Eric Burdon. 'So he had two things in his mind that he really wanted to do in life,' Mayall reasoned. 'One was to play the blues in the right environment, and the other was to go to America. With Burdon, he got the offer to go to America; and with me he could play the music that he loved. Thankfully, the music took precedence. He really wanted to go to America, but he came with me.'

Green made the correct decision. Mike Vernon once reflected, 'Other people played the blues. Peter felt them.' But Mayall himself admitted that his own sense of urgency, the desperate need to push the Bluesbreakers as fast as possible into the new era that was forced upon them, left him with little time to consider any other player.

Hughie Flint continued, 'there were several gigs where [Eric] just didn't turn up, so we played as a trio. It was pretty dire, but John insisted on carrying it off, and getting paid, and all the rest of it. But two solid hours of John Mayall, John McVie and myself must have been pretty heavy when most of the people wanted God.'

It took two weeks of constant cajoling before Peter Green finally agreed to join the Bluesbreakers, which in turn meant that Clapton still had two weeks of his notice left to serve. According to Flint, however, Mayall wasn't interested in waiting any longer. 'He turned round to Eric and said "Well, you can leave tomorrow because we've got another guitarist." So he actually fired Eric.' Clapton's last Bluesbreakers gig was at the Ricky Tick in Hounslow on 15 July; Green made his debut two nights later at the Bexley Black Prince.

The sordid end to his stint with the Bluesbreakers remained an unresolved issue in Clapton's mind for close to forty years. In the mid-1990s, Hughie Flint told the BBC's *Rock Family Trees* programme, 'Eric had amazing charisma at that time, and I think he realised, as he was getting more and more of a star billing in the Bluesbreakers, that that was where he was destined; that he wanted more personal success.' But it was not until 2003, and the eve of his guest appearance at Mayall's seventieth birthday concert in Liverpool, that Clapton himself finally acknowledged, 'I sense, as the years go by, that I definitely used [John]'s hospitality, his band and his reputation to further my own career, and I felt I'd never given him credit for that personally.' His appearance at that concert went some way towards salving an ancient wound; at the time of his departure from the Bluesbreakers, however, the discomfort was almost palpable.

Clapton was quick to proclaim Green a worthy successor. When *Record Mirror* asked him that same June, whom he rated most highly among his fellow guitarists, Clapton had no hesitation in nominating Green alongside the Yardbirds' Jeff Beck – and the fact that both had replaced him in their respective bands doubtless had nothing to do with his praise. (Besides, he was scarcely polite about Beck and the Yardbirds' own latest album, the so-called *Roger the Engineer*. He warned the paper's readers, 'I just don't want to know.')

Even with Clapton's endorsement, however, Green was scarcely stepping into an enviable situation, as Mayall admitted. 'The thing that was difficult for Peter was, when Eric first left, audiences thought he was still in the band and gave Peter a hard time. But that didn't last very long, fortunately, and it didn't really take us very long to gel as a band. The rhythm section was the same, the formula was the same, it was just the songs that changed.

'Any time we got in a new musician, we would change the repertoire, change the songs around because it's not a good thing. If somebody's really made a song their own, it doesn't work for someone else to try and do it. As an example, Eric kind of took possession of Freddie King's "Hideaway", which was almost a guitar signature tune. So when Peter came into the band, we never did "Hideaway". But to continue with the Freddie King instrumental theme, we did "The Stumble", and that became Peter's thing. And Peter composed quite a few tunes, so it was a different repertoire.'

Manfred Mann, too, recovered quickly from their loss. By the time 'Pretty Flamingo' finally left the chart in mid-June, the group had already ushered in Bruce's replacement, Beatles associate Klaus Voorman, and waved goodbye to Paul Jones as well, as Mike D'Abo stepped in from the Band of Angels. Bruce was present at this new line-up's first session, on 8 June, adding backing vocals to a couple of cuts. But, no less than Bruce himself, as he came together with Baker and Clapton, Manfred Mann were embarking upon a new era of their own.

The *Melody Maker* story did not name the new group; that task was left to Robert Stigwood, as he issued his own first formal statement a few days later. 'They will,' he announced portentously, 'be called the Cream.' The name was Clapton's idea. 'He always said it was meant to be descriptive of the sound,' Bruce explained, although he admitted that he, personally, had his doubts about that. 'I thought it was a good name, [though]. We had to call it something [and] we were quite arrogant and full of ourselves in those days!'

Stigwood outlined further plans for the new group: a debut at the National Jazz and Blues festival at the end of July; a forthcoming single; and so on. Of course, the group would record for his own label, Reaction.

Following its chart-busting beginnings, Reaction had slowed down considerably over the past six months. With the Shel Talmy lawsuit still dragging on, the Who were constrained from releasing any new records whatsoever, throwing Stigwood back on the label's other resources.

Intent upon emulating one of the Immediate label's most successful traditions, of establishing a 'house brand' around a community of musicians (Jimmy Page, the Stones and the Small Faces all fulfil that function in the Immediate story), Stigwood turned to his own in-house talent for further assistance. He had recently signed a south London act, the Cat, to the label; although they never saw a record release, their drumming songwriter, John 'Speedy' Keene, had in turn signed with Pete Townshend's own Fabulous Publishing company, and Stigwood was keen to utilise him.

Of all the label's 'discoveries', by far Stigwood's favourite was Paul Beuselinck, a former member of Screaming Lord Sutch's Savages, and the son of Oscar Beuselinck, a music business lawyer whose clients included the Who. As the pseudonymous leader of Paul Dean and the Thoughts, Beuselinck's first single, 'She Can Build a Mountain', proved a minor hit on pirate Radio London's weekly chart; weeks later, he followed through with Speedy Keene's 'City Of Lights'.

The record was released under another pseudonym, 'Oscar', which inevitably prompted Stigwood to flood the music industry with specially commissioned promotional replicas of the Academy Awards statuette of the same name. And, though this release fared little better than its predecessor, Oscar remained Reaction's Man-Most-Likely-To, as a string of further 45s spun out to further propagate the family circle: his second single, 'Join My Gang', was an otherwise unreleased Pete Townshend number; his third, 'Over the Wall We Go', was written by another Fabulous songwriter, the then unknown David Bowie.

(Oscar did not fade from view once his Reaction career was through. As Paul Nicholas, he maintained a long connection with Stigwood, featuring in the London productions of *Hair*, *Jesus Christ Superstar* and *Grease*; starring as the vicious Cousin Kevin in Stigwood's film version of the Who's *Tommy*; and ratcheting up a quartet of mid-70s hits for Stigwood's next label, RSO. Today, he co-owns his own theatrical agency, in association with partner David Ian.)

Cream, too, were expected to benefit from the wealth of talent that flowed through the Reaction offices. Very early on in their career, Clapton was thrilled to report that Pete Townshend intended writing a tune for them; and, though that particular pairing never materialised, still Reaction remained an environment in which Cream were free to spread their wings and to do so, Stigwood assured them, completely at their own pace. He knew how precious a commodity they were. He would never rush them into anything.

In early July, Cream agreed that it was time to finally meet their public or, at least, a very select portion of it. The band had taken over a school hall in northwest London's Kensal Green, rehearsing around the activities of the local Brownie troupe. It was a peculiar combination, but it worked – the Brownies were old enough to be impressed by the presence of a pop group, but too young to care for the players' pedigrees. If a less finicky audience could have been mustered to witness Cream's first rehearsals, it is hard to imagine where they might have come from.

The group's repertoire remained locked deeply into the blues, an attribute that not only gave Clapton an upper hand of sorts, but also confirmed that, in terms of bums-on-seats, his was the biggest name in the band.

There were musical reasons behind the decision, of course. As Bruce has acknowledged, what Clapton took from the blues, he and Baker habitually took from jazz – 'fugitives from Ornette Coleman', as he so memorably put it. They both played blues, they both knew more than enough to get by on, and both had accrued powerful reputations within that field. But Clapton lived and breathed the music and, no matter what fusions Baker and Bruce might eventually bestow upon the music they played, it made more sense for them to impose their jazz sensibilities onto the blues, than to try and work the other way around.

Bruce mused,

Everybody had a different idea of what the band was. We didn't sit down and say 'this is the band policy' or anything. Eric probably thought it was a blues band, with a rhythm section to back him up. In fact, I thought of Cream as a sort of jazz band, only we never told Eric that he was really Ornette Coleman. Kept quiet about that.

Looking back from 2004, he continued:

I think what I've done throughout my career is bring the things I love into rock music. With Cream, we very much brought free jazz improvisation in, which was kind of a dirty word in those days. Ginger and I, in particular, brought that approach in, and with Eric we brought country blues in, which again nobody had done before. Before that, there was a lot of pop, a lot of rhythm and blues, but there was no real country blues and this was something I wanted to do, to emulate one of my great teachers, Charles Mingus, who brought country blues into jazz.

Clapton's role in achieving this fusion was immeasurable. 'Eric was very good at teaching us both, introducing us to people like Skip James and Robert Johnson. I didn't have a great knowledge of blues music at the time ... delta blues, which is what we were playing at the beginning. So I had to change a lot, simplify my playing and become interested in new things, but I was also full of big ideas of what we could do ... rewriting the blues!'

Publicly, all three remained adamant that Cream's music could never be pigeon-holed. 'We call it Sweet And Sour Rock'n'Roll,' Bruce told Chris Welch when he became the first writer to witness one of their rehearsals; a few years later, Baker continued, 'we were always having rows with reporters because they wanted to name [our music]. I've never put a name to music. You play *yourself*. I just play what feels natural for me to play. If music is enjoyed by the people, then I'm happy. It was just *our* music.'

He said as much to Welch in 1966, when he told him that the quest for a suitable repertoire had them 'digging back as far as we can' in search of material, before leading his bandmates through an old jugband number, 'Take Your Finger Off It'. So far as the remainder of their set was concerned, Bruce copped to Robert Johnson and Son House, but also mused aloud on the possibility of trying an old Hollywood Argyles number that Manfred Mann had occasionally played around with, 'Long-Haired, Unsquare Dude Called Jack'.

Bruce had also written his first song for the group, an edgy, amphetamine-laced chant that he titled 'NSU', which most observers readily assumed paid tribute to the NSU Quickly Moped, the German-built veteran of the Mods and Rockers wars. He allowed that misapprehension to stand; it was only later that he confessed that the title was really based upon a notation he saw scribbled on a bandmate's (rumour insists it was Clapton's) medical chart, where 'NSU' was an abbreviation of the venereal ailment 'non-specific urethritis'. But then you listened to the lyric itself, and it really didn't seem to concern either topic.

The clock was ticking. Rehearsing through July, Cream looked towards their official live debut at the National Jazz and Blues Festival, at its new home in Windsor, which was scheduled for the final day of the month, the crowning evening of a three-day bash that danced through the peerless best that the British R&B scene could muster: the Small Faces, the Spencer Davis Group, the Who, Chris Farlowe, the Move, Gary Farr and the T-Bones, Alan Bown, the Action. Georgie Fame was topping the Sunday bill, but the bands to beat would already have made their mark by then. As the day grew closer, Cream began to hanker nervously for some kind of warm-up.

At such short notice, beggars could not be choosers. Joe Tex and his American Showband were scheduled to play John Mayall's old stomping ground, the Twisted Wheel in Manchester, on 29 July, but had called off at the next-to-last moment. Cream were promptly despatched up the country to replace them, driving up with all their gear in the back of their newly acquired black Austin Princess, with the ubiquitous Ben Palmer at the wheel to fulfil his first ever duty as Cream's roadie. (And that is roadie in the singular: it would be some months before he had even one more body, Mick Turner, to help him haul the band's equipment around.)

The Princess herself was a beautiful vehicle, equipped with what was widely regarded as the very apex of in-car entertainment systems, a portable gramophone player into which individual 45s were slotted with the same ease that a modern motorist might slide a CD into the player. The mechanics of the machine prevented the needle from skipping or slipping as the car drove on and, with one of the band playing DJ, and everybody throwing in their favourite 45s, Bruce said, 'we'd be singing our hearts out all the way to wherever'.

The bassist continued:

> The first gig at the Twisted Wheel – there was hardly anybody there because it was unannounced. We got in there and it was really to warm up for Windsor. I think [the show] was pretty good, although we had hardly any original material, so a lot of it was blues covers. We played pretty short in those days, but sets *were* pretty short in those days ... people didn't play three-hour sets back then, they played 45 minutes, then had 15 minutes off, then played another hour, and that was a gig. And it was nice ... like LPs were nice, because you had to make a statement in a very confined amount of time; you couldn't just fill them up for hours and hours like they do nowadays, fill them up with one decent song.

'Steppin' Out' was reprised from Clapton and Bruce's share of the *What's Shakin'* compilation; Howlin' Wolf's 'Spoonful' was co-opted from the Butterfield Band's portion. 'Cat's Squirrel', 'Lawdy Mama' and the Brownie McGhee staple 'Meet Me in the Bottom' followed. Then came Buddy Guy's Chess Records debut 'The First Time I Met the Blues', Skip James' 'I'm So Glad', Bruce's Organisation favourite 'Train Time' and Baker's percussive showpiece 'Toad'. It was a nervous performance, but a tight one, and the audience seemed to approve – although, Bruce shuddered, it was too late to change things, even if they hadn't.

Just three days later, Baker, Bruce and Clapton were walking onstage at Windsor and, was it an omen? or just misfortune? – but, just as Cream appeared on stage, the heavens dumped their finest deluge onto the audience's head. Or maybe it was neither omen nor misfortune for, from the moment the band started playing, 15,000 people forgot their discomfort, forgot the damp, and roared the group through its paces; kept on roaring, too, even after Baker plaintively admitted, 'Sorry, but there are no more numbers.' Twenty-four hours earlier, England's football team had been crowned Champions of the World at Wembley Stadium. It would have been a brave soul who predicted that Cream were not destined for a similar accolade.

The following week's reviews confirmed the crowd's delight. The festival had served up some stiff competition, not least of all the

Who, whose set not only ended with the usual demonstration of auto-destruction; but with the audience getting in on the act as well. With the air thick with smoke bombs and the squeal of dying guitars, the fans smashed up so many seats that even Keith Moon, the arch-destroyer of rock, professed himself impressed by the aftermath. 'The whole place looked like Attila the Hun had ridden through it.'

That was what Cream were up against, but sufficient onlookers were impressed that, close to forty years on, readers of Q magazine rated their show among the hundred greatest concerts ever staged; and that without even a low-fi bootleg recording to compare against their memories. Cream had triumphed.

8. HOW DOES A HAT STAND FEEL?

S prawling, vast and immensely influential, the Windsor festival was not the kind of gig Cream – or any other group, for that matter – would be playing on a regular basis, at least in the UK. As Jack Bruce pointed out, 'There wasn't a lot going on in those days, festival wise; there weren't a lot of places to play like that.' Such future open-air institutions as the Isle of Wight and Glastonbury, or even one-off legends like Weeley, were still some way off in the future; the very art of putting a bunch of bands on a stage in a field was still in its infancy, fraught with more problems than it was even worth addressing.

Neither were promoters paying any attention to the handful of exhibition halls that dotted the landscape. Wembley's Empire Pool *was* in occasional use for concerts, but it tended to be reserved for special events – the *New Musical Express*'s annual Poll Winners' concert was staged there, for instance. The first rock concert was not held at the cavernous Earls Court, however, until 1973; and even Alexandra Palace and Olympia were not press-ganged into service until 1967. The concrete stadia and amphitheatres that, by the late 1970s, were established as the doyen of the domestic concert circuit remained a cultural catastrophe still waiting to happen.

Even at the top of the tree, the Beatles and the Stones were still confined to the British theatre circuit, the two-to-three-thousand-seater cinemas and music halls that then highlighted every town and city's local night life; for performers at their particular peak, giant shows were measured in terms of prestige – the London Palladium, the Royal Albert Hall – rather than in terms of size.

Lower down the feeding chain, the most frequently available outlets for a night out were the clubs, pubs and church halls that had always been the bread-and-butter of the jobbing musician, and it was to this circuit that Cream naturally, inevitably gravitated. Indeed, as Cream's own agent within the Stigwood office, Robert Masters, started piecing together their schedule for the next few months, almost every gig he set up returned Cream to precisely the same venues the members had played with Graham Bond and John Mayall, and the only indication that their stature had risen even a little lay on the financial side. The Organisation traditionally went out for £40 a night. Cream were clearing £45.

The difference was, Bond (and Mayall) concerts did well to fill up on the night. Cream's first London shows were oversubscribed from the moment the queues began forming at the door. Two days after they stunned the hordes at Windsor, Cream headlined Klook's Kleek and arrived to find the audience already spilling through the downstairs bar and into the street. If people couldn't actually see the band, then at least they'd listen through the walls.

'Until Cream, I had no idea that Eric was as popular as he was,' Baker later admitted. 'I liked him very much, and I loved his playing. But when we started gigging . . . we took over the old Graham Bond circuit, but where we'd had 800 people with Graham, when we played with Cream, we had 800 people in the gig, and another 800 outside the gig.'

Baker exaggerated those numbers – there were few venues on that circuit that could hold even half that many people. But his point was made and it was a crowd that the three musicians already knew well. 'There was a certain type of audience in those clubs that wanted to hear [blues],' Clapton mused, 'and they were educated because they'd been hearing the Stones, John Mayall, Georgie Fame and all kinds of people playing jazz and R&B.' What they were less accustomed to, as Cream realised when they first started gigging, was hearing that music from a mere trio.

John Mayall later swore, 'If you'd heard the first Cream gigs, you'd bet money they would never make it. It was chaos, three people playing their own thing in all different directions. When I saw them down Klook's Kleek, Eric's amp blew, so you practically had a half-hour drum solo.'

However, he admitted that the new band had promise. 'It was very exciting to hear them playing together. You could see the possibilities and it didn't take long before it gelled together, and they found the things that didn't work . . . and the things that did, and took off from there.'

Baker himself later compared the fusion that Cream delivered to the early days of Blues Incorporated, as they, too, clashed two musical forms in a fashion that nobody had envisioned before. There was more to Cream's impact than their free-spirited approach to the music, however. Danny Adler, the American blues guitarist who played alongside Bruce in the mid-1980s Rocket 88, explained, 'Jack was great. He's kind of a busy bass player and I thought I'd find him a pain to play alongside, getting up in the guitar's register and ignoring the bottom end. But to play with him was marvellous, because he had such a broad frame of reference, he's schooled in harmony, he has great ears, he could follow you into any kind of harmonic thing.' Or, if the mood took him, lead you there. It was within the interplay that resulted that the true genius of Cream was to be found.

Despite these promising portents, Jack Bruce confessed that Cream's early days were riddled with nervousness, as they stepped into the virtual unknown territory of playing rock'n'roll with such a slimmed down line-up. 'There was a lot of insecurity, because we'd come out and there were bands that had four horns and two drummers ... there were only three of us, and a lot of the bands that we used to play with on the same bill, they were "proper bands", you know, so we would feel pretty insecure about following them. It was only after a while we realised we didn't have to ...'

Sometimes the nerves really did get the better of them; Clapton never forgot one gig 'where Jack had what appeared to be a semi-epileptic fit because of the adrenalin. He got in such a state that he actually passed out. Ginger and I played for about half an hour without any bass.'

Clapton himself was very aware of the extra demands that the trio format placed upon the players. 'More is expected of me in the Cream ... I have to play rhythm guitar as well as lead.' He was adamant, however, that even in the mere months since his departure from the Bluesbreakers, 'my whole musical attitude has changed. I listen to the same sounds and records, but with a different ear. I'm no longer trying to play like anything but a white man. The time is overdue when people should play like they are, and what colour they are.'

Clapton's audience did not necessarily welcome the change in emphasis. Ben Palmer told biographer John Pidgeon, 'every time Eric [did] something new, there were more people who were disappointed because they didn't hear what they wanted him to do, than there were who took immediately to [it].'

Cream certainly fell into that category. Clapton was still God – the graffiti remained on the walls around the country and had become a virtual catchphrase for anybody wanting to underline their allegiance to the modern British blues. But God has certain responsibilities – answering his believers' prayers, for example. When Clapton played a solo, he did that. He reckoned he was merely extemporising on runs he'd been playing his entire career, yet he never seemed to follow the same line twice, and he never repeated himself, even when the band found itself playing the same number twice in one set. 'We did that a few times,' Bruce admitted. 'But we played them so differently that I don't think anybody even noticed.'

A Cream gig was not all about Clapton, however. His colleagues, too, took off on flights of instrumental fancy, and their interludes could be as boring for the Claptonites, as his excursions were for those people who'd gathered to witness Bruce or Baker alone. Still, Clapton was in no doubt about the sheer power of the combination; nor about the marked impact his bandmates had had on him.

'Jack . . . has had a tremendous influence on my playing – and my personality. It's a lot easier to play in a blues band, than in a group where you've got to play purely your own individual ideas. You have got to put over a completely new kind of music. Jack, Ginger and I have absorbed a lot of music, and now we're trying to produce our own music. It's hard, [but] it's also original. It's also more satisfying, and a lot more worthwhile.'

BBC television director Tony Palmer, a friend of Clapton's since they met back in the Yardbirds days, caught the infant Cream in concert on several occasions, and reflected on the band's musical immensity, even at this stage of their development:

> The first time I saw them I was swept away and, really, I effectively became a groupie, in the sense that I went to lots and lots of their concerts. It was just extraordinary musicianship. I'm attracted to great musicians and, to me, it doesn't matter whether they're Eric Clapton or Yehudi Menuhin, as it were; I just admire that utter devotional skill. And those three had it, absolutely had it in abundance. And they could keep on going, come hell or high water. They realised, quite early on, that they didn't like each other and, to some extent, that helped them become the great group they became. And it was perfectly clear when you watched them, I think, that they're not wanting to be outplayed by the other two. And that's what made them really fire off.

Still in north London, Cream found themselves at the Cooks Ferry Inn in Edmonton on 5 August, crushing through a mob that was there for Cream, but was intent on enjoying the support act as well – Kim Simmons' Savoy Brown Blues Band. Another of Mike Vernon's discoveries, the Blues Band had just cut their first single for Purdah (by the new year, they had moved on to Decca), and the producer makes no secret of his admiration for the Savoys: 'Theirs was a style that took no prisoners.' With Jamaican vocalist Brice Porteus accenting even the most familiar blues with a strong Caribbean flavour, and Simmons' assaultive guitar churning riffs into so much mulch, the Savoy Brown Blues Band were one of

London's most spectacularly brutal attractions; and, on this particular evening, they were absolutely blazing.

The watching Clapton was certainly impressed. According to one onlooker, he turned to one of his own companions, gestured towards the stage and asked, 'How am I supposed to follow him?'

Melody Maker's review of the proceedings suggests that he didn't; not at first, anyway. Although the opening 'Lawdie Miss Claudie' received 'a concert-style reception', and 'solos from Eric, Ginger and Jack had the crowd in raptures . . . enthusiastic shouting and cheering were reserved for the second half of their act, when they dropped their nerves and reduced the gap between numbers.' Prior to that, the band had done little more than stumble.

Neither, it rapidly became clear, had Cream – or even Clapton's – fame necessarily translated itself beyond London. The evening after the Cooks Ferry show, the band was in Torquay, Devon, rivals to the traditional Saturday night seaside diversions. But the Town Hall was scarcely half full for the show, and Ben Palmer continued, 'for a long time, there was no suggestion that we were ever going to be a very big band. We weren't going out for much money, the public interest was not great.'

Back in London, however, Cream packed Wood Green's Fishmongers Arms on 9 August; and hit the Marquee for the first time seven days later. By now, according to Clapton, a gorilla had replaced the stuffed bear on stage, and the group's tentative dada ambitions took another leap into the unknown with the addition of 'dry ice, freaky things. No meaning, no purpose . . . just lunacy!'

It was a passing fancy, however; Cream had the unadorned stage to themselves once more when they made their west London debut on 19 August, cramming Kingston-upon-Thames' Cellar Club beyond its bursting point. One onlooker that night, nineteen year-old Kevin Michaels, returned home after the show to discover that the very dye had sweated out of his Levis, staining his legs a dark blue. 'And they weren't even a particularly new pair.'

Playing just a handful of gigs a week, Cream faced a relaxed schedule compared to the routines that the trio had undergone with past bands. But still it was capable of testing them to the limit, as they found on 27 August, when the schedule threw up two shows in one evening, half a city apart; at the Ram Jam Club in Brixton, and the Flamingo in Soho.

As befitted its location in the heart of south London's West Indian immigrant population, the Ram Jam was the centre of the British ska and R&B circuit, an ethnic dance club in the parlance of the day, where audiences were more accustomed to the sounds of Derrick Morgan than Elmore James, Tommy McCook than Phil Seaman. The first thing Cream were asked when they arrived at the club was, 'where's your organ?'; the handful of white acts that had performed there since the Gunnell brothers opened the club earlier in the year (the Animals were the first), had all made a point of throwing a Hammond into their musical mix.

Cream possessed no such luxury; as they stood on the boards, looking out at the audience that stared contemptuously back at the sparsely furnished stage, all three wondered whether they should have invited Steve Winwood to join the group, after all.

The gig began nervously and never really shook off its fear. The jam-packed floor wanted to dance, but you cannot skank to 'Crossroads'. They wanted to carouse, but a five-minute drum solo can shatter any mood. Cream could have pulled out every musical stop in the book, and the biggest roar of the evening would still have been reserved for the Prince Buster single that the DJ spun once they'd left the stage.

Back into the Princess, their gear stowed in the back, Cream shot across the river to the Wardour Street womb of the Flamingo – familiar territory, safer ground. Friends were there, and friendly journalists, people who wouldn't be seen dead crossing south of the Thames to watch a band; and that skews memories of the night a little. In Brixton they bombed, but at the Flamingo, Cream went down a bomb, and the following week's music papers celebrated their triumph accordingly. Reviewers didn't like going south of the river, either.

Cream's live schedule continued spottily. They were at Manor House's Friday night Bluesville 66 club on 2 September, and the Ricky Tick – still in Windsor, but now at the Thames Hotel – two nights later. Attempts to begin scheming their debut single and album were just as sporadic. Although all three musicians were very aware that they needed to get down to some serious recording, so far they had managed no more than two days in the studio, taking over Rayrik Studios in Chalk Farm first in early August, then again at the end of the month.

Neither were the fruits of those sessions especially overwhelming. Most of the first date was spent working on just two songs, a distinctly Yardbirds-esque take on future Heads Hands & Feet mainmen Tony Colton and Ray Smith's 'The Coffee Song', and a peculiar little rocker that Bruce had just written with the Organisation's old associate, poet Pete Brown, 'You Make Me Feel Like a Hat Stand'.

Brown was initially invited into the Cream framework by Ginger Baker, as a possible lyricist for what he, Baker, intended to be the musical collaborations of all three band members – 'we'll write the music between us, Pete will put the words in, and Jack will sing them. Simple.' Unfortunately, things would not work out as he planned.

Born on Christmas Day 1940, Londoner Brown started writing poetry when he was 14; he was first published when he was 18; and, at 25, was as firmly established on the poetry circuit as Cream were in the musical firmament. Yet the term 'poet' only began to describe Brown's oeuvre; he was still a teenager when he hit on the notion of enhancing his readings with a jazz accompaniment, to lend colour and emphasis to his performances – and they *were* performances, manic modernist hybrids that were skewing off in fresh directions even before fellow poet Michael Horowitz launched the poetry magazine *New Departures* in 1959, and did indeed send the British poetry world spinning off at a whole new tangent.

Brown himself became involved with *New Departures* immediately after the first issue hit the streets; according to legend, he first met its founder at that summer's Beaulieu Jazz Festival, introducing himself by walking past mumbling, 'Horowitz, ecch! Horowitz, ecch!' Soon, Brown, Horowitz and a third poet, Adrian Mitchell, were staging their own *Live New Departures* revues, tapping the vast reservoir of jazzmen that haunted the Café des Artistes in Fulham for an ever-changing army of accompanists.

New Departure's *pièce de résistance* was 'Blues for The Hitch-Hiking Dead', described by Horowitz as 'an endless English jazz poem of the road'. He and Brown wrote it while hitchhiking to the Edinburgh Festival shortly after they met, and the series of 'spontaneous exchanges' that form the soul of the poem would, in turn, cue in the wildest improvisations from the accompanying musicians. Ginger Baker, Graham Bond and Dick Heckstall-Smith all fell into *New Departures*' orbit during this period; they remained involved when Brown convened a one-off Big Band to accompany his Jazz & Poetry Concert at St Pancras Town Hall in 1961; and when the *New Departures* team took to invading the Marquee, to busk 'Hitch-Hiking Dead' (and others) between the scheduled band's sets, invariably one or more of that same trio was alongside them.

Mixing media long before the two words were conjoined into one, Brown and his allies attracted other artists. Pioneering lighting engineer Mark Boyle, whose illuminations coloured the London psychedelic scene of the late 1960s, was soon a regular fixture, bathing the performers in light with such skill that Boyle himself asserted, 'We would make the light show into another instrument.' Art installations were erected, then dismantled while the show went on; conjurers and magicians accompanied the poetry with their own acts – when the Marquee staged its first Spontaneous Underground event on 30 January 1966, Brown was there, accompanied by a collapsible silk top hat he had liberated from his father's wardrobe, so that a duo called Poison Bellows could juggle with it.

But the lifestyle that was demanded by these bold new directions was markedly less than comfortable – a world of beatnik affectations in which home was whichever slum or squat offered the most convenient floor; drink and drugs were the two major food groups; and existence itself blurred into that haze of filthy, stoned self-abuse that outsiders regard as so romantically bohemian, but which they rarely adopted for themselves. Brown revealed that, by the time Baker got in touch, just days after Cream's first gigs, he was close as Christmas to touching rock bottom, physically, spiritually and emotionally.

Baker's selection of Brown was not wholly down to personal friendships. He knew that Brown was one of the few poets on the scene at the time who was purposefully writing within a musical framework; who was familiar, furthermore, with the jazz, R&B and blues-style influences that Cream drew upon. Indeed, it was an indication of Baker's confidence that the first time Brown was invited down to meet the band (at Rayrik Studios), he was confronted with a completed backing track and the request that he put words to it. Brown came up with 'Wrapping Paper', and the band recorded it that same afternoon.

Soon, Brown was joining the group at their regular rehearsals, taking up residence in a small studio on the Finchley Road as it winds through Swiss Cottage (the local branch of Waitrose stands on the site today) and firing off lyrics to the themes that Cream's jams suggested.

It was immediately apparent, however, that it was Bruce's musical ideas that lent themselves most closely to Brown's lyrics, just as the combination of the two went some way towards fulfilling the Dadaist brief that Cream had set out in their very earliest days together, but which (stuffed wildlife notwithstanding) had yet to reach any kind of fruition. Not only did the pair share a sense of humour that stepped straight out of *The Goons*, they were also keen disciples of the Bonzo Dog Doo Dah Band, the anarchic vaudeville jazz troupe with which Viv Stanshall, Neil Innes, 'Legs Larry Smith' and co. had devoted the last year or so to bedevilling the trad scene with pinpoint parody and vicious humour.

'Jack was a wonderful friend in the early days,' Stanshall reflected in the late 1980s. 'Peter and Eric, too, but Jack was there from the beginning.' Indeed, when the Bonzos found themselves looking for new management in late 1966, it was Bruce who pointed them in the direction of Gerry Bron, manager (with his wife Lillian) of Manfred Mann.

Retrospect positively refuses to ever imagine Cream as contemporaries of the Bonzos; as an act whose own sense of humour (both musical and verbal) could conjure up such gems as 'Jazz: Delicious Hot Disgusting Cold', 'Cool Britannia' or 'Mr Apollo'. However, both Clapton and Bruce went on to record with a subsequently solo Stanshall ('Labio-Dental Fricative' and 'Real Leather Jacket' respectively), while the Bonzos delivered their own tribute to Clapton in 'The Intro and the Outro', a hilarious roll call of (purely fictional) guesting musicians that includes Adolf Hitler on vibes, the Incredible Shrinking Man on euphonium, and Eric Clapton on ukulele. Clapton, in addition, recruited Legs Larry as Master of

Ceremonies on his 1974 American tour. And, with all that in mind, it is not at all difficult to align some of Cream's more whimsical songwriting efforts as gleeful soulmates of the Bonzos.

The warmly harmonic piano and echo-draped 'Wrapping Paper' lovingly parodied precisely the same kind of old time musical hall numbers that the Bonzos so juicily deconstructed. 'You Make Me Feel Like a Hat Stand' revelled in the irresistible joy of placing everyday objects in absurd situations; while another song – sadly never recorded, but still recalled with affection by Bruce – opened with the line 'He started off in Canada, selling fridges to the Eskimos.' The Bonzos would have been proud.

Brown has described such efforts as 'one of the stranger components of the band', and history itself is probably relieved that few of them ever saw the light of day during Cream's own lifetime; those numbers that did leak out played havoc enough with the group's reputation for serious virtuosity. But all concerned have since conceded that Cream's own output, not to mention their very lifespan, might have been mightily improved had they themselves acknowledged *all* of their strengths, as opposed to merely those that the public most admired. Unfortunately, they were swept along on the tidal wave, as much as any of their fans, friends and even foes.

From the outset, then, it was clear that there was a chemistry between Brown and Bruce that didn't spark with either Baker or Clapton. Yet, despite the crucial role that Brown was to play in Cream's make-up, the poet's close involvement with the group was not necessarily to Bruce's bandmates' liking. Ginger Baker, in particular, felt distinctly put out, partly because he viewed the majority of Cream's songs as the product of all three members' musical contributions, rather than the back-room scribblings of two writers alone; but also because he had recently ignited the promise of his own writing partnership with, of all people, Jack Bruce's wife Janet Godfrey, only to see it overwhelmed by the sheer quantity of material that Bruce and Brown were producing.

Bruce explained, 'Pete and Ginger had come over to my place to write; the idea was that they would write something together, but it wasn't happening. But Janet was there and she was throwing ideas into the pot and suddenly she and Ginger were writing this song together. I always say I got Pete Brown, Ginger got my wife, and we've all been living happily ever after.' Cream's maiden visit to the BBC, recording a session for *Saturday Club*, proudly unveiled one Baker–Godfrey co-write, and the pounding rock of 'Sweet Wine' galloped on to prove one of the nascent Cream's most popular live numbers.

Bruce, too, wrote with Godfrey; the slow blues 'Sleepy Time Time' was one of theirs. But Brown remained his most regular partner, both through Cream's gestation and on into the group's future and, as September 1966 got under way, so the band was back in the studio, to record another song that was far more indicative of the partnership's potential than any of the numbers Cream had taped so far, 'I Feel Free'.

All chant and harmony, toe-tapping tempo and percussion that crashed like breakers on the beach, urgent bleeps and a guitar that sliced out of left field to whip the top of your head away, 'I Feel Free' was cut at Ryemuse Studios in South Molton Street, a stone's throw from Stigwood's own Brook Street headquarters, and one of his own favourite set-ups. Stigwood himself was nominally the producer, although the band members prefer to recall themselves as handling the nuts-and-bolts of the session, learning technique as they worked, and relying on studio engineer John Timperley to keep the tapes rolling.

Owned and operated by the Spot label (hence its occasional, erroneous designation as Spot Studios), Ryemuse Studios was a tiny and, from the outside, unprepossessing-looking establishment. The ground floor of the building was occupied by a chemist's shop; the studio itself stood two flights of stairs up, and there wasn't even a lift to help get the gear up there.

Inside, too, Ryemuse was a daunting prospect. Timperley cautioned future historians that it was 'quite a home-made set-up', a single four-track Ampex reel-to-reel recorder operated from a custom-built consul. The control room and the band room were separated by a corridor, ensuring that there was no visual communication whatsoever between the two rooms, and the whole place was so small that claustrophobics were well advised to get in and get out quickly. But the acoustics of the room were fabulous, and the records that came out of Spot – the Who's 'Pictures of Lily' and John's Children's 'Jagged Time Lapse' among them – still testify to the power of the environment.

Bruce himself has since professed himself astonished that Cream ended up sounding as good as they did, even as he acknowledged that they should have been better. And, as for Stigwood's involvement in the actual process, only one memory seems to stick out – the time that Baker, frustrated at another nowhere-bound recording session, knocked a can of Coke over the mixing desk.

Cream's first UK tour was scheduled to kick off on 15 September, a veritable Reaction Roadshow headlined by the Who, but also featuring Cream, Oscar and the MI-5 (the Merseys and comedian Max Wall completed the bill). Sold out across the country, the tour was to kick off in Hanley, move on to Derby and, from there, spread to all four corners of the country.

From the outset, however, the fates were conspiring against the outing. Three new Reaction label releases were scheduled for release that same mid-September week: the Who's 'I'm a Boy', Oscar's 'Join My Gang' and Cream's 'Wrapping Paper'. But whereas those other two ploughed ahead without a hitch, a foul-up at the pressing plant left Reaction with no alternative but to postpone the Cream single. Some 10,000 copies of the record were junked, and Cream were already pondering the wisdom of even embarking on the tour when the tour itself was scrapped.

The Who were offered a ten-day promotional visit to the US and, having spent months complaining about a lack of support from their American label, it would seem worse-than-churlish to turn it down. The package tour was sacrificed instead; tickets were refunded, for all but the first two shows, and then the band discovered that American Immigration had turned down their visa applications, and they'd be staying at home after all.

Cream only played the tour's opening night in Hanley (they were replaced in Derby by the Magic Lanterns), and the group embarked instead on a clutch of their own shows – Hitchin's Hermitage Ballroom, Grantham's Town Hall, the Blue Moon in Hayes, the Star Club in Croydon and back to the Marquee on 27 September, where the support act, the Herd, were still breaking in their own latest recruit, guitarist Peter Frampton, as they neared the end of a spectacularly successful summer residency at the Marquee.

It was there that their soon-to-be manager Steve Rowlands caught the Herd for the first time; there that the music press came firmly down on the group's side; and there that they played alongside some of the year's most significant newcomers – the Move and the VIPs included. Cream, however, were something else entirely and Frampton watched spellbound as the trio ran through their set, and he carried the memory for the next two years. When the Herd finally ran their course, and he went off to form Humble Pie with Steve Marriott, Clapton and Cream remained paramount in Frampton's mind. 'When everyone else was listening to the Bluesbreakers and Cream for Eric Clapton ... so was I.'

The question, had anyone cared to ask it, was: who was Clapton listening to? Sitting on a trans-Atlantic airliner, flying home from a US tour with the future of rock'n'roll in his pocket, Animals bass player Chas Chandler knew he had the answer to that particular poser.

9. A SPOONFUL OF WRAPPING PAPER

On 23 September 1966, Jimi Hendrix left New York for London. On 23 October, he recorded what became his first single, 'Hey Joe'; on 26 December, he wrote the follow-up, 'Purple Haze'. He'd been in Britain for ten weeks, and he'd not only reinvented himself from a flashy rhythm guitarist who once worked with Little Richard, to the flashy lead guitarist who even made God feel humble; he'd also laid the foundations for the reinvention of rock'n'roll.

Though so much of what he achieved in the years thereafter was technically better, musically stronger and, in almost every way, more audacious than those first two months of creation and realisation, still if one were to remove those ten weeks from the time stream, it would not only alter history. It would change the face of everything we have listened to since then.

It is impossible, from a distance of almost four decades, to appreciate just how powerfully Hendrix impacted upon Britain. Fact and fiction have become so inextricably intertwined that any story could be true, even the ones about him landing in Hyde Park aboard a silver spaceship, from a planet where music was regarded as an aphrodisiac. He once said that he never figured out why people liked what he did, but he conquered the world regardless.

A more considered approach adheres to the pragmatic tale of a young black American guitarist who graduated from sundry low-rent club acts to a smattering of solo nightclub gigs, who was spotted by a passing English bass player, and whisked off to another country where, literally overnight, he learned how to write great songs, play great guitar and, almost as an afterthought, convince the Swinging London glitterati that he was some kind of Second Coming. All that, of course, is far more feasible. But still, when Jimi Hendrix and Chas Chandler first came in contact with one another, neither had an inkling of just how volatile the ensuing alchemy would prove.

Chandler was introduced to his protégée by a mutual acquaintance, the English fashion model Linda Keith, who cornered him in Central Park, where his band, the Animals, were playing one of their final shows. The group was crumbling, and Chandler had already decided his future lay in production and management. All he needed to decide was, who exactly would he produce and manage? Linda Keith answered that question. According to Hendrix, 'he came down where we were gigging, and asked would I like to come over to England?'

'I remember thinking, this cat's wild enough to upset more people than Jagger,' Chandler remarked years later; Hendrix, for his part, was simply thrilled when Chandler promised to introduce him to Eric Clapton.

Over the years, until his death on 17 July 1996, Chandler remained perhaps the one man in Jimi Hendrix's immediate orbit who never allowed his judgement, or his memories, to become embroidered by nostalgia and posthumous glory. The first time Chandler saw the guitarist, and the last time he thought of him, the bluff Geordie's vision of Hendrix was unwaveringly complete: a rebel, a savage, the ultimate showman, the ultimate sex machine. 'Here was a guy who was going to turn on all the chicks, and crucify every blues guitarist in the world.'

What was even more important, however, was Hendrix's willingness to follow Chandler's intuition. Until Chandler showed up in his life, Hendrix confessed, 'I was ready to take the phone and call my old man to get him to send money, so I could get away from New York and home to Seattle.'

Instead he was on his way to London, and if Hendrix needed any further confirmation of just how seriously Chandler was taking him, it was waiting when the plane touched down. Chandler's business partner, Mike Jeffery, had already begun arranging auditions at London's Birdland niterie, and Hendrix was thrown straight into the rehearsal room with the Bluesbreakers' latest drummer, Aynsley Dunbar, and pianist Mike O'Neill. Five days later, he had his first bandmate, as guitarist Noel Redding turned up to audition for Eric Burdon's New Animals, and found himself handed a bass instead. Drummer Mitch Mitchell, followed, to complete what Hendrix had already determined would be a Cream-shaped trio, the Jimi Hendrix Experience. Before that, however, Chandler set about fulfilling his first ever promise to Hendrix, by introducing him to Eric Clapton.

With the once-delayed release of Cream's debut single, 'Wrapping Paper', now realigned for 7 October, Baker, Bruce and Clapton were gearing up for their most concerted burst of gigging yet, a slew of shows around the fringes of London that commenced with a 2/6d-a-head performance at the Central London Poly on 1 October.

Clapton and Bruce were backstage, getting ready for the show, when Chandler turned up in the dressing room, with a young Black American standing quietly just behind him. The lad was new in town, Chandler explained, but a white-hot guitar player. Would it be alright if he sat in with Cream for a couple of numbers?

Hendrix was not a total stranger to the band; in fact, Bruce had met him a couple of hours earlier in a nearby pub, although he'd all but put the encounter out of his mind; people often wandered over and asked if they could jam with Cream, and Bruce, ever the diplomat, usually said with a shrug, 'Well, you'll have to ask the others.' If this latest supplicant had not looked so distinctive, Bruce would probably have forgotten him altogether.

Clapton, too, was aware of this young American, although he'd never met him. When Linda Keith returned to London a few days ahead of Chandler, she was full of praise for the new discovery and quickly passed on the news to other friends. Brian Auger had mentioned him as well; a couple of nights earlier, Hendrix and Chandler had turned up at a Trinity show at Blaises, and the guitarist sat in with them for a while.

He made an impression, but he'd also played it cool. 'I told him not to do anything wild,' Chandler detailed in the mid-1980s. 'I wanted him to save the real thing until the Cream gig. And Eric really wanted to hear him play. Jack was "well, if it's alright with the others", but Ginger wasn't at all happy, they'd never had anyone sit in with them before and, so far as he was concerned, one guitarist was enough. But Eric was, "yeah, why not". So we plugged Jimi's guitar into a spare channel on Jack's amp and off he went.'

In fact, Baker was positively hostile towards the introduction of the interloper. He had still to arrive at the venue when Chandler made the introductions; the first he knew of their plans was when Bruce told him, 'Hey man, Jimi Hendrix is here and he wants to sit in with us.'

'I said "Who the fuck's Jimi Hendrix?" Jack said, "He's this great American guitar player"', and, even in years to come, Baker thought how funny it was, the way everybody believed that, on nothing stronger than the word of the man's would-be manager, a star-struck super model and a few late night club-goers. 'I said "Yeah, but we've got a guitar player ... Eric's a guitar player." Nobody ever sat in with us, before or afterwards. It took some convincing.'

They discussed what numbers Hendrix could come out for – Howlin' Wolf's 'Killing Floor' was one of them – and Cream took the stage. If the watching presence of the stranger beside the stage even registered in their minds, it was nothing more than the fervent hope that he was as good as Chandler insisted he was. The show was going well, the audience was going nuts. The last thing Cream wanted to do was bring the mood crashing down by transforming the night into amateur hour.

In fact, it was they who were brought back to earth. Jimi walked out, Ben Palmer plugged him in and, Clapton was thrilled: 'He did his whole routine, playing the guitar with his teeth, laying on the floor, playing behind his head and doing the splits, the whole thing.'

It wasn't an altogether unfamiliar routine; such trickery was a staple routine in the arsenal of any number of American guitarists. The difference was, it tended to be older players and showmen who played with their teeth or behind their heads as a special treat at the end of the show. It was flash, but it was staged. Hendrix looked like he did that kind of thing as naturally as he strapped on his instrument in the first place – plus, he was young; 'He was *our* generation,' marvelled Clapton, 'and he wasn't in a suit.

'Everything that he did for the rest of his career,' Clapton continued, 'he did . . . in those two songs. It just blew the audience away; they'd never seen anything like it before.' And in one burst of manic energy, all that Cream had achieved over the past six months, all the plaudits and honours that had crowned them 'the greatest band in the world', were no longer worth the newspapers they were written on. There was a new kid in town.

Hendrix's impact was immediate. 'You know English people have a very big thing towards a spade,' Clapton explained to *Rolling Stone* a year later. 'They really love that magic thing, the sexual thing. They all fall for that sort of thing. Everybody and his brother in England still sort of think that spades have big dicks. And Jimi came over and exploited that to the limit, the fucking tee. Everybody fell for it. I fell for it.'

Indeed. Word of mouth spilled from the Cream concert immediately, but Hendrix was not about to rest upon his suddenly bestowed laurels. Evening after evening, Chandler made sure Hendrix was seen around town, but not to play, just to be seen. Occasionally, he'd bounce up to jam with someone or other but, for the most part, he was content to simply hold court, flanked by an already-expanding entourage, including Chandler, Redding, Mitchell, and the girl he met on his first night in town, and remained with for much of the rest of his life, Kathy Etchingham.

Everywhere, a bevy of devotees was waiting to marvel at his poise. Jeff Beck, in the throes of launching his own solo career following his departure (at last!) from the Yardbirds, bemoaned, 'Suddenly, you couldn't do anything remotely flash or clever, because people would just say you were ripping Hendrix off.'

Beck was among the witnesses to Hendrix's performance alongside Cream, and was as awe-stricken as Clapton. Until then, he too had believed in the pecking order that the music press had laid out for the world's greatest instrumentalists; had grown accustomed to seeing his name in lights, alongside Clapton and Townshend, the Bluesbreakers' Peter Green and his own replacement in the Yardbirds, Jimmy Page.

'We all wanted to be Billy Big Bananas,' he confessed, laughing. Then, 'along comes Jimi, who ... upsets the whole apple cart – playing with his teeth ... circus tricks with the guitar. Even if it was crap, which it wasn't, it got to the press. People wanted that. They were starved for theatre and outrage.' Not one of the guitar glitterati of the day 'realised that someone [could] come along and whip the carpet out from under us, in quite such a radical way', and there was little they could do about it now that someone had.

That was the dilemma that Cream in general, and Clapton in particular, now faced, as Jack Bruce realised. 'It must have been difficult for Eric to handle, because he was "God" and this unknown person comes along and burns.'

He admitted, 'I never liked Hendrix's band, I only ever liked Hendrix, I thought of him as a soloist really; the two guys were just there because he had to have something, he couldn't really go out on his own at the time. I never reckoned ... I don't think any of us ever reckoned them as a band; they certainly weren't up to Jimi's standards; and it's a pity he didn't have better musicians to play with.'

Bruce's criticisms of the Jimi Hendrix Experience find willing echoes among other musicians. But, even if Mitchell and Redding did nothing more than place Hendrix's fretwork within what the mainstream adjudged a palatable framework, still the group completely upset Cream's perception of what they were doing – and what they could be doing.

Clapton admitted that, through the first couple of months of Cream, 'I was still pretty uptight by the fact that we weren't playing 100 per cent blues numbers.' One glimpse of Hendrix, however, the manner in which he reshaped the blues to fit his own image, and Clapton knew that that was what he, too, needed to be doing. 'It just sort of opened my mind up to listening to a lot of other things, and playing a lot of other things.' Soon he was able to say, without a trace of self-consciousness, 'I don't think I really represent the blues any more. Not truly. I have more of that in me and my music than anything else, but I don't really play blues any more.'

The problem was, how long would it take before he could confidently exploit what he was playing? Cream were already halfway through recording their debut album, the long-awaited *Fresh Cream*, and suddenly it was looking and sounding grotesquely old-fashioned. Hendrix was the future; *Fresh Cream*, by comparison, was rank cheese. And the band knew it. The day after the Hendrix gig, said Bruce, Cream convened for a few hours' rehearsal. 'I've got

a tape of it. Eric was trying to play [like] Jimi, and failing miserably.'
A Spot Studio take on 'Sweet Wine' also survives, and Clapton's
fascination with Hendrix is written all over it – he scarcely plays his
guitar at all, preferring instead to let nature take its course, and
feedback over the entire tape.

Into the midst of this period of sonic re-evaluation, 'Wrapping
Paper' was released on schedule, on 7 October; and, had they only
exercised control over such things, Cream would have thought
nothing whatsoever of canning the entire exercise. A ditty that
seemed an ironic gesture when it was first put forward, a debut that
had nothing to do with its creators' mighty reputation, now felt like
a pale, failed joke; one that lay far, far away from even beginning to
address the challenge that Hendrix had so publicly thrown down.

The first reviews of 'Wrapping Paper' were already in and they did
the record few favours. A handful had kind words for the B-side, a
near-instrumental take on 'Cat's Squirrel', so dramatically
rearranged that Cream actually slapped their own pseudonymous
identity into the writing credits: trad. Arr S Splurge, completely
overlooking bluesman Doctor Ross's own composing credit.

'Wrapping Paper', however, scarcely scraped a word of praise, and
the critics were not alone in their disdain. The record-buying public,
too, proved absolutely underwhelmed, while an appearance on
television's Ready Steady Go left Bruce in no doubt whatsoever over
the size of the massive misstep Cream had taken. Manfred Mann
were guesting on the show as well, and Bruce glanced over at them:
'You could see them giving us looks, as if to say, "They've blown
it."' And it was true – they had.

It took two weeks for 'Wrapping Paper' to even gnaw at the
national chart. It finally limped to number 34; and, though pirate
Radio London was to show some support for the record, even
there its progress was slow. The single bowed onto Big L's Fab 40
chart on 23 October at number 23; and, over the next fortnight,
it climbed to number 8, Reaction's most successful single outside
of the Who since the label's inception. But still it foundered far
below the latest efforts by the Hollies, the Manfreds, and Cliff
and the Shadows; moreover, its success was further overshadowed
by the growing furore that surrounded Big L's own airplay
practices, as the British music industry lurched into a season of
payola-scented recriminations, and accusations of a wholly
unsporting 'pay-to-play' policy at this most influential of offshore
radio stations.

The heart of the problem lay in the nature of Radio London's
chart. Unlike those operated by the BBC and the music press, the
Fab 40 was calculated not according to sales, but by some nebulous
combination of the station staff's own predictions and preferences;
Radio London frequently claimed its chart was some six weeks
ahead of those published on the mainland, a testament to the hit-

picking *nous* of its resident disc jockeys, whose own tastes supposedly dictated each week's lay-out.

The suspicion, however, that advertisers, sponsors and plain old record pluggers had just as much influence on the listings was never far from view, all the more so since certain labels – Reaction among them – never seemed to have any problem placing records on the Fab 40, regardless of their performance on other charts. Indeed, by the time 'Wrapping Paper' made the Top Ten in early November, Reaction was in the midst of a truly remarkable run during which *every* single they released had charted, as opposed to the meagre three (two by the Who, one by Cream) that made the mainland listings. Furthermore, by the time the label folded in late 1967, every Reaction single released prior to Radio London's closure that August made the Fab 40; and not one of those issued thereafter even dented any other listing.

Few names were ever named as the payola scandal rumbled on, lending infinite credence to Radio London's own insistence that the pirates' many enemies invented the entire affair, in an attempt to discredit them in the eyes of a supportive public and industry. The Marine Offences Bill was to pass into law in August 1967, but the government still had a long way to go if they were to convince the country that the ruling was anything less than a totalitarian dictate. Painting the pirates as a nest of corruption was just the clumsiest element of the ensuing campaign.

In fact, Cream had their own suspicions about 'Wrapping Paper's' success on both the Radio London chart and its scarcely spotless official counterpart, as Pete Brown openly acknowledged. 'We heard that it had been bought into the chart, and I see no reason to disbelieve that.' Clapton, too, expressed some surprise at the various chart ratings that the band racked up with 'Wrapping Paper', as he conceded, on BBC radio, that the record maybe wasn't the most obvious choice for Cream's debut.

DJ Brian Matthews started the exchange: 'I think [your following] expect a certain kind of music from you, a kind they didn't get on . . . "Wrapping Paper". Would you agree?'

'I do agree because we did want to surprise them in a way, because we didn't want them to just accept us as just a blues band; we wanted to be something more than that.'

'Yes, you certainly did,' replied a supremely deadpan Matthews.

The *New Musical Express* was even more inquisitorial, reminding readers of Clapton's departure from the Yardbirds, 'a man sacrificing fame for musical principles', and then demanding, 'How does he regard his new-found fame as a pop person?'

'There's no compromise,' Clapton insisted. 'We're playing exactly what we want – it just happens to be very commercial, in this case.' Bruce agreed; 'There are a lot of developments to come out of us, and we think it's going to be successful.'

He acknowledged, elsewhere, that the very existence of a Cream single had surprised several writers. The tidal wave of 'album-oriented artists' that stormed the scene later in the decade had yet to emerge, but already a fine dividing line was being drawn between those groups that thrived on hit singles, and those whose work was a little more precious. The advance word on Cream made few bones over precisely where the group stood, and continued to do so once it became apparent that Cream weren't even featuring 'Wrapping Paper' in their live set. Bruce, however, shrugged such leprous criticisms aside.

'You shouldn't be limited by only recording material that you can play on stage. People who come to see us in clubs may not buy records, and record-buyers may not go to clubs, so we please them both.' Besides, he says today, 'singles success was. . . it was like it is now, you want to get played on the radio and you have to have things that will be played on the radio. You had to have [singles] in order to get played on the radio; it was important. Although the albums probably sold more . . . well, definitely more . . . the singles were important, too.'

If 'Wrapping Paper' opened to reveal a side of Cream that no one was expecting, a closer approximation of what audiences demanded from the band emerged from their next set of studio sessions, back at Spot in mid-October, and as guests on Alexis Korner's BBC General Overseas (later World) Service series *Bandbeat* a few days on.

Korner began hosting the fifteen-minute show – one of several BBC gigs he secured – in 1964, ensuring that every broadcast pushed the very best live blues into homes across the globe. The Stones, the Yardbirds, John Mayall, Spencer Davis, Zoot Money and Georgie Fame were among the myriad guests who pulled off some grandstanding performances for the show, and Cream, acting fast to counter the shockwaves of Hendrix's emergence, were to be no exception.

Those two Janet Godfrey co-writes, 'Sleepy Time Time' and 'Sweet Wine' were both on board; while Clapton's personal tastes saw Cream try their hand at 'Rollin' and Tumblin'', a classic slice of Depression-era delta blues (the song was written by Hambone Willie Newbern in 1929) that he first heard on a Muddy Waters collection. Fronted by Bruce's wailing harp, the performance was already a powerful live favourite. A hammering version of 'Spoonful' was likewise cut as a taster of the group's concert repertoire, with Bruce and Baker deliberately stepping back a little to allow Clapton to shine.

The recording itself was subdued; even as Cream arrived at the studio, news was coming in of a major disaster in the Welsh mining community of Aberfan, as one of the coal slag heaps that towered over the houses gave way, collapsing onto the village school. Close to 150 bodies, 126 of them children, were pulled from the rubble, and every ear in the studio was half-tuned to the regular radio updates coming in from the shattered village. 'I've never seen the building so quiet as it was that day,' one of the Beeb engineers said. 'People were walking around in tears, unable to believe what was happening. We had two or three bands in that day and I honestly cannot remember any of them. I'm amazed any work got done at all, everybody was so upset.'

But, though no tape recording survives from the *Bandbeat* performance, people who claim to remember the broadcast (it aired one month on, on 21 November, with two repeats later in the week) reckon that Clapton blazed that afternoon.

Danny Adler is one of the many listeners who, though not the greatest fan of Cream's live work, was nevertheless bowled over by their BBC performances. 'What I like about hearing them is, it reminds me of bed-sits and people with roll-ups, just jamming together, with Eric holding it all together, because he's not as abstract as the other two. And you really hear that in the BBC sessions, because he brought a voice to the band, and a shape to the band, that the concert stuff loses.'

Clapton's playing is equally dramatic across what is believed to be the earliest live recording of Cream in existence, a tape recounting seven songs from their return to Klook's Kleek on 15 November. It is, by no means, the entire show – the group were playing two, even three, 45-minute sets a night. Neither is the sound quality up to what modern ears have come to term acceptable, and that despite the recording being undertaken from the Decca studios next door – lines were literally run through the windows, from one building to the other. Even the best-equipped studio of the day could not handle the sheer volume at which Cream were habitually playing, and distortion literally flooded out of the tape.

But that does not negate its impact in the slightest. Comprising versions of 'Steppin' Out', 'Lawdy Mama', 'Sleepy Time Time', 'NSU', 'Sweet Wine', 'Crossroads' and 'Meet Me in the Bottom', there is a savage beauty to the recording, one that is so many miles removed from the almost polite stylings of the group's studio work that one can readily understand why, warts notwithstanding, Cream themselves were seriously considering releasing a four-track EP from the show.

Indeed, plans were sufficiently advanced for the *New Musical Express* to spotlight 'Spoonful' as one of the tracks destined for the EP, but the scheme ultimately got no further than talk, as Cream turned to inspect the increasingly parlous state of the market for EPs. Having once enjoyed a major share of the audience, overall sales of the EP format had declined so dramatically that what was once a thriving Top Twenty chart, published weekly in *Record Mirror*, had already been cut back to a Top Ten only, and would disappear altogether within another year. Similarly, though Reaction's one other foray into those waters, the Who's *Ready Steady Who* EP, effortlessly topped that chart for the month leading up to Christmas 1966, its actual sales were scarcely a fraction of those attending the band's latest single, 'Happy Jack'. The EP was dying, and Cream did not intend attending the funeral.

Instead, they turned their attention back to the album, completing *Fresh Cream* with one last burst of recordings at Spot in early November. It was not a task they necessarily relished; each of them was well aware that the group they called Cream was, in fact, two very separate entities: the adventurous trio they had formed less than six months earlier, around a notion of playing the music they liked, to the best of their abilities; and the one that they needed to become if they weren't to suddenly slip behind the times.

Ginger Baker touched upon this dilemma when he told Chris Welch, 'there *were* two bands. A lot of the studio stuff we hardly ever played live.' What he didn't add was the reason for that omission. On stage, it remained possible to dazzle the audience with virtuosity. On vinyl, however, you needed to give the listener something more than that, and too much of *Fresh Cream* fell short of providing the necessary pizzaz.

'I am not happy about [the album]; it could have been better,' Clapton remarked sniffily as the LP hit the streets. 'We were working on it so long ago, and we have greatly improved since then. I'm [also] not completely happy with the production.'

With the Bruce–Brown writing team still finding its feet, *Fresh Cream* emerged a tentative offering at best. For all Clapton's hopes that Cream might 'surprise' people, fully one half of the album mined precisely the same blues repertoire that he (and so many others) had built his entire reputation on – Robert Johnson, Muddy Waters, Skip James, Willie Dixon, and the ubiquitous 'Cat's Squirrel'; Jack Bruce turned in a couple of solo compositions, the still-mysterious 'NSU' and the shockingly slight (but sweetly harmonic) 'Dreaming'; Ginger Baker unchained five minutes of 'Toad', the latest in his growing menagerie of spectacular solo vehicles. 'Sleepy Time Time' and 'Sweet Wine' were inevitably on board. But the one song that Cream possessed that might truly have stunned their listeners was, amazingly, left off the LP altogether.

Although Clapton professed himself deeply unhappy with his playing on the finished take, Bruce/Brown's 'I Feel Free' had already been scheduled as the group's second single, and sensibly so. The guitarist's misgivings notwithstanding, this intricately constructed performance encapsulated everything that Cream had promised, without ever dipping into the grab bag of all that might be expected from them.

The decision to omit it from the album naturally followed 'I Feel Free''s selection as a single; it was a couple of years more before any

British act, even the Beatles, felt truly comfortable about stacking their LPs with singles (strangely, the opposite was true in the US; there, 'I Feel Free' replaced 'Spoonful' on the long-player); but the result was to lend *Fresh Cream* a one-dimensionality that it certainly didn't deserve, at a time when everything around Cream was exploding into Technicolor madness.

London in the last few months of 1966 was an incredibly fertile city. Music, fashion, film, the arts apparently revolved round the city. Once quiet shopping strips, King's Road in Chelsea and the slightly more designer-conscious Carnaby Street in the West End, were household names the world over. Clubs and pubs which had flickered through the past decade or so, the Marquee and Ronnie Scott's, the Scotch of St James and the Bag O'Nails, were now virtual shrines for brigades of visiting tourists.

A new Royalty held sway, an Aristocracy of Youth that rose from humble working-class beginnings to rule the roost from the far side of a vinyl platter. The Beatles were Kings, the Rolling Stones (dragging up for their latest promo film) were Queens, and around them cavorted a host of princes and knights, dukes and earls, gods and goddesses.

You can still get a sense of all this from the music. In September 1966, the Beatles remained a couple of months away from recording 'Strawberry Fields', and *Sgt Pepper* was little more than a few half-realised fragments. But 'Eleanor Rigby' was out there posing her musical questions, and scholars were already rooting around Liverpudlian graveyards, trying to ascertain her truths.

In terms of strict chronology, mere weeks divided the Small Faces' 'All Or Nothing' and the Troggs' 'With a Girl Like You' from the Yardbirds' 'Happenings Ten Years Time Ago' and the Stones' 'Have You Seen Your Mother', but musically they were light years apart; on the one hand, the clunking, earnest sounds of the British Beat Boom; on the other, the forging of whole new frontiers, into a world of conscious expression which bled into experiment, sonic avant-gardisms within three-minute pop.

In tiny church halls and unsuspecting provincial nightclubs, Pink Floyd, with the genius of Syd Barrett present and *compos menti* correct, were thrashing their first wild steps out into the cosmos. In the Midlands, that one-time scourge of Robert Stigwood's pocket book, maverick mastermind Tony Secunda, was fashioning the rudimentary R&B of the newly formed Move into an aural assault that would one day shake (or, at least, really annoy) the government.

And in London, where Cream continued gigging in the run-up to the new records' release (both *Fresh Cream* and 'I Feel Free' were scheduled for simultaneous issue, on 9 December), Jimi Hendrix had raised the bar even further.

10. MUDDY WATERS ON MARS

Ten weeks had passed since the American Hendrix first stepped into Cream's lives – ten weeks, into which he had crammed a lifetime's worth of influence. Four days after the Polytechnic show, on 5 October, the Experience played live for the very first time, a private showcase which ran through renditions of 'Have Mercy', 'Green Onions' and 'Everybody Needs Somebody to Love'. Immediately, the wisdom of the three-man format was confirmed; Hendrix himself called it the smallest unit that could make the most noise.

Although his appearance upstaging Cream had already alerted the London media to Hendrix's presence, Chas Chandler refused to move too quickly. For a start, he had not even secured the guitarist's British residency; Hendrix entered the UK on a one-week visa, which Chandler had so far managed to extend to one month. Although he was assured that further extensions were little more than a formality, he was smart enough to know that, if the worst did come to the red-tape-enveloped worst, any investments he sank into Hendrix now might well be worthless.

Not that he had unlimited funds at his disposal to begin with. Moving Hendrix into his, Chandler's, own apartment at Hyde Park Towers, was one way of keeping costs down; so was booking the fledgling Experience onto a short French tour. Rather than spend hard-earned cash on rehearsal rooms, Chandler reasoned that provincial soundchecks and concerts would serve exactly the same purpose. On 13 October 1966, just eight days after their first-ever rehearsal, the Jimi Hendrix Experience opened for former French pop idol Johnny Halliday, in Evreux.

Their live set indicated their lack of experience. Even with just fifteen minutes at their disposal, the group did little more than jam a few R&B classics and that was fine for starters; onstage, a great showman could get away with a lot. But, on record, he needed to give a lot back. When Chandler asked Hendrix what he intended for his first B-side, the guitarist suggested taking on one of the established classics he'd been playing for years, 'Killing Floor', maybe; or 'Land of a Thousand Dances'. Chandler, however, was having none of it; he wanted an original composition and, when Hendrix complained that he had never written a 'proper' song in his life, Chandler snorted. 'Well, you've got to start sometime, so it might as well be tonight.'

That evening of 24 October, returning home from a night at the Knuckles Club, and invigorated by the reaction he received when he got up to jam with Dave Mason and Jim Capaldi's highly rated (but barely remembered) Deep Feeling, Hendrix settled to the task. By dawn, he'd finished. 'Stone Free' was the result. Within a week or so, he had also composed 'Can You Hear Me', and had the basic elements of 'Fire' in place. The master guitarist was now mastering songwriting.

He was granted the opportunity to show off the first of those compositions the night after it was written, as the Experience played a private showcase at the Scotch Of St James. The audience was wall-to-wall superstars.

'Chas brought all his friends along to see me,' Hendrix told the Danish magazine *Vi Unge*. 'Mick Jagger, the Beatles, Eric Clapton, Jeff Beck. Mick told me that I was the sexiest performer in the world, after himself . . . whatever that means.' Still reeling from his own first exposure to the American's magic, Clapton followed through by describing Hendrix as the greatest guitarist he'd ever heard. Pete Townshend admitted that the first time he saw Jimi play, he wanted to give up there and then.

The accolades poured down like rain, and Hendrix lapped them up. Once, the pop glitterati was concerned with nothing more taxing than outdoing one another. Now they were fighting to discover who could place the most outrageously extravagant crown on Hendrix's head, and a full month before the Jimi Hendrix Experience launched into its first, admittedly tentative, string of London club dates, Hendrix himself was the talk of the town.

Again, clothes maketh the man. While Chandler busied himself securing the Experience a record deal, eventually going with Kit Lambert and Chris Stamp's still-gestating but quickly solidifying Track label, Hendrix went shopping. By the time most people caught their first glimpse of the wildman, rolling out on *Ready Steady Go* to promote 'Hey Joe', he was swamped in the most spectacular psychedelic peacockery that London could provide. But

Kathy Etchingham remembered a time when such tremendous togs were the furthest thing from the wardrobe.

'Chas's original idea, and you can see this in photos from the French tour; he wanted Jimi to wear a stage suit, a two-piece suit. But Jimi hated it. He hated this damned thing. I remember a conversation in the bar of the Hyde Park Towers hotel, where I was wearing one of those Mary Quant outfits with trousers and a little fitted jacket; Chas and Jimi were discussing stage clothes, and Chas was saying "something not unlike what Kathy's wearing". Jimi just goes "Well, it's alright on a girl."'

Hendrix got his way, in the fashion stakes as in everything else. No costume was too garish, no clothes were too way-out, and there wasn't a designer or boutique owner in town who was not happy to hand over free samples of their wares, the moment Hendrix's name was mentioned. The very possibility of Hendrix digging threads from their emporium was worth a fortune in advertising.

Where Hendrix went, Clapton didn't necessarily follow, but he certainly kept abreast, pushing his own wardrobe a little further towards the psychedelic roundabout every time he left the house. He haunted the strip of fashionable boutiques that snaked around the World's End kink in the King's Road – Granny's, Dandy's and Hung On You – his jackets growing brighter, his shirts more colourful, his trousers more flared. Clapton had never been a total scruff – whether besuited in the Yardbirds, or sporting the sharpest trouser-crease in town on the cover of the Bluesbreakers' album, he had always dressed well. Now, however, there was a distinct impression that maybe he was overdressing or, at least, overcompensating. There was only room for one king of the guitarists, and Clapton did not intend to be dethroned.

Jack Bruce is adamant that the 'rivalry' that so many subsequent historians have attempted to paint between Cream and the Experience, was not an emotion that either group entertained. 'Absolutely not, there was no rivalry whatsoever with Jimi. We recognised him as a one-off and a great, but he was such a nice person that you would never want to compete with him. He was never a rival to us, and he never thought of us that way; I've never thought of music as being the Football League or something.' But still, when Hendrix upped the ante, Clapton had to match it.

Once short and well-mannered, the American's hair suddenly exploded from his skull in a wild, furry Afro. His bandmates marched to the same stylist's drum, a roar of coiffeured unity that caught on as quickly as their threads. You could always tell when Hendrix was out and about, by the number of new 'dos being sported by the audience – and, as time passed, by his peers, as well.

Disc & Music Echo, one of the leading music papers of the day, ran its own observations on the subject: 'for weeks after Jimi Hendrix's explosive arrival, no one could talk of anything but ... his guitar-playing, his stage-act, his voice and, inevitably, his hair. Immediately, the "Hendrix style" – otherwise known as the fuzzy-wuzzy, the freak-out, the Greek God – caught on as the biggest thing to happen to hair since Samson . . . [and] overnight, huge curly heads of hair sprouted on . . .': and, thereafter, there followed a roll call of all the musicians who'd heeded the siren call of the Permanent: 'Twink of Tomorrow, Ace and Trevor of the Move . . . Kiki Dee . . . Blinky Davison and Dave O'List of the Nice. And Eric Clapton of the Cream.'

Clapton disagreed, albeit unconvincingly. It was March 1967 before he finally unveiled his own fuzzy-wuzzy, a perm that clung tenaciously to his skull like a small (and, it must be said, very ill-fitting) animal. But it was inspired, he insisted, by Bob Dylan, bubbling from the cover of the previous year's *Blonde on Blonde* album; it had nothing to do with Hendrix.

Skewing the time frame with outrageous disregard for such niceties as chronology, Clapton explained, 'I liked Dylan's hair [so] I went and had my hair curled. Then Jimi came on with the curly hair and his band did it to complete the image, and everybody else did it because they dug Jimi and other people did it cos they dug me, I guess. It became quite a trend in England to have curly hair.'

Jack Bruce knew the truth, though. 'When Jimi Hendrix came on the scene, Eric said "One of us has to have a hairdo like that." I said, "OK, so long as it isn't me," so Eric went and got a perm.'

Not every observer was thrilled by Clapton's tonsorial extravagance. 'I don't know *why* he's grown his hair that way,' the defiantly straight-haired Jeff Beck tutted. 'He doesn't need it. The short crew-cut, Levis with paint on them and sneakers were always his scene.'

Clapton remained stoically unphased. Indeed, interviews of the day catch him having a whale of a time playing down the comparisons with Hendrix – well aware that such denials only added further fuel to the flames. 'I think [they] started because Jimi is more in the public eye than I am,' he mused to *Beat Instrumental*. 'Also, the British scene is so small. Everybody knows what everybody else is doing, and the whole thing thrives on competition.'

But it could become very frustrating, sometimes. 'Some nights, after a good gig, I think "Well, after that, no one could possibly compare me with Jimi Hendrix." But I always get someone coming up and saying I sound like him.' Unspoken, but pleadingly apparent in his words was the request that someone, anyone, reassure him that he didn't.

Clapton – and Cream's – sense of urgency was only heightened following the release of 'Hey Joe' on Polydor on 16 December, one week after 'I Feel Free' hit the stores. Although most of the necessary mechanism was already in place, Track Records would not be opening its doors for business until March 1967. Neither Kit Lambert nor Chas Chandler, however, was prepared to wait that long before unveiling Hendrix upon the record-buying public; 'Hey Joe' was ready to go, the guitarist was chomping at the bit. An interim deal was worked out with Track's distributors, Polydor, one which would slam 'Hey Joe' onto the streets in time for the busiest week in the record-buying calendar. With luck, and sufficient radio play, they could be seeing in the New Year with a bona fide hit.

In fact, luck was not going to have too much to do with it. Taking full advantage of (and, confirming the reality of) pirate radio's still-notorious susceptibility to a little payola, Chandler's partner, Mike Jeffery, was already out signing away portions of Hendrix's 'Stone Free' royalties in return for guaranteed airplay on Radio London and Radio Caroline. Shortly after, Track's business offices relocated to Caroline's own central London headquarters, Caroline House; and, from the moment the first copy of 'Hey Joe' arrived on board the Radio London and Caroline vessels, both its A- and B-sides were press-ganged into rotation.

The record had only just gone on sale, and 'Hey Joe' was already nestling at number 34 on the Radio London chart, with 'I Feel Free' poised nine places higher, the week's fourth-highest new entry (the Troggs, Cliff Richard and another Reaction release, the Who's 'Happy Jack' all topped it). Hendrix, strangely, stalled the following week, while 'I Feel Free' leaped to number fifteen. But any sense of superiority that Cream might have gleaned from those statistics was swiftly shattered. Big L's Christmas Day chart saw Hendrix begin to climb, while Cream commenced their fall and, by mid-January, 'Hey Joe' was in the Top Five, and 'I Feel Free' was nowhere in sight.

Neither were those figures another example of the pirate compilers' customary eccentricity. On the 'official' BBC charts, too, Hendrix soared to number six, while Cream could only knock on the door of the Top Ten. In this first great battle of the giants, Hendrix had clearly come out on top. But there was also a shared accomplishment to be drawn from the two singles soaring so high.

Neither, after all, was exactly the stuff that major pop hits were traditionally made of. On a chart dominated by Tom Jones's lament for 'The Green Green Grass of Home' and the Seekers' 'Morningtown Ride' (neither of which had *anything* to do with smoking marijuana, no matter what the counter-cultural conspirators might have mumbled); where the Who ('Happy Jack') and the Kinks ('Dead End Street') continued promulgating their makers' traditional vignettes of whimsy; where Ireland's rocking chair-bound balladeer Val Doonican remained a committed hit-maker, and the Monkees were still brand-spanking-new and *ever* so exciting, 'I Feel Free' and 'Hey Joe' were total anomalies, oddly constructed slabs of sound that made pop-buyers out of people who'd not bought a hit single in years.

Again in years to come, history would look back on 1967 and imagine that the entire year was constructed from acid and flowers. In fact, 'Hey Joe' and 'I Feel Free' weren't simply the first even nominally psychedelic records to make the UK chart. For a long time

... until the end of February, when the Beatles delivered 'Strawberry Fields Forever'... they were the only ones. And Hendrix, at least, was revelling in the accomplishment. 'The bomb exploded,' he reflected. '[The song] was a hundred years old and there are a thousand versions of it. But I made version 1,001 and it exploded.'

Away from the pop charts, and the *Battles Royale* therein, gigs were coming more regularly now that *Fresh Cream* was finally complete, the traditional round of hotels, pubs and universities swollen by the group's first steps onto larger stages – East Ham Town Hall, the California Ballroom in Dunstable, the public baths in Sutton. Cream also took their first trip abroad – interviewed on BBC radio's *Saturday Club* in early November, Clapton was already looking forward to the upcoming trip to Paris, a weekend that saw them make live appearances on local television and radio, before headlining the famed La Locomotive Club.

Cream returned home on 18 December; the following day, they motored out to Camberley for another ballroom appearance, at the Agincourt. They had, according to Baker, been contracted to play for an hour, for the usual £45. But, when a rapturously received performance was over, promoter Bob Potter asked if the trio would play another set.

Baker, in his self-appointed role as on-the-road band leader, agreed, but only if the group was paid a further £45. Potter demurred, but Baker was adamant, even after Clapton and Bruce weighed in on Potter's side.

Finally, the drummer had had enough. He packed up his gear, walked out of the club, and went home, leaving Bruce and Clapton behind at the club, to spend the next hour entertaining the masses with a drummer-less set that was no less well received than their earlier, full-strength performance. Then, as they came off stage, the pair made a decision that could have ended Cream there and then – or introduced an entirely new dimension to the group. Baker was to be fired.

It was not, on the face of it, that big a deal. Again in his role as the group's leader and spokesman, particularly when it came to collecting monies owed, Baker had long ago proven himself a sometimes-unnecessarily argumentative asset, pushing the group into confrontations that the more liberal Clapton and Bruce would have preferred to avoid. On stage, too, he still delighted in playing those little musical jokes that had so dismayed Bruce during their days with Graham Bond, prolonging his solos by just enough to upset his colleagues' rhythm, or dismissing rehearsed themes to fly off on another tangent entirely.

In many ways, that was good. Such diversions kept the band fresh and on their toes, they ensured that a Cream performance was never going to sink into the abyss of painting-by-numbers. At the same time, however, both Bruce and Clapton agreed that it might be nice to get through a day or two, even a concert or two, without feeling that their feet were forever walking on eggshells.

There must, they were sure, be another drummer, a calmer, saner, cleaner drummer, somewhere in London, who could step into the volatile redhead's shoes?

Very likely there was. Jon Hiseman, Baker's own full-time replacement in the Graham Bond Organisation, was a name that quickly came to mind, not only as a terrific player and a dedicated organiser, but also as somebody who knew his way around the studio. Bond's most recent set of studio recordings, a dozen-strong demo taped for Polydor at Olympic Studios, was overseen by Hiseman and emerged among the finest recordings of Bond's entire career.

Dick Heckstall-Smith was certainly unstinting in his praise of Hiseman, claiming that his arrival in the Organisation 'marked the end of the who-dares-wins outward-bound trial-by-ordeal fearless-in-the-face-of-oncoming-disaster stage of my life. From then on, things began to get easier.' Just 21-years-old, Hiseman was 'incurably sane'.

But there was also the small matter of Cream's own immediate schedule. Their album was fresh on the shelves, and their next show, on Worthing Pier, was just two days away. The tantalising prospect of recruiting Hiseman was abandoned (in tandem with Heckstall-Smith, the drummer soon moved on to the next batch of Bluesbreakers, before forming his own group, the stellar Colosseum). Instead, possibly reluctantly, but certainly inevitably, Bruce and Clapton agreed to reinstate Baker to Cream, under one condition. He was no longer the leader of the band, even in his own mind. From hereon in, Cream would be an absolute democracy.

Baker agreed, but laid down his own condition. If Cream was to be a democracy, so was everything about it, including the writing. No more individual credits – if the group worked on something together, then it should be agreed that they wrote it together, regardless of who did what. Cream were not, after all, the Beatles or the Stones, bands who had built their careers around *songs*. Cream was a feeling, a mood, the improvisation of the moment, and the numbers they performed and recorded reflected that.

It was a reasonable request. Across *Fresh Cream*, Bruce had his name attached to four songs (including co-writes), Baker two and Clapton just one, a credit for the distinctive arrangement of Robert Johnson's 'Four Until Late'. Yet nobody ever claimed that Clapton was somehow a lesser member of Cream than his colleagues, simply because he wrote with his guitar, not a pen.

Bruce, however, backed away from such an arrangement. No matter what his bandmates put into a number once it was written, still it had to be written in the first place and, in an age when even the biggest band was routinely expected to kick out a couple of albums and a handful of singles a year, at the same time as spending every day they could on the road, writing was not a task that came easily.

Moreover, Bruce acknowledged, although he was happy to offer his songs to the group, they remained *his* songs. 'I was so possessive. I'd have an idea, and it was mine.' At one point, he cosseted his compositions as though they were children, painstakingly nursing the melody out in manuscript form, then creating his own arrangements before anyone else – even lyricist Pete Brown – had a chance to hear them.

Though the dispute rumbled on for the remainder of Cream's career, Baker and Clapton finally acceded to Bruce's insistence – if not necessarily willingly, then because there were so many other things to occupy their minds, beginning with a two-night stand in Birmingham on the very edge of Christmas.

Outside of London, Birmingham and the Midlands had shifted to take centre stage on the British beat and blues scene. The Moody Blues, the Move and the Spencer Davis Group had opened the floodgates; now a swarm of new bands was buzzing through the gap: Stan Webb's superblues Chicken Shack was already pecking at the outskirts of London; within eight months, they were selling out the Marquee. Steve Gibbons's Uglys, Dave Pegg and John Bonham's Way of Life, Jeff Lynn's Idle Race, all were suddenly powering the city through a musical renaissance that apparently knew no bounds.

Cream's arrival in Birmingham saw the entire scene pour out to greet them. Savoy Brown's Dave Walker caught them at the Swan in Yardley, one of the region's premier live venues and, according to local legend, the biggest pub in Europe. 'Seven shillings and six pence (37½p) at the door. They were fucking loud! I saw them again at Wolverhampton Civic Hall and they were loud even in there, but they were deafening at the Swan. And I remember you already had the silly buggers genuflecting in front of Clapton, which must have embarrassed the piss out of him!'

Back to London, Cream took Christmas off, then began preparations for the biggest gig they'd played since the Windsor festival, American scenestress Suzy 'Creamcheese' Zieger's two-day (or, rather, two-night – 10 p.m. until dawn) year's end Double Giant Freak-Out Ball.

Although tickets for the event were sold through some of the most respected outlets on the counter-cultural scene of the time, including the underground organ *International Times*' Indica bookstore lair, the Double Giant Freak-Out was in fact originally set up by what journalist, author and musician Mick Farren pointedly described as 'opportunistic hoods'; it was close to the last minute before any real organisation came into play, as Tony Secunda took over the reins and, in typical style, alchemised an event that the infant underground could be proud of.

Of course it was all a far cry from the vast and sprawling psychedelic extravaganzas that the *International Times* itself unfolded over the next year or so, as such frenzied combatants as the Purple Gang, the Crazy World of Arthur Brown and the Jimi Hendrix Experience brought psychedelia into the mainstream language. But the scene itself was still learning to walk; the UFO Club, so soon to emerge as the nerve-centre of Psychedelic London, had opened just a few days earlier, and was still utterly uncertain as to what it was intended to be; that first evening, there were as many curious onlookers dropping in from the Berkeley Cinema upstairs, as there were denizens of the realms of hobbits, goblins and elves.

Neither, at this point in time, could the organisers even muster anything approaching the senses-shattering bills that dominated those future events. Pink Floyd were up and running, but were still so inexperienced that they lay bottom of the second night's bill, below the Move and, to see in the New Year with their traditional rousing aplomb, the Who. Cream, on the other hand, were positioned midway between sets by Geno Washington's R&B soaked Ram Jam Band, and the similarly blues-and-soulful Alan Bown Set.

But the DJ promised 'psychedelic psounds' from the Mothers of Invention, the Fugs, the Brain Police and the Radiophonic Workshop, while the 15s (75p) a-night ticket also entitled participants to 'come and watch the pretty lights [of] Psychedelicamania'. And, knowing that there were a lot of people out there who really wouldn't understand a word of that, advertising for the event even patiently explained precisely what a 'freak-out' entailed – 'a large number of individuals gather and express themselves creatively through music, dance, light patterns and electronic sound ... dressed in their most inspired apparel, [they] realise as a group whatever potential they possess for free expression.'

Again, compared to the wild excesses of such future events as the 14-Hour Technicolor Dream the following April, and Christmas On Earth twelve months hence, the Double Giant Freak-Out Ball looks hopelessly naive, and fundamentally freak-*less*. Inspecting the bill with the benefit of hindsight, one is reminded of the beginners' guide to psychedelia with which *Melody Maker* presented readers a couple of months earlier: the Monkees ('a unique experiment in pop'), the Count Five, the Association, the Left Banke. . . .

But the Chalk Farm Roundhouse, the former railway turntable shed and Gilbey's gin warehouse that north London's arts community had co-opted just a few months earlier, was decked out for the occasion regardless, while Secunda's entrepreneurial zeal ensured that the entire event passed off with spectacular aplomb, even as the speed with which he'd salvaged the show fired torpedo after torpedo into the event.

From the outset, it was apparent that nobody was going to be making any money from the event: Farren recalled, 'The Roundhouse was such a ruin that most people got in for free, by crossing the railroad tracks and walking through the holes in the walls.' There was no security in place; there wasn't even a lock on the doors that led to the Roundhouse's maze of junk-filled cellars, condemning what Secunda described as 'the Lost Tribe of Hippy' to spend half a night roaming the darkened corridors, searching for a way out.

There were no bars or refreshment stands, no toilets and, though it was the bitter end of December, no heating. Gales of wind swept in alongside the gatecrashers and whipped up the thick dust and oily odours that coated every surface. *Melody Maker*'s Nick Jones shivered as he wrote, 'If to get high ... you first have to suffer frostbite, malnutrition and nausea, give me the *At Home with the Fugs and the Brain Police* album any day.'

According to Farren, the only way for anyone to keep warm was to sneak out again, and visit one of the local off-licences to stock up on whatever warming liquor they could find. And still catastrophe piled upon indignity, as the rented generator spluttered and sparked through the weekend, before finally packing up during the Who's last-night set. Hastily, somebody jerry-rigged it back into life, but it was only a temporary fix. Twice more, the power cut out on the band; but still, said Farren, 'The Who went bananas with Townshend hurling himself bodily in his stacks.'

Elsewhere, the Move demolished a '56 Cadillac with sledge-hammers for an encore, and Pink Floyd spooked everyone with an 'Interstellar Overdrive' that bleeped, whirred and roared in all the Roundhouse's darkest recesses. But it was Cream who made the most lasting impression, as they overcame the greatest obstacle of all – the sheer incompatibility of the three acts on the first night's bill, and a Roundhouse filled with Moddish hordes who were sure they were going to have Cream for dinner.

It should have been a slaughter, the Ram Jam Club debacle (which itself was named in tribute to Washington's band) multiplied by *pi*. The Alan Bown Set escaped unscathed; a tough R&B combo, they knew the audience as well as the headliner. Cream, on the other hand, were completely wrong-footed, and the catcalls were rising even before they plugged in.

But, bathed in Psychedelicamania's madly flashing lights, the colourful slides and flickering film footage that submerged the entire stage area within a heady glow of psilocybic bliss, Cream blotted out the howls of the wolves on the dance floor, and locked instead into the purity of their own playing. And, suddenly, everything they'd worked towards, dreamed about, hoped could happen, clicked into place.

Musical passages that might once have been described as mere 'blues work-outs' were suddenly transformed into psychedelic journeys; lyrics that once appeared bizarre now verged upon the Byzantine. It was Muddy Waters on Mars, Robert Johnson's rocket trip, a deafening, dazzling, delirious feast that left the audience stunned, and silenced even the loudest cat-calls. All Cream had done was play their usual set, but it was context, not content, that won the day. Now what they needed to do was figure out how to keep that alchemy alive.

11. THE SUNSHINE OF YOUR BLUES

It was noses to the grindstone time. Although Clapton found the time to catch Jimi Hendrix's bag of tricks at the Bag O'Nails on 11 January, standing with Pete Townshend and still wracked by disbelief, the remainder of the month saw Cream either on the road or in the studio constantly.

The band was practically living at the BBC. They were there on 10 January, to cut a session for *Saturday Club*; back again six days later for *Monday Monday*; again on 25 January for *Parade of the Pops*; and once more the following afternoon, for *Top of the Pops*, a performance that offered many viewers their first and, in a lot of cases, only opportunity to see Cream 'live'.

Bernie Tormé was a schoolboy in Dublin, Ireland, at the time, a city – indeed, an entire nation – that the group never visited. (They journeyed no closer than Belfast, in the North.) But still he was 'a huge fan. I bought *Fresh Cream* when it came out, bought the "I Feel Free" single, and the reason I first saw Hendrix was because I heard Cream were gonna be on *Top of the Pops* doing "I Feel Free". Imagine that; *Top of the Pops* with Cream and Hendrix! Changed my life.'

Changed a lot of people's.

January also brought another swing through the English Midlands, and John Fiddler, soon to find fame as the frontman for Medicine Head, also hankers nostalgically for a time when pop was still eminently capable of surprising you. He caught Cream's show at Willenhall Baths, 'a swimming pool, where they put a floor over the pool, and held gigs there', attending with a couple of friends, and happily drinking at the bar with Ginger Baker before the show. 'Cream were superbly good, as you would imagine – and so were the support act, a band called Listen, whose lead vocalist just happened to be Robert Plant. Ahh, those were the days!'

The release of 'I Feel Free' in America, on Atlantic's Atco subsidiary, meanwhile, prompted the trio to set about shooting a short promotional film to accompany it. Following in the footsteps of the ever-pioneering Beatles, a number of acts – the Kinks, the Stones and the Pretty Things among them – had already taken to filming little song-length clips, both straight performances and more fanciful sequences, for the benefit of television shows they might otherwise not be able to grace.

Reaction had already dabbled in the same waters with the Who – their latest, for 'Happy Jack', saw *Ready Steady Go* director Michael Lindsay Hogg helm the slapstick antics of four cake-loving burglars, and it was that innocent goofiness that Cream's effort, supervised by Stigwood, was intended to replicate. With the trio clad in monkish robes and cowls, running and playing in Richmond's Old Deer Park, the result (by modern standards) is little more than quaint; though its immediate influence can certainly be seen in the surreal film Pink Floyd shot for 'The Scarecrow' later in the year, the 'I Feel Free' film said nothing for the song, nothing for Cream – and would say nothing to its intended audience, either, as American television clocked the band's antics, then placed the film on the shelf. Ever-conscious of the increasing sensitivity of sundry religious fraternities, producer after producer deemed the combination of monks, fun and, in one scene, some suspiciously jointlike cigarettes, too provocative for broadcast.

Over at Atlantic, however, Ahmet Ertegun knew that the fate of the single was largely immaterial; that it was the album charts that would determine Cream's future, and album-buyers who would ultimately decide whether the union between three of the most legendary musicians in British blues was capable of bursting through on a worldwide level. With the aforementioned exchange of 'I Feel Free' for 'Spoonful' set to open the album on the highest note possible, the Stateside edition of *Fresh Cream* was lined up for an early March release. Now all Atlantic needed to do was persuade Robert Stigwood that it was time to despatch the band across the ocean.

Cream certainly agreed with that. For weeks now, the UK music papers had amused themselves by repeating vague murmurs of an impending American tour, but Cream had long since tired of discounting them; there was always one rumour or another floating around and, as the new year gathered pace, an American tour seemed as unlikely as the other popular legend of the day, that the trio would be appearing, as musicians *and* actors, in a forthcoming movie – title, plot, and any other cogent details to be announced. Clearly, Stigwood's office was feeling especially creative when it let that tale out, yet Stigwood himself had far more on his plate than trying to pacify Cream.

On 13 January 1967, he and Beatles manager Brian Epstein announced the merger of their two companies into one. With the Beatles having retired from the live circuit the previous summer, in order to spend more time in the studio, Epstein had decided to free up more of his own routine as well, and step back from the day-to-day running of the NEMS Enterprises empire he'd been controlling since 1963.

The announcement stunned the industry. Over the years, Epstein had turned down any number of offers for a share in the company, including several American dollar deals that must have looked like international telephone numbers when compared with the assets that Stigwood could lay on the table. But Epstein was not interested in the money, so much as ensuring that his company, his baby, remained in good hands. Stigwood was already a long-time friend; he was also a well-respected businessman.

No matter that, according to the whispers round the offices, Epstein was the only person at NEMS who actually supported the merger; in mid-January, Stigwood was appointed NEMS' co-managing director, with access to all of the company's resources, financial and otherwise – in fact, one of Stigwood's first moves was to record a single with one of NEMS' earliest-ever clients, Merseybeat survivor Billy J Kramer. Hitless for so long it hurt, the once all-conquering Kramer suddenly found himself riding high (at least on the Radio London chart), as the ensuing 'Town of Tuxley Toymaker' became his most successful single in two years.

Neither was Stigwood's role at NEMS the summit of his ambition. There was talk of Epstein stepping aside as the Beatles' manager, and installing his new partner in his stead, and it very likely would have happened, had the Beatles themselves not shot down the notion. According to Paul McCartney, 'We said, "If you do, if you somehow manage to pull this off, we can promise you one thing. We will record 'God Save the Queen' for every single record we make from now on, and we'll sing it out of tune. That's a promise. So if this guy buys us, that's what he's buying."' Epstein backed down, and Stigwood stepped back – but only for as long as it took him to discover something that, in his mind, might well turn out to be an even better bet than the fractious, and slowly fracturing, Beatles themselves.

A few weeks earlier, towards the end of December 1966, Polydor had picked up the opportunity to release a one-off single ('Spicks and Specks') by a British-born, Australia-based group called the Bee Gees. Already a major hit in their adopted homeland, the single not only had a certain charm, it also lent itself to one of those peculiar marketing moves that record companies love so much, as one of the biggest records of the moment was 'Friday on My Mind', by another Aussie combo, the Easybeats. Could there be an Antipodean Invasion a-brewing? Polydor was keen to find out.

In fact there wasn't, and the record flopped. But, when a copy of 'Spicks And Specks' found its way to Stigwood, he, at least, was convinced that the Bee Gees were precisely the kind of act he was looking for. On 24 February 1967, three weeks after the Bee Gees' brothers Gibb ringleaders arrived in London, they became Stigwood's first NEMS signing and, so far as many industry observers were concerned, the only ones he truly cared for. Over the next six months or so, Reaction was wound down (significantly, Stigwood placed his new charges directly onto Polydor); the bulk of its roster similarly faded; and even his involvement with Cream decreased exponentially, as the Bee Gees commenced their own mercurial rise.

Ginger Baker was certainly mistaken when he complained that this particular conflict was there all along; that even the *Melody Maker* announcement of Cream's formation was overshadowed by 'a full page advert for the Bee Gees' – Stigwood had never heard of the group in June 1966, and the ad proclaiming 'the most significant new musical talent of 1967' did not actually appear until March 1967.

Nevertheless, once the Gibbs did walk into his life, to spellbind the world with such falsetto-flavoured hits as 'New York Mining Disaster 1941' (the brothers' own tribute to the Aberfan tragedy), 'Holiday' and 'To Love Somebody' (not to mention Billy J Kramer's 'Town of Tuxley Toymaker'), Cream certainly found themselves with stiff competition for Stigwood's attention, and the resentment did not fade with time. A decade on, as the cameras rolled for Clapton's 1978 tour documentary, *Rolling Hotel,* the guitarist turned to Stigwood, still on board as his manager, and snapped, 'If it wasn't for me and Ginger and Jack, you wouldn't have been able to bring the Bee Gees over from Australia, would you?'

The Bee Gees were even bigger in 1978 than they were a decade earlier, riding the disco wave to absolute world domination, yet Stigwood, who had remained their manager too, acknowledged the reality that lay behind Clapton's outburst. 'It's true,' he replied, but while Clapton walked away triumphantly, Stigwood turned towards the camera. 'And now that I've earned so much money and have become so unhappy . . . after you finish filming this, I might strangle him.' (Stigwood was replaced as Clapton's manager later that same year.)

For all the ill-feeling, however, still Cream remained well placed to take advantage of Stigwood's newly attained position.

Among the NEMS organisation's most far-sighted and recent acquisitions was The Fool, Dutch-born designers Josje Leeger,

Simon Koger and Marijke Posthuma, whose bright and beautiful designs were the closest thing you could wear to a full-on acid trip. Epstein was introduced to the group in late 1966 by Barry Finch, a consultant at Epstein's (and, coincidentally, Stigwood's) favourite PR company, Mayfair. At the time, Epstein was looking for an artist to design weekly concert programmes for another NEMS project, regular Sunday night shows at the Saville Theatre on Shaftesbury Avenue; so enamoured by the Fool was he, however, that a team that was once thrilled to design clothes for various of Finch's other clients, now found themselves charged not only with the concert programme, but with redecorating the Saville itself.

Soon, all of fashionable London was beating a path to the Fool's Montagu Square headquarters – the Hollies, Marianne Faithfull, Procol Harum and Donovan wore their clothing; the Beatles took them into their homes to repaint George's fireplace and John's Rolls Royce; deeper into the year, the Fool were even commissioned to create the massive mural that bedecked the Fab Four's Apple boutique on Baker Street. (Naturally, their fabrics stocked the store as well.) Later still, the Fool cut their own album, numbering Graham Bond among the contributors.

Cream were among the Fool's earliest clientele, as Stigwood set the team to work redesigning the band from the booties up. Clapton's butterfly transformation was already in full swing; now Bruce and Baker joined him in acquiring bright new wardrobes, all flamboyant satin and flowing, flowered kaftans. The group's instruments and amplifiers were spirited away, then returned in brightly painted colours and patterns, dayglo designs that screamed for attention. 'Cream may be a blues band,' one reviewer punned, 'but they are all the colours of the rainbow as well.'

So was the Saville Theatre; audiences streaming in for the first of the Sunday night concerts on 29 January, which featured the Who and the Jimi Hendrix, were as spellbound by the décor as they were by the prospect of the actual music. Volume triumphed over velvet in the end; Clapton and Bruce were in the audience that night and were so blown away by Hendrix's performance that Bruce went straight home and came up with the most powerful riff he had ever conceived. Later, he joked, 'that was the night Jimi . . . nearly got in tune', but still, insisted Clapton, what became the foundation for 'Sunshine of Your Love' was 'strictly a dedication to Jimi'. (The wheel turned full circle following Cream's decision to split, when Hendrix took to featuring 'Sunshine of Your Love' in his own set, as a tribute to the trio.)

Having arrived with such a vivid splash, the Saville was scarcely out of the music press headlines. The Bee Gees made their live British debut there on April Fool's Day, opening for Fats Domino and another NEMS veteran, Gerry and the Pacemakers; Steve Winwood's Traffic played their first-ever concert at the Saville in

September, while the Bonzo Dog Doo Dah Band, the Crazy World of Arthur Brown, Fairport Convention, the Incredible String Band and Pink Floyd all graduated out of UFO's all-night cellar shows to play their own part in cementing the theatre's legend.

It was there, too, that the home-grown guitarists whose own thunder and renown was so comprehensively stolen by Jimi Hendrix commenced their fight back. Jeff Beck appeared there with his own eponymous group, coming onstage with his twelve-string Telecaster tuned to the then utterly-unfathomable depths of D. 'No one had ever done that,' Beck celebrated. 'It was very low and gritty, a real "fuck off" sound. It was like a bloody ten-piece orchestra, it was so powerful, and so absolutely happening. [Pete] Townshend was watching, and he was wetting himself; he came back and said "The best thing about tonight was the sound of your twelve-string Tele."'

Clapton himself adopted that same growling key for Cream's own Saville symphony, 'Sunshine of Your Love'; in the meantime, he was busy making his own stab at upstaging the flashy newcomer, the night he suspended his guitar from the ceiling with chains, then left it howling ear-bleeding feedback into the stalls – and the stalls, of course, went wild. The night that Hendrix set fire to his guitar, onstage at the Astoria Theatre at the end of March, a lot of people said he'd taken guitar-driven showmanship to its ultimate limit. In truth, following on from Pete Townshend smashing his instrument, Marc Bolan (as a member of John's Children) whipping it, and Clapton hanging it high, what else could he have done to it?

Cream made their Saville Theatre debut on 5 February, supported by Motown newcomer Edwin Starr, and Reaction labelmates Sands (their single 'Mrs Gillespie's Refrigerator' was poised for release that same month); and, although they returned to the venue on just two further occasions (2 July and 29 October 1967), still those shows are revered among the band's UK following as the best gigs they played, in the best possible surroundings.

Jack Bruce, too, remains thrilled by his memories of that 'fantastic venue', both as a player and as an audience member, yet Cream's first appearance there was all the more remarkable when one remembers that the group was operating on almost zero sleep. Less than 48 hours earlier, Cream had headlined another all-night show, when Leeds' Queen's Hall staged its own All-Night Rave, sharing the bill, once again, with Pink Floyd, together with a bevy of go-go dancers, a fairground, an all-night barbecue and, as the music wound down at 6.30 in the morning, a free breakfast for all. The organisers also promised to release a live gorilla into the audience at midnight, before safety concerns forced them to make alternative arrangements.

Live gorillas or not, it was a billing that absolutely thrilled the Floyd. Recent months had seen the group take some astonishing leaps forward, as guitarist Syd Barrett stepped out from beneath the cloak of lengthy, spacey improvisation around sundry butchered blues that was the quartet's earliest approach, and commenced writing songs that were as short, succinct, and eminently delicious as those that Jack Bruce and Pete Brown were now turning their hands to.

Behind Barrett's visions of underwear-thieves, scarecrows, gnomes and bicycles, however, there remained a pulsating musical generator, and both drummer Nick Mason and bassist Roger Waters admitted that it was Cream who, as Mason put it, 'were the one band that made me really think, "*That's* what I want to do." The idea that you could have a band that was actually based on music ... power music ... rather than [one] that was based on whether they looked lovable and had nice Beatle jackets.'

Clapton was a confirmed Floyd fan. 'I like [them] very much,' he told *Rolling Stone* in 1968. 'A very strange group. Very freaky. They're not really psychedelic. They do things like play an hour set that's just one number. They are into a lot of electronic things. They're also very funny. They're nice, they really are a very nice group. They give you a nice feeling watching them.'

Jack Bruce was somewhat less favourable. Although they shared several concert bills, 'I never saw Pink Floyd ... crap, I always thought. But there again, I didn't like anybody. Buddy Guy I loved, BB King, Albert King, I loved a lot of those people. I'm afraid my tastes are incredibly eclectic and always have been. I studied classical music, I studied classical Indian music, I played with jazz musicians, I know Beethoven's string quartets note for note, I know the Shostakovitch symphonies very well. But Floyd and all those bands - no thanks.'

Still the influence continued to cut both ways. Pete Brown, no stranger whatsoever to the psychedelic underground, admitted that Barrett's decision to perform songs 'that dealt in an English accent with English cultural obsessions and English fetishes' had an incredible influence upon his own lyric-writing. 'There had never been anything like it; everyone had been behaving like Americans.' Without Syd Barrett, he told Floyd biographer Nicholas Schaffner, masterpieces like his own 'White Room' 'wouldn't have happened'.

At the end of February 1967, Cream made their German debut with two nights at the Star Club, Hamburg, combining the journey with a performance for Radio-Bremen television's Saturday night pop show, *Beat Club*, to lip-synch their way through 'I Feel Free'. Early March then brought Cream to Scandinavia, where they suffered the same fate that apparently awaited most musicians setting foot on Danish soil for the first time.

Arriving at Copenhagen airport, the band was refused entry to the country while the authorities investigated an apparent irregularity over their work permits; it took three monotonous, red-tape strewn hours for the matter to be sorted out, although Cream could count themselves lucky. At least they'd taken a quick flight to Denmark. A year later, in April 1968, the fledgling Deep Purple received the exact same treatment at the end of an exhausting, all-night ferry crossing.

Nevertheless, Scandinavia would, along with West Germany, become one of Cream's few regular ports of call during 1967, as it was for so many other groups of the time. Though thriving markets existed elsewhere, and for all Danish customs' attempts to make life difficult, there was an established routine in those northern European lands that had already scythed through much of the bureaucracy that normally accompanies any trip to foreign climes. Furthermore, as Clapton pointed out, Scandinavia in particular was renowned for its love of blues and jazz, a romance that even prompted many black American musicians to make their homes there. It was only natural that any British exponents of the same roots should be equally well received.

Danish rock photographer Jorgen Angel was at the first Danish show, at the Falkoner Centre in Copenhagen. Still a schoolboy, whose future renown was still mere ambition, he recalled, 'it was a bit like the story about the bumble bee. You know, it can't fly, but it doesn't know that, so it flies. I didn't know I was not supposed to walk into Eric Clapton's dressing room after a Cream concert, so I just walked in and said, "Hi, can I take a photo?" In no way did I look professional. I was a schoolboy with my mother's holiday camera.' Sadly, the photographs Angel took that day have long since been lost, but Clapton's own kindness to the boy has remained an abiding memory.

On returning to England, Cream, at last, were told of a major development. On 11 March, just as the group were setting out for their next show, at the Tavern Club in East Dereham, Norfolk, Stigwood finally delivered the news they'd been waiting for. They were going to America, and the first show was exactly a fortnight away.

Stigwood never explained why it took so long for him to set up an American tour. It was one of the markets Cream had targeted back before they were even a band, and they'd confidently expected to be there before the end of 1966. Instead, they'd spent almost nine months rattling around the UK, while Stigwood did his best to pacify them with talk of waiting till the right offers came in, or striking while the iron was hot.

It was Ahmet Ertegun who finally pushed him into action. The US edition of *Fresh Cream* was now just a couple of weeks away, and Ertegun was convinced that, with the right muscle behind it, it could fill a musical void that the local music industry had spent several months eyeing hungrily. American music was in the process of an almost formidable change, opening up both musicians and audience's minds towards the boundless possibilities that suddenly seemed inherent within rock'n'roll.

Dylan had broken the three-minute barrier, the Stones had shattered the ten-minute roof; Dylan, again, had smashed past quarter-of-an-hour – 'Sad Eyed Lady of the Lowlands', the final track on *Blonde on Blonde,* had devoured one entire side of vinyl, a sound painting that doubled as a three-course meal for listeners who hated having the mood broken every radio-friendly couple of minutes.

And, where Dylan ventured, others followed. Jack Bruce has spoken affectionately of the station KMPX in San Francisco, the first albums-only broadcaster he ever encountered, 'and that was great, that was a nice thing to do'. But elsewhere, too, FM Radio – a growing force in American entertainment as the mid-1960s inched forward – was spinning entire sides of new albums as an unbroken block of music; Dylan gave them an unbroken block of sound to air. Though a lot of artists were now looking to follow the master's lead, however, precious few had truly stepped forward to take advantage of it.

San Francisco-based acts like the Grateful Dead and the Jefferson Airplane were off and running; others, like Big Brother & the Holding Company and the Quicksilver Messenger Service, were bracing for action and, in every case, their live performances had long since expanded into protracted orgies of feedback, improvisation and, indeed, psychedelia. Yet their appeal was still very localised – outside of the Bay Area, neither their wild music nor their hippy reputation was making any mark beyond the deepest underground clubs. On record, they remained bound by convention, two- or three-minute pop and folk songs, no reason to get excited at all.

Fresh Cream did not vary wildly from that format, but when it did step out of bounds, it did so with abandon – 'Rollin' and Tumblin'' rolled and tumbled for almost five minutes; 'Toad' crashed and thundered for a little more; and 'Spoonful', though you could only hear it on imports of the LP, rocked out for six.

Equally importantly, Cream had a pedigree, at least one of the members was already a 'known quantity'. Even among those industry types without an ounce of understanding of the blues, Eric Clapton's name was familiar, by weight of reputation alone. Throw in a few British press cuttings describing the union as rock's first ever supergroup, add the accolades of such respected spokesmen as Paul Butterfield, Paul McCartney, Pete Townshend and John Mayall and, even before Atlantic launched their own marketing campaign, there was a curious buzz surrounding the band.

It was just a buzz, however. Contrary to those oft-repeated claims that *Fresh Cream* had charted in America before Cream set foot in the country, it was mid-May before the album gnawed the lowest reaches of the Top 200, by which time Cream's American debut had come and gone, and the band's own thoughts had turned wholly towards their second album. Yet the potential was there all the same, and Ertegun burned up the trans-Atlantic phone lines waiting for Stigwood to finally spring into action. Now he had. The only problem was, a lot of people found themselves wishing that he hadn't, after all, bothered.

12. MUSIC IN THE FIFTH DIMENSION

Cream's first US visit was no ordinary tour. There would be no long hours spent gazing out of the window of a tour bus as the strip malls, corn fields and industrial parks raced by; no glimpses of the landscapes of Sonny Boy Williamson, Muddy Waters and Howlin' Wolf. Rather, the group was not even to leave New York. If America wanted to see Cream, it had to come to them.

Cream's entire visit was consumed by a nine-day series of shows at the RKO Theater on 58th Street, organised by New York disc jockey Murray 'the K' Kaufman. 'Live in person!' bellowed the ads; 'Music In The Fifth Dimension – Total Audience Involvement!' And the bill for the season was spectacular, as the Who flew over to join Cream in keeping the British flag flying; Wilson Pickett and Smokey Robinson brought some soul to the proceedings; party-time rocker Mitch Ryder unveiled his newly designed Mitch Ryder Show, and the Blues Project . . . well, they played the blues.

There would be guest appearances from Phil Ochs, Simon and Garfunkel, the Blues Magoos and the Young Rascals; one-hit wonders like Jim and Jean and the Chicago Loop; light relief from the Hardly Worthit Players; and even a fashion show, supplied by Murray's wife Jackie, and her K Girls. All in all, it sounded like one helluva lot of bang for your buck.

Then you looked at the small print, the part where it mentioned that each performer had just five minutes in which to strut their stuff, and that the whole show would be over in an hour. Then the theatre would empty, a new audience would file in, and the whole show would go through the motions once again. Five times a day, for nine days without a break.

Cream's own involvement in the circus came about via a remarkably circuitous route. Of all the acts on the bill, it was Mitch Ryder whom Murray the K was most desperate to recruit. Ryder, however, was not at all keen, and instructed his own promoter, Frank Barsalona, to price him out of Murray's reach. But every condition Barsalona delivered to Murray, be it an extortionate fee or a freshly painted (all blue) dressing room, was accepted with barely a murmur. So was Ryder's final demand, that his own favourite British act, the Who, be invited to appear alongside Ryder on the bill. Murray could not be deterred.

Barsalona, however, remained dedicated to extricating Ryder from the show. Before Murray could even pick up the phone to call Stigwood, still acting as the Who's booking agent, Barsalona was on the line, asking the Australian to set his own sky-high bar.

Stigwood agreed. The Who, he insisted, would cost Murray $5,000. No problem, replied the K. They also wanted to bring over their own special guests, at a cost of another $2,500, and that was fine as well. By the time the negotiations were over, Barsalona and Stigwood were both scratching their heads in stunned disbelief, and Murray the K had landed both the act that he wanted, and the American debuts of two of the hottest British combos around. How could his festival fail?

How indeed?

From the outset, it was clear that the entire event was destined to become a logistical nightmare. Intending to utilise the theatre's own PA system, Murray told the various performers not to bother carting their own gear along. But, of course, it didn't work like that. Cream arrived in New York, the paint still sticky on their Fool repainted instruments, to discover that the theatre was not supplying any equipment, after all.

Cue an immediate exodus of harassed and frenzied roadies, descending upon every hire shop in the vicinity, in search of a suitable set-up. Ben Palmer wound up at Manny's on 48th Street, but quickly realised that his charges could blow through its entire fee, in hiring equipment alone. How fortunate, then, that the Who had ignored Murray's advice from the outset, and brought their entire PA rig with them. Cream borrowed that for the duration of their stay.

The sound system was not the only hassle. No matter that the entire performance was timed down to the last nano-second, with a rotating stage that allowed the road crew to set up for one act while another was still playing, it quickly became apparent that the tight choreography of each show was never going to survive. Several of the scheduled performers, including Smokey Robinson and Simon and Garfunkel, failed to turn up, but still, across the course of the first day, the final show had to be cancelled altogether, as the earlier ones overran by a total of eighty minutes.

Cream, inevitably, played their own part in the ensuing chaos. Without a hit single to their name, they were usually the first turn on each show (occasionally they swapped positions with the Who), with instructions to play just a couple of numbers – Murray the K's own favourite 'I'm So Glad', after he fell in love with the snatch of the *1812 Overture* that had worked itself into the live arrangement, and one other, for the most part, 'I Feel Free'.

Occasionally, for a taste of variety, they'd throw another number into the mix; Blues Project organist Al Kooper described hearing 'Spoonful', 'Train Time' and 'Crossroads' at different points as the season rolled on. But anyone who believed that any of those songs could be squeezed into just a couple of minutes was sorely mistaken. 'We started off with two songs,' Jack Bruce reported. 'Then we were playing one, then they said "Can you take a bit out of that one?" ... by the end, we were playing half a song a set.'

If the routine of the shows was unchanging, neither was there any room for deviation in any of the actual performances. Whether by choice or circumstance, Murray the K had selected acts that were capable of driving an audience to a frenzy, and each was under strict instructions to pull out all the stops, every performance.

Cream's required reprise of the *1812 Overture* was, compared to what some people had to put up with, scarcely worth even complaining about. Mitch Ryder, for example, had recently taken to performing from atop a massive castlelike stage set, complete with battlements and towers. Murray demanded the entire edifice be recreated at the Theatre, knowing that it looked great for the audience. For the roadies who had to tear it down and then rebuild it five times a day, the novelty swiftly wore thin.

The Who, too, found you can have too much of a good thing. 'Five times a day, every day,' John Entwistle and his bandmates 'would go out there and play our couple of songs, wind up with "My Generation", and then Pete would have to smash his guitar. Every time, because if he didn't, or if he forgot, Murray would be backstage screaming the moment we came offstage, that we'd let the kids down.'

They *were* kids as well. The shows themselves were timed to coincide with the local schools' spring break; each day's first performance started at ten in the morning, to catch children coming into the city for the day. They could watch a show, be out before lunchtime, and then have the whole afternoon to go sightseeing and shopping. There was another performance *at* lunchtime; one in the afternoon, one in the evening and, finally, one for the after-dinner folk. But even they were not offered anything more than an easily digestible hits routine. 'The word "soul-destroying" comes to mind,' Entwistle sighed.

Such rigours mattered little to the audience, however. Ivan Kral, future guitarist with the Patti Smith Group, was among the throngs feeding into the theatre that week, and was instantly taken by the first band of the day. 'Cream played more serious rock and rhythm and blues than most bands, I thought; very, very serious and also very dark music. Not many lights on stage.

'Baker was the wildest drummer, skinny, crazy-looking, who seemed to overplay every measure on his kit. Eric and Jack just stood still singing tight into their mikes. A big change after watching the Who smashing and trashing their instruments! I stayed for four shows that day, and filmed a few seconds of each band with my little Super 8 camera. And the next day I went out and bought *Fresh Cream* for $1.29.'

Arriving at the theatre in a hired limo, teenaged singer-songwriter Laura Nyro was in the audience as well, accompanied by her cousin Alan Merrill. 'It was a big moment for me,' said Merrill. 'The harmonies were spot on in "I Feel Free", the a cappella intro. Laura loved it, and so did I. They had that three-part down pat and smooth.'

Better was to come. The *1812 Overture* interlude during 'I'm So Glad' 'sounded, to my teenaged ears, like a thunderbolt. It was powerful. Rock to classical, back to rock. I thought of Roger McGuinn doing "Jesu, Joy of Man's Desiring" in "She Don't Care About Time" at that moment. Rock music was growing, and anything was possible. The parameters of what was acceptable as rock music were widening every day, it seemed.'

Equally impressive were the musicians' costumes, a consideration with which Merrill himself became familiar a few years later, as frontman with the Anglo-American glam heroes Arrows. 'They were wearing very Carnaby street psychedelic clothes. Lots of colours, satin. Tight fitting. Clapton was starting the "Armadillo in the trousers" look. I'm sure he'll cringe at the memory, but he *did* like to tease the groupies with the tight trousers. There are photos that prove this!' Indeed, Clapton himself acknowledged the allure of the armadillo when he reflected on how he felt, standing on stage 'with thousands of little girls screaming their heads off. Man, it's power! Whew!'

Groovy times for the audience, then. But backstage, the mood was one of almost relentless gloom. Mindful of the schedule, Murray the K expressly forbade musicians to even think about leaving the theatre between sets – much of the time, they were banned from leaving their dressing rooms. And, just to make sure his injunctions were obeyed, security guards were posted alongside every exit, with strict instructions to let nobody pass.

Players were permitted to stand in the wings and watch the other acts run through their performances, but there were only so many times one could stand and listen to Jim and Jean before the novelty began to wear off. Soon, the players' thoughts began turning to mischief. But even there, they were stymied.

Murray himself did not feel his demands were unreasonable. 'Musicians can be like children,' he once explained. 'Let them loose and you don't know where they'll get to, and we had a very strictly timed show to run.' But Entwistle continued, 'Murray ran the show like a Parade Ground Sergeant. Every so often a rumour would go round that somebody – usually Keith [Moon] and Pete [Townshend], but Ginger was often in there as well – was planning something, and Murray would run in screaming that if *anything* happened, we wouldn't be paid.'

Cream didn't know what hit them. The Who, as Entwistle pointed out, 'had been around for a few years at that point, we'd done all the silly tours and mad packages, where you go out and find you're supporting a dancing bear and a juggler. But Cream had never been in that environment – the Bluesbreakers, Graham Bond, the Yardbirds, they were club bands, playing to audiences who knew what they were about, and suddenly they were dropped into this Christmas Pantomime environment, with a couple of thousand thirteen-year-olds eating sweets and reading comics. It really was rather ridiculous.'

It was only when the final show of each day was over that the musicians could escape to sample all that New York had to offer. Bruce affirmed, 'Going to New York for the first time . . . it's like it is for everybody, it's sort of like going home, because you know it so well from the movies and especially from the comics we used to get, which always had those wonderful drawings of New York.'

There were delights, however, for which the comics never prepared them: the television channels that never closed down, the bars that never slept. Back in London, the tightly controlled all-nighters were the only place you could get a drink 'after hours'. In New York, there was no such thing as 'after hours'. At home, 'Sunday trading' was strictly enforced; entire law codes existed simply to document the handful of things that a shop was allowed to sell on the Sabbath, and the millions more that they weren't. In New York, every shop was open every day, even on Wednesday afternoons, a break in the work week that was so deeply ingrained in the British psyche that there's even a football team named after it.

Everything was faster, everything was bigger, everything was brighter. London taxis were funereal black; New York cabs were canary yellow. London neon flickered and fizzed; the New York lights hadn't dimmed in decades. 'And I'm not even going to mention the groupies,' Entwistle confided. 'Except to say, I never met an American groupie named Deirdre.'

Clapton, on the other hand, was only too happy to talk about them. Although the so-called groupie scene was still very much in its infancy compared to the peaks it attained during the early 1970s, still he had no hesitation in describing it as a 'red-hot' situation, and one in which he dabbled as much as any other twenty-something single man might.

He remained, however, a gentleman, refusing to do more than kiss-lightly and tell. 'As a rule, they're the most incredibly warm people. I mean, there are a few exceptions – chicks who are just out to be superstar groupies because it's the "in thing" to do. But, in the early days, they were just chicks who wanted to look after you when you were in town. If making love to you was going to make you happy, they'd make love. If you were tired and didn't want to make it, they'd cook you a meal and make you feel at home. They were really "ports of call".'

Mountain drummer (and future Bruce cohort) Corky Laing, however, has less prosaic recollections of Clapton's attitude towards groupies. Visiting the guitarist in his hotel room, Laing 'invited one of my favourite girlfriends along ... [and] after a few hours of talking with us, he gracefully hinted to me to get the fuck out, so he could spend some quality time with [her].'

Such diversions notwithstanding, the majority of the trio's spare time was spent absorbing the city. Baker found a virtual home-from-home at a tiny jazz club on 47th Street, where he hung with Wilson Pickett's drummer, Buddy Miles, and jammed entire nights away.

Teaming up with Mitch Ryder, Clapton was frequently to be found in one or other of the myriad clubs and water-holes that dotted Greenwich Village, sitting in with whoever else might be around at the time – Al Kooper, blues great BB King, and the Mothers of Invention, in town for their newly opened *Pigs and Repugnant/Absolutely Free* extravaganza at the Garrick Theater, upstairs from the Cafe Au Go Go. Bruce also caught the Zappa show on a number of occasions, and came away astonished by the brutal brilliance of a concert that changed its dynamic, its content, its very *raison d'être* every single night. How far away it all seemed from the RKO Theater, and how close, in so many ways, to the principles that guided Cream when they first set out.

Clapton and Bruce escaped the clutches of the K once more on Easter Sunday, dashing out after their lunchtime set to link up with some fellow runaways from the Blues Project, to attend New York's first ever Human Be-In, in nearby Central Park's Sheep Meadow.

Picking up on a craze that had already swept San Francisco, the city's freaks and underground had spent weeks gearing up for the event, and the day did not disappoint. On the Lower East Side, artist Joey Skaggs erected a massive crucifix sculpture, built from telegraph poles and incorporating a human skull, a barbed wire crown and a long metal penis; in Central Park itself, musicians, artists, street performers and mimes came pouring out of squats and suburbs alike to celebrate the largest organic gathering in the city's entire history: 'Twenty thousand people,' Clapton marvelled, 'just having a good time. There were no stages or admission fees. . . [just] a reaction against materialism.'

There was also a lot of LSD floating around, as Jack Bruce readily discovered. 'I remember this little girl coming up and giving me all this popcorn, which I thought was quite generous . . . but of course it was very spiked, and that was my introduction to acid. In retrospect, I can tell that story and you know what's coming. Now I know, because I was spiked a few more times. But that time, I had no idea. Of course, the other guys, Blues Project, they thought . . . me being this British psychedelic character, I must really know what I was doing. But I didn't, and I ended up being so wrecked that they were taking me round doctors, just trying to get me down to play the next set of shows.'

Easter Sunday also marked the last day of the concert series and, back at the theatre, Cream prepared to make their exit by making a cake. Or, at least, that's what they looked like they were doing, as they smuggled a few dozen eggs, and some 14 lb bags of flour into their dressing room. In fact, they were planning to redecorate the stage, waiting until Jackie and the K Girls shimmied out for their final fashion parade, and then letting loose an endless barrage of the Sticky Mixture From Hell.

It was not to be. Long before it was time to attack, Murray the K picked up a rumour of the madness afoot, and made it quite clear that the consequences of even *considering* such a stunt would be very protracted and painful. The band redecorated the dressing rooms instead.

Throughout the run of concerts, Murray's severest threat, his most devastating punishment, revolved around the musicians' fee for their performances. The bulk of the payments were to be made at the end of the series, by which time he expected to have more than recouped the estimated $30,000 that he sank into the shows. In fact, he barely scraped back one-tenth of that sum.

Few of the performances sold out, and those that were full were largely populated by kids like Ivan Kral, who took advantage of the ticket's generous all-day offer; once you were in the theatre, you could stay and watch as many shows as you wanted. According to Chris Stamp, the only band that received any money whatsoever was the Who; and that, he said, was only because 'I was so skint that, every day, I had to go and see Murray the K and get another advance from him. We got paid because we needed to eat.'

Cream, on the other hand, looked like making precisely nothing out of the entire dispiriting affair, a situation that Stigwood knew would lead to bitter recriminations the moment they returned home. The shows were just winding down, then, when roadie Ben Palmer received a call from Stigwood, holding out an olive branch that he was convinced would make amends. He'd just been talking on the phone to Ahmet Ertegun; Cream were booked into Atlantic's own studios on West 60th and Broadway, with Ertegun himself lined up to produce them. The first session was scheduled for 3 April, the day after the final Murray the K show.

Cream had commenced work on their sophomore album shortly before leaving for New York, back at Ryemuse Studios in mid-March. Bruce and Brown were now turning out new material at a phenomenal rate, with each fresh batch of compositions seemingly eclipsing the best that they had mustered before.

Certainly that was the case with this latest crop: there was the bizarrely titled (and equally strangely worded) 'She Walks Like a Bearded Rainbow', with its trippy images of moustachioed paintings and a honking harmonica solo amidships, and the martial romp of 'The Clear-out' – a staccato riff in search of a song. There was the flirtatiously acrid (and, lyrically, vaguely Beatles-esque) 'Hey Now Princess', with its frenetic jazz percussion, and Clapton's guitar undergoing a catastrophic meltdown; and, most promising of all, 'Weird of Hermiston', a song that sounded so compulsively quirky that, a decade or so on, it could have been the blueprint for just about everything the Police ever did.

Pete Brown was especially enamoured with that particular number. 'I think "Weird of Hermiston" has a very Scottish feel. Robert Louis Stevenson's last novel was called *Weir of Hermiston*, and he never finished it. That novel has a feeling of doom, which is enhanced even more by the fact that [it] remained unfinished. Jack is a great reader, and we both looked to literature for inspiration, and it was reflected in this song.'

Not one of the four tracks would accompany Cream into Atlantic Studios. With their visitors' visas about to expire, Cream were granted just one day with Ertegun. But that was time enough to lay down a thunderous version of 'Lawdy Mama', and make arrangements to return to New York to record in greater earnest the following month. Then it was back to the UK to try and figure out precisely what they had gained from the entire American experience. Almost forty years later, according to Jack Bruce, they're still not certain.

13. MY AUNT JEMIMA'S CHRISTENING DRESS

With ten days to go before their next scheduled live show, at the Newbury, Berkshire, branch of the Ricky Tick, Cream took the opportunity to revamp their entire live show, rearranging old favourites, introducing new material and, to give them a ground floor view of exactly what they sounded like, arranging for at least one of the shows to be recorded by one of the band's friends, blues enthusiast Ian Shippen.

Setting up a pair of mikes in front of the stage, leading back to a reel-to-reel tape recorder, Shippen captured what is possibly the definitive document of Cream as they finally shifted out of blues gear and into the realms they would inhabit for the remainder of the year.

Their confidence shines through every moment of the tape, from the opening hypnotics of the brand-new and barely road-tested 'Sunshine of Your Love' – faster and, if you follow the guitar, far more frenetic than the familiar studio version, but already glorying within Jeff Beck's 'fuck off' key of D; through to a newly tumultuous 'Toad' that brought every drummer in the house to the front of the stage, to watch Baker bake. Of course the old classics were still in place: a sprawling, brooding 'Spoonful'; a supremely lazy rumble through the Mississippi Sheiks' early-30s blues dirge 'Sitting On Top of the World'; and a dramatically locomotive 'Lawdy Mama'.

But, without even appearing to have lent more than half an ear to the music that was cascading around them, the monstrous transformations that saw such beat boom renegades as the Pretty Things, Brian Auger, the Who, even the Beatles and the Stones slip into an entire new musical gear, Cream had made that same transformation themselves, and had done so entirely on their own terms.

Their model, in many ways, was the Jeff Beck Group – the only other band on the scene that, without ever shaking off the blues tag, had nevertheless squeezed out of the narrow bottleneck that so many other groups had clogged, and were now exploring the untapped mysteries that awaited on the other side.

'We used to take things like John Lee Hooker and Muddy Waters and all the great bluesmen, and play them our way, which is the way to do it,' Rod Stewart reflected, while Beck continued:

> The blues shuffle stuff was a prerequisite in those days. Everybody was doing it, Peter Green and all; nobody wanted their music fucked around with. So bands were very hard pressed to get anything other than very authentic blues going, because there were people like John Mayall around, playing completely authentic Chicago blues and, unless you really had a handle on things, you were going to get a bit of a rough time of things.
>
> But we were trying a lot of covers of less well known songs off the Stax label, Otis Redding things, anything to break out of the blues mould. We were doing things like 'Neighbour Neighbour', some Jimmy Ruffin stuff, stuff that we could take and supercharge a little. It was a very minimalist feel, but it suited us and, although we did get a lot of shit thrown at us, that just made us all the more determined to do things our way.

Primitive though they are, live recordings of the Beck Group's first summer together certainly pre-empt several of Cream's own, subsequent, musical manoeuvres. It was only natural, then, that Cream should absorb the lessons of the Beck Group's first shows; combine them with their own untested ideals; and, like Beck, emerge with something altogether new.

Bruce told journalist John McDermott:

> With the blues things we were doing, we just played them and, because of the interaction between the three of us, they took on a different structure. 'I'm So Glad' was one of the first examples, and certainly 'Spoonful' was something that we made our own.

He reiterated Beck's contention that:

> At that time, bands like Mayall ... were trying to recreate the sounds of Chicago blues. Doing that was completely valid, but

it was something I didn't want to do. Those original blues records had been done so well, which meant you could only ever be second best. But, if you treated those songs with a great deal of love and respect, you could remake them into your own.

Clapton's guitar playing had long since slipped the anchor of his Bluesbreakers days and, if the blues continued to consume the lion's share of Cream's repertoire, the mood of the times was necessarily impacting as well. Pete Brown's lyrics were spinning ever more elaborate fantasies around the very meaning of the words he used, while the band were now decked out as fashionably as the hippest kid on the block – Bruce and Baker were even contemplating perms of their own.

The psychedelia that Cream posited, however, owed little to the visual finery and Carroll-ian wordplay that fired other dreamers' imagery; owed little, even, to Jimi Hendrix's own personally skewed vision. There were no sugar-lump-eating Jacks, third stones from the sun or fourteen-foot spider-suits in Cream's iconography. In the hands of those other artistes, psychedelic music was intended to expand the mind. Cream, in full flight, asked why it had to stop there.

Compared to Cream's schedule earlier in the year, gigs that spring were sporadic, amounting to nothing more testing than a day trip to Bristol; a return bout with the Who at the Brighton Arts Festival; and a charity bash at the Royal Agricultural College in Chippenham; plus two events that, for a few fleeting moments, brought the misery of the Murray the K gigs screaming back into focus.

Twice in the course of three weeks, Cream found themselves lining up at the Empire Pool, Wembley, as the British music industry conducted its annual celebrations of its own popularity: the *Record Star* Show on 16 April, followed by the *New Musical Express* Pollwinners Concert on 7 May, alongside the Beach Boys, the Jeff Beck Group and a cast of almost-hundreds.

Scheduled, with almost monotonous inevitability, to follow Geno Washington and the Ram Jam Band onto the stage, Cream ran through competent renditions of 'I Feel Free' and the rarely aired 'Wrapping Paper', but the audience, including watching journalist Keith Altham, seemed more intrigued by Clapton's 'embroidered, white dangling cloak that looked like my Aunt Jemima's christening dress'. The band themselves 'were a bit too way out ...' for the occasion; their performance greeted 'with what I'd call a stunned silence'. They may have won a poll, but they did not take the night.

Cream themselves scarcely noticed. Their own focus was now wholly on their return to New York on 10 May, where they intended recording their entire new album. And, if their company at the last session, Ahmet Ertegun, was illustrious, this time it was even better, as Tom Dowd stepped forth from the annals of legend to oversee the proceedings.

Clapton confessed that he wasn't overly impressed by Dowd's presence – it was musicians he cared for, not the backroom boffins who placed their sound onto record; in his own experience, after all, that was all a producer really did: switched on the tapes and made sure that the balance was right. Neither were first impressions any more revealing. Bearded and bespectacled, Dowd still looked like a trendy version of the nuclear physicist he had once almost become; as a student at Columbia University during World War Two, Dowd was one of the army of researchers involved in the Manhattan Project, the scientific think-tank that created America's atomic bomb.

He had fallen into the music industry only when his career in physics was derailed by red tape; but, having made the switch, he readily established himself as one of the most precise, and precognitive engineers around.

Cutting his teeth in the jazz era, then linking with Atlantic Records just as rock'n'roll began taking hold, Dowd echoed his mentor, Ahmet Ertegun and his passage through every significant act on the label's roster, from the Coasters and the Drifters, to Aretha Franklin and Otis Redding. Now, with the label taking its first steps into the new rock era, Dowd was again the logical choice to oversee the sessions.

'Ahmet called me up . . . and told me he wanted me to meet this English group, who were arriving that afternoon, over the next three days, because they had to be on a plane at seven o'clock on Sunday evening, which was when their visa would expire.'

The roadies and the gear arrived first, and Dowd recalled watching as the amps piled up, the double speaker cabinet for Bruce's bass, the mountain of Marshalls for Clapton's guitar. 'I thought, "that's all well and good, but where do I put these things . . .?" Then I saw the drum kit go up with two bass drums and five cymbal trees . . .

'All of a sudden, these tons of equipment started coming into the studio, and I'm wondering how big this group can possibly be, but it was just Eric, Jack and Ginger.'

Famously, Dowd spent many years insisting, 'We started on the Friday morning, and they got into their limousine at five o'clock on the Sunday, with the album done.' In fact, the session was somewhat more relaxed than that, as subsequent researchers have placed the group in the studio for anything up to ten days. Neither, though he was certainly in charge of the sessions, was Dowd officially present as anything more than engineer. The role of producer, at Ertegun's insistence, went to one of the rising stars of the contemporary New York scene, the Youngbloods' producer Felix Pappalardi.

'Ahmet was buying insurance with Felix,' Dowd told a BBC interview a decade-plus later. 'I was recording predominantly blues and that type of record and, while Ahmet wasn't worried about my ability to record Cream, he was concerned about my being sensitive to what they were doing and where they were coming from. So Ahmet ran [Felix] in to ensure that, if there was a hole, a communication problem, or a taste consideration to which I might not be sensitive, he would be on it.'

Pappalardi himself explained, 'I had sort of taken Phil Spector's place at Atlantic, as Ahmet Ertegun's protégé. I'd gone over there and Ahmet and I really hit it off. I was in [his] office one afternoon, and Tommy Dowd and Arif Mardin came in and said there were three boys from London and – I don't remember the exact thing, but would I go into the studio and attempt to take over?'

Interviewed by *Rolling Stone* fifteen years on, Pappalardi's own manager, Bud Prager, claimed it was his idea that the aspiring youngster introduce himself at the label, and confessed that the young man's first major commission scarcely filled him with glee. 'I figured if he stayed around there, maybe he'd end up producing Sonny and Cher. Then, one day I got a call from him and he was so excited. He said, "You'll never believe what happened." I thought, "Oh my God, he got Sonny and Cher." And he said, "I'm producing Cream." I had never heard of them and I was so depressed. I couldn't wait for him to get through with it, so he could do something worthwhile.'

In fact, the newcomer swiftly proved himself extraordinarily worthwhile. On their first night in the studio, Cream had barely finished recording Clapton's latest rearrangement of 'Lawdy Mama', than Pappalardi was asking if he could take the tape home with him, to see if he could come up with any fresh ideas for it.

Somewhat taken aback by the request – who was this guy, anyway? – the group agreed. The following day they were thoroughly astonished when Pappalardi returned with an entire new set of lyrics that he and his wife, Gail Collins, had knocked off overnight. Dropped straight onto the 'Lawdy Mama' backing track, 'Strange Brew' became the first song to be completed towards the new album, and that despite the final performance leaving Bruce feeling distinctly uncomfortable.

'There's a bum note in there, and it annoys me every time I hear it. They grafted these lyrics on top of the backing track, and it had a different chord change. If you listen to the song, it sounds like I'm playing the wrong bass line. That's because I'm playing a different tune! I cringe every time I hear it.'

The session got off to a flying start, then, only to hit a brick wall of sorts as Dowd tried to explain to the bemused Englishmen that everything they thought they knew about recording was wrong, or, at least, ten years out of date. Visiting London earlier in the year,

Dowd himself was astonished to discover that even the best-appointed UK studios were still recording on nothing more advanced than a four-track recorder, and that most bands, the Beatles included, were still utilising just two or three tracks, as Ryemuse engineer John Timperley explained. 'We recorded the backing track on all four tracks, then mixed that down to a Philips mono tape machine. We then recorded that track onto another four-track tape and filled up the other three tracks with overdubs.'

Dowd, on the other hand, had spent close to a decade working with twice that many, with Atlantic Studios second only to the ever-enterprising guitarist Les Paul in taking delivery of an Ampex 8-Track recorder. It was Dowd, too, who pioneered the use of sliders, instead of knobs, to control volume and balance on those eight tracks. When Cream walked into the studio for the first time, and saw the equipment at Dowd's disposal, the effect was akin to stepping onto the bridge of the *Starship Enterprise*, the hero of American television's smash-hit sci-fi series of the year, and no less incomprehensible, either.

Even after Dowd explained all that his equipment was capable of, Clapton, Bruce and Baker refused to take it on board. 'They recorded at ear-shattering levels,' Dowd marvelled. 'I never saw anything so powerful in my life and it was just frightening. I don't think they were cognisant of the fact that they had more tracks.'

Nor, according to Bruce, did they need to be. Every basic track on the session was recorded live, played through in no more than a take or two. He and Baker, after all, had cut an entire Graham Bond Organisation album in three hours; to them, anything more than that was profligacy at its most inexcusable. Dowd was mystified. 'They just went about recording in their own method.'

If the group's chosen studio system was archaic, however, ears within the assembled Atlantic hierarchy considered their actual material to be suffering from precisely the opposite problem. They were meant to be a blues band, so what, Ertegun demanded to know, were they doing messing about with what he bluntly dismissed as 'psychedelic hogwash'.

'Sunshine of Your Love' was the worst offender; the old veteran simply could not see any virtue whatsoever in that number, and it swiftly became apparent, at least to Bruce, that Pappalardi's function in the studio had less to do with liaising between the musicians and Tom Dowd, than convincing them to stick with what their reputation (or, at least, Ertegun's interpretation of that reputation) demanded they did best: blues, blues and more blues.

It took a passing Booker T to finally reprieve 'Sunshine of Your Love', after he dropped by the studio and offered up his opinion of the work-in-progress – he loved it. Otis Redding, too, professed himself heartily impressed, while Tom Dowd, who sat quietly through Ertegun's objections, added his own magic to the number when he suggested Baker look beyond the somewhat pedestrian drum beat that underpinned the song in its earliest form, and think, instead, of Cowboys and Indians. The tribal pattern that Baker responded with became one of the recording's most remarkable features. 'I was extremely impressed with Tom Dowd,' Bruce enthused. 'He wasn't just an amazing engineer, it was like having another musician in there with you.'

Pappalardi, too, was invaluable. 'Felix usually sat out in the studio while I was recording in the control room,' Dowd told McDermott. 'Especially during playbacks. He would point out certain things to each member where he felt improvements could be made. There was a lot of dialogue between Felix and the three of them. Some of it was specific to the session, but it also included exposing them to the styles of different artists and sounds from other records.'

Ertegun accepted the wisdom of his workmates. But another battle still lay ahead, as Jack Bruce stepped up to the microphone to voice one lyric or another, only for Ertegun (again!) to demand to know what he thought he was doing. Wasn't that Clapton's job?

Slowly, the story came out. When Atlantic Records signed Cream, it was in the belief that they were picking up Eric Clapton's new group; that the guitarist was the star name in the band, just as he was in the Bluesbreakers and the Yardbirds beforehand. And stars, Ertegun insisted, should sing, even if they were playing lead guitar at the same time.

He had a point. Though neither meant anything in America at the time, Jimi Hendrix fronted the Experience in every conceivable way, and even Jeff Beck was forced to stretch out his tonsils before he grabbed the solo hit single he so richly deserved. High on the UK chart as Cream sat in the studio, 'Hi Ho Silver Lining' had utterly sidelined the Jeff Beck Group's regular vocalist, Rod Stewart, and pushed Beck up to the microphone instead.

Bruce, however, would not budge and neither would Clapton. As he proved with a readily aborted struggle through Ginger Baker's melancholic singalong 'Blue Condition', though he could sing, he hated doing so, and avoided it at every opportunity. (Baker himself eventually voiced that song, bequeathing a lugubrious vocal that matched the lyric perfectly.)

Neither, Clapton almost proudly pointed out, was he writing material. 'I really didn't have knowledge of theory, or how to go about it. To me, writing a song was a miracle. At that stage, I was good for about a song a year.' In fact, of the new Cream numbers to which he even laid a co-claim as composer, one was that slice of psychedelic hogwash, 'Sunshine of Your Love'; and the other was a spookily rhythmic riff (the Lovin' Spoonful's 'Summer in the City' revisited), to which Clapton's Australian flatmate, pop-art artist Martin Sharp, had added some dreamily Floyd-ish lyrics, 'Tales of Brave Ulysses'. Maybe Ertegun thought that was hogwash, as well?

Martin Sharp was a relatively recent addition to Cream's immediate entourage, the brilliant Australian-born graphic designer at the underground *Oz* magazine; indeed, it was *Oz*'s founder, fellow-Aussie Richard Neville, who made the introductions, one night at the Speakeasy, and who preserved the meeting for posterity in his own memoirs.

'After a brief discussion [about] snakeskin boots, the must-have footwear of the day, Martin brought out a crumpled envelope.' He had just returned to London from a holiday visit to Formentera, in the Balearic Islands – the place where, according to legend, the Greek warrior Ulysses encountered the sirens, the sinister singing spirits who lure sailors to their doom.

'"I've just written a song," [Sharp] announced.

'"That's great," replied Eric. "I've just written some music."'

Days later, Clapton and his girlfriend Charlotte Martin (the future Mrs Jimmy Page) were moving into the Pheasantry, the King's Road, Chelsea, flats where Sharp, photographer Bob Whittaker, Australian filmmaker Philippe Mora and (in a flat downstairs) feminist writer Germaine Greer, among others, were already living.

It was there that 'Tales of Brave Ulysses' took shape and, though its recounting of the ancient myth might have appeared an odd subject for a pop song, still it readily attracted its admirers; within weeks of its eventual release, songwriters Ken Howard and Alan Blaikley made their own grab at the Greek classics, adapting the legend of Orpheus for the Herd's 'From the Underworld'.

Ertegun knew none of that, of course. But Clapton's insistence that he was simply the guitar player finally got through to him. He backed down, and Cream got on with their album.

The band and their production team were not alone in the studio. In keeping with the free-and-easy atmosphere of the times, the doors were open to all-comers most of the time Cream worked, for who knew when an outsider might have something to contribute? Jenny Dean, one of the queens of the local groupie scene, was among the visitors; she cheerleads the party atmosphere that rattles so raucously behind 'Take It Back'.

The future Mrs Paul McCartney, photographer Linda Eastman, was around; Tom Dowd recalled one evening when, at her request, the studio lights were turned up 'and we'd suddenly realise there were about fifteen people crashed out against the wall, digging the session, Janis Joplin and all kinds of people'. The Blues Project's Al Kooper dropped by and turned in a few keyboard flourishes, although any contributions he might have made to the proceedings have never seen the light of day. Bruce played all the album's keyboard parts.

The most innovative newcomer, however, was the wah-wah pedal that Clapton and Pappalardi happened across, while paying a visit to Manny's instrument store. Cream were attempting to nail down

Above (*left to right*) Fresh-faced Jack Bruce, Ginger Baker and Eric Clapton – 1966
(COURTESY OF REX FEATURES)

Right Cream in their prime – 1967
(COURTESY OF REX FEATURES)

Right The early London blues scene: Cyril Davies, Charlie Watts and Alexis Korner performing at the Ealing Club – 1962
(COURTESY OF REDFERNS)

AUTHENTICITY IN

R&B

THE
GRAHAM BOND
ORGANIZATION

THE
BLUE BOTTLES
WITH MIKE PATTO

Both represented by the agency for REAL Rhythm & Blues
CHARLESWORTH PRESENTATIONS
1a Westbourne Road, Newlands Park, S.E.26
Tel.: SYDenham 9661

Left Graham Bond advert draws attention to mid-60s 'real' R&B debate – 1964
(COURTESY OF PICTORIAL PRESS)

Below The Graham Bond Organisation: Jack Bruce, Graham Bond, Dick Heckstall-Smith and Ginger Baker – 1965
(COURTESY OF PICTORIAL PRESS)

Above John Mayall of The
Bluesbreakers
(COURTESY OF REDFERNS)
Right Pete Brown performs poetry
with percussive accompaniment
(COURTESY OF JORGEN ANGEL)

Below Eric Clapton (*right*) in The
Yardbirds – 1964
(COURTESY OF REDFERNS)

Above Performing on TV programme 'Ready Steady Go' – 1966
(COURTESY OF PICTORIAL PRESS)

Above Backstage at the Windsor Festival – 1966
(COURTESY OF REDFERNS)

Above Geno Washington and the Ram Jam Band at Windsor – 1966
(COURTESY OF GETTY IMAGES)

Right Hippies at Windsor take in the atmosphere
(COURTESY OF GETTY IMAGES)

Left The Clapton afro –
1967
(COURTESY OF REDFERNS)

Below In the recording
studio – 1967

(COURTESY OF REDFERNS)

Above At London airport on the way to Los Angeles – 1967 (COURTESY OF GETTY IMAGES)

Below Performing at the Fillmore, San Francisco – 1967 (COURTESY OF CORBIS)

Above The band united at the farewell concert, 26 November 1968
(COURTESY OF REDFERNS)

Below Farewell concert inside the Royal Albert Hall, 26 November 1968
(COURTESY OF PICTORIAL PRESS)

'Tales of Brave Ulysses' at the time, but a final shape for the song wasn't gelling. Hoping that a change of scenery might spark some fresh inspiration, Pappalardi recalled, 'Eric and I took a walk and ended up at Manny's. They'd just got a bunch of Vox wah-wah pedals in, so we bought one . . . [and], as it turned out, the wah-wah was perfect for "Ulysses".'

It was also perfect for keeping up with the Joneses. Clapton admitted that the deciding factor for him was being told that Jimi Hendrix had just bought a wah-wah for himself (he debuted it on his next single, 'The Burning of The Midnight Lamp'); that, Clapton acknowledged, 'was enough for me'.

Once he got the device back to the studio, however, he quickly fell in love with it, taking an almost childish delight in the speech-like sound that the pedal emitted; indeed, as he put it through its paces, the watching Americans stared blankly at one another as Clapton started raving about Sparky the Magic Piano. But his bandmates' peels of laughter proved that Bruce and Baker knew exactly what he was talking about.

In many ways, the wah-wah crystallised everything that Cream hoped to achieve with this new album, formulating a sound that wasn't merely willing to confront the future head-on, it was demanding the opportunity. Of all the complaints levelled at *Fresh Cream*, the most damning – but also the most accurate – was that it really didn't *do* anything new; you could play it alongside almost any British blues record of the past two or three years, and it blended in seamlessly.

These current sessions, on the other hand, breathed scorching innovation from every pore, with almost every song pushing the boat far away from the expected Blues Central, to reflect Cream as they now were, not as their admirers thought they ought to be; only one number, Clapton's arrangement of Blind Willie Reynolds's 'Outside Woman Blues', even glanced towards the group's stockpile of old classics.

Elsewhere, 'She Walks Like a Bearded Rainbow' was now referred to by the more economic, if no less baffling, 'SWLABR', and proved one of Cream's most vital team efforts. Pappalardi and Collins bequeathed another of their own co-compositions, 'World Of Pain'; Baker turned in 'Blue Condition'; 'Sunshine of Your Love' was pinned down with awe-inspiring precision; 'Tales of Brave Ulysses' likewise. And the mid-March demos were plundered for two more tracks, Bruce's 'We're Going Wrong' and 'The Clear-Out' – at least until the night that Baker and Clapton found themselves in nearby Martin's Bar, entertaining the natives with their repertoire of half-remembered Cockney drinking songs.

Suddenly, one of the pair seized upon the short, sad tale of the gin-soaked mother who washed her baby down the plug 'ole, one of those old music hall favourites that seemed to have been around forever. Paul McCartney used to entertain the Germans with it during the Beatles' days at the Star Club in Hamburg; more recently, Anglo-transplant Ian Whitcomb had included a version on his second album, *Mod Mod Music Hall*, so when a few of the bar's patrons joined in, it shouldn't have been a surprise; Whitcomb was selling a lot of records in those days.

The drunker the evening became, the more attractive the song sounded. By the time the group reconvened in the studio, the decision was made. 'Your Baby Has Gone Down the Plug-Hole' – retitled, for some reason, 'Mother's Lament' – would wrap up the album; and, when somebody pointed out that the record would wind up with one number too many, the pair had an answer to that as well. They would sacrifice 'The Clear-Out' and share the new recording's 'traditional' credits between the full band.

'The Clear-Out' was joined on the putative scrap heap by a clutch of other Bruce compositions. Clapton may have raved in the pages of *Melody Maker* about 'Weird of Hermiston', but it never appeared on record during Cream's lifetime. Neither did 'Hey Now Princess', nor another song that today is regarded among the Bruce/Brown team's most majestic accomplishments, 'Theme For An Imaginary Western'.

Of all the excisions, it was the latter that shocked Bruce the most. 'I think that would have made a great Cream number.' He'd written the music back in 1962, and it formed the perfect backdrop to a Brown lyric that, far from lionising the American West that its title apparently conjures, was instead, almost autobiographical. Brown explained, '[it] was about the early British R&B bands, seen as cowboys and pioneers. We'd all grown up with Western movies and, in a way, I think the musicians on the British R&B, jazz and blues scenes all thought of themselves in that way. Musically, the Graham Bond Organisation were like pioneers, and [the song] was a mythologisation of that band, really.'

Bruce ultimately held onto 'Theme From an Imaginary Western' until 1969, when he finally rerecorded (and released) it on his *Songs For a Tailor* solo album, and he admitted, 'In a way, I think it was good that it ended up [there], as it's one of the things I'm most proud of.' He returned, too, to 'The Clear-Out' and 'Weird of Hermiston' during those same sessions and, again, he had good reason to be grateful that the songs were still available to him; widely heralded as a stone cold classic though it is, *Songs For a Tailor* would certainly have been poorer for the absence of so many jewels.

As for the songs' desertion by Cream, Bruce blamed nothing less than jealousy. No matter the sheer quality of what he was offering the group, if Cream had recorded every number that Bruce and Brown handed them, there'd have been no room (and, consequently, no songwriting royalties) for anyone else.

Besides, the album was already shaping up to be an absolute triumph; and, as the band finally flew back to London, all were congratulating themselves on a job done well indeed, and were ready to face their next decision, the release of a new Cream single – a much-needed new Cream single.

Close to five months had elapsed since 'I Feel Free', a lifetime during which the pioneering trail that Cream had beaten in the first weeks of the year had become a firmly paved, and well-travelled motorway. Hendrix had scored his second monster smash with the unalloyed freak-out drama of 'Purple Haze'; the Small Faces had abandoned their beat group heritage and were coyly toying with psychedelic culture at its most vibrant, 'Here Comes the Nice' being a paean to their amphetamine dealer. The Move, too, were smirking cheekily – 'I Can Hear the Grass Grow' could be taken in any number of ways, but the enhanced sensations that could be derived from LSD was certainly among the commonest.

Elsewhere, groups that had scarcely been recordable back in January were now scoring major hits – Pink Floyd had already tripped through the Top Twenty once, with their debut single, 'Arnold Layne'; now they were readying the follow-up, a celebration of the massive concert they'd just headlined at Queen Elizabeth Hall. Everywhere, new warlords were springing up like magic mushrooms, and every one had its own psychedelic gimmick: the Purple Gang, with their manic washboard solos; John's Children, with a stage fringed by massive silver screens; and the Crazy World of Arthur Brown, newly signed to Lambert and Stamp's Track label, who set their singer's head on fire, as a regular part of the show. How could Cream – how could *anyone* – follow that?

Cream's choice for their next release was 'Tales of Brave Ulysses'. Hendrix had yet to reveal his own wah-wah on the world so, if they moved quickly, they could beat him to unveiling it. Stigwood, however, was less certain. Let the musicologists argue over who did what when; he wanted a sure-fire hit and, the moment he heard 'Strange Brew' he knew he'd found one. A great tune, a catchy chorus and, almost as an added bonus, a lyric that could be as innuendo-laden as anything the Move or the Small Faces had come up with.

But he did slap 'Tales of Brave Ulysses' on the B-side, for anyone who cared to pursue that particular debate; and, with the single lined up for release at the end of the month, the best of Cream's activities over the remainder of May were devoted to ensuring it received as great a response as 'I Feel Free': a BBC radio session for *Saturday Club*; a quick trip to Germany for a return to *Beat Club*; then bang up to Manchester, to appear on Simon Dee's Saturday evening variety show, *Dee Time*.

The first voice ever heard on a British pirate radio station, when he announced Radio Caroline's arrival in March 1964, Dee was also the first former pirate to be 'legitimised' by the Beeb, as he shipped off the ocean and into the television studio. *Dee Time* kept time with its namesake's reputation, by paying little more than lip-service to the established tenets of tea-time television; its host was hip, and his guests were hipper still (Hendrix appeared on the very first show). Of all the programmes that were available to the in-demand pop group of the age, *Dee Time* was a veritable feather in the cap, and Cream did not disappoint.

Beat Club, on the other hand, proved a less than gripping exercise, as the oft-circulated footage of the performance proves. Decked out in his most fulsome Fool-made *peau de soie*, Clapton looked distinctly uncomfortable, while neither he nor Bruce appeared at all sure which one of them was meant to be mouthing the words. But such performances did the trick regardless.

A Top Five hit in *Beat Club*'s German homeland, 'Strange Brew' breached the pirate charts on 4 June; the BBC chart just four days later; and, within weeks, it was revelling from its respective peaks, number four on Radio London, number seventeen on the national listing. And, in the wee small hours of 15 August, it was one of the records with which offshore DJ John Peel mourned the final night of his *Perfumed Garden* underground showcase, before Radio London was closed down forever.

Jimi Hendrix reviewed 'Strange Brew' for *Melody Maker*; every week, the paper's 'Blind Date' column called in a performer and asked him to comment on a clutch of new releases, without being told in advance who they were by. Some excellent commentary has been preserved in those pages: a fortnight on, upon hearing David Bowie's 'Love You Till Tuesday', Pink Floyd's Syd Barrett quipped, 'Very chirpy. But I don't think my toes were tapping at all.' Hendrix, however, knew precisely what he was hearing, and exactly how to respond. 'Ooh, that's nice. I like this record because I like the way [Clapton] plays . . . his solo is just like . . . Albert King.'

Yet, for all their apparent pre-eminence, for all Hendrix's enthusiasm and their superstar supporters, Cream remained outsiders – if not so far as the general public was concerned, then at least within the hallowed halls of the underground movement that they themselves were so fervently embracing. The fans they had were influential: producer Joe Boyd, DJ John Peel and publisher Richard Neville were all firm and vocal supporters. But they were also out-numbered, swamped by a growing rumble that insisted that the very existence of Cream was, in some unforgivable manner, a sell-out.

It was an age in which artists rose and fell (or appeared to rise and fall – in showbiz, after all, appearances are everything) in a state of organic purity; where groups existed because they needed to, and the music they made flowed from that need. To those observers who most cherished the utopian ideals of the counter-culture, Cream were phonies. Where other bands experienced natural births, Cream were a mere composite, pieced together with scientific methodology and unparalleled condescension – three players, deeming themselves the crown princes of their instruments, united not because they liked one another, but because they liked one another's stature. No less an admirer than Pete Townshend was willing to accuse, 'the machine created Cream. It *really* did'; while Clapton himself was certainly thinking about Cream when he mused, thirty years later, on the need to form a band out of friendship, not ability.

Naturally, the straights, that is, the vast majority of onlookers, were taken in by it all. To a pop mainstream that itself paid mere lip-service to the latest fashions (are *you* going to San Francisco?), Cream looked psychedelic, they dressed psychedelic, they even, on this latest single, *sounded* psychedelic. But when it came to actually getting their hands dirty, mucking in down in the trenches where the movement *really* moved, they were nowhere to be seen.

By now, Cream's pulling power was such that, at last, they had outgrown the clubs that had hitherto nurtured them. Their Marquee show on 23 May, on the very eve of the new single's release, was so oversubscribed that the line at the door reached almost to the 100 Club, up on Oxford Street; while the temperature inside the venue was so high that the pirate recording that has survived of the night captures the sound of the instruments all but melting.

But when Cream were invited to appear on the 14-Hour Technicolor Dream, at Alexandra Palace in April, the grandest gathering of the psych clans yet, Stigwood turned it down. They were offered other, similar events in the provinces. He turned them down. Again and again, promoters called RSO with offers that any other manager would have grasped with both hands. They were all rejected.

Even the group's friends professed themselves mystified by the stance. 'Jimi loved Cream ... we all did,' Experience bassist Noel Redding said in 1996. 'But through that whole Summer of Love psychedelic movement that was going on in 1967, we were in there, playing all the Happenings and the Freak-outs; it was our scene. Cream just watched from the sidelines, played the odd one or two when it suited them, but you got the feeling that the whole thing was somehow below them. Whether it was bad management or the band's own decision, they didn't feel a part of it, they didn't want to be a part of it. They had their own agenda – and good luck to them for pulling it off.'

Today, divorced from the petty squabbles and rival factions that were the true face of the so-called Summer of Love, such observations are easy to overlook, and certain Cream records are inescapably a vital part of the soundtrack to 1967. 'I Feel Free', 'Strange Brew' and 'Tales of Brave Ulysses' in particular, should turn up on any self-respecting *Best Psychedelic Album in the World ... Ever* type compilation, while as far back as April 1975, when *New Musical Express* journalist Charles Shaar Murray set about documenting the greatest records of the entire psychedelic genre, he had no hesitation over including 1968's 'Anyone for Tennis' in the mix, describing it as the only *great* Cream number to have escaped 'the attention of the trained armadillos who slave away in Robert Stigwood's basement endlessly permutating old Eric-Jack 'n-Ginger tracks'.

Yet Cream (or, again, their management) not only distanced themselves from the nuts and bolts of the psychedelic movement, they did so with a deliberation that bordered upon arrogance. It wasn't only the Happenings that the group steered clear of. Almost alone among the major bands of the day, Cream never played UFO or the now-swinging Middle Earth, the pulsating hearts of British psychedelia. They never lent their support to any of the counter-cultural causes and fund-raisers with which the era was peppered; they seldom raised their voices over the issues of the day.

Even the Vietnam War, certainly the most crucial, and divisive, conundrum facing the underground during 1967, all but passed the group by. Two or three key lines amid Bruce and Brown's 'Take It Back', a rollicking juggy-blues number recorded in New York in May, may have prompted some listeners to direct its sentiments towards the anti-war movement, but until one heard Bruce himself confirm those intentions, the song could have been about almost anything.

Yet Cream's failure, as musicians, to immerse themselves in the scene was not necessarily their own decision, although it was only afterwards, as Bruce surveyed the catalogue of refusals that was issued in Cream's name, that people realised that the band were as mystified by their non-availability as everybody else. 'To be honest, we were too busy working to notice the places where we *weren't* working. We were a really hard-working band at the time, so there wasn't a lot of time to sort of hang, and find out what else was going on.

'I expect we were offered all kinds of big events that we never got to hear about, that maybe we should have played. And instead, we were doing some terrible little gig somewhere else.' Robert Stigwood, he concluded, could be 'very unimaginative'.

Besides, though Cream themselves seemed to have little time for political revolution, audiences were more than capable of drawing them into the ferment regardless. Their visit to Germany in May, for instance, plunged them into the midst of the student uprisings that were tearing apart that nation's fragile post-war constitution, to find themselves adopted among the leading flag-wavers of the looming revolt.

Holm Kogel was a student at West Berlin's Free University, the nexus of the incipient revolution, and he detailed how 'I Feel Free' was unanimously grasped as an anthem by 'everybody who wanted to feel free themselves'. Cream's appearance at the local Stadion nightclub on 20 May 1967 became a rallying point not only for West Berlin's music lovers, but also for everybody planning the city's next mass protest, against the Shah of Iran's upcoming (early June) visit to the city. Following the concert, Kogel was among the 'several hundred' students who 'remained behind in the club, still singing "I Feel Free". We believed, if only everybody sang those words, then the world would become a better place.'

It didn't. Twelve days later, the rally that was so fastidiously planned at the concert ended in tragedy and death, as the Berlin police hustled their distinguished visitor into the Opera House, then turned on the protestors with a violence unseen in that city, several cringing commentators observed, since the last days of World War Two. Twelve protestors were hospitalised, one was shot and killed, and the German student movement was finally launched onto the path that ultimately climaxed in the terror campaigns of the Baader-Meinhof Gang.

Cream themselves saw little of the turmoil seething beneath the surface of the city, but they tasted the day-to-day oppression of the divided Berlin all the same. Bruce and Baker decided to take a quick trip into East Berlin, 'to check it out,' as Bruce put it. 'We got as far as Check Point Charlie, saw all the Russian troops, got the horrors and decided not to bother!'

Instead, they returned home to discover that RSO had booked them to appear at an event in Oxford that was surely the corollary of all the fervent revolution being schemed elsewhere, the Pembroke College student's May Ball. There they lined up alongside the similarly discomfited Who, to perform before an audience that was already drunk before the music began, and was destined only to get even drunker. Finally, in a desperate attempt to liven up the rows of living dead men who stared out from the audience, Keith Moon hurled his drums with such superhuman abandon that he wound up giving himself a hernia. Cream, for their part, contented themselves with hauling a coal-scuttle full of vomit through the darkened halls of learning, and watching while Baker rode a bicycle pell-mell through the bar.

Socially, Cream's isolation from the psychedelic pulsebeat was far from their minds. Pete Brown was riding his own renown as Cream's lyricist by staging a succession of jazz, poetry and rock fusion events around the underground club circuit, a routine that ensured Cream maintained a high profile, even if they weren't attending the events themselves. His First Real Poetry Band, convened with guitarist John McLaughlin, were regulars at Middle Earth in Covent Garden where, Brown declared with a laugh, 'We certainly frightened a few people.' Canny promoters quickly realised that even a mention of Brown's Cream connections on a playbill drew in an army of extra observers.

All three band members, too, were regularly out and about in London, hanging out at the Scotch of St James and the Bag O'Nails; they knew what was going on, they were friends with the people who were going on with it. They showed up at favourite bands' gigs, and dropped by their recording sessions – Donovan's 'Someone Singing', from his masterpiece *A Gift From a Flower to a Garden* album features a wonderfully characteristic Bruce bass line; Bruce was also included among the cast of superstar thousands that anonymously populated poets Roger McGough and Mike McGear's eponymous debut album, a spectacular guest list that also included Hendrix and Noel Redding, John Mayall, Graham Nash and Dave Mason.

Unfortunately, as John Entwistle pointed out, 'it doesn't matter who the musicians know. It's who their management know, and their booking agents know, and the people who make the real decisions know.' The Who were lucky. Their management team, Kit Lambert and Chris Stamp, were among that brave breed of young entrepreneurs who arrived on the music scene without any under-standing of its traditions and rules whatsoever – and made damned certain that they kept it at that. The Move's Tony Secunda, too, saw the established industry as a castle to besiege, not a palace to relax in, and his charges flowered accordingly.

'But Stigwood,' Secunda once accused, 'he was old guard. Even though he didn't come along that long before the rest of us, and he made his own little dent in the establishment when he started, he never updated his address book. The gigs he got for Cream were the same as he'd got for Graham Bond, and he'd have done the same with the Who if Kit hadn't stopped him. That Murray the K thing was just an embarrassment for everybody . . .'

Cream agreed, with even the customarily non-reactive Clapton once remarking that the band was successful *despite* Stigwood, not because of him. More bluntly, Jack Bruce snapped, 'He was a wanker. People think of him as this big Svengali character, but he wasn't. It was bad management.'

But Stigwood cannot be held responsible for every perceived slight and calumny that befell Cream, with one of the greatest injustices being history's (and numerous writers') insistence that he turned down an invitation for the group to play the Monterey Pop Festival, an event that the same history (and writers) now regard as a crucial watershed in the development of late 1960s rock.

Even Clapton, Bruce and Baker themselves are convinced that Stigwood was solely responsible for Cream's non-appearance at the event; that he insisted, instead, that when the time came for Cream to break in America, they would do it in their own right, not on the back of some open-air event, even if it was the most spectacular meeting of the tribes that rock had ever witnessed.

The bill spread across the entire spectrum of modern music, from the folky strains of Simon and Garfunkel and co-organiser John

Phillips's Mamas and the Papas to the acid rock of Jefferson Airplane and the newly Americanised Eric Burdon; from the soul of Otis Redding to the Eastern mysteries of Ravi Shankar; from the hefty blues of Janis Joplin to the bluesy heft of the Butterfield Band; and on to the Who – making their first American appearance since the Murray the K debacle; and Jimi Hendrix – making *his* first since he grasped fame.

Staged over the weekend of 16–17 June, and then replayed on cinema screens for the rest of the decade, Monterey elevated both British imports to a status bordering upon superstardom, in the days when it was still possible for one gig, by word of mouth and the enthusiasm of the press, to do so; established, too, the infamous rivalry between the two bands that played its own part in confirming their renown. If any event would have suited Cream, muse history's accusers, it was Monterey; if any event can be said to condemn Stigwood's handling of their career, therefore, it is Monterey.

In fact, the group was never even considered for the event, as one of the festival's own advisors, Andrew Loog Oldham, has since acknowledged. 'Paul McCartney and I suggested the English acts and only the Who and Hendrix were ever in the running.' Cream didn't even cross their minds.

Neither, in the festival's immediate aftermath, might they have felt especially despairing over that fact. The Who and Hendrix *did* become superstars. But both bands underwent their own trial by mismatched fire in the months before they truly ascended to that position, as Hendrix was sent out on the road as the opening act for the Monkees, and the Who went out with Herman's Hermits, acts whose intended audiences were as unsuitable to the support acts, as the Murray the K concerts were for Cream . . . more so, in fact, as the teenyboppers positively recoiled from the volume and violence that preceded their idols, and made their impatience heard with incessant chanting. As Roger Daltrey remarked once the Hermits tour was over, 'It got us around America, but it did us no good at all.'

If Cream were to be spared that particular ordeal, however, still their schedule scarcely befitted an act of their purported magnitude. While the Who and Hendrix were duelling at Monterey, Cream were enjoying a few weeks off; while the American media hastened to praise both bands' triumphs, Cream were upstairs at the Manor House in north London. And, on the day 'Strange Brew' was released as a single in the USA, they were playing to an 8/6d (42½p) a head crowd at the Upper Cut in Forest Gate. It was with a brave face indeed that Clapton was moved to enthuse, 'after all the early criticisms, we have got through to audiences. And what really surprises us is . . . not only do fans welcome the blues things, they like the things Jack has written as well. They like our whole programme . . . Things,' he concluded, 'are swinging along beautifully.'

14. HEY, HEY, WE'RE THE CREAMIES

Cream did make it to one psychedelic happening as the spring of 1967 drifted into the Summer of Love, and it was both ironic and extraordinarily unlucky that it might well have been the one they'd have been better advised to skip.

The quaintly titled Barbecue 67, staged at the equally pleasingly named Tulip Bulb Auction Hall in Spalding, Lincs, on 29 May, boasted a spectacular bill. Hendrix was there, riding his third hit single, the luscious 'Wind Cries Mary', and celebrating the success of his just-released debut album, *Are You Experienced?*; Pink Floyd were aboard, packing all the punch of their own finest hour-so-far, the sparkling second single psych of 'See Emily Play'. Geno Washington and Zoot Money were on hand to send some driving R&B through the festivities; the Sounds Force Five were there to warm everybody up; and the venue itself had the kind of name that oozed Flower Power from every last drop of mortar.

Unfortunately, the floral industry that gave the hall its name had withered long ago. These days, the vast barn was more frequently used for cattle sales and, on a hot day like today, it smelled like it. With dung underfoot, cow in the air, and 4,000-plus people squeezing into a windowless space through one sliding door, Jack Bruce described the event as 'totally mad'.

But it was totally torturous, too, as the air grew so heated that even the Marquee looked air-conditioned by comparison and, by the time Hendrix took the stage, it was so hot that he could barely tune his guitar, or rely on the amplifiers not to sputter and die. So he played a furious set, then disembowelled his instrument, before kicking over the amps, and promptly fusing all the lights in the shed. The disgruntled crowd was left to feel its way out in a reeking darkness broken only by the glow of cigarettes and joints, and Cream – whose own performance had passed off with little more than heat-exhausted competence – never braved another provincial English 'happening' again.

There was little respite from the gnarling crush of the regular circuit, however. The Ram Jam in Brixton, the Starlite Ballroom in Greenford, Bluesville 67 at Manor House were all packed to fainting point, and the only break in the monotony was simply another of those infuriating quickly on-and-off-again showcases at which the sheer weight of participants somehow compensated for the fact that none of them had time to play more than a couple of songs. French television's *First Festival of Pop Music* also featured the Troggs, the Pretty Things, John Walker, Johnny Halliday and Dave Dee, Dozy, Beaky, Mick & Tich, with each band given time enough to perform just a couple of numbers. Cream served up 'I Feel Free' and, with surely purposeful irony, 'We're Going Wrong'.

Of course Cream did register a few of the year's most epochal moments. The release, on 1 June, of the Beatles' *Sergeant Pepper* album, for example, could not have passed anybody by. But whereas so many others on the scene set off in slavish imitation of all that the Beatles had seen fit to invoke, Cream remained musically untouched.

'I thought *Sgt Pepper* was brilliant, oh sure,' affirmed Bruce. 'But I thought the Beach Boys' *Pet Sounds* ... if you want to compare things, at the time I thought *Pet Sounds* was the more influential of the two albums, which are quite similar in a way.'

Freshly released as Cream themselves got under way – that is, a full year before *Sgt Pepper* – *Pet Sounds* bowled Bruce over, with both its musical content and with what Clapton described as 'Brian Wilson's viewpoint ... Jack saw it as the new Bach.' Indeed, Clapton himself waxed very eloquently on the subject, when *Melody Maker* corralled a clutch of contemporary stars ('pop people' in the paper's parlance) a few weeks after the album's issue, to ask whether it was really 'the most progressive pop album ever? Or as sickly as peanut butter?' 'All of us, Ginger, Jack and I, are absolutely and completely knocked out by *Pet Sounds*,' Clapton averred. 'It encompasses everything that's ever knocked me out, all rolled into one. We're all gassed by it.'

Bruce retained his affection for *Pet Sounds*; almost four decades on, he continued, 'Although it wasn't quite as famous at the time, I always thought *Pet Sounds* would last longer [than *Sgt Pepper*], and be more famous, and it has turned out that way really. Plus, I wasn't a big fan of the Beatles. Their music was a bit trite for me, especially the early stuff. As they went on, I did get to like them a lot, their later stuff I thought was great.' Nevertheless, he was never going to make the mistake of assuming that anything the Fabs could do, Cream could do later. While he conceded that 'we were all very influenced by Lennon and McCartney, their skill at writing great pop songs', he was also adamant that 'I only wrote pop songs when that was what I was doing. When Cream had a chance to sell a couple of singles, that became an aim, to try to write a successful pop song. I suppose "White Room" or "I Feel Free", those two are quite successful attempts at writing a pop song. But I only did it when I had to.'

Another number that fit that bill was 'SWLABR', an effort, Bruce once revealed, that 'was definitely influenced by the Monkees'. There was something about the song's bridge, he said, that was inescapably conjured out of the Prefabricated Foursome's music; and there was something about the way Bruce smiled as he said it that suggested he knew precisely how far up people's noses it would go, to hear him utter a sacrilege like that.

Cream returned to the Saville Theatre on 2 July, for a show that *Melody Maker* insisted confirmed the band's supremacy over all contenders. Opening performances by beat boom survivors Jimmy Powell and the Dimensions, John Mayall and the Jeff Beck Group scarcely raised reviewer Nick Jones's temperature a single degree: 'the Bluesbreakers playing the blues like they've always played the blues . . . [Beck] also playing yesterday's blues, only a bit louder . . .'

But, 'from the first quiver of "NSU", the Cream obliterated what had gone before', while the closing number in the set, 'I'm So Glad', raised the roof even higher, as Cream dismissed their continued (and, thanks to Hendrix, chastened) reluctance to allow guests onto the stage, and ushered on Beck, Mick Taylor (the now-departed Peter Green's replacement in the Bluesbreakers) and the Dimensions' Red Godwin for a 'freaking . . . four-guitar feedback finale'.

Most of Cream's set now comprised new – or, at least, still-unreleased – material and, in late July, it was announced that the group's second album was to be titled *Disraeli Gears*, so-named after a slip of the tongue by roadie Mick Turner, during a discussion of a racing bike's 'Derailleur gears'. (Hitherto, the album was referred to, simply, as *Cream*.) A release date, however, had still to be confirmed, as Robert Stigwood and Ahmet Ertegun sought to line up Cream's next American visit, a full tour this time, as opposed to a fleeting spot on a cabaret bill.

So far as Cream were concerned, it was a repeat of the protracted nativity of *Fresh Cream*; impatient to maintain their own momentum, the group returned to the studio in mid-July 1967, flying in Felix Pappalardi to oversee a couple of covers, 'Sitting on Top of the World' and 'Born Under a Bad Sign', a Booker T composition that had just made its debut on the latest Albert King album; plus the Bruce–Brown composition that the lyricist insisted might never have existed without Syd Barrett's influence, 'White Room'.

The song was another of the numbers that Ertegun dismissed as 'psychedelic hogwash', and, in this instance, the American was correct, in the first half of that assessment, at least. It was very psychedelic.

Brown wrote the lyrics to 'White Room' during those months immediately before he hooked up with Cream, a period within which poor health and the incessant jangle of the alarm bells at the neighbouring fire station combined to push him to the brink of a nervous breakdown.

But the white room ... with black curtains ... near the station ... itself was no product of his fever; rather, it was a physical description of the tiny Baker Street flat in which he was living at the time, and where his life finally bottomed out in a tangled mess of alcoholic binges, dope-addled comas and long, rambling conversations with the furniture.

Starting life as an eight-page poem, 'White Room' was only gradually whittled down to a manageable length, but it never lost its foreboding power and menace; indeed, the abbreviation might even have amplified the song's strengths. 'Fuzzy and raucous,' raved the *New Musical Express* when it first encountered the claustrophobic nightmare, 'with wowing guitar and walloping beat. As ever, the boys dispense a gripping, electrifying sound ...'

Brown had long since left the white room behind him. The money flowing in from 'I Feel Free' alone was sufficient for him to rent a new pad in fashionable Montagu Square, just a few doors away from both The Fool's centre of operations, and the basement flat shared by Jimi Hendrix and Chas Chandler; 'White Room' was soon adding to his riches.

The sessions were not wholly obsessed with the group's next album, however. Another studio visit that summer was booked so that Cream could fulfil their half of one of Stigwood's most audacious deals yet, a tie-in with the American beer company Falstaff.

It was not an altogether unique adventure. Over the past couple of years, the Coca-Cola company had wrung jingles out of several dozen different turns, ranging from Leslie Gore and Wayne Fontana, to the Supremes and Stigwood's Bee Gees. The audience that was being envisioned for Cream, however, lent itself to a somewhat stiffer beverage than Coke; and, though the band could scarcely have relished lending themselves to anything so crass as a beer commercial – Clapton had quit the Yardbirds for less, after all – still they turned in an impressive performance, and positively the heaviest, loudest advert that American radio could hope to hear, at least until Coke recruited the Vanilla Fudge.

'Eric didn't want to do it, neither did Ginger,' Jack Bruce confessed. 'I hated Falstaff, it was the worst imitation of beer ever. But I remember Ginger saying, "I'm old, I'll be skint, we've got to do this for the money." So we agreed to do it and it was a good song, if we'd done it without the "Falstaff Thirst-Quencher" bit.' In the event the ad went unaired, but any disappointment that the band may have felt was salved when their long-awaited American return was finally confirmed for late August, with the release of *Disraeli Gears* set for November.

Cream's homeland schedule, meanwhile, remained as patchy as ever. There was a short tour of Scotland in mid-July; another BBC session, for bandleader Joe Loss's Light Programme show; and a return to the Windsor Festival, this time to headline the entire weekend. But there were also rumours afoot that Cream might not actually make it that far. It was no secret, among fans as much as friends, that the three musicians were growing increasingly weary of the band's apparently directionless journey through the clubs and swimming baths of the English hinterland, and the fact that Windsor also marked the first anniversary of the band's inception only reminded everybody how little Cream had actually achieved over the past twelve months.

It was so easy to look around at other groups, the Who and Hendrix were only the most obvious candidates, and compare their career trajectories with Cream's. Even leaving aside Monterey and the United States; even forgetting the demands and desires of the 'psychedelic scene', both had released more records, scored more hits, and played a lot more worthwhile shows than Cream. Even the *Melody Maker* poll seemed to conspire against the group. Bruce, Baker and Clapton all topped the individual musician listings, of course. But Cream itself ranked no higher than fourth, behind the Beatles, the Stones, and – it's that man again – Hendrix.

The group itself had not stalled; indeed, as the last round of recording sessions proved, musically, Cream were still ploughing ahead as determinedly as they ever had. But the long bouts of inactivity interspersed with sudden flashes of boredom and routine, were taking their toll regardless.

'It just wasn't really happening [for us] in England,' Bruce admitted. 'We were stagnating in a way, because we hadn't got over certain gaps. And there was a limit in what you could do if you didn't get beyond a certain point.' That early summer, Bruce said, he and his bandmates made a decision. If things didn't start to turn around quickly, 'we were going to split the group up'. When Bruce received a call from Peter Green, asking if he'd be interested in meeting up for a chat, the bassist didn't need to give the offer a second thought.

Green's departure from the Bluesbreakers was in the air for several months before it actually occurred, the guitarist conspiring long into the night with bassist McVie and new drummer Mick Fleetwood, but never actually taking the bit between his teeth until Mayall fired Fleetwood for one drunken transgression too many, in May 1967. A month later, Green followed him out of the band, and what became Fleetwood Mac followed soon after, but not before Clifford Davis, a booker at the Gunnell agency, suggested Green first experiment with an entirely different configuration of musicians, to see what might transpire.

Crazy Blue was an act of inspired genius, pure and simple. With Mike Vernon producing, as he set about launching his Blue Horizon label as a full-time outlet, Green was joined by drummer Aynsley Dunbar, and vocalist Rod Stewart, as he pondered (not for the first time) breaking out of the Jeff Beck Group.

That just left one position open, and all were in agreement over who they wanted to see fill it – Jack Bruce. And Bruce, though he never actually committed to anything more than playing a session, just to see how things went, agreed.

Set loose upon an unsuspecting world, there's no telling what such a partnership might have achieved. One session produced three recordings: two versions of Buddy Guy's 1962 hit 'Stone Crazy', and one of 'Fly Right Baby', with Bruce forsaking bass for piano. 'I think Brian Auger was there as well,' said Green. 'I think he came in and did a guest organ.'

The notion that they had a new supergroup on their hands was never far from anyone's mind, Green admitted. 'That came up, yeah. It was a possibility. I was Fleetwood Mac-ing at the time, Jack was with Cream . . . I don't know where Eric was, that day! Aynsley was about to start his band [Aynsley Dunbar's Retaliation] . . . and Rod was with Jeff Beck, so the idea did come up.'

Unfortunately, it was not to go any further. 'We just did the session,' Green continued, 'just did the two tunes, and that was it.' Mike Vernon assumed that 'the chemistry between the combatants was not a success', but Green disagreed: 'Everyone just mucked down to it. It was good.' He believed that other forces played their part in the drama, other managers, other concerned observers, and pointed out that legal difficulties have continued to relegate Crazy Blue to a minor footnote in the history of rock.

One of the versions of 'Stone Crazy' turned up on a Blue Horizon retrospective LP during the 1970s, where it was credited, strangely, to Dunbar's Retaliation, but when Vernon tried to include both Crazy Blue numbers within 1997's *Blue Horizon Story* box set, he was stymied by what he diplomatically described as 'problems of a legal nature'. 'I heard one of the other guys didn't want them coming out,' Green explained. 'So he stopped it. A shame.'

Neither would Crazy Blue ever reconvene, as all four musicians drifted apart. But they were reunited just days later at Windsor.

Now long-windedly christened the National Jazz, Pop, Ballads & Blues Festival, the Bank Holiday weekender packed a line-up that, today, seems almost impossible to believe: the Small Faces, the Move, Tomorrow and Marmalade on the Friday; the Nice, Paul Jones, Arthur Brown, Zoot Money, Dunbar, Ten Years After, Amen Corner and Time Box on the Saturday; and, wrapping it all up, Cream, Beck, John Mayall's Bluesbreakers, PP Arnold, Alan Bown, Chicken Shack, Donovan, Denny Laine, Blossom Toes, Pentangle and, following firmly in Cream's own footsteps, by making their own public debut at the festival, Fleetwood Mac.

For all that, the three-day event was not an especially well-starred occasion. The following Monday's newspaper headlines were consumed with reports of the near-riot sparked by the Crazy World of Arthur Brown, after fans took his invocations of 'Fire' too literally and caught light to a pile of rubbish. When firemen moved in to extinguish the blaze, and press photographers closed in to capture the action, the night turned ugly, and a hail of bricks and bottles was showered indiscriminately down upon everyone.

From a musical point of view, meanwhile, the darkest talking point was the abysmal sound quality. WEM, who provided the venue's PA, supplied what was virtually a state of the art set-up, capable of emitting a then-staggering 1,000 watts. Yet even that was insignificant when disseminated over an outdoor multitude of 20,000 people; especially when a succession of technical problems saw almost every performance interrupted by one malfunction or another. (Arthur Brown, again, provided the most spectacular. His traditional flaming headgear was whipped into such frenzy by the wind, that it needed to be extinguished before the rest of the singer went up in smoke.)

Melody Maker, its observer one of many awaiting a veritable feast of guitar-playing genii, grimly commented, 'A host of guitarists like Peter Green, Eric Clapton, Jeff Beck and David O'List [of the Nice], had their sound reduced to a near pathetic level.' Nevertheless, the newspaper's verdict was unassailable. Though 'Peter Green's Fleetwood Mac made an impressive debut; [and] John Mayall was received with fervent enthusiasm . . . Eric Clapton is still 240 miles ahead of the other guitarists in his field.'

Cream closed the festival with an hour-long set; but the crowd, as though somehow aware that this would be its last opportunity to see the band for a good three months, might have let them play all night – and Cream could have, if the local residents committee hadn't already slammed so many injunctions upon the festival that, to proceed any deeper into the night, would likely have seen the lot of them slung in jail. The Festival never returned to Windsor.

Windsor was not Cream's final UK showing of the season – that honour went to a long-standing date at the Redcar Jazz Club in Cleveland, the night before they left for California. Three days before that, meanwhile, the group received at least a taste of the welcome they could expect in America, when Frank Zappa took it upon himself to introduce them at a late-night Speakeasy show. In town himself for a handful of shows, Zappa was thrilled to welcome 'this dandy little combo', and to wish them luck on their forthcoming adventure. As it turned out, however, they scarcely needed it.

15. THE MOST INCREDIBLE PERFORMING BAND I'VE EVER SEEN

Commandeering the teetering pile that, forty years before, was built as the Majestic Academy of Dancing, on the corner of Fillmore and Geary, Bill Graham opened the Fillmore Auditorium in San Francisco with three nights of the Jefferson Airplane, at the beginning of February 1966.

His autobiography, *Bill Graham Presents*, chuckled at the opening naivety of what became one of the Summer of Love's most cherished institutions, the rudely printed handbills that heralded 'three dance concerts ... Sounds of the Trips festival'.

Within a matter of months, however, the Fillmore had tapped wholeheartedly into what history now refers to as the San Francisco Explosion, the sudden upsurge of new talents that, eschewing the borrowed British Invasion licks of the past four years of new American talent; dismissing, too, the lyrical folkiness of the post-Dylan protest brigade, had set out instead to carve their own unique direction through the world of pop, one that retained elements of all that had gone before, but blended them with so much that was new as well.

There were no limits, no boundaries, to the innovation that was now free to roam. In London, the psychedelic scene that Cream left behind as they boarded the flight to San Francisco was increasingly built around a distinct set of images, a fast set of rules – whimsical and weird, childlike and nostalgic, a world wherein nursery rhymes were as valid as poetry, and jingles as sweet as symphonies. In America, on the other hand, or in San Francisco, for that was the tightly knit focus of the new movement, the pictures were wholly in the audience's heads, with the music merely providing the canvas upon which they would be daubed, by an experience that pounded every available sense.

The Fillmore first fermented, then cemented that doctrine, transforming simple gigs into vast multi-media experiences, where even the posters on the door were magnificent works of art, the audience was a living installation, and the lights . . . smoke . . . the very odour of the Fillmore conjured up all the magic, promise and freedom inherent in the word 'psychedelia'.

It was the percolating renown of the Fillmore that the *International Times* crew was trying to re-create with their Freak-Outs and Technicolor Dreams; which was the model for the All Night Rave, and Barbecue 67, and for all the other, greater and lesser, Happenings that occurred across the Western world throughout 1967. But, as Pete Brown remarked, 'When you're dealing with your information second-hand, it all gets very distorted. You produce a strange version of the thing that inspired you.'

With its Beardsley imagery, Pooh Corner word play, Edwardian grandeur and sci-fi flying sorcery, the British underground had a unique charm and magic that could not have occurred any place else. But it wasn't until you actually set foot inside the Fillmore itself, and breathed in air that was heavy with the sex and drugs and rock'n'roll of so many past nights, that you realised just how far off the mark those other events were. In London, New York, Paris and Berlin, the Happenings were planned; they were brought together in deliberate emulation of a legend. The Fillmore, however, was the real thing. Its ambience was not imported from elsewhere, it simply happened on the night, every night.

Bill Graham had wanted to book Cream into the Fillmore from the moment he first heard about them, while reading through the extortionately priced, and several-weeks-old copies of *Melody Maker* that made their way out to the west coast. Paul Barrata, Graham's partner in the venue, remembered, 'We kept hearing so many things about this band called Cream, [and] Bill, God bless him, had the intuition to pick it up. If it had been me, I would have booked Cream for a week. Bill booked them for *two* weeks. He called Robert Stigwood in London, and paid Cream $5,000 for the two weeks.'

Still, as they departed London on 21 August, Cream had absolutely no idea what lay in store for them. Even their itinerary was a mystery, with the only confirmed concerts that fortnight in San Francisco. From there, they would play it by ear, check out the response, see what was offered, and then make their move from there. It seems a remarkably chaotic approach today, in a world where the industry insists that everything is preplanned with military precision. At the time, however, it was standard practice –

when the Who and Hendrix played Monterey, neither knew they would wind up proving so sensational that promoters were banging on their hotel doors all night, but both left windows open in their schedules, just in case. So it was with Cream.

Neither was the one destination they were aware of any less of a mystery. They had heard of the Fillmore, of course – both the Who and Jimi Hendrix had already played there, as they made their own ways around America, and their reports were certainly enough to arouse Cream's curiosity. But, some twenty years on, Clapton could still recall his astonishment that first night on the hallowed stage, when he discovered that nothing he'd ever been told about the place could prepare him for its actuality.

'When we played the Fillmore for the first time, the band was *in* the light show. If you were in the audience, you didn't know *who* was playing. Not at all. It was a sensory thing.' As Cream's opening set progressed, that night of 22 August 1967, the trio was initially shocked, and rapidly mortified, to realise that scarcely anybody was dancing to their music, and hardly more were even applauding. It was only as the evening wore on that they realised that the audience wasn't sitting there hating them. It was listening, and Clapton described the night as the first time 'I experienced the kind of more introverted or serious or introspective attitude towards our music, which seemed to go hand-in-hand with hallucinogenic drugs, or grass, or whatever. It was more into a "head" thing.'

The shift in emphasis that Cream now embarked upon was not necessarily deliberate, and it certainly did not take place overnight. The band had long since established a live set that ranged between 45 minutes and an hour in length, and had already staked out their show-stopping rendition of Skip James's 'I'm So Glad' as a nine- or ten-minute monster. But it was an exception, not the rule. Other numbers came in at five or six minutes tops, with the 'hits' (on the occasions they chose to play them) rarely exceeding the dimensions of their vinyl counterparts.

Perhaps it was the smoke, perhaps it was the vibe, perhaps it was the realisation that America represented a whole new plane of existence for the group, a rebirth that had scarcely heard of 'Wrapping Paper', 'I Feel Free' and 'Strange Brew'. But something about the Fillmore convinced Cream that none of the conventions that had hitherto bound them counted for anything any longer.

According to Procol Harum's Gary Brooker, 'The Fillmore was the absolute making of [Cream]'s whole style. They only had a few songs. They had their set. Which, in England, was alright. It did you fine for an evening. But once you got to America, it was all a bit boring to play the same set twice in a night, so you would make variations ... people had to extend themselves.'

Clapton's solos soared to the skies, just as they always had in the past, but with so much more space in which to manoeuvre. Nor was he alone in his peregrinations. More than they ever had even in their jazzier days, Baker and Bruce, too, found room to stretch out into the limelight, both as soloists (Baker's 'Toad' was soon extending towards the quarter-hour mark) and alongside their bandmates. As Jack Bruce put it:

> The beauty of Cream was that any instrument could be the lead instrument. It might be the guitar playing the melody, it might be the voice, it might be the bass, it might be the drums.

And it didn't matter which it was, for the effect was always the same.
Bruce continued:

> That was the influence that San Francisco had on us ... or the drugs, or a combination of them both. We suddenly ... when we hit the Fillmore, we started to play those long improvisations ... because we didn't know hardly any songs! It was partly a repertoire, and partly a product of the times, because all the audiences were stoned out of their collective bonces. That was what they wanted us to do, they just encouraged us to do that, and it was very successful. It just sort of happened and we liked it, obviously.

Before the first show, Bruce confessed:

> We expected that it would be the same kind of thing [as England]; nobody knowing us [or] wanting to know us. [But] we got there and we played and it was amazing, because the whole place had come to see us. We'd just been doing three-, four-, five-minute versions of our songs, and we were very, very nervous because this was something really big for us, and also it was almost the first time we had played to a full house – the others were festivals, with loads of bands, or else they were tiny pubs and clubs. But all these kids had actually come to see us, and it was the first time we'd had our own audience on that scale, and they were just shouting out things like 'play anything, just play, we love you' and stuff, and the whole thing ended up with us just playing these incredibly long, improvised things.

Clapton dived headlong into the experience. He told *Hit Parader* magazine:

> We don't do anything straight. We're into music much more now, as much as jazz musicians are into music. There are no arrangements, except for arrival and departure points. Sometimes, we just play free for half an hour.

If Clapton was to discover an entire new dimension to his music during Cream's two-week run at the Fillmore, however, he is convinced that America learned something as well:

> There weren't many bands doing what Cream did. I don't know how we got the courage to do it, in a way – we went out there and took on San Francisco, and we didn't even know what we were in for, or what we were up against. [But] even though there were the Grateful Dead and the Jefferson Airplane and Big Brother and all that, they were kind of playing pop music. They weren't relating to their own roots too well. They were trying to get away from it all. What we were doing, basically, was bringing their music back home and showing it to them for the first time.

Cream were not the only blues act in town that fortnight. Aware that not everybody in town might be as familiar with the group's reputation as he was, Graham scheduled Cream as the second act out of three for their first five nights in town, sandwiched between the opening Electric Flag, and Paul Butterfield's Butterfield Blues Band.

The three combos swiftly formed their own mutual appreciation society. Electric Flag, Clapton raved to *Rolling Stone*, were 'just the heaviest thing around. An incredible band.' But though Butterfield and Electric Flag played the blues, that was all they seemed to do. Even as he acknowledged his personal admiration for the two groups and all who sailed in them, Clapton could not help but view them as some kind of throwback to the earliest days of the R&B boom in Britain, players whose devotion to the blues *form* was so fervent that they forgot they could take it further.

It is not for nothing that rock histories frequently refer to Butterfield as the American answer to John Mayall (or vice versa); nor that the Butterfield Blues Band is so regularly mentioned in the same breath as the Bluesbreakers. It wasn't that they played the same kind of music. It was the fact that they played it in the same kind of way, with respect, with restraint, with regard for its history. Cream, on the other hand, had dispensed with the restraint, and were now realigning the respect and the regard. If blues was to live, it had to be seen to be alive. And the Fillmore, through the last nights of August and the first days of September 1967, was where that life came alight.

What Cream had to offer, and what precious few other bands even dreamed of, was summed up by John Mayall. 'They did start off with a lot of Eric's input, and that [showed] up in all the blues things that maybe Jack and Ginger weren't quite as familiar with. Then the improvisational thing, that's a jazz quality, and that's totally where Ginger and Jack came from, a jazz background, so that was their forte.

'Eric, of course, was never playing the same any night in the Bluesbreakers ... none of my musicians ever do, because blues is a part of jazz and we improvised all the time. But the free form aspect of it, where you abandon the changes or appear to abandon the changes, that's a jazz device and that was right up the alley of Jack and Ginger.'

Other performers went in for lengthy improvisations. Filmmaker DA Pennebaker once explained away the Grateful Dead's absence from his film of the Monterey Pop Festival by recalling with amusement that 'We decided to film one song by each band. After ten minutes, they were still on their first song and we ran out of film.' But there is a vast difference between simply extending a song, a riff, an idea, which is what the Dead (and countless others) were doing, and actually abandoning all such forms, to play on the *inter*play of the musicians.

Cream's early notions of transplanting dada-ism into the blues had long since been dismissed; their plans for 'weird things happening on stage' were a far-away memory. Yet an inkling of that mindset remained, as Clapton swore. 'The idea is to get so far away from the original line that you're playing something that's never been heard before' – and, nightly, it seemed, the actual 'song' part of any given number seemed to get shorter and shorter, as all three players drove pell-mell for the instrumental break, and the opportunity to open up on all cylinders.

'When I saw Cream for the first time, I thought they were the most incredible performing band I had ever seen in my life,' Jefferson Airplane's Jorma Kaukonen told his group's biographer, Jeff Tamarkin. 'That might still be true.'

The Airplane missed the first Cream concerts – to their absolute horror, they were scheduled to play a string of shows elsewhere around California that weekend; and, just to make it worse, the man who'd booked them into those gigs was the same man who brought Cream over, the Airplane's own manager, Bill Graham. But Kaukonen was in no doubt over the effect the British trio had on him, once he was able to see them. 'As a guitar player, I wanted to be able to do stuff like that' – and he did. A few nights later, continued bandmate Marty Balin, 'We were playing and Jorma just took off. He started playing amazing and it was just real and free. Pretty soon, we got to a place where the music was playing us. We weren't playing it. That's where you want to get to.'

Overnight, the streamlined Airplane of 'White Rabbit' and 'Somebody to Love' was buried. In its place came the vast flying experimentation of *After Bathing at Baxters* and *Crown of Creation*, the sound of a band that had tasted freedom, and wanted now to devour it.

Yet, though Jack Bruce appreciated Cream's obvious influence and impact on the Airplane and more, he remained adamant that the efforts of other local, California, performers did little to impress him. 'Nah, they were crap. All those bands . . . none of them were any good, they were all so many weekend hippies. Not so much the Grateful Dead, I never saw the Dead at that time, but all those other bands . . . the Doors, crap. All of it. I'm trying to think of a band that impressed me. I was kind of impressed that the Doors didn't have a bass player, but their sound was thin and they just weren't in the same league, really. I think a lot of the bands . . . when they saw us, they just wanted to give up. And maybe they should have.'

Clapton sympathised with his disdain, albeit phrasing it a little more generously. Though he laughed at Pete Townshend's description of the Dead as 'one of the original ropeys', Clapton agreed with that summation. 'I don't think the quality of their music is as high as a lot of other good recording bands. People are more concerned with live music, maybe, than with recording. [But] if the Grateful Dead are one of the best [groups around], they're not doing a very good job on recording.' The Dead, he concluded, were 'not really my bag'.

The Dead were staunch supporters of Cream, however, while certain members of their entourage were also in attendance at most of the group's area shows – most notably Augustus Owsley Stanley III, the pharmaceutical mastermind behind the Acid Tests that turned on great swathes of Bay Area youth during the mid-1960s. (LSD remained legal in the United States until October 1966, by which time the law was powerless to halt its appeal.) 'He showed up at all our gigs,' Clapton recalled, and he rarely travelled without a hefty sample of his prize wares. Cream were happy to sample them. 'We did a lot of acid, took a lot of trips,' Clapton told *Rolling Stone* in 1985, adding, to *Uncut* magazine a decade on, 'I don't know how many times we tried to play while using acid, but there were a few.'

Bruce shared his enthusiasm. 'San Francisco! The first time we went there, that was pretty mind-expanding. It was a very interesting time because, obviously, it was 1967, the famous year; and, though we never thought of ourselves as a hippy band, obviously we were quite influential. The west coast in general was kind of nice . . .'

Still, he insisted that one of his own favourite memories of the group's time at the Fillmore was finding himself with enough ready cash to purchase a new car. 'I bought myself this amazing convertible Stingray. I went into the shop and paid for it in dollar bills, this big bag of fives and ones, just emptied it out on the guy's desk.' The car's engine ran far too hot, but still Bruce had a grand time, 'driving around in it, posing a lot!'

Word of Cream's arrival spread fast – according to Bruce, a local chapter of Hell's Angels was waiting at the airport, to give them a motorcycle escort into the city. But word of their success spread faster. Paul Barrata reported, 'They opened on a Tuesday night. On Wednesday morning in New York, everyone knew what a sensation they were. Elmer Valentine called from the Whisky A Go Go in LA and said, "I understand Cream was sensational. I'd like to put them on." And we were saying, "How the *fuck* do these people know?"'

They knew because people arrived home from the gig and called up all their friends. They knew because journalists were phoning their reviews into the following morning's newspaper before the audience was even back out on the pavement. And they knew because it was their business to know; because every major promoter had his spies in other cities, in the hope of pouncing on the next hot thing before his rivals got to hear about it. By the time Cream had spent a week in the country, their visit had already been extended to a month, as shows were booked for three-, five-, even twelve-day residencies in LA, Boston, New York and Detroit, plus a few one-nighters or two-nighters in between. It wasn't simply beyond their wildest expectations; even Robert Stigwood seemed shocked by the group's impact.

Clapton was still reeling when he sat down with *Rolling Stone*'s Jann Wenner for an interview (to be published in *Melody Maker*) later in the tour. 'We seem to be a lot more popular here than I had imagined. I'd heard that we'd been heard of through the under-ground thing. Yet I really didn't imagine that we'd be this popular, or that we'd be accepted as readily as we were, because an American band like Butterfield can go to England now, and just die at all the places.' Indeed, Butterfield's late 1966 British tour was an almost unmitigated flop, a succession of barely attended concerts and, though collectors covet it today, a half-share in one of John Mayall's worst-selling records yet, the *Bluesbreakers with Paul Butterfield* EP. Even in the straitened climate that now haunted the EP, the long-awaited follow-up to *Bluesbreakers with Eric Clapton* really ought to have done *something*.

Cream were expecting much the same kind of treatment. Instead, the San Francisco scene took Cream to its heart. Clapton flashed through some of his favourite recollections: 'the hippies in Sausalito, meeting the Grateful Dead, meeting Big Brother. All night long in Sausalito, where it was *very* hippy, these guys would be outside our window with bongos and congas . . .'

Back at the Fillmore, Graham had already upgraded Cream to headline status, retaining Electric Flag and adding the Gary Burton Band to open the show – a move that would, in turn, add another name to the growing list of life-changing encounters that Cream could now have been compiling. Jack Bruce acknowledged, 'We did encourage a lot of people – I remember the Gary Burton Band . . . that had Larry Coryell in it, and also Steve Swallow on bass. Steve was playing double bass at the time, but when he saw us, he went out the next day and bought a bass guitar and he's never gone back to playing double bass.'

But they discouraged some folk as well, as Bruce mourned. 'The Electric Flag had just formed, and it was embarrassing because we went down so well that the whole audience left and didn't bother to wait for the Electric Flag, so they split up.'

The group's trip to Los Angeles was no less successful than San Francisco. Cream played three nights at the Whisky, and left promoter Elmer Valentine cursing that he had not booked the band for any longer. But it was too late. The group flew out of California on 7 September; the following evening they were in Boston, headlining the unlikely named Crosstown Bus Club, in the suburban Brighton Center, as the first of a couple of warm-ups for their main gig, seven nights – and fifteen shows – at the more centrally located Psychedelic Supermarket.

Situated on Commonwealth Ave, just beyond Kenmore Square, the venue itself was uninviting: 'It was a parking garage that had been vaguely done up and turned into a venue,' Bruce recalled with a shudder. Even worse, however, was the discovery that Cream's Californian reputation had *not* preceded them. A local audience that might have packed the club for a couple of shows was spread hideously thin over fifteen, making it very easy for any passing detractors to hit these latest British Invaders very hard. Boston music fan John Donovan remembered one local reviewer drawing parallels with the city's own historical past, by opining 'We showed the Brits what we thought of their tea when we dumped it in the harbour in 1776. Now Boston has shown them what they can do with their cream as well.'

Bruce is correspondingly ungenerous in his own recollections of Boston:

> I think we were among the first bands to wear psychedelic clothes in America; we were the first ones to arrive wearing clothes by the Fool, stuff like that. Because, although the Who were there before us, and the Beatles, they weren't psychedelic-looking and I remember we used to get a lot of stick from people, walking around and being at airports or whatever, being dressed the way we were, especially in Boston.
>
> Boston was the worst place I'd ever been at that time, because it's a redneck town – it has this reputation for being very sophisticated, but when you go there, actually it's more redneck than Birmingham, Alabama . . . well, maybe not quite. But I remember being there; we stayed in our hotel for ten days while we played this one little club, and we never left, we just went from the hotel to the gig because the World Series was in town.

That same week, the local Redsox were challenging the St Louis Cardinals for baseball's ultimate crown (unsuccessfully, it might be added), filling the city streets with several tens of thousands of sports-loving, hippy-hating ruffians. Bruce concluded:

You just couldn't go out. It was too uncomfortable.

He whiled away his time writing and, once he returned to England, his tales about his incarceration in a Bean Town hotel quickly inspired Brown to put words to one of the new tunes, a brief, jazzy snippet that Bruce had titled 'Plastic Eye'. The result was 'Boston Ball Game 1967', another number that was destined to lay on the shelf until *Songs For a Tailor*, but that captures Cream's cultural dislocation with inestimable ease.

Cream flopped again a few nights later, when a pair of shows at the Action House in Long Beach attracted no more than fifty onlookers – and that despite the presence on the bill of a band that the American industry was already convinced was set to become the Next Big Thing, San Francisco's own semi-supergroup, former Airplane drummer Skip Spence's Moby Grape.

More indicative of Cream's future was the group's return to New York City, for two shows at the Village Theater, and a record-breaking dozen nights at the Cafe Au Go Go, one of those legendary Greenwich Village watering holes where the trio had only jammed during their last visit. Now they were the stars, and the other stars poured out to greet them, jamming the tiny club and reeling as Cream, their PA cranked as high as it would be in venues two or three times the size, sledgehammered them with the sound.

'The trio,' *Billboard* magazine agreed, 'thunders towards musical destruction at high amplification.' But, in 'tearing down all precon-ceived musical ideas, ideals and forms', they were simultaneously 'building . . . a series of melodic structures, each self-contained but connected as a song'.

Even more chaotic was the crush that occasionally developed despite everybody's best efforts. One night at the Village Theater, sundry technical problems ensured that Cream could not start their first set, scheduled to kick off at 8 p.m., until 9.30, which meant that they were still playing when the doors reopened to allow in the audience for the second show. Neither was the crowd at all patient during the changeover. The opening act, Tiny Tim (one of Martin Sharp's all-time heroes, incidentally), was barely a couple of numbers into his set when a huge metal padlock came flying out of the audience, and only just missed him. A direct hit could have been lethal.

Once again, the band members took advantage of all the diver-sions New York City had to offer, although history records most of them as bus-man's vacations. The group had hoped to schedule some more recording time at Atlantic, only to discover that Aretha Franklin had got in there before them. Clapton quickly found solace, however, when Tom Dowd invited him into the studio regardless, to lay down some guitar on Franklin's 'Good to Me As I Am to You'.

Similarly, when Frank Zappa, back in town to record his *We're Only in It for the Money* album at Apostolic Studios, heard that Clapton was around, he issued his own invitation to come down and play. Zappa being Zappa, however, he decided to present a side of Clapton that very few people had ever heard. 'I invited him over to do [a] rap. People think he's playing on [the album], but he's not; the only thing he's doing on there is talking.'

The group's itinerary wound up with their maiden trek into the American Midwest, for two shows in Ann Arbor and three at Detroit's Grande ballroom – home turf for such super-heavy garage grinders as the MC5, the Stooges and the Frost. But Cream had no time for respecting local reputations, if they were even aware of them, playing with such force that more than one critic, reflecting back upon Cream's entire American career, has suggested it was Detroit, not the Fillmore or New York, that truly confirmed the group's impending pre-eminence.

On the coasts, after all, vast cosmopolitan audiences will turn out for the opening of a bottle if the pre-show buzz is loud enough. In the vast expanses of the heartland, however, the working-class sprawls that are the hub of American industry and agriculture, concerts are not events for the kids to be seen at, they are a mass to submerge within, a chance to forget the shit of the dead-end day, to get drunk and shout, to unwind. And, if an act doesn't fulfil that need, then they might as well never come back. Cream, of course, *would* be back.

Local scribe Ben Edmonds wrote, 'The appearance of Cream was ... a watershed weekend. The ballroom was jammed well beyond legal capacity; the shows were magnificently performed and rapturously received. It was an engagement that was talked about for months afterwards, and Cream soon rivalled the Beatles and the Stones in local popularity.'

Neither was he alone in predicting that, at this rate, they might soon eclipse them both.

16. ALL HAIL THE BLUES MESSIAHS

If there was any downside whatsoever to the American tour, it was that *Disraeli Gears* was still awaiting release. Cream were back in the United Kingdom, and settling back into the old routine of now frankly anti-climactic provincial shows, before the album was finally in the stores at the beginning of November.

Fresh Cream was still out there, and its slow rise up the American chart, following its lowly entry in May, was inestimably furthered by the live shows. But it was no longer even loosely representative of all that Cream represented, as even the best of its contents were transformed on stage, while Atlantic's decision to finally release 'Spoonful' in America, carving its six minutes across both sides of a platter, barely registered on listeners who were now accustomed to hearing it spread out to three times that length.

Disraeli Gears was unlikely to sate those urges either. Eleven tracks ranged in length from under two minutes ('Mother's Lament') to barely four; indeed, even the longest song on the record, 'Sunshine of Your Love', came in at no more than four minutes ten seconds – again, a far cry from the leviathan into which it was transformed on stage.

Even before the album's issue, complaints that the musicians did not stretch themselves, did not lay down shattering solos and soaring instrumentals, were whispering through the industry and, once again, Cream found themselves facing a new record release in the knowledge that, in terms of their own development, it was already very old.

'It's a good record, a great LP,' Clapton hurriedly assured *Melody Maker* readers. But he was also honest enough to admit, 'It was recorded last May, and it's not indicative of what we're doing now. When I hear it, I feel like I'm listening to another group. It's an LP of songs and there's no extended improvisation.'

Instead, he directed his readers' attention towards the moments of innovation that did percolate throughout the record. 'We're Going Wrong', for instance, 'was [recorded] in two different keys, but we mixed them in such a way that it's not very noticeable. You're supposed to dig the overall effect and atmosphere of the number, not the fact that it's in two keys. I mean, it wouldn't work if you did notice it.'

Elsewhere, he praised Felix Pappalardi's production for so dramatically realigning the very sound of the band. But even there, there were drawbacks. Todd Rundgren, a member of the Nazz at that time, detailed how hearing *Disraeli Gears* prompted his group scrapping their own plans to recruit Felix Pappalardi as producer of their debut album. 'We thought [*Disraeli Gears*] sounded too echoey, and it didn't have the punch of the first album.'

Jeff Beck, too, was dismissive, gnashing to *Disc & Music Echo* that there was 'nothing new' in there (a criticism he subsequently retracted, claiming he'd been grotesquely misquoted). When the reviews were good, they were drooling: the ever loyal *Melody Maker* proclaimed *Disraeli Gears* a definite, if not exactly giant step up from *Fresh Cream*, 'a more quality-heavy package of ... super-power', with Clapton's guitar sinking 'serpent-like deep into the ... varied and hypnotic musical journeys'. *Billboard* applauded the 'wall to wall rock', and *Crawdaddy* headlined Richard Meltzer's rabid assessment 'What a Goddam Great Second Cream Album'.

But still *Melody Maker*'s Nick Jones was prompted to ask, precisely who Cream were aiming itself at: 'The hangover of hard blues appreciators who ... still have "Telephone Blues" ringing in their ears? The hippies sifting through the pop scene in search of new heroes and villains? The new Cream fans attracted by the image and the gloss – and the hit with "I Feel Free"? Or, maybe, themselves?'

Rolling Stone, meanwhile, seemed more interested in what it perceived as the album's weaker moments, cited as 'Blue Condition', 'We're Going Wrong' and 'Dance The Night Away' – compositions that highlighted the group as writers, technicians and musicians, as opposed to blindingly brilliant soloists, and that was a far firmer indication of just how dramatically different an effect Cream's music, and reputation, had already had on American ears. In Britain, after all, the group was known for the short songs, even if fans were impatient for the long ones. The American response, as crystallised by *Rolling Stone*, however, was rooted in a peculiar narrow-mindedness that was to have dramatic repercussions as the next year of Cream's life played out, all the more so since Clapton himself seemed destined to follow this same line of thought.

Although it would be who-knew-how-long before anybody actually heard the group's most recent recordings (which themselves were anything up to six months old, now), he hastened to remind *Rolling Stone* '[*Disraeli Gears*] was a collection of songs. The stuff we're writing now is really more a series of jumping-off points, rather than just songs.

'Personally, I've written a lot of things that have a lot of different sections, and I'd like to play these sections all together in one song, but be able to improvise freely on each section.' He was also 'certain' that 'a lot of the numbers will be a lot longer on this new album', and mused aloud on the possibility of recording a double album.

Bruce, on the other hand, hit out at the critics who grumbled that *Disraeli Gears*, for all its musical brilliance and eccentricities, offered nothing 'new'. 'We do a lot of new things,' he replied. 'In fact, that's our scene, getting into new things. In a lot of ways, we do things that are completely new. It's just that they're not inclined to be things as spectacular as the Stones' 3D sleeve'; that band's latest album, *Their Satanic Majesties' Request*, had just been released within, indeed, a sleeve that bore a 3-D image and, in the first few weeks as listeners attempted to assimilate the album's seriously lysergic ambience, it was the art work that garnered as much attention as the music itself.

Yet Cream's sleeve design was no less spectacular, a Martin Sharp collage that still epitomises the pop-art sensibilities of the psyche-delic age, that took a simple group portrait by a fellow Pheasantry resident, photographer Bob Whittaker, and positively overwhelmed it with minute and fascinating details.

Sgt Pepper had set a new standard for album art, as Peter Blake's sprawling spread of cut-out heads set nigh-on iconic standards for the rest of the world to catch up with. Sharp, his eye for colour and detail already honed by the brilliance of his work for *Oz*, and his regular productions for UFO and Middle Earth, seemed destined to raise the bar even higher.

The intricate red and gold portrait of Dylan that was constructed, almost wholly, from tightly wrought circles; the multi-coloured Hendrix that contrarily shimmered from a mass of messy splashes; the Picasso-esque alien that lured spaceheads to the Roundhouse to see Jeff Beck; the cartoon Mick Jagger that graced the cover of *Oz* issue 15; these images gazed out from billboards and newsstands across London and, whereas other poster art seemed to blend into its surroundings, Sharp's flavoured them, no less than the work of Rick Griffin and co. was absorbed into the fibre of the Fillmore.

Yes, the Beatles had recruited a better-*known* artist. But Cream had befriended a better-adapted one; and, even today, *Disraeli*

Gears' mysterious mélange of passing peacocks, antique watches, green-faced ladies and sculptured tree trunks continues to be eye-catching, enervating and almost precociously redolent of the age in which it was executed. The elitist overlords of Psychedelic London may not have warmed to Cream. But even they could not stop themselves gazing at them.

The music within that sleeve, too, remains a time capsule that captures a Cream far-removed from the leviathan that is their twenty-first century reputation; that mocks the suspicion with which the hip glitterati regarded the group, and reminds us just how self-crucifying the group's subsequent development turned out to be.

The wisdom of the intervening decades has placed a handful of 1967's new releases atop a glittering pedestal from which they will never be dislodged – *Sgt Pepper*; the Pretty Things' *SF Sorrow*; and, completing a triumvirate of albums that were recorded all but simultaneously at EMI's Abbey Road studios, Pink Floyd's *The Piper at the Gates of Dawn* debut.

On the second tier lie the subjective also-rans, the albums that thrill as many ears as they painfully repel: the Who's *Sell Out* tribute to the recently outlawed pirate radio stations; the Kinks' sweetly evocative *Something Else* – incredibly, the last of that band's regular (as in non-compilation) albums ever to make the UK album chart; Chad and Jeremy's bizarrely bewitching *Of Cabbages and Kings*; the Jeff Beck Group's earthy *Truth*. And below that is a free-for-all of individual critical favourites, and hopeless obscurities that barely anyone remembers (*Elmer Gantry's Velvet Opera*, anyone?), but which were masterstrokes regardless.

Depending upon the dictates of the fashions most prevalent on any given day, *Disraeli Gears* usually makes it aboard the second level, but has occasionally splashed overboard to the third, both overlooked and undervalued in the years since its release, and swamped, perhaps, by the rapacious stream of Cream (and related) compilation albums that have punctuated the decades since their demise. It rarely bothers the modern critical craze for 'all time Top 100s', is seldom represented in discussions of the era and, though its attendant singles do soundtrack the year, the album itself is forgotten.

Contemporary audiences were more welcoming. *Disraeli Gears* peaked at number five in the UK, one place above *Fresh Cream*, and it might have climbed even higher had Cream only been able to promote it. But, coming off an exhausting American tour, Cream had little interest in embarking upon any kind of promotional routine, no interest whatsoever in launching a gruelling bus-ride up and down the United Kingdom.

Instead, their itinerary continued on the same sporadic pathway as it had through the summer. The group returned to the Saville

Theatre at the end of November, to share the bill with their good friends in the Bonzo Dog Doo Dah Band. They headlined the correspondingly unglamorous Silver Blades Ice Rink in Streatham, south London. There was a short burst of gigging through Scandinavia, and a couple of dates in the English north. And every single one of them reminded the band why America had felt so exciting.

Playing Morecambe's pier-end Marine Ballroom, Clapton groaned, was like travelling twenty years back in time. 'A ballroom on the end of a pier! The whole thing was like being in another era, you know? I couldn't play there at all. There was nothing familiar for me to grab hold of. It was like being stuck in another time.' Another show at the Animals' old stomping ground, Newcastle's Club A Go-Go, left him equally bemused, as he returned to 'a club which I used to play in with the Yardbirds, [and] it was the same now as it was then. The same audience!'

If European gigs were at a premium, even more remote was the possibility of Cream releasing a new single, either from the album or else from the growing stockpile of unreleased material – but *not*, this time, because Cream couldn't be bothered. Rather, as with their decision to abandon the Klook's Kleek live EP the previous autumn, it was because they didn't believe the 7-inch format had long left to live.

'I'm a great believer in the theory that singles will become obsolete and LPs will take their place,' Clapton prophesied to *Melody Maker*. He hated, he said, 'all that running around to get a hit', and he knew that a lot of Cream's contemporaries felt the same way. The Rolling Stones had spent close to six months working on *Their Satanic Majesties' Request,* and had not now released a new British single in just as long; neither had they another one planned.

The Beatles' most recent 45, 'Hello Goodbye', was simply excerpted from a longer work (the *Magical Mystery Tour* television soundtrack), and Clapton knew from his conversations with Pete Townshend that the Who's next opus was to be a single piece of music, absorbing no less than four sides of long-playing vinyl – a veritable rock opera. Everywhere, artists appeared to be in agreement; that trying to squeeze 'any good music in a space of two or three minutes requires working to a formula, and that part of the pop field leaves me cold'.

Rather, Clapton outlined a perfect world scenario in which LPs would replace singles altogether and appear with the same regularity. Cream's own recording schedule, after all, was already moving towards precisely that plateau, and he knew other bands were in the same boat, piling up new material that might not see the light of day for months to come.

Instead, he said, they should 'record an LP every two months, or every month. Then record an Extended LP that would be on 16 rpms. Do that twice a year. Singles are too expensive for what they are. What I would like to see is an LP for the price of a single, and an Extended LP for the price of the present LP. It's optimistic dreaming, maybe . . . [but] it would be much better for the public.'

Better than what? If you wanted to see or hear Cream at the end of 1967, you had to either buy the album, or turn to the radio or television. On 24 October, they visited the month-old BBC Radio One to tape their first-ever session for *Top Gear*, the station's flagship underground rock show. With Cream's old Radio London flag-waver John Peel making his own debut as the show's regular host, Roy Harper, the Kinks and Jeff Beck were in session alongside them. But Cream's performance alone would be repeated no less than three times before the end of the year, such was demand from starving listeners.

There were more broadcasts during the group's visits to Denmark and Finland, while London's Revolution Club staged a super-secret invitation-only concert for the benefit of French television. Then it was back to the BBC on 25 November, to mime 'We're Going Wrong' for television's *Twice a Fortnight*, directed by Clapton's friend Tony Palmer.

Originally envisioned as a visual equivalent to the radio comedy *I'm Sorry I'll Read That Again* (and featuring many of the same cast – Bill Oddie, Eric Idle, Michael Palin and Terry Jones), *Twice a Fortnight*'s ten-week run through late autumn 1967 is equally well-remembered today for the musical interludes that, once a week (twice a fortnight, in fact), interrupted the comedy sketches and films. Cat Stevens, the Small Faces and the Who all made memorable appearances on the show, although not, according to Palmer, without some complaint from the cast. 'Bill Oddie *always* objected to the rock groups, but I said . . . one time, I was telling him we had Cream coming on, and he replied "Cream what?" I'll always remember him saying "Cream what?" And I said, "Well, actually, these guys are rather good."'

It was a brief performance and, under normal circumstances, should have been a relaxing one. So far as Ginger Baker was concerned, however, even the mildest exertion was a step too far. For several weeks he'd been suffering from a series of only loosely definable aches, pains and unpleasant sensations, an affliction that nagged, rather than crippled, but which was capable of sending him reeling all the same. The Lime Grove Studios session was still under way when Baker suddenly collapsed.

He was rushed to the hospital, and the first suspicion was that he was suffering from an ulcer – many of his most overt symptoms certainly pointed in that direction. Tests were ordered up, and the drummer was ordered to bed. Cream's last scheduled British performances of the year, at the Marquee and the Top Rank, Brighton, were cancelled, alongside a return appearance on Alexis

Korner's *Rhythm and Blues* radio programme. It was not, however, an ulcer that laid Baker low. 'After exhaustive tests,' Stigwood was able to announce, 'it was found that Ginger ... collapsed through exhaustion.' After that, even he was forced to acknowledge the group's wisdom in refusing to push themselves through a fresh promotional regimen.

Baker was sidelined for no more than a week; by the first days of December, he was back in the rehearsal room, and pushing himself as hard as ever, as Cream prepared to fly back out to New York to resume the sporadic, but so satisfying series of recordings they had inaugurated back in June.

Atlantic's New York studio was now firmly established as their base of choice; Tom Dowd and Felix Pappalardi as their favourite engineer and producer. Baker continued, 'We're all temperamental, but Tom ... and Felix ... manage to get rid of that temperament. It's not even the sound we get that encourages us to record in America, just those people. The sessions are relaxed and everybody's working. We spend a long time in the studio, so we don't have to rush. We usually talk for hours before we record anything, then we play, think and add sounds.'

Pappalardi was equally enamoured by the process. Having very much learned on his feet during the *Disraeli Gears* sessions, he told *Crawdaddy*:

> Now I know what I dig to do, and how I like to go about it, as a producer. Which is like not spending a whole lot of time with the electronics, the equipment, but with the music. That's why the engineer is so important to me. Like Tommy Dowd, he's invaluable. Because I don't have to worry about him, he's got it covered. At any rate with Cream, we agreed, without even really talking about it, how they should be recorded. It was an untalked-about agreement; he heard the band the same way I heard the band. It's a natural sound is what it really is.
>
> Basically I like to get totally involved with the music, to the point where I'm involved in the band. When I work with Cream, for the two or three weeks that I work with Cream I totally join them as a musician. I know this is contrary to a lot of the ... not the stock methods ... but the very important methods of recording self-contained bands. I just feel that you should go after the record, the experience, in both making it and listening to it, that's right for that moment, regardless of what you draw upon.

Reels upon reels of tape had already been consumed as Cream laid down take-after-take of the songs they intended to comprise their next album. 'We've [already] got too many numbers written,' Clapton admitted to *Rolling Stone* at the outset of the sessions.

191

'And we've recorded three already. I should think between the three of us, we've got about three new LPs.'

Such assurances were deceptive, however. Of all Robert Stigwood's decisions for, and on behalf of, Cream, his refusal to allow Pete Brown to travel with the group was the most perverse, dismissing as it did the possibility of ever forging the solid association between the writer and the musicians that Ginger Baker had hankered for a year before.

Brown himself agreed that writing partnerships with both Clapton and Baker might have developed had he only been permitted to spend more time with them – there are, after all, precious few distractions to occupy one's mind on an all-night car or bus journey; songwriting might well have been one of them, had the musicians only had someone to nudge them in that direction. Brown is adamant, too, that the sole reason for his exclusion was pure dislike; that Stigwood regarded him, at best, as 'a necessary evil'. Yet one can question even how 'necessary' Stigwood perceived that 'evil' to be, when the only constant writing team within the group was regularly shattered, at a time when everybody concerned was convinced it could only grow stronger.

Thus, while Cream were left wholly to their own devices on the road, Brown remained behind in London, merely dreaming of the free and easy atmosphere of Cream's first months together – the nights they sat up all night, so alive with ideas that, even the rising of the sun could spark a new idea: years later, Brown recalled that early morning when, as Bruce picked out a riff he'd recently written on his double bass, a glance out of the window inspired Brown towards one of the best-known opening lines in rock – 'It's getting near dawn'.

Those opportunities never came any more; he and Cream had not parted, but they were apart anyway, and Brown was no less a spectator to the band's latest activities than any other member of their audience.

From Stigwood's point of view, such personal feelings mattered little. With or without this mythical super-songwriting partnership, the new material was mounting up: by December, 'Born Under a Bad Sign', 'Sitting on Top of the World' and 'White Room' were all more-or-less complete; so was 'Pressed Rat and Warthog', a truly brilliant slab of demented doggerel dreamed up by Baker and jazz pianist Mike Taylor, as they pursued a writing relationship that was both as compatible as the Bruce–Brown pairing, and as eminently capable of ear-tripping wonder.

Like so many of the other players on the periphery of Cream, Taylor was among those truly unsung heroes who occupied the driving seat as British jazz was propelled headlong into blues, rock and, ultimately, into the fusion experiments of the decade's end. Colosseum's show-stopping 'Jumping Off the Sun' was a Mike Taylor composition – indeed, that band's Jon Hiseman and Tony

Reeves were themselves former members of Taylor's mid-1960s Quartet, while Jack Bruce, too, played alongside the pianist, during sessions for Taylor's 1966 album, *Trio*.

With its emphasis firmly in a rock/pop-toned territory, Taylor's union with Baker had little in common with the unerring purity of his own solo efforts. But it certainly worked in the context of Cream, producing no less than three of the group's most distinctive latter-day numbers: as the Cream sessions rattled on into the new year, 'Pressed Rat and Warthog' was joined by 'Passing the Time' and 'Those Were the Days', with Baker clearly relishing both the opportunity to pursue his own flair for off-the-wall lyricism, and the chance to work closely with a partner who was as legendary in his circles, as Brown was in *his*.

Neither was Baker alone in challenging the supremacy of the Bruce–Brown team. Clapton and Martin Sharp, too, had sparked an at least occasionally fruitful partnership, as the guitarist dismissed a casually convened attempt to write a new song with Pete Brown, and took his tune back to the Pheasantry instead. There, he and Sharp came up with a ditty that, though it would not make the new LP, nevertheless emerged as another of Cream's best-loved numbers, the possibly allegorical (but certainly surreal) 'Anyone for Tennis'.

The song was specially commissioned for director Richard Rush's forthcoming biker flick *The Savage Seven*, a somewhat laughable attempt to mythologise Hell's Angels' culture that may or may not have spun out of rumours that Phil Spector and Peter Fonda were just commencing work on their own variation on that theme, *Easy Rider*. Starring Robert Walker, Larry Bishop and Joanna Frank, plus several of the kids who went on to the equally risible *Hell's Angels on Wheels*, *The Savage Seven* revolved around a gang of bikers who descend upon an Indian reservation in search of a sport of mindless violence, only to find themselves drawn into the equally violent, but somewhat more calculated, world of local racist politics.

A clunking, lumbering slab of misplaced social commentary, *The Savage Seven* was certainly more fascinating because of its sound-track, with 'Anyone for Tennis' (an almost gleefully inappropriate theme for such a relentlessly sensationalist picture) joined by similarly out-of-place contributions from Iron Butterfly, Barbara Kelly and the Morning Mood. But, if *The Savage Seven* fails as a slab of gritty realism, it does stack up as an enjoyable snapshot of a peculiar moment in Hollywood history; the point when the studios stopped trying to portray pop groups as happy-go-lucky japesters stumbling into a succession of ever zanier adventures, and drew on them instead as a vérité soundtrack to vital cultural issues.

From *Homer* to *Zachariah*, and on, indeed, to *Easy Rider*, the next few years saw rock soundtracks increasingly become a serious vehicle with which to drive an audience into the cinema, and *The Savage Seven*'s certainly placed a few additional bums on seats. But there comes a time in every movie's life when the film itself needs to rise above the music that accompanies it, and *The Savage Seven* never stood a chance. 'Anyone for Tennis', on the other hand, remains a jewel in Cream's crown.

Felix Pappalardi was visiting London as the song came together. '"Anyone for Tennis" happened pretty much like it exists, in Jack's living room in London. I was playing bass, and Jack was playing drums with Ginger; Ginger was playing these big giant maracas and Eric was playing guitar and singing. The change that we made when we got to the studio was that Jack played bass and I played viola lines over the finished record, and the ocarina and cello duet that Jack and I did was something that we had planned, just as a thing we wanted to do, we wanted to try.' Clapton himself had that song in mind when he mused, a few years later, 'The strange thing about Cream was that every time we went into the studios to record, we formed another group, adding violins or another guitar or something.'

'Anyone for Tennis' was among the songs scheduled for completion on Cream's pre-Christmas trip to New York, yet the band had just three days in which to record, before boarding another plane, this time bound for a return engagement in Detroit. Buoyed by the reception to their Grande Ballroom appearances in October, Cream were invited back for a pair of shows during Christmas week (they also hit Chicago as they headed west). And, if their last appearance in the city suggested that they were more than a match for any local competition, on these nights they confirmed it, as the MC5 themselves turned out to support them and were left reeling by the experience.

Cream were back in New York on Christmas Eve, tying up some loose ends from the previous week's recordings; back in London by the New Year, they then threw in a handful of shows, luxuriously spaced throughout January: the Redcar Jazz Club, the London University Union, St Mary's College in Twickenham. There was also a triumphant appearance at the University College, London for its *Carnival 68* show, billed above Two of Each, the Millionaires and the Soundtrekkers, and viewed by one of the largest gatherings the band had ever entertained in their home town.

But, again, the British bread-and-butter circuit seemed impossibly dull after the venues they'd visited in America, and, as Stigwood's plans for the group's next US tour began taking shape, a fast-filling date sheet that overflowed with some of the most evocative names in the rock'n'roll lexicon – the Fillmore, the Family Dog, the Shrine Auditorium, Winterland – the pleasures of a European winter began to pale even further, reaching their absolute nadir in early February, when Cream travelled to snowbound Copenhagen to play movie stars for a day.

If *The Savage Seven* represented the modern American ideals of the moviemaking mind-set, *Det Var En Lordag Aften (On a*

Saturday Night) remained firmly locked into the earlier age of *Gonks Go Beat*. Directed by Erik Balling, the 43-year-old director of the Danish slapstick cinema legend *The Olsen Gang, Det Var En Lordag Aften* starred singer Daimi and the young future superstar Morten Grunwald in a slice of flower-power cultural commentary, within which Cream were to cameo as real-life rock accompaniment to a couple of pivotal moments in the action; other musical contributions were provided by the movie's cast itself, from lyrics by author and poet Klaus Rifbjerg.

Cream's own appearances are powerful enough, though nobody could ever compare their role to, say, the Yardbirds' scene-stealing cameo in Antonioni's *Blow Up* – brief, brutal and destined for immortality. Still, there is a fire to their performance that, as Bruce shivered, blazed in absolute defiance of the frigid auditorium in which they mimed through 'We're Going Wrong'; and that was the warmest point of the exercise.

Apparently concerned that the group had not yet experienced the full bite of a Danish midwinter, Balling then ushered them onto the back of a truck, and drove them through the streets of Copenhagen, while their frozen fingers tried to pluck out 'World of Pain'. Few songs, Bruce remarked afterwards, could have felt so aptly titled.

The temperature was not always so frigid, of course; indeed, there was one moment during that Danish sojourn when life in the band almost literally became too heated for Clapton to handle any longer. Driving to the venue, an argument between Bruce and Baker exploded so vehemently that Clapton was literally reduced to tears. 'I was a stripling of a lad, remember. It really got to me. Between Jack and Ginger, it was pure love–hate. Their anger was so vicious. I'd never experienced any words like it. It never reached blows in my presence, but the language, the venom, was so powerful . . .'

By the time the band reached their destination, the spat was forgotten – or, at least, filed away in the psychic vault where Bruce and Baker both stored their grudges. But Clapton never forgot the moment when he finally realised 'This is a big band going out of anybody's control.' Instead, he tried to bury it, by concentrating instead on the sense of sheer camaraderie that he hoped bound Cream together despite their eruptions.

The six months that lay on either side of *Disraeli Gears*, he said, 'was the peak of the mountain when we were so together, and so tight, and loved one another so much ... We were talking in tongues at that point. We'd invented a language that no one else could get in on. We just never spent a minute apart from each other's company.'

Unfortunately, such close quarters were soon wreaking a very different set of responses and emotions, and the conflict that erupted as they drove through Copenhagen was soon to become a way of life.

17. SEVEN MINUTES TO MIDNIGHT

On 9 February 1968, Cream played their final show before returning to the United States, at Leicester University's Arts Ball. The gig itself passed off no more or less remarkably than any other club or college date; it was only later that it began assuming a Brobdingnagian air of poignancy, as the next few months passed by, and the three musicians realised that it might well have been the last regular concert Cream would ever play in Britain.

The group flew to New York the following morning, and headed straight from the airport to the studio to kick off their most intensive round of recording yet, ten days during which they nailed down final masters of every song they'd already begun, together with a couple of new ones: the so-magnificently titled 'Deserted Cities of the Heart', Baker–Taylor's 'Those Were the Days' and 'As You Said', an adventurously exotic Bruce–Brown composition whose open-tuned acoustic guitar puckishly pre-empted Led Zeppelin's third album in its entirety. Bruce, who played the guitar on that track, was quick to credit singer-songwriter Richie Havens with teaching him the tuning: 'I was always embarrassed about my acoustic guitar playing, especially when you had Eric Clapton in the band. [But] I wanted that guitar sound on the track.'

And, finally, there was a song that the group themselves had only cemented into place a few weeks earlier – 'Politician'. In its original form, 'Politician' was another of Pete Brown's pre-Cream epics, a snarling slice of bitter discontent with enough verses to stretch a simple recital to more than seven minutes in length. Brown himself had already recorded a demo of the song with the First Real Poetry Band; Bruce, however, loved the lyric and readily earmarked it for Cream. But he did not find a use for it until 9 January 1968, while the band was recording their latest (and, as it turned out, final) session for *Top Gear* at the BBC's Aeolian Hall studios.

Four songs were already in the bag, 'SWLABR', 'We're Going Wrong' and 'Blue Condition' from *Disraeli Gears*, and a brand new arrangement of 'Steppin' Out', a song they had not attempted in the studio since their BBC *Saturday Club* debut back in November 1966, but which had developed, since then, into a lavish live favourite. They still had time to record one more song and, while they pondered what it should be, Clapton and Bruce started jamming around a riff that the bassist had just stumbled upon, a ponderously threatening motif that was as impressive, in its own way, as that which underpins 'Sunshine of Your Love' (and which has since been plundered just as frequently, too).

Begging Clapton to hold the thought, Bruce produced the 'Politician' lyrics and began tentatively to wrap them around the riff. In no more time than it took to sing the song, the number was complete. 'There was no big writing session or anything,' Bruce intimated with a shrug, 'it came together quickly, and we performed it for the first time on that radio show.'

Neither did the number require more than a modicum of refinement; just a handful of live performances separated the creation of 'Politician' from its final recording in New York the following month, while Bruce's riff proved so immovably powerful that even Brown was unable to resist reprising it when he recut the number, replete with ranting poetic prelude and elephantine horn work, for his own 1969 album, *A Meal You Can Shake Hands with in the Dark*.

Kicking off at the Santa Monica Civic Auditorium on 23 February 1968, the US tour that stretched before Cream was vast, and would grow even vaster as time passed; it was mid-June before the group finally came off the road, by which time they wouldn't merely have played an exhausting 70-plus shows in 115 days, they'd also have torn the laws of American touring asunder for all time.

Though it always seemed that way from the cosy confines of the Ricky Tick or the Flamingo, Stateside venues had not always been huge; they were, in fact, still dominated by a theatrical circuit that really did not offer much more room than the Gaumonts and Astorias of its British counterpart.

Ever since the Beatles turned established practice on its head and crammed close to 56,000 keening screamagers into the Shea Stadium baseball park in August 1965, however, local promoters had fought to out-gross one another, not necessarily in terms of size – it would be a mighty draw indeed that could ever shade the Beatles' attendance records – but certainly in terms of workload.

Cities, towns, even tiny communities were scoured for buildings large enough to stage a modern pop concert, with the most unlikely halls being press-ganged into use; on more than one occasion, Cream arrived at a venue to discover the roadies setting up on a jerry-built stage at the far end of a high school auditorium. And not only high schools.

In Scotch Plains, New Jersey, the band found themselves playing a very exclusive, private Catholic school, where monks and nuns stalked the corridors and the pupils' parents paid a fortune in the apparently mistaken belief that they were insulating their offspring from the evils of the outside world. An evening in the presence of Cream and *their* audience was probably not what mom and pop had in mind, but the evening was clearly a success. Over the next couple of years, under the guidance of schoolboy promoter Ty Nutt and headmaster Brother Vincent, the Who, Chicago, Vanilla Fudge and even Black Sabbath all played the school.

Disraeli Gears was already setting the scene for the tour. Having entered the US chart in early December, the album was soaring, even breathing new life into *Fresh Cream* as it rose. That set eventually halted just inside the Top Forty; *Disraeli Gears* soared to number four. But that wasn't all. From the moment the first promotional copies of the LP hit the radio stations, 'Sunshine of Your Love' was pumping out of every FM transmitter in the land. Now Atlantic had sprung it as a single in its own right and, though it initially sailed no higher than number 36, at a time when America's own music scene was flexing every muscle it had, and foreign groups (even British ones!) were finding it increasingly difficult to break into the US market, even that was already a triumph.

Cream's own itinerary could barely keep pace with ticket demand. The band was no more than a week into the outing, checking into their hotel for their return to San Francisco, and extra shows were already being added to the date sheet, devouring the few free days the musicians had planned on enjoying, and burrowing ever deeper into an American hinterland that even the road crew's roadmaps had trouble documenting.

San Francisco, naturally, was all but home territory, with Cream booked in for no less than eight two-shows-a-night concerts, spread across two weeks. Of course they were returning to the 900-seater Fillmore, but Bill Graham had now moved into a second venue as well, the almost five-times-the-size Winterland. It was there that Cream opened their residency, and it was there, too, that Robert Stigwood discovered just how out-of-touch with the new rock hierarchy he had become.

Graham tells the tale in his autobiography. Arriving in town three nights into Cream's run, Stigwood initially caught Graham's eye when he became 'the first guy ever to wear his full-length coat into Winterland *over* his shoulders. Nobody even wears a coat in San

Francisco. Much less over the shoulders with the hat *and* the dicky scarf wrapped around his throat. Like he'd come in from Pluto, and the natives on Earth were alien to what he represented.'

Graham's two sisters and their own families were in town for a few days that week, and their host had arranged the best seats in the house for them, a row of six on the side of the stage. Stigwood, however, couldn't understand how a mere promoter's family could take precedence over his own entourage, not only demanding that the seats be surrendered to him, but dispatching a relay of lackeys to Graham's office to remind him just how *important*, just how *powerful* and, now, just how *insulted* Mr Stigwood was by Graham's continued refusal to kick his sisters into the stalls.

Finally Graham had had enough. Storming up to this 'Simonised version of Errol Flynn', he offered Stigwood two choices. 'You can walk out of the building right now, or we can carry you.' Then, before Stigwood even made his decision, 'two of my guys on either side of him . . . walked him through the audience, [and] out through the side door to the outside of the building.' Then Graham headed backstage to let the band know what had happened: '"I have some bad news for you. We had to just throw out your manager." [And] in one sentence, Ginger Baker said it all . . . He said "Really? That's marvellous. That is *marvellous*."'

'We thought it was hilarious,' Clapton continued. 'We thought it was *incredible*. Because we all knew what Robert Stigwood was. God bless his soul, I still think the world of him. But he did try to strong-arm it quite a lot . . .'

The performance that Stigwood missed was one that Cream would be honing to perfection over the next week in town, as they psyched themselves up for the road trip of their lives; it was that process that Atlantic hoped to capture when it was suggested that the group record a few of their shows – not necessarily for immediate release, but for the sake of posterity regardless.

Cream's past experiences with live recordings were primitive to say the least. Even within the most professional surroundings that Europe could muster, still the basic set-up relied upon little more than a couple of strategically placed microphones, as though technology had stubbornly refused to advance from the days when the Yardbirds taped their first album at the Marquee.

But when the band members peeped inside the Hertz rental truck that Tom Dowd and engineer Bill Halverson had converted into a mobile studio, they could scarcely tell it apart from the Atlantic Studios themselves. There was a full studio consul, a bank of four speakers and two separate eight-track recorders, each linked to a battery of strategically placed, and wholly unobtrusive microphones. And, to ensure that they captured the very best of Cream, no less than eight of the group's sixteen San Francisco concerts were recorded, to be spilled out over a host of future releases.

Even with so much sophisticated gadgetry to hand, however, Cream were never wholly satisfied with the final results; never believed that the excitement that unquestionably bled from the recordings could compensate for the shortfall in the actual sound quality; and certainly did not agree that the recordings came even close to capturing the 'true' sound of Cream.

The recording equipment, after all, could only handle so much volume, and so much leakage, and Cream were now playing so loud that, even during their quieter passages, the recording needles were dancing in the red. Cautiously, Dowd offered up a handful of suggestions (he was too diplomatic to suggest that the band make actual compromises), altering the tone of Clapton's guitar, for example, but though the group agreed, they clearly were not happy.

Even more damning was the combo's own belief that, no matter how many nights Dowd and Halverson recorded, they never captured those when Cream were truly on form. The tapes, Bruce said, were 'a fair representation of the band on an average night, but not on one of the nights when we really took off'. Those shows, unfortunately, survive only in the minds of the people who saw them.

Not that there was any shortage of them. In quiet moments, as the tour pulled out of San Francisco, en route for the almost daily change of scenery that comprised the remainder of their visit, the trio asked themselves how things had grown so immense so suddenly, and the only answer they could find was, people genuinely wanted to hear them.

No accusations of hype or payola buzzed around the grapevine. Nobody hinted that wheels were being greased, or palms crossed with silver. And nobody suggested that Cream were pandering to some cleverly identified common denominator. Indeed, the group's own assessment of their live show's integral components left them grasping for any kind of explanation for their popularity: twenty-minute drum solos, fifteen-minute guitar solos, and a core repertoire of blues songs that was essentially old as mud. What kind of musical mainstream could ever adopt that as an ideal?

Yet it had, and Cream had no alternative but to accept that; accept, too, that for great swathes of the audience, the very proximity of the three virtuosos was enough. The actual virtuosity of their playing was almost irrelevant.

Jack Bruce realised that on that infamous night when Cream took the stage amid a hail of accidental feedback, and received a standing ovation on the spot; and had it reinforced the evening when the vocal mikes failed, and Cream inadvertently played an all-but instrumental set; and had it confirmed at the show when the gremlins took out the sound of the guitar, and the audience grooved to drum and bass alone. No matter how hard a concert might stumble or fall, the response never wavered.

Even *Rolling Stone* magazine was not immune to the hysteria. Writing at the end of February, at the very outset of the tour, journalist Nick Jones (the *Melody Maker* regular) mused, 'There's something just formidable about the Cream. Maybe it's the multi-talented [trio], brimming with musical confidence and religiously slaying their audiences with a bedazzling hurricane of technique, drama, emotion and zooming spirit. Maybe it's that hairy Satanic aura, the cool hard gaze of Eric Clapton from beneath that under-world of hair, the deep colorful mystery of their flowing robes. Maybe it's the creamy texture of both the group and their music.'

Whatever it was, it had hypnotised America, and Cream were duty-bound to maintain the illusion. Quickly, the group fell into a routine – in the most soul-destroying, grinding, meaning of the word. Whether they flew or drove to their next engagement, the mechanics of the day barely varied. They checked in at whatever the local equiv-alent of the Holiday Inn might be, drove to the venue to soundcheck – or, at least, waited around in the hope that the stage would be set up in time to permit them that luxury; they would play the show; go to bed; and then start the whole thing again the next morning.

The traditional perks of a life on the road were always there, of course, but even the groupies lost their lustre after a time, while the lines of local acolytes who queued outside the hotel, or spilled into the dressing room to spend a few moments with the idols, became so predictable in their worship that, before long, the musicians found themselves answering questions before they'd even been asked: 'No, I don't think Jimi's blown it'; 'Yes, they should get out of Vietnam'; 'Maybe you should ask Bob Dylan himself.' And so on.

Just weeks into the trek, all three players agreed that the entire tour, vastly successful and hugely profitable though it was, was a mistake. Reiterating what had become an almost monotonous mantra, they had joined together in order to play the music that they loved, in the manner they chose. It sounded glib, even pretentious, when they said it, but the money really wasn't important; Cream was formed to allow three musicians, at the peak of their powers, to play to the best of their abilities – and beyond. But what opportunity could there be for such lofty ideals, as they dragged from day to day around the American countryside, playing not because they wanted to, but because they were contractually obliged to?

Even the luxury of residences in single cities was beyond them now, and with it the opportunity to do more than simply glance out of the window as another conurbation rushed by. In San Francisco, both the previous autumn and again on their return, Cream had succeeded in putting down some roots; making their way into the local culture and, even if only for a couple of weeks, forging relationships and friendships that might last a lifetime. New York, too, offered a home-from-home; when recording sessions wound down, the band members would be out on the town, meeting new people, reuniting with old friends.

Now, however, such comforts were far beyond them. The previous year had seen record sales in America reach an all-time high; $1 billion-dollars worth of music shifted meant profits had more than doubled in a decade. For the first time, too, LP sales were outstripping singles, and Atlantic, for whom 1967 had proven spectacularly successful, were intent that 1968 should push the profits to even greater heights. And so Cream were put to work. From Sacramento to Fresno, Phoenix to Anaheim to Denver to Beliot, Wisconsin – who in their right mind ever chose to go to Beliot, Wisconsin ... and what would they find when they got there? The place was barely even on the map.

Back in London, Cream's thoughts were full of the new groups they would get to see, the new musicians they would meet, the sensational jams into which they might fall. Instead, Bruce mourned, 'Obviously, we did play with people; whenever possible, we went to see people. But we were too busy working to see a lot of people ... if we happened to be in a town and there was somebody playing when we had a day off, obviously we'd go along ... or I'd go along, because we didn't hang as a band. But that didn't happen very often. I did see some pretty interesting things, but not that many.'

In fact, some nights it wasn't even safe for the group to leave the security of the venue or their hotel, shades of Boston and the World Series, all over again. America was a powder keg and the Cream tour seemed to stumble over another fizzing fuse every time it touched down.

The façade of love and peace that had sustained youth fashion through 1967 had finally been punctured. The three-year-old Vietnam War was turning ever uglier every day, with the previous year's death toll – 9,353 Americans were killed there during 1967 – more than double that of the first two years combined. The launch of the Tet Offensive at the end of January 1968 suggested that, this year, the numbers were climbing even further.

The anti-war movement was gaining momentum; the Civil Rights movement was gathering arms. Again the previous year, race riots had become commonplace throughout the inner cities, but now the rioters were lethally organised, as Dr Martin Luther King's dream of peaceful Black Equality was translated into the gun-toting Black Panthers' cry of Black Power.

The world outside America, too, was changing, but there, it was positive action, not negative reaction that seemed to be making the headlines: in France, where the students were agitating loudly against the de Gaulle government's ambition of exemplifying law and order in an increasingly lawless world; in Czechoslovakia, where Slovakian-born, Chicago-conceived Alexander Dubcek took over the leadership of the local Communist Party, and ushered in a Prague Spring of enlightenment and ... dare the people even breathe the word? ... freedom; in Spain, where the Fascist

Government was experiencing, for the first time, the lashings of a pro-democracy movement, rising in furious disbelief at General Franco's decision to stage a Mass for Adolf Hitler on the dead dictator's birthday; and in Germany, where a young generation was asking what *their* elders did during World War Two.

Its sense of domestic indignation already blazing at fever pitch, American youth now arose in open support, or, at least, vocal emulation, of each of these movements, and more. In February in Brooklyn's Bedford-Stuyvesant, eighth grade students all but rioted in protest at the quality of school dinners; in March, Columbia University was stricken by a daylong boycott of classes, in protest over the war.

The establishment responded in kind. The police were fighting back. In Los Angeles, the Sheriff's Office was contemplating the purchase of a fleet of armoured cars; in Detroit, they purchased an army-surplus half-track; and, from the depths of the bunkers where the nuclear arsenals grow, *The Bulletin of Atomic Scientists* prepared for Armageddon by pushing forward one hand on the Doomsday Clock, their own iconic contribution to the shaky state of the world. For more than four years, since the days that drove Dylan to warn of Hard Rain, the hands were frozen at twelve minutes to twelve. Now they hung at seven.

A country that was founded on the principles of freedom, was suddenly being ruled by fear, at least if you were young and longhaired. Hippy was a dirty word; student, pacifist and protestor likewise. Visiting California the previous year, Cream had expressed their own astonishment at the freedom that seemed to permeate the very streets. True, not every passing cop was willing to look the other way when he stumbled on a gang of kids taking a crafty toke, but he wasn't about to start cracking skulls with his nightstick, either.

How different it all was now. In LA on 20 March, Clapton hooked up with Jim Messina, Neil Young and Ritchie Furay of the Buffalo Springfield, for a party at Stephen Stills' ranch in Topanga Canyon. Of course it turned into an all-day jam session, with Clapton and Stills on dual lead guitars and the surrounding mountains, said another guest, Linda Stevens, 'were ringing. The Marshall amps were stacked.'

The session was loud; so loud that, inevitably, a neighbour called the police. They arrived, however, to discover something more than a party. There was marijuana on the premises as well, and the entire party (Stills aside – he was already out of the window) was arrested.

At the LA County jailhouse, the men were booked, then stripped down and sprayed with DDT, a disinfectant that was universally believed to be the only known antidote to dirty, filthy hippies – 'It was a time,' Jim Messina recalled, 'when long hair was not cool.'

With his British accent and his bright pink boots, Clapton seemed to especially intrigue the officers – they let him keep his footwear, but otherwise stripped him naked, and stood him in front of the rest of the gang. But the guitarist, according to the Springfield's road manager Chris Sarns, handled his predicament 'beautifully. Typical British stiff upper lip. "Oh well, we've got good lawyers. We'll be out of here by morning."'

And so they were; not only that but, for the most part, even the drug charges were eventually reduced to one of disturbing the peace. But all the time the initial action hung unresolved over him, Clapton knew that there was a lot more than a $300 fine that was at stake. A drug conviction, in those days of draconian visa restrictions and requirements, would inevitably have resulted in his deportation, and that would have ended his entire American career. Cream's entire American career.

Breaking out of California, the temperature continued rising. Cream's arrival in Beloit, Wisconsin, was overshadowed by the authorities' fears that unrest at the nearby University of Wisconsin in Madison might spread to other campuses – there, anti-war protestors had planted 400 white crosses on the lawn outside the administrative buildings, beneath a notice that proclaimed them 'the class of 1968'.

Days later, security shadowed, and came close to out-numbering, the audience at Hunter College in New York, as reports continued filtering through of a major student uprising at Bowie State College in Maryland, while at least two of Cream's scheduled shows were cancelled outright, as University authorities clamped down on anything that might provoke any kind of unrest. Naturally, rock'n'roll music was universally regarded among the most potent flashpoints of all.

Amid such unrest, Cream's own personal politics – Baker's basic conservatism, Bruce's broad socialism, and Clapton's staunch traditionalism – were agitated by all that they saw and heard. On at least one occasion, in Indianapolis, Bruce and Baker left a venue barking abuse at one another, after the drummer overheard his bandmate commiserate with a fan who'd had his skull cracked by riot police during a student sit-in earlier in the week. 'Serves you right,' Baker supposedly muttered, prompting Bruce to wheel on him furiously.

On another occasion, being interviewed by a student journalist, Baker allegedly tired of his interrogator's constant harping on about the injustice of the military draft, and snapped, 'if you feel so strongly about it, get a gun and get out to Washington, and shoot the fucking lot of them', and that, too, sparked a battle in the band, as Cream abandoned their attempts to even feign unity, and took to warring over every minor incident, every misplaced word, every askance glance.

History has hauled out an endless queue of onlookers, spectators and observers, all willing to testify to the increasingly fraught state of the group: the semi-public fights into which relations had deteriorated, the trigger-happy tempers that could erupt at the most innocuous comment; the night Ginger Baker was spotted apparently trying to shove a hotel fire-extinguisher up Bruce's bum; and the evening Clapton left a sold-out gig, and sat crying in a darkened park.

In his own autobiography, Corky Laing tells of the afternoon he arrived at the band's hotel to learn that 'Jack Bruce was apparently in the ... hospital after an alleged failed suicide attempt. It was rumoured he was depressed because of a terrible review of *Disraeli Gears* in *Rolling Stone* ...' Or perhaps he was just hiding away, seeking any respite from the merciless routine whose only escape valve was rage and abuse, violence and misery.

All of these tales, or variations thereof, doubtless have their basis in fact. But even the psychological insight that other commentators have brought to bear on such tidings only scale the foothills of the monumental psychic disaster that was now taking place, as each of the musicians retreated into his own world. Bruce, Baker and Clapton had long enjoyed the luxury of separate dressing rooms. Now, one persistent legend insists, they actually demanded separate hotels, so sick of the sight of one another had they become.

For each of them, the very mention of Cream conjured up nothing less than the sheer loss of opportunity that the band represented; and, no matter how vast the cheques they were paid for playing, the knowledge that being paid to play also meant being told *what* and *how* to play had sucked the last vestiges of joy out of the entire project.

On 4 April, the assassination of Civil Rights leader Martin Luther King left inner-city America teetering on the very brink of Civil War. As Cream drove into Boston for the first time since the Psychedelic Supermarket debacle, any trepidation they may have felt about returning to a city that had proven so unwelcoming the last time around, was only amplified by the very real prophesies of imminent apocalypse that swirled around them now.

Some 120 American cities had already exploded into violence, 40 erupted into all-out rioting and Boston, though it still lay calm, was itself regarded as a prime candidate for warfare. Only the quick thinking of City Councillor Thomas Atkins and Boston Mayor Kevin White quelled the flames before they could start burning; mindless of any other counter-attractions in town that weekend, they scheduled a special performance by soul legend James Brown at the Boston Garden for the following evening; arranged, too, for the entire show to be broadcast live on local television.

Cream themselves considered cancelling their own show as a mark of respect to the slain MLK – or, at least, two-thirds of Cream did. Baker, however, insisted that the show go on and not, according to a fly on the wall, for the sake of the audience alone. There was a pay-cheque to think about as well.

Of course, the possibility that they might have to brave blazing streets filled with rioting negroes would still deter some people from attending Cream's Back Bay Theater outing; as would the venue's own fears that the Brown concert might not prove sufficient incentive for any potential revolutionaries to lay down their Molotov cocktails.

Bostonite John Donovan was one of several would-be audience members who turned up for the Cream concert, only to be told that it was cancelled. He went home disappointed, but the gig did go ahead. Doug Yule, the young Boston guitarist who, a few months later, replaced John Cale in the Velvet Underground, was there that night and he recalls the show 'almost as clearly as I remember where I was when Kennedy was shot'.

The venue wasn't packed, but it was crowded and, long before Cream took the stage, all eyes were turned towards what Yule admiringly described as 'two stacks of Marshall cabinets with the largest kit of drums I'd ever seen in between them. It looked like two walls. We were at a stage in Boston at that time where owning a twin reverb was like winning the lottery. Having a wall of Marshalls was beyond comprehension. But the thing that made the set for me was the sound. Baker's drumming was totally without precedent for me; much more pitch-oriented, almost like a marimba at times, but thick and fat. He looked a little crazy. Years later the *Muppets* character Animal always brought back Baker's aura.

'The other outstanding things that grabbed me were the sheer sound pressure, like being pinned up against the wall by volume, and the sound of Clapton's guitar. He was playing an SG, the deluxe white one, and he made a sound that I had never heard before, like a cross between a violin and a guitar. That was the best Clapton ever sounded to me.' Indeed, Yule admitted that he immediately dedicated himself to trying to replicate 'a sound like that' in his own playing. He did get there in the end, 'but only at the expense of a number of amplifiers!'

The following evening, Cream were in nearby Lowell; the day after that, they hit Rochester, New York. Shows as far afield as Ottawa, Philadelphia and Toronto, in that absolutely logic-defying order, lay immediately ahead of them; and, alongside them, who knew what other disturbances, riots and mayhem? 'They were working us to death,' Bruce sighs wearily. 'It was nonstop, and there really didn't seem a point to any of it.'

Cream were at the end of their tether – possibly even beyond it. One day, pacing the floor of one more anonymous hotel room, Clapton caught a glimpse of himself in the mirror. 'I looked like death.'

He checked his weight and was horrified to discover it had plummeted to nine stone. And, though some people might have laid the blame on self-abuse, he knew it was self-neglect. Trying to keep pace with the group's schedule, trying to keep up with his colleagues' constant demands and squabbling, the most perfect band in the world had turned into the most imperfect nightmare imaginable. A world of troubles such as he had never experienced, or even envisioned, was barrelling down upon him, and crushing the very will to live.

Bruce, too, was afraid to do more than glance at his own reflection – and he was absolutely terrified to look at Baker. The drummer had recovered from that crippling bout of exhaustion that struck him down at the end of 1967. But, no sooner was he given the all-clear by his doctors, than he was back working harder than ever before; gigging harder and, because that was the nature of Cream's music, playing harder. Some nights he came offstage looking as though he'd physically passed out hours before, and continued drumming courtesy of some unstoppable instinct for rhythm and mayhem.

'We all looked like we were at death's door,' said Bruce, 'but I'm sure that a lot of people came to see Cream to see if Ginger would die. Whereas they'd go to see other bands because they thought the singer was sexy, they'd come and see us and shout through the window, "You gonna die tonight, Ginger?"'

Baker could not answer that question; sometimes, he admitted, he couldn't even hear the words themselves. 'When we first went out, Eric and Jack had one Marshall speaker cabinet each. Then it became a stack, then a double stack, and finally a triple stack. I was the poor bastard stuck in the middle of these incredible noise making things. It was ridiculous. I used to get back to the hotel, and my ears were roaring.'

All three members of the band placed calls to Stigwood, begging for some kind of reprieve from the routine, but their pleas went unanswered. Every time, the Australian asked them to give things 'one more week' – it was always 'give it one more week'. Though nobody knew it, that week was now up.

Cream had just crossed the border into Canada when Bruce's patience finally snapped. The tour was a little over six weeks old – it was 8 April 1968, and Cream were playing the Capitol Theater in Ottawa, a relatively cosy venue, but one which supplied an even cosier PA. Looking it up and down, rubbing a throat that was already raw from so many nights bellowing to be heard through the tiny systems with which every venue seemed to present the band, Bruce mused aloud on Cream's need for their own PA system, a monster set-up that could travel around with them, and make sure that wherever they played, they could be heard.

Baker's response appalled him. 'He said we can't afford it. And I was ... then what is the point of any of this?' Six weeks on the road already, another six weeks ahead of them; a Top Ten album, a Top Forty single, and they couldn't afford their own PA? 'So I just said "That's it, I'm going home."'

Storming out of the venue, Bruce made his own way to the airport, bought a ticket back to England and was just about to board his flight when a couple of the band's roadies appeared, and reminded him there was a gig that night. Then, Bruce laughs (he laughs now; he didn't at the time) saying, 'They almost physically carried me back.'

The gig went ahead, but the tour could not. Again they called Stigwood and, this time, there would be no concessions, no arguments. Cream played one more concert, a manic dash to the finishing line at Yale University's Woolsey Hall on 10 April, then cancelled the next ten days worth of shows, three in Philadelphia, and one in Montreal. They were going home, and even Stigwood finally had to admit that they deserved a break. 'The schedule I arranged was too intensive.'

Yet, exhaustion was not Cream's only problem, any more than the irascibility that had long been a part of the group dynamic. Cream had spent almost two months forging into unknown territory. Plenty of performers had undertaken long tours of the United States in the past, and homegrown bands did it all the time. But Cream weren't homegrown, they were homesick. Their schedule did its damnedest to absorb every one of their waking thoughts, or at least swamp them in the novelty of mental and physical exhaustion. But still the band missed the comforts that, in London, they'd taken for granted, and whose absence they'd never even contemplated.

Try and find a jar of Marmite in late 1960s' Indianapolis. Or a bedtime mug of Horlicks in Houston. A pint of beer, a packet of crisps, the latest *Beano* or *New Musical Express*. The football results. Little things that, at first, you don't miss, take on marathon proportions when they're far enough away.

Strangers in a very strange land – no matter how much certain elements of American culture had infiltrated the British landscape, still there was an entire world out there that was completely new, that they'd never even heard hints of before: the poverty, the provinciality, the sheer perversity of the richest country in the world harbouring some of the filthiest ghettos on the planet.

Racism wasn't merely endemic, it was so deeply inculcated that even the most liberal of Liberals could not help but let it out occasionally. A few weeks before Cream hit New York, John Mayall's latest batch of Bluesbreakers were playing their own first shows in that city, when Dick Heckstall-Smith was invited out to jam at a late night club in Harlem.

He didn't think anything of it; 'It was just like the Flamingo all-niters, only more so. Black music, black faces.' But when he returned to Manhattan and told people where he'd been, they could scarcely believe he'd lived to tell the tale. Cream were themselves in America before Mayall returned to England, and hadn't had a chance to compare notes with Heckstall-Smith. But they quickly discovered the same story for themselves, and were as astonished by its reality as he was.

Culture shock can wear off after time. Not so the sheer logistics involved in hauling the band from one coast to the other; the alarm calls that dragged them from bed only a few hours after they'd collapsed into it, so they could beat the traffic to the next day's venue; the hours they spent waiting while the gear was set up, only to be torn down again a few hours later; the days they spent watching another cornfield-the-size-of-a-small-country pass by.

Again, other British bands had undertaken massive American tours, but this outing surpassed all past efforts. It wasn't, after all, simply the number of shows that was an issue. It was the weight of expectation that accompanied each one. Somebody pays five bob to see a club gig and, if it doesn't go as planned, it's a disappointment, but it's not a tragedy. Somebody pays five bucks, however – or even more – and they not only expect a razor-sharp show, they demand it, whether they're front row, stage centre, staring up the guitar player's nose, or half a mile back in the last row of the omnidome.

Other groups can hit that plateau, can find a rhythm, a level, a formula, and rattle along without a hiccup for weeks. Everybody plays what they're meant to play, one neatly fitted piece in a jigsaw puzzle that is so smoothly programmed that even the ad-libs are painstakingly rehearsed, and the hardest part is remembering which town you're in tonight.

Cream, however, did not work like that, and probably couldn't have, even if they'd tried. Whether they wanted to use such imagery or not, Cream were unique, not simply as the first rock group to become internationally renowned and obscenely successful without the easy entry of a hit single, but as the pioneers of an entirely new style of music, one in which a programmed set list was simply the launch pad for a decidedly unprogrammed exploration of the outer limits.

Pioneers need to do more than walk where no one else has ever journeyed. They also need to travel where they themselves have never been before, for their own sake if nobody else's. So, every night the show was different; every night, Baker, Bruce and Clapton were pushing one another to hit a note, execute a run, chase a spectre they had never chased before. One hundred per cent creativity, one hundred per cent of the time. And suddenly, they'd run out, of the spontaneity that is needed to fly to the moon every night, and the patience to deal with an audience that cheered every note, regardless of whether the mission ever got off the launching pad. 'It just wasn't enjoyable any more,' admitted Baker.

In years to come, both Baker and Bruce reflected upon conversations they shared with Clapton in Texas, at the end of March, as the guitarist looked them wearily in the eye and confessed 'I've had enough.' Both recall answering 'Yeah, so have I.' What neither of them realised until later was how fervently they meant what they said.

18. THE ELEPHANTS ARE DANCING

Shortly before Christmas 1967, a remarkable new Bob Dylan album began circulating around the London cognoscenti. Dylan himself had spent the last year out of action, ever since he tumbled off his motorcycle in July 1966 and effectively declared himself *hors de combat* for as long as he wanted to take.

He remained in seclusion, but he was scarcely inactive. Sequestered within his basement in Woodstock, a then-unknown idyll in upstate New York, Dylan surrounded himself with the musicians he knew best, the same gang he'd been working with for the year before his accident, and began working up some new songs.

Robbie Robertson, Richard Manuel, Garth Hudson, Rick Danko and Levon Helm – four Canadians and one Arkansasian (Helm) – had started life as the Hawks, backing rockabilly god Ronnie Hawkins as he toured through the early 1960s. They first hooked up with Dylan in 1965, after he heard them playing in a Greenwich Village club, and accompanied him on the road as he launched the so-controversial, electrified phase of his career. Now they rejoined him, renting their own communal haunt, the Big Pink, in nearby West Saugerties and, over the next six months, the perpetually rolling tape recorder captured what Dylan chronicler Clinton Heylin justly describes as '[possibly] Dylan's greatest collection of songs'.

'Million Dollar Bash', 'Tears of Rage', 'Down in the Flood', 'The Mighty Quinn', 'This Wheel's on Fire', 'I Shall Be Released', modern bootlegs of the unexpurgated proceedings stretch across five well-stuffed CDs; Dylan's own label's eventual (1975) attempt to make sense of the mass was spread across four sides of vinyl. The tape that reached the streets in late 1967, however, comprised just fourteen songs, brought together by Dylan's music publisher, Dwarf Music, to showcase the latest material that he was offering up for cover versions.

The tape had an immediate impact on its intended audience and far, far beyond. Within six months of its appearance, Fairport Convention, Manfred Mann, the Julie Driscoll–Brian Auger Trinity and many more had hit the recording studio with songs that Dylan himself was all-but throwing away, and each would reap the rewards of so doing. But *The Basement Tapes*, as the cassette was quickly becoming known, was crucial for more than the clutch of new music that it featured.

There was something about the very execution of those songs that thrilled everyone who heard them; an indefinable something that not one of the subsequent covers, no matter how brilliantly they were delivered, was ever able to recapture. They were relaxed, but never sloppy; they were at ease, but never easy – some of the lyrics rating among Dylan's most obtuse yet. And they were informal, without ever losing the sense that here was a band that was so comfortable with its abilities that the musicians did not even need to try and show off. There were no solos, there were no grand finales, no grandstanding athletics or musical gymnastics. Just song after song, all played so naturally that the songs themselves did not even seem to have been written. Rather, the musicians reached into the trees and plucked them fully formed from the branches.

For a while, there was only one copy of the tape in circulation in London – Brian Auger was on the receiving end of a very excited call from Giorgio Gomelsky one day, telling him about a collection of new Dylan songs that would be arriving any day now. 'I asked him where it was now, and he said, "Oh, bloody Manfred Mann has it"' – Dylan's love of the Manfreds, and all they had brought to his songs in the past, was well known, and the Manfreds justified his faith with their own recordings of this new material.

Extra copies of the recording soon began surfacing, however; Eric Clapton received his first exposure to the tape around Christmas from a friend named David Lipenhoff; the legend captures the pair lying around somebody's apartment, puffing on some hot, new Mexican weed, while Dylan strummed through the speakers.

Clapton was captivated immediately, but he was furious as well. What he heard on the tape was the same music he had once heard in his head, way back when he first agreed to form a partnership with Jack Bruce and Ginger Baker; way back when he believed that Cream's future was as wide as they made it.

In the pell-mell of the group's career so far, Clapton had forgotten those founding ambitions. But now they came hurtling back at him and, no matter how much he loved the music he was hearing, he was simultaneously fighting to control the ... well, as Dylan himself sang towards the end of the tape ... 'Tears of Rage' that built up within him, as he realised just how skilfully the American had taken his dream, and brought it so vibrantly to life.

Clapton's own copy of *The Basement Tapes* accompanied him to America in January; it was quickly joined in his luggage by another clutch of recordings, this time an extremely pre-release copy of the forthcoming first album by Dylan's accompanying players, now portentously renamed The Band. *Music from the Big Pink* was highlighted by a clutch of the Band's own compositions: the instant classic 'The Weight', the foreboding 'To Kingdom Come', the pure Americana of 'Caledonia Mission', and then a recycling of several Dylan songs; and, though Dylan himself was now absent from the recordings, the mood, the vibe, the general feel of the songs remained the same.

Clapton revealed, 'I got hold of a tape of [*Music from the*] *Big Pink* from somewhere ... and I used to put it on as soon as I checked into my hotel room, and listen to it, and then go and do the gig and be utterly miserable. Then [I'd] rush back and put the tape on and go to sleep fairly contented, until I woke up the next morning and remembered who I was and what I was doing. It was that potent. And I thought, "Well, this is what *I* want to play – not extended solos and maestro bullshit, but just good funky songs."'

The objects of his desire agreed with him. 'We were trying to do a type of timeless music,' Robbie Robertson explained. 'We were thinking, hopefully, you could listen to this in twenty years or fifty years; we'd admired so many people whose music had lived on, regardless.'

Clapton met Robertson for the first time in Los Angeles; anxious now to learn more about the music and the musicians behind it, Clapton took a trip up to the group's headquarters in Woodstock, on one of Cream's days off at the end of March. He came away no wiser for the encounter, but no less impressed, either. The five musicians, he said, 'looked like the Hole In The Wall Gang', sitting around their rural hideaway in their denim, buckskin and sneakers; a far, far cry from the self-confessed 'psychedelic loonie' who arrived at their front door in all his rainbow gaudiness.

Conversation was apparently stilted, or maybe there was no need to talk. Interviewed almost twenty years later, bassist Rick Danko reckoned the two parties spent most of the time 'just sitting around not speaking, just checking each other out. We put on some records, we ate; Eric didn't say much, I think he just wanted to soak up whatever atmosphere he thought he would find there, and then he left.' Clapton, for his part, mused, 'They just turned out to be great people – very intelligent, very tight. And [I've been] in awe of them ever since.' (Eight years on, Clapton was among the performers guesting at the Band's *Last Waltz* farewell concert.)

In his mind, Clapton cast around for faces to blame for Cream's failure to pursue the vision that the Band were so effortlessly mapping out; he found them alongside him every night. And the more he thought about it, the more the blame piled up. It continued building through what was left of Cream's lifetime; it was still agonisingly palpable more than 35 years later, when he sat down to talk with *Uncut* magazine. 'I was absolutely certain,' he said, 'if we had engaged . . . Steve Winwood, we could have gone in that [same] direction, but done it in a very English way.'

He flashed upon a remark Jimi Hendrix made to *Melody Maker,* back at the beginning of 1967, ruminating on the likelihood that he and Clapton 'think along the same lines', but mourning the diffi-culty of 'getting [that] across to the other musicians. I'm not sure if Eric is playing exactly what he wants to . . .' At the time, Clapton laughed that observation off. Now he wasn't so certain.

Almost before the flight from New York touched down in London on 11 April, rumours were flying that Cream were breaking up; that tempers had finally frayed beyond all hope of reconciliation, that the tight proximity of three monstrous egos had crushed the group between them.

Stigwood was quick to quash the growing insistence. 'Nothing,' he announced, 'could be further from the truth.'

But circumstances elsewhere seemed to back up the whispers. Clapton was a regular guest at Rolling Stone Keith Richard's home in Cheyne Walk, Chelsea, at a time when the grapevine was rife with reports that Bill Wyman was on his way out of the group. The Stones had always admired Clapton's playing. Was it really so unlikely that Clapton might curtail his time with Cream, so that he might join the Rolling Stones instead?

It was, if it meant he'd be replacing a bassist. 'I know nothing about it,' Clapton insisted. 'But it's all pretty strange to me. I'd have to play lead guitar, anyway.'

A clue? Again, it was no secret that the Stones were rapidly tiring of Brian Jones, that his spiralling disintegration was creating any number of problems within the band. Perhaps Clapton was being lined up to replace him instead?

Another dead end. 'The five Rolling Stones remain the five Rolling Stones,' Mick Jagger announced. 'There is to be no alteration.' Nor would there be, at least for the time being. It was another year before Jones was finally removed from the group (to be replaced by the Bluesbreakers' Mick Taylor), and eighteen months on from there before Clapton finally fulfilled so many people's ambition and played with the Stones themselves; when Keith Richards staged his 27th birthday party at Olympic Studios in December 1970, Clapton was on hand to slash some ferocious guitar through an early take on 'Brown Sugar'. In spring 1968, however, he insisted that he was no more likely to join the Stones than he was going to walk on the moon. Or, for that matter, leave Cream.

Interviewed that same month by *Melody Maker*'s Chris Welch, Clapton insisted, 'All the rumours are denied. I'm happy with the group.' Of course there was some strain placed on the relationship, but that was wholly down to the group's workload. 'We've been doing two-and-a-half months of one-nighters, and that is the hardest I have ever worked in my life. Financially and popularity-wise,' he continued, however, 'we're doing unbelievably well in America.' And, if those were the only goals that mattered to Cream, then maybe his words might have stilled the murmuring. But they didn't, and Clapton knew that. Why else would he have concluded his denial by turning his entire statement back on its head with the acknowledgement, 'If we hadn't had this holiday, we might have broken up.' And why else would he so wistfully have allowed Welch access to a private world that itself was far away from the frontiers of Cream?

Writing in his own biography of Cream, *Cream: The Legendary Sixties Super-group*, Welch recalled, 'He played me some of Bob Dylan and the Band's recordings ... which had clearly made an impression. "I think this music will influence a lot of people ... everybody I have played it to has flipped. All my values have changed."'

He was not given the opportunity to elaborate. Cream spent a little under a week at home; by 19 April, they were back on the road, and facing a second round of dates that was no shorter, and no less seething than that which had pushed them to the brink in the first place. Rescheduling the four cancelled shows dragged the tour into the second week of June; almost automatically, a further handful of dates appeared a few days after that. The final concert was now set for 16 June, and only a long-standing booking at Atlantic Studios for the following day prevented the itinerary from spilling into the summer festival season.

The shows were spaced a little further apart during this leg of the tour, however, and there were a few more distractions to look forward to, amid the customary jungle of school gyms and converted cinemas, beginning with three nights at Philadelphia's famed Electric Factory, a former tyre warehouse that now boasted a fluorescent miniature playground, a bank of reclining body racks, and even a parade of boutiques and head shops. Another highlight loomed in Chicago on 27 April, as Cream found themselves sharing the bill with the Mothers of Invention – a crazy musical misalignment for sure, but guaranteed entertainment for Cream themselves, both at the show and during the after-hours jam that inevitably followed the actual gig.

Into the midst of all this, Atlantic released Cream's latest single, 'Anyone for Tennis', a record that could scarcely have been further removed from the portrait of the band that the past three months had daubed across America. Still it was a gem, a semi-acoustic romp that delighted in some truly violent imagery, but also layered in an irresistible chorus, a haunting middle-eight – everything, in fact, that a hit single could require. And then somebody had the bright idea of ruining the whole thing by concocting a promotional film to accompany the release, with Baker, Bruce and Clapton dressed as American policemen, miming the song on tennis rackets, while a handful of frogs leaped around on some lettuce – frogs that would, before the film was finished, be nailed into place by a man with a hammer.

Totally unaware that such slaughter had even been contemplated, the band was absolutely disgusted; you can see it in their faces in several of the shots, and they continue to distance themselves from the film even today. 'There's one part where Eric looks like he's about to throw up,' said Bruce; while American television, for whom the film was made in the first place, was not especially enamoured either. The film was archived, all but unseen, while the single itself barely limped to number 64, with an ill-at-ease appearance on the Smothers Brothers comedians' television special, *The Summer Brothers Smother Show*, in mid-May, stubbornly failing to jog it any higher.

Looking more discomfited than ever before, Cream performed two songs, 'Sunshine of Your Love' and 'Anyone for Tennis'. Throughout, Clapton stood at the microphone mouthing words he might never have spoken before, while playing a song he might never have heard. But, if the performance was an embarrassment for the viewers, it was even more nightmarish for the band. Baker admitted, 'The Smothers Brothers thing [looks] hilarious now, but I think way back then, it was probably far from it. That was probably when we knew it was all over. I'm glad it wasn't something I was singing.'

Clapton agreed with him. Referring, of course, to Stigwood, he reflected, 'We were being governed by a particularly lunatic man who, God bless his soul, was just ready to put us anywhere at any time for any old reason. And we would just turn up and play and count the costs later. I think that, really, the guy you were looking at on that Smothers Brothers show was just the result of too many situations where I was out of my depth, to the point where I just didn't know who I was, where I was or what I was doing any more.'

'Anyone for Tennis' fared a little better in the UK, at least sniffing the Top Forty before a total lack of promotion sent it tumbling again. Cream's first single on the Polydor label, following Stigwood's decision to shut down Reaction, it was irreparably hamstringed by the group's absence from the country; and further crushed by its proximity to a clutch of higher-profile releases elsewhere in the Polydor family: the Crazy World of Arthur Brown's imminent chart-topper 'Fire', and the Julie Driscoll–Brian Auger Trinity's brilliant reinvention of one of Clapton's own most-beloved *Basement Tape* numbers, 'This Wheel's on Fire'.

It was those groups, not Cream, that supplied the soundtrack for Britain in 1968, and the menacing mood of their music that captured the spirit of the age – the Vietnam rally-turned-riot that was fought out at the gates of the American Embassy in Grosvenor Square; the anti-Fascist demonstrations that beset German press magnate Axel Springer's UK distribution centres; the rising tide of anti-immigrant verbiage being spilled from the Keep Britain White brigade. No more than two years had passed since Cream formed, and already they seemed old and staid, the last clinging remnants of a world that had otherwise fallen off the edge of the planet.

Cream could handle that. They were not the only group, after all, to be written off by the media, then turn around to prove that their best was still to come. The Beatles and the Stones had spent years dodging the bullets, with the latter's own 'Jumping Jack Flash' single not only obviating the obituaries that accompanied *Their Satanic Majesties' Request*, but obliterating the obituary writers as well. As Cream contemplated the mass of still-unreleased material that they were slowly easing into shape for their next LP, they knew that their own reinvention was just a matter of months away.

Noel Redding, Jimi Hendrix's bassist through his most vital years, once hypothesised, 'The things that killed Cream were the same that killed Jimi. If one person had booed while Jack was tuning his bass, or Eric hit a bum note, then they'd have known that people still cared about what they played. Instead, they were allowed to get away with everything, until finally it didn't matter what they did. And the moment they realised that, it was the end.'

That realisation and, accordingly, that end, was delivered by *Rolling Stone* magazine, just a couple of weeks after Cream returned to the road. Though it was little more than a year old at the time, *Rolling Stone* had completely torn asunder the kind of music reporting that had passed before it ('and here's the latest happening sound by those good-looking groovers who call themselves Cream'), replacing it with the considered criticism that any serious art form – as the magazine's founder, Jan Wenner, determined rock music to have become – deserved. On 11 May, in the same edition that headlined its cover with Wenner's own exclusive Eric Clapton interview, journalist scribe Jon Landau devoted a full page to reviewing a Cream show ... and he ripped them to shreds.

He did not do so overtly, and certainly not gratuitously. 'I don't believe there are more than a handful of American bands that come within miles of Cream,' he wrote. In every arena one could name, from 'technical equipment' to 'the understanding of their instruments', Cream were streets ahead of the competition. So far, so fawning.

But, having set the trap, Landau then sprang it. Clapton, he wrote, was 'a master of the blues cliché . . .'; Baker's showpiece 'Toad' was 'terribly boring' (to differentiate it from 'NSU', which was simply 'terrible'); and Cream as a whole was so hung-up on its ideal of virtuosity that the entire affair was rendered redundant and aimless. '[But] the greatest pitfall that stands before them is that an over-accepting audience in the United States will lull them into a complacency in which they increase their virtuosity at the expense of their own involvement. It would not be difficult for a group of this caliber to start making it all sound like scales.'

It was not Landau's first assault on Cream; the previous summer, he reviewed *Fresh Cream* for the *Crawdaddy* fanzine, pairing it with a belated mention for the *Bluesbreakers with Eric Clapton* album, and his disdain for Cream wasn't merely apparent from the opening sentence ('The first of these albums is by far the best'), it set the stage for virtually all he wrote in his *Rolling Stone* assault. *Fresh Cream* contained 'too much chaff, too much unfulfilled experimentation. Things like "I Feel Free", "NSU" and "Sweet Wine" just aren't very good songs to begin with. And, regardless of how fine a drummer Ginger Baker is, "Toad" is just another drum solo.' The difference was, *Crawdaddy*'s circulation was under 20,000 at that time. *Rolling Stone*'s was maybe ten times that.

For anybody brought up on the pop press of the 1980s and beyond, who knows it only as the generally toothless mouthpiece of whichever media conglomerate is buying this week's round of drinks, it is difficult to imagine a time when the press wasn't merely opinionated, it was also massively influential – when it wasn't merely capable of making or breaking a band, but took an active joy in exercising that capability.

That era lasted little more than a decade. *Rolling Stone* started it; punk rock essentially ended it, as a new generation of journalists became so obsessed with their personal ideologies that the actual quality of the music became a less-than-secondary consideration. But while it flourished, it could be ruthless, with even the most flippant of its assessments capable of seriously impacting upon an artist's ego.

Clapton himself was mortified, but not by Landau's words alone. He was horrified by the knowledge that somebody else was thinking – and writing – thoughts that Clapton imagined were his and his alone. Of course Bruce and Baker were both well aware of his infatuation with *Music from the Big Pink*; had heard it often enough that they knew half the songs by heart, whether they wanted to like them or not. But Clapton had not told them how he felt about Cream becoming the unwitting corollary to all that The Band represented; wasn't even convinced he'd explained it to himself. And now here were his own most private, innermost thoughts, spread across every reading table in America.

Clapton was in a restaurant when he read the piece, 'and I fainted. The ring of truth just knocked me backwards.' After he'd picked himself up, he returned to his hotel, and put on his so-well worn copy of *Music from the Big Pink*. He knew now what he needed to do.

The end of the tour was in sight. A month ... three weeks ... a fortnight... until, at last, it was June, and the tour was into its final stretch. A couple more shows in Canada, the make-up dates from the mid-tour break, and then one last dash to the finishing post: Hempstead, New York; Wallingford, Connecticut and, finally, the Camden County Music Fair in Cherry Hill, New Jersey, just outside Pennsylvania.

It was a gorgeous day in a delightful, and surprisingly intimate, setting, 400 fans within a tented theatre 'in the round', that was itself as accustomed to staging mainstream Broadway musicals as hosting visiting rock bands. But Cream were scarcely even paying attention. 'At the time, I thought it was the greatest show I'd ever seen,' said Camden native Brian Paige – one of an army of twelve- or thirteen-year olds who clambered under the tent flaps to watch the show. 'But later, after I'd heard some other live recordings, I started to notice things: none of the solos went on for very long, a lot of the songs were played a bit faster; now, I think back and it almost feels like they couldn't wait to get the gig over with.'

He was correct, they couldn't. Yet even in their darkest hour, Cream retained the ability to impress, to overwhelm, to positively reinvent all that they surveyed. As Cream departed the American live circuit, the Jeff Beck Group flew in, and Beck himself was immediately aware of just how all-encompassingly the conquering heroes had reshaped the American scene. Nine months earlier, Cream had complained that American blues were tightly rehearsed, overwhelmingly faithful. Now, it was America that was spreading its wings and, inverting Cream's earlier debt to his own group, Beck was happy to ascribe the shift to their unprecedented impact.

Suddenly, 'There was this serious underground thing going on, with Steppenwolf, Vanilla Fudge, Blue Cheer, all that stuff. In Britain, the blues were everything; straight, unadulterated, faithful blues. But anything would go in the States, they were ready for anything. They were expecting it. They didn't particularly want [bands] to play blues, they wanted progressive rock.' The Jeff Beck Group, the only true forebears to all that would subsequently be undertaken in the name of the heaviest rocking blues, from Led Zeppelin to Grand Funk Railroad, made sure they got them.

Cream did not head home straight away. Rather, they returned to New York to put the finishing touches to their new album, barely a fortnight away from its scheduled release. Clapton, at least, also entered into a social whirl of sorts. Jeff Beck's US tour kicked off with more than a week of shows in New York and, with Jimi

Hendrix in town as well, the Scene, at West 46th and 8th, became the site of a veritable summit meeting, as Hendrix, Beck and Clapton joined together in one mighty jam on 18 June. 'Jimi and I always had a friendship from a distance because we never really spent a lot of time together,' Clapton mourned. 'Only during the acid period I used to see him a lot. Occasionally we'd spend time alone together just raving about, but, I mean, it was always a distant friendship. Playing together was something else.'

True to Clapton's prophecy earlier in the year, *Wheels of Fire* was to be a double set, resplendent in another graphic Martin Sharp-designed sleeve, a gatefold silver canvas across which disembodied body parts splashed and splurged within some vast, surreal machinery. (Sharp revisited the same image two years later, in colour this time, for the dust jacket of Richard Neville's *Playpower* study of the underground, while *Wheels of Fire* itself earned him the New York Art Directors Prize for Best Album Design for 1969.)

Only half of this eye-catching new package drew from the studio recordings Cream had spent the last year working on. The remainder would be boiled down from the live shows recorded earlier in the year.

Even so, the clock was ticking, and when Tom Dowd walked into the studio, long inured to Cream's traditional fractiousness, even he was shocked by the tension and impatience that sparked between the three musicians. He put it down to road weariness, but he readily admitted, 'There were times when I thought they were going to kill each other.'

Baker was insistent that the flare-ups were simply the way Cream operated, that they portended nothing more than a reflexive letting-off of steam. 'It's alright most of the time. I tend to be bad-tempered, [but] I think it's a load of crap when people say we aren't working out as a group. We have had some plays that have been absolutely tremendous. We are three totally different personalities, and none of us thinks alike. But we get more and more together musically. It's a world class band, and I don't think there are three other musicians to touch us.'

Dowd, however, was not so certain and neither, following its release, was *Wheels of Fire* to offer anything that dismissed the swirling rumour mill. A brilliant album, a stunning achievement, a Herculean melding of craft and creativity, its centrepiece was nevertheless the dichotomy that dogged Cream throughout their career; the uneasy marriage of, on the studio disc, a succession of sharp, tight rock songs and, on the other, four sprawling jams, epitomising the half-life that this most life-enhancing of line-ups had suddenly found itself condemned to endure.

To modern ears, accustomed as they are to the 'legend' of Cream, the two faces are not so extreme. Journeying through the strangely Yardbirds-y 'Passing Time', the haunted neo-orchestrations of 'As

You Said', the lumbering 'Politician' and the eerie 'Deserted Cities of the Heart', we can slip from the whimsy of the studio record's 'Pressed Rat and Warthog' to the thunder of the in-concert 'Toad' and understand that the same man wrote them both.

At the time, however, they were as divisive as any other facet of the group. Reiterating the complaints it had slung at *Disraeli Gears*, *Rolling Stone* opened its review of the album with the admonishment, 'Cream is good at a number of things; unfortunately songwriting and recording are not among them. *Disraeli Gears* was far better.' The live record, on the other hand, was the food of the Gods. Preaching at a time when the vast majority of live albums were little more than contractual obligations, poorly recorded and even harder to listen to, the review insisted, 'This is the kind of thing that people who have seen Cream perform walk away raving about, and it's good to, at last, have it on a record.' Such enthusiasm still holds true. In 2003, *Classic Rock* magazine published its critics' choices of the Top Fifty live albums ever released. *Wheels of Fire* came in at number fifty.

But still the divide between the two discs was disconcerting. Even Polydor were so nervous about the LP's schizophrenia that, for the British release, the scheduled double album was also released as two individual discs (the snappy *In the Studio* in August, and the lumbering *Live at the Fillmore* in December), so that fans of one would not perforcedly be saddled with an unwanted other. Neither was it a wasted gesture. While the full weight *Wheels of Fire* marched to number three on the UK chart, the slimmed down *In the Studio* soared almost as high, to number seven. *Live at the Fillmore*, on the other hand, did not even make the listings.

The record was even bigger in America. The most eagerly awaited new release of a summer that was already girding for fresh albums from the Dead, the Airplane and Vanilla Fudge, and which had finally noticed Jeff Beck's year-old *Truth*, *Wheels of Fire* was released in America in July, and marched straight to the top of the chart, bumping brassman Herb Alpert out of the way in the process. It remained there for a month, until the latest by the Doors came to push it off its perch, but it was still in the album chart close to one year later.

'Sunshine of Your Love' was soon racing to join it. Originally released back in January, the single had dropped quietly out of the charts at the end of March. Now it had staged an absolutely unexpected revival, unstoppable until it breached the Top Five, and established itself in the process as the biggest-selling single in Atlantic's history so far. So much for psychedelic hogwash.

'White Room', the towering cathedral of sound that ignited *Wheels of Fire* itself, was swift to follow it up the chart and if, at the end of June 1968, Cream had chosen to mark their second birthday with any kind of celebration at all, it was in the knowledge that – in the words of the blues that cut through the studio disc – they were 'Sitting on Top of the World'.

There was no party, however; and no celebration of Cream's achievements. Rather, the group flew home to let it be known that all of Robert Stigwood's fears, Tom Dowd's misgivings, and the churning rumour mill's continued insistence had come to pass. Back in May, the UK press were full of reports that Cream were set to tour Britain during the summer; and as late as the end of June, the *New Musical Express* was confidently predicting 'concert tours for the next couple of months'. It was even reported that the band had already left the UK for Australia, where they were to headline a British blues festival. But it was all so much smoke. Instead, the 13 July issue of *Melody Maker* led with Chris Welch's world-exclusive report, CREAM SPLIT UP.

19. FARE THEE WELL

The break-up would not take place immediately. There would be a farewell tour of the United States, and two final concerts in London. There would be a memorial movie and one last LP. And there would be a future of music from all three members, with the possibility that, at some point, they would join forces once again.

People wondered when the decision was made, but in truth, it never was; the day the magic left the building and the fun sunk out of the bottom of the glass was not one that anybody could readily put a date to. But hindsight insisted that those conversations in Texas had a definite air of finality about them; one which Bruce's attempted escape out of Canada, a few days later, both emphasised and confirmed. Even the week-long vacation in April was now seen not so much as a rest, more a chance to cool off, as though Cream had already called it a day and then called Stigwood to tell him the news. But the holiday did not change their minds. It only strengthened their resolve.

Clapton was quick to confirm both the finality of the decision, and the reasons behind it. 'The Cream have lost direction,' he informed *Melody Maker* and, while Stigwood emphasised the trio's intention to 'follow their individual musical policies', the guitarist explained what that meant for him. 'With the Cream, solos were the thing, but I'm really off that virtuoso kick. It was all over-exposed. I went off on a lot of different things since the Cream formed, a lot of different directions all at once. But I find I have floated back to the straight blues playing. I've returned to what I like doing as an individual, and that is playing exploratory blues. I am and always will be a blues guitarist.'

He was already planning his next move, as well. 'I've already had plays with a few people, and I know the musicians I want,' he revealed. 'I'll start work on a new group in November.'

Clapton's bandmates were equally at ease with the decision to split up. Still seething over the songwriting division (or absence thereof) that had shattered Cream's original vision, Baker pointed out, 'If you listen to *Wheels of Fire*, there are none of Eric's things on it, which is wrong. What it boils down to is, we all like to write and get our musical ideas across, and it seems the only way we can do this is separately.'

Bruce, too, sympathised with Clapton's dilemma. Recalling the nights he spent quietly listening while Clapton prosletysed on behalf of The Band, Bruce acknowledged, 'Suddenly he was wondering what he was doing in his huge power rock band, when he could be doing something more subtle.' Lest it should somehow appear that the disintegration of Cream was wholly down to Clapton's own change in direction, however, he confessed that Clapton was not alone in questioning that fate.

As he gathered confidence as a writer, Bruce naturally looked to Cream as a vehicle for even his most ambitious compositions. But the group's success had narrowed those options beyond any comprehension – the merciless microscope that incredible success focuses upon an artist's work had already seen Cream come in for some violently personal criticism, merely for doing what they'd set out to do; reviews of 'Anyone for Tennis', for example, savaged the song for its simplicity, as though a fifteen minute bass solo might have made a more appropriate 45.

Personally, Bruce was aching to broaden Cream's remit even further. But he also knew that to do so would be to subject themselves to even more vicious attacks. And the band couldn't withstand any further assaults.

Clapton's own ambitions were the first to find a willing echo, via his friendship with Beatle George Harrison. He, too, knew how it felt to be playing in a group whose direction was lost; on the surface, as they worked towards *Sgt Pepper*'s long-awaited follow-up, the Beatles remained as strong as they'd ever been – but personal tensions were tearing them apart all the same, while Harrison's own dissatisfaction leaped up one further notch every time he brought another song into the studio, only for his fellows to barely give a second look.

The two guitarists had known one another since the Yardbirds played the Beatles' Christmas concert back in 1964; it was Harrison who invited Clapton to join the cast of almost-thousands that accompanied the Beatles on the live telecast of 'All You Need Is Love' at the end of June 1967; and who recruited him to the sessions for the movie soundtrack *Wonderwall*, where Clapton – appearing, on Ringo Starr's suggestion, beneath the fiendishly ingenious pseudonym of Eddie Clayton – layered some hard rock guitar against Harrison's eastern raga inflections. (The real-life Clayton was the eponymous frontman for one of Ringo's own first-ever bands, a Liverpool skiffle group in the late 1950s.)

Harrison and Clapton were to spend much of this latest summer together, both listening to music and making it. Their homes were practically next door to one another in the Surrey suburbs; many mornings, when both had business in London, Clapton drove them both into town. Inevitably, given their friendship, that business occasionally coincided. Just days after Cream returned to London, Clapton was dropping by Trident Studios, where Harrison was producing the debut album by Apple Records artist Jackie Lomax.

'Clapton did like five tracks with us, which was, to me, incredibly generous,' Lomax recalled. 'I knew Eric quite well, but I could not have used my influence to get him into the studio to record with me. George could, [and] Eric was great. He worked for hours.'

Clapton himself was so thrilled with the recordings that, again during that *Melody Maker* interview, he cued-up the backing track for one of the songs, 'Sour Milk Sea', to illustrate his own plans for the future. Warning his interrogator 'You can't say who it is' (Welch correctly guessed Harrison, Ringo Starr and Nicky Hopkins), he left the excited journalist commenting, 'If this is any indication of the sound Eric wants in the future, disappointed Cream fans can look forward to a great new group in replacement.'

A few days on, Clapton and Jack Bruce together paid a visit to the Decca Studios in West Hampstead, where Mike Vernon was recording the first album by singer Martha Velez, *Fiends and Angels*.

With Mitch Mitchell on drums, Brian Auger and Christine McVie on keyboards, and Jim Capaldi adding percussion, the pair played through four tracks, including Velez's forthcoming single, a marvellous take on Dylan's 'It Takes a Lot to Laugh, It Takes a Train to Cry'. For both, the opportunity to relax, side-by-side, into a simple song was one that they had not enjoyed in far too long, and maybe, for a moment, both realised that it wasn't a new band they needed, it was simply a new name, and a fresh start, for the group they already had. But both understood that there was no going back.

The best-remembered of all Clapton's collaborations came towards the end of the summer, on 6 September, when he and, again, George Harrison convened at Abbey Road's Studio Number 2 to complete a song that the remainder of the Beatles had all but written off.

Speaking of 'While My Guitar Gently Weeps', that most delicately moving of all his Beatle contributions, Harrison mourned, 'The [others] were not interested in it at all.' He alone seemed convinced that 'it was a nice song', but take after take passed by, and the performance was nowhere near completion. 'The next day I was with Eric, and I was going into the session, and I said, "We're going to do this song, come on and play on it."'

Clapton was horrified at the suggestion. 'I can't do that. Nobody ever plays on the Beatles' records.' But Harrison was adamant. 'I said "Look, it's my song and I want you to play on it." So Eric came in . . .'

Clapton, studio engineer Brian Gibson told Beatles historian Mark Lewisohn, was 'very quiet, [he] just got on and played. I remember [him] telling George that Cream's approach to recording would be rehearse, rehearse, rehearse, spending very little time in the studio itself, whereas the Beatles' approach seemed to be record, record, record and then eventually get the right one.' According to Abbey Road's own session log, 'While My Guitar Gently Weeps' ran to 44 separate takes, although Clapton was involved with only one, take 25.

The final performance wasn't merely destined to emerge one of the most timeless songs in the Beatles' entire catalogue, it also represents one of Clapton's own most beautiful guitar solos, one that has excited the imagination and admiration of fellow players ever since, as Peter Frampton explained, after he covered the song for his 2003 album *Now*.

'I started doing "While My Guitar Gently Weeps" on the *Rock Symphony* tour with Roger Daltrey and Alice Cooper. I don't do many covers, but that was one I'd always wanted to try. We tried to simplify it. John [Regan]'s bass line is a lot simpler than McCartney's, and I was never going to try and compete with Eric [Clapton]'s solo.' The end result, *Goldmine* magazine enthused, was 'a scratchily energetic number that ranks alongside . . . Siouxsie & the Banshees' version of "Blue Jay Way" in the realm of genuinely worthwhile Harrison covers'; praise to which Frampton could only respond, 'Well, it has to be worthwhile. You have to make it your own, otherwise you might as well just play the original record.'

While Clapton hovered in the limelight, his bandmates were somewhat less visible, although neither was inactive. Ginger Baker spent much of his summer in the company of Phil Seaman and, on 10 August, the second day of that year's National Jazz & Blues Festival, the advertised 'special guest appearance' of Ginger Baker was revealed as a gigantic drum duel between the two masters – with added Eric power. Clapton appeared on stage a few minutes into the first number, unrecognised by the vast majority of the watching crowd. Then compere John Gee ran onto the stage and grabbed a microphone. 'And who's this?' he asked the audience. 'It's Eric Clapton!'

'Most of what they did was spontaneous improvisation,' *NME* reviewer Keith Altham taunted stay-away readers the following week, '[and] most of it was bordering on the realms of musical genius. Poor Arthur Brown, [who] had to follow that.'

Jack Bruce, too, was soon itching for some kind of return to action and, one evening in early August, he found himself back on stage with Dick Heckstall-Smith and Jon Hiseman, playing through the interval at the 100 Club.

The pair was busily assembling Colosseum at the time, but the opportunity, as Heckstall-Smith chuckled, to 'blast hell out of some music somewhere', with Bruce alongside them, was a notion he'd been 'fancying for quite a time. It was just a short set, filling in the support spot for a band about which I can remember nothing, except that, in the matter of styles, it was a wild contrast to the kind of thing we were up to.' *That*, he continued, was 'a real rip-roaring, take no prisoners set with only the barest of perfunctory nods towards anything like a tune, and all three of us were dripping with sweat and ecstasy when our half-hour was up. We fell, ululating, on one another's necks, and swore we must do it again.'

In the event, the trio never returned to the stage. Just days later, however, Bruce was on the phone to Heckstall-Smith, explaining how Stigwood had just given him the money to make a solo album, and he wanted to record it with the trio. In fact he wound up with a quartet when, leaving IBC Studios after the first day's recording, Bruce spotted John McLaughlin walking down the road, 'with his guitar in one hand and his amplifier in the other, so I stopped my Ferrari and asked him what he was doing'. The following morning, McLaughlin was in the studio with the others.

True to the determination that helped pave the way for Cream's dissolution, Bruce intended his first solo flight to travel in directions that the band could never have countenanced. He had already amassed an impressive stockpile of songs, both offerings that Cream had rejected, and more personal efforts he had never even presented to them. But there was also a crop of compositions, jazz pieces for the most part, that dated back, he said, to when he was eleven. 'Composers don't ever throw anything away – you never know when you can recycle things.'

His primary goal was to return to his roots, something he had not even glanced towards in longer than he cared to remember. 'I had always wanted to make a jazz record ... [and] I was keen to go back to my earliest compositions, because I think it's when you're very young that you develop the ideas you continually rework to form the basis of the rest of your life.' It was, he confessed, 'strange' returning to material he'd not played in fifteen years; but enlightening, as well. 'One thing that struck me was that I must have been a pretty sophisticated eleven-year-old!'

Completed in just three days, and mixed within a fourth, the ensuing *Things We Like* LP was described by Dick Heckstall-Smith as 'one of the very few recordings I've made that *I* like'. It was, however, scarcely likely to wring the same effect from Bruce's own, regular audience; as with the 100 Club show, it barrelled along with madness but rarely a melody, with even Heckstall-Smith's showboating medley of Milt Jackson's 'Sam's Sack' and Mel Tormé's 'Born to Be Blue' barely distinguishable as the sum of its part. Bruce himself described the record as little more than 'a pet project I had wanted to do ... to get a jazz record out of my system', while Polydor were certainly in no hurry to release it to the world. *Things We Like* remained on the shelf for the best part of two years, before finally being pushed out as a successor to *Songs For a Tailor* – Bruce's 'official' solo debut album.

Around so much activity, the summer passed too quickly. Barely had Cream celebrated another strong showing in the latest *Melody Maker* readers poll, third behind the Beatles and the Stones in both the UK and International Best Group lists, than their final, *Farewell*, American tour was scheduled to kick off at the Oakland Coliseum on 4 October.

Cream arrived in California to find that the mania they left behind them in June had only become more frenzied. 'White Room', the first single from *Wheels of Fire*, was en route to number six, while its chart-topping parent was still exploding out of FM radio, as jocks across the country dropped seven minutes of 'Train Time', or seventeen minutes of 'Toad' into their airplay schedules, knowing that their listeners would be glued to every minute. Atlantic were even contemplating issuing the live version of 'Crossroads' as the next single; short though it was, still its four-minute lifespan encapsulated all the hyperbolic intensity of Cream in full flight.

The latest tour itinerary reflected back those statistics. Unlike their last American outing, this new round of shows felt no need to dwell on the minor markets that had so congested the spring undertaking. There were no school auditoriums or town halls this time, even if the promoters were able to afford the $60,000 or so that the band now commanded *per night*; and, such was the demand for tickets that just twenty shows in seventeen cities ensured Cream ended the year as the biggest concert draw on the entire American circuit, with even their closest competitors – Hendrix, the Doors and the Who – leagues behind them.

Familiar faces awaited them at Oakland Coliseum, as Felix Pappalardi and Bill Halverson flew in to record the first of the four shows that would be preserved for posterity; the other three, in Los Angeles and San Diego two weeks (but only four Midwestern concerts) later, ensured that the band's entire farewell repertoire could be eased out over any number of future releases. In LA, too, the group had the opportunity to meet one of the new British groups that would, within just a couple of months, be vying to plug the immense void on the Stateside live circuit that Cream's demise would produce.

Deep Purple, a new sessioneer super-gang formed in London earlier in the year, were just coming down from their first American hit, a flamboyant rendition of Joe South's 'Hush'. They would be joining the Cream tour for the remainder of its run, before heading off on their own headlining outing.

The musicians nodded their acquaintance – guitarist Ritchie Blackmore traced his career back to Screaming Lord Sutch's Savages; Clapton had run into them often during his Yardbirds days. Drummer Ian Paice and singer Rod Evans had shared Robert Stigwood as a manager, when their last group, the Maze, recorded a single for Reaction; and each of the other members, organist Jon Lord and bassist Nick Simper, had rattled around the periphery of vision for at least a few years.

Yet it was not to be a happy reunion. By agreeing to share the cost of the mobile studio, Purple's label, Tetragrammaton arranged to set the tapes rolling a little earlier, to capture their show as well. Released some three decades on as *Live at the Forum*, the ensuing tape found the newcomers unexpectedly opening their show with the hit, before turning the rest of their performance into an endless jam through the self-penned pieces, 'Mandrake Root' and 'Wring That Neck'.

It was a stunning performance, as loud as it was dynamic, as solid as it was skilful; and that, voices in the Deep Purple camp mused afterwards, might be why the group's tenure on the tour was cut so brutally short; *not* because Deep Purple were upstaging the headliners, but because they could be seen to be trying to. Either way, Deep Purple survived just three nights on the tour, two at the Forum and one in San Diego, before they were invited to take their leave.

The dismissal was not, Purple keyboard player Jon Lord insisted, anything to do with Cream. 'We got on well with them. They had no idea we were to be taken off the tour. They were too stoned!' Besides, at the time the fateful decision was taken by an assortment of promotion, record company and management staff, Cream themselves had far more pressing matters to worry about, such as how to get Jack Bruce and half of the road crew out of jail.

Travelling down the Californian coast, San Diego is the last American city before the Mexican border and, following the show, Bruce, wife Janet, and a few of Cream's roadies leaped into the bassist's car and headed south.

Mexico itself was something of a legendary counter-cultural destination at the time – a few years earlier, word seeped out about a Mazatec healer, Mariá Sabina, and a potent crop of magic mushrooms, that were to be found around Huautla, in the southeastern corner of the country. Since that time, any number of rock glitterati had made the pilgrimage to El Fórtin, her home ... Donovan namechecks it in 'Mellow Yellow'; Lennon and

McCartney supposedly wrote 'The Long and Winding Road' about the journey to the village; Dylan and Pete Townshend allegedly dropped by to visit.

With them, and around them, there arrived hundreds of others: hippies, drop-outs, stoners, the flotsam of the flower-power movement come to sample the region's wares, and discover why Donovan claimed to be 'mad about Fórtin'. Instead, they discovered why 'Fórtin's mad about me'. Deluged by the dregs, the locals declared virtual war on the invaders, while back at the border, American customs officials grew so accustomed to hauling over another in-coming camper van packed to the ceiling with bags of magic mushrooms, that any vehicle heading towards America with a cargo full of hippy-types was considered fair game for a bout of stop-and-search. Especially when the occupants were clearly out of their heads.

Bruce and company did not travel to Huautla; they did not even come close to it. Rather ... the chain of events was foggy, but somehow the party wound up in the company of a group of shepherds, and spent the day drinking in a tiny bar in the absolute middle of nowhere.

Desperately intoxicated, they eventually turned for home, but as they neared the border crossing, the sudden realisation that drunk driving was a serious offence in the United States persuaded Bruce to do something very foolish indeed. He stopped the car and hid the keys. He remained in the driver's seat.

The consequences were inevitable. The entire party was swept away to the local police station, to the accompaniment of Bruce's impassioned insistence, 'You can't do this, I'm number one in the charts!' And it was that insistence, more than its reality, which saved the day. Within minutes, word of the arrest was spreading throughout the neighbourhood and an army of hippies was descending upon the police station, intent upon springing their idol from his cell, and redecorating the entire place with flowers. By the time word got back to the rest of Cream, waiting and wondering back in San Diego, the police were about ready to release their prisoners then and there.

Two shows at the Rhode Island Auditorium, on 4 November, concluded the American farewell tour. The true climax to the outing, however, arrived two days earlier, at Madison Square Garden, New York, not the biggest stadium in America, but certainly one of the most iconic. The fourth New York stadium to bear that name, this latest incarnation of the showpiece Garden had opened just nine months before; Cream, in fact, were the first rock band to play there, and it was there that the trio finally realised precisely how far their journey had taken them.

Bruce described standing with Clapton at the back of some auditorium or another, gazing towards the tiny spots that were barely visible on the stage, and remarking 'We've come a long way from the Twisted Wheel.' But it was at the 220,000 capacity Garden that the full extent of that voyage was brought home to them.

On a revolving stage that made Bruce feel like he was a boxer ('I should have been in the blue corner'), each musician was presented with a platinum disc, to represent two million dollars worth of records sold, the first such award ever issued.

Leonard Bernstein, no friend or fan of rock in general, came out in support of Cream. 'I mean, they've got a drummer who can really keep time!'

Caroline and John Jr, the children of assassinated President John F Kennedy, were formally introduced to the group; and the corridors outside the dressing rooms were filled with paraplegics and cripples, all begging to be touched by their idols – see me, feel me, heal me. In the beginning, only Eric Clapton was God. Now all three of them had ascended to the same insane status.

Cream's remaining lifespan could now be measured in days, not weeks. It was time to start wrapping things up. The day after the Rhode Island show, the trio flew back to California, to bunker in at Wally Heider's studio in Los Angeles for a final bout of recording, the triptych of instrumental backing tracks that formed the framework of a last will and statement.

When all concerned first began discussing what would become Cream's final album, the original concept was to serve up another double, repeating *Wheels of Fire*'s proven formula of half live, half studio. It was obvious, however, that the group had neither the energy, nor the inclination, to put together an entire disc's worth of new material. The album was trimmed accordingly; there would be just three new songs, and the tape that travelled back to London with the group titled each one according to its author: 'Eric's Tune', 'Jack's Tune' and 'Ginger's Tune'.

Cream flew into Heathrow on a moist November morning, and they knew they were home the moment they stepped off the plane, as customs caught one glimpse of their stash of platinum discs and started to calculate the duty that was owed on them. It never dawned on the officials – or the band, for that matter – that one of rock'n'roll's most treasured honours is no more sincere than a lot of the industry's other baubles, but one day Jack Bruce removed one of his discs from its frame, and tried playing it on his stereo. It was a mispressed Louis Armstrong album, with metallic paint daubed over the grooves.

Felix Pappalardi was in the studio with Leslie West and Corky Laing at the time, producing and playing on the momentous sessions that ultimately spawned the American power trio Mountain. Wrapping up that project, he flew to London and Cream reconvened for the next-to-last time at IBC Studios a day or two later, to complete recording the three songs they'd begun in Los Angeles.

It was a hurried occasion; in fact, the band was actually in the studio and recording when Pete Brown received a midnight phone call from Bruce, playing the tape of 'Jack's Tune' down the telephone, and asking for lyrics as quickly as possible.

Holding a microphone to the handset, Brown taped the tune on flatmate Dick Heckstall-Smith's Grundig, and asked Bruce what the song was about. 'He said it was autobiographical. As I played [the tape] back, I wrote most of the words around the few that Jack already had, and then I phoned them back to [him]. We made some small adjustments during the call, but that was "Doing That Scrapyard Thing".'

Baker's contribution had metamorphosed into the wryly titled and so-lovably barrelling 'What a Bringdown', while Clapton's composition was now paired with a set of George Harrison verses that he, too, completed in the studio while the band was recording, but which he never quite got around to titling. 'I wrote most of the words,' Harrison explained, 'and Eric had the bridge and the first couple of chord changes. I was writing the words down and, when we came to the middle bit, I wrote "bridge". And from where he was sitting, opposite me, he looked and said, "What's that – 'badge'?" So he called it "Badge" because it made him laugh.'

It also became one of the best-loved songs in Cream's entire canon, an indelibly funky bass line married to spectral melody, a chiming guitar line, not a lick, more a gentle nuzzle, and a lyric that revealed far more than it said before sliding into a scintillating Clapton solo and then, at 2.14, a heartstopping chord change before the final verse ... 'talking about a girl that looks quite like you'; if you could bottle that moment and sell it to songwriters, there'd never be another lousy record made again.

Bruce supplied the piano that runs through the song, but it was Harrison, not Clapton, whose guitar powered the first half of the song. 'Eric doesn't play guitar up until [that] bridge,' Harrison continued. 'I played the rhythm chops right up until the bridge, at which point Eric came in on the guitar, with Leslie. And he overdubbed the solo later.' To avoid any contractual wranglings surrounding his performance, incidentally, Harrison renamed himself L'Angelo Misterioso for the occasion.

Clapton was not the only band member to be impressed by Harrison's presence. Bruce, too, was overwhelmed. 'I first had the privilege of working with him on the *Goodbye* sessions and his wonderful rhythm guitar work on "Badge" prompted me to ask him to play on "Never Tell Your Mother She's Out of Tune" on *Songs for a Tailor* [another credit for L'Angelo Misterioso!]. He took the session so seriously that he arrived at the studio an hour before anyone else, in order to be prepared for the live recording!' Speaking shortly after Harrison's death in November 2001, Bruce also joked, 'I always felt a special empathy with him, the "Quiet Beatle" as I guess I was also the "Quiet Cream"!'

For all Cream's relief over being so close to the end of the road, the run-up to the final concert was nerve-wracking all the same. Stigwood had booked the Royal Albert Hall for the occasion, two shows on Tuesday 26 November. But it was so long since Cream played their last British show that they doubted whether anybody even remembered who they were.

Time passed a lot slower in those days – a few months out of the limelight, and even the most successful act could find itself dead in the water before it returned; the streets were littered with the carcasses of performers who'd set out to break America, and broken their homeland fans' hearts instead. Even Jeff Beck, no stranger to keeping his own fans waiting, warned Cream that, 'If they [don't] look after their public in this country, they might lose their tremendous popularity.'

But the moment tickets went on sale for the Cream farewell concerts – one in the afternoon, one in the evening – the queues that had patiently built up outside the stately Victorian hall over the previous two or three days devoured every one of them. Other troupes might find themselves forlornly forsaken, but Cream, it seemed, were unforgettable.

Opening sets by two of the hottest young acts on the London circuit of the day, Rory Gallagher's Irish blues renegades Taste, and the symphonic ambitions of Yes, warmed up the audience for the main attraction, the former on the back of an acclaimed debut album, the latter still aching to be offered the chance to begin theirs. Robert Stigwood had already expressed an interest in Yes and had arranged for them to open the Cream show as an audition of sorts. Yet it was not a test that Yes especially relished.

Guitarist Pete Banks complained, 'We didn't have very long to play, thirty minutes ... and we were not happy about that. I remember the show being very rushed, and we didn't have a sound-check because Cream was the headline band, and they had equipment everywhere. I mean, there were Marshall stacks coming out of the walls, as many as you could imagine. So we had to fit around all of this. We weren't allowed to do an encore, [and] they kept most of the house lights on during our set ... people were still arriving, and you could see them trying to find their seats and what-not, so it was very uninspirational.'

Nevertheless, they acquitted themselves well – so well, in fact, that Stigwood was left behind in the ensuing race for Yes's signatures, pipped to the post by Ahmet Ertegun's Atlantic. Yes's own stellar rise to the top commenced there, just as Cream's demise played out its final act.

To memorialise an unrepeatable moment in time, *Twice a Fortnight* director Tony Palmer was recruited to film both shows for a documentary, *Farewell Cream*, to be broadcast in the UK within the BBC's weekly *Omnibus* arts digest, before receiving a full-on cinema release around the rest of the world. 'I had no idea that they were going to split up,' said Palmer. 'But I suddenly got this call from Eric saying he was pretty sure that the Royal Albert Hall concerts would be their last, and could I film it? Well, if you really want me to . . .'

It was an astute decision. More than twenty years before MTV arrived to revolutionise the way we look at music, 'pop television' was a very rare commodity, the preserve either of the weekly half-hour dedicated to the likes of *Top of the Pops* and BBC2's newly launched *Colour Me Pop*, or guest appearances on variety, comedy and family shows.

More scholarly ventures, such as the magazine-style *The Look of the Week* existed, but they tended towards the darkly disapproving – oft-repeated in the years since its original, May 1967, broadcast, Pink Floyd's encounter with classical music critic Professor Hans Keller set the tone for a lot of what passed as 'serious' music television in those days, as the fiercely disapproving Keller criticised everything from the Floyd's volume ('terribly loud') to their very approach to music ('a regression to childhood'). The idea of being able to turn on the television, or turn up at the cinema, to catch a full-length, non-aggressive consideration of any pop act whatsoever was a nigh-on impossible dream.

It was Palmer himself who set the ball rolling towards a more fluid approach, one that would, within a couple of years, see films and documentaries shot around any number of groups and performers (Palmer's own subsequent list of subjects includes Fairport Convention, Colosseum, Frank Zappa, Leonard Cohen, Rory Gallagher and Tangerine Dream). Around June 1967, he recalled, 'I was asked by [BBC head] Huw Wheldon, "You know about rock'n'roll . . . could you make us a film that explains it?" It was as simple as that.' The result was *All My Loving*, still one of the greatest rock documentaries ever made.

Palmer credited John Lennon, one of his closest friends, for suggesting the framework that assured *All My Loving*'s immortality. 'I went to him and said, "If we do this film, what should we do?" And he said the most important thing we could do was get onto the screen the groups that could not, at that point in time, get on – such as Frank Zappa, such as the Who *really* going crazy, such as Hendrix, such as Cream. So I made a film that included them all' – the Cream footage was shot live at both Winterland and the Fillmore in February 1968.

All My Loving was broadcast for the first time just three weeks before the Royal Albert Hall concerts; and, though only a couple of Cream clips were seen in the show, even those mere moments of 'Toad' and 'I'm So Glad' contributed much to what the *Daily*

Express described as 'a disturbing piece of television . . . which no parent could afford to miss . . . a psychedelic experience which ten years from now will be the definitive document of its time. How often,' demanded reviewer James Thomas, 'does television *really* make you sit on the edge of your chair?'

Palmer's brief was different this time around. *All My Loving* concentrated on the powerful presence of rock in general. *Farewell Cream* was centred on the majesty of one group alone, with Palmer taking full advantage of the two scheduled shows by filming them both for absorption into one. He succeeded admirably. Although modern sensibilities might be somewhat bemused by the interview sequences which separate the songs, as Bruce, Clapton and Baker in turn discuss their music and musicianship, the live footage itself is spectacular; even on those occasions when, to take advantage of a better camera angle, the edit switches from one concert . . . and, hence, one set of stage clothes . . . to another.

Yet, in future years (and certainly in past Cream biographies), it was reported that the musicians themselves loathed the finished film; that Clapton vowed never to speak to Palmer again, so disgusted was he with *Farewell Cream*. The director himself, however, had a very different take on the group's dissatisfaction.

> I know one thing they did get upset about, that they did object to, was that when it was released in the cinema, it was not thought to be long enough. So somebody added in some scenes, which had nothing to do with me. One of the technical problems that we faced when we shot the film was, when they said they wanted it filmed, I said the way to do it was on video tape. But this was 1968, very primitive times technologically speaking, and the problem with video at that point was, colour video tape had only just started and you couldn't edit the damned stuff. The only way you could do it was with a razor blade, and then it wouldn't necessarily join up. So the only thing we could do was cut it as we were going, which I did, I cut it myself.
>
> We filmed an 85-minute version, but *Omnibus* was only about 52 minutes, so we cut it. But when it was released in the cinemas, when it was transferred to 35-millimetre film, it was not thought to be long enough. So somebody in Stigwood Land went back and got the sound recordings, then fitted them to the pictures – which meant it wasn't in synch. There was a film cameraman there as well, so they added in that material, which became even more bizarre because it looks completely different. So the whole thing was a bit of a mishmash.

However, the extent of Cream's true response to *Farewell Cream* can be measured from their own future relations with Palmer.

> The first thing that happened after the Cream film was, Jack had bought this island off Scotland and wanted me to go shoot him up there, so we made *Rope Ladder to the Moon* (another *Omnibus* special), which he absolutely adored. Then Ginger got rather cross about that and said, 'Well, what about one with me?' So we went off to Lagos via the Sahara Desert and did some amazing shooting of him and Fela Ransome Kuti, among others – and that became *Ginger Baker in Africa*; and Eric was hovering in the background, and we were always talking about doing something, but we kept putting it off and putting it off for one reason or another.

Besides, it's unlikely that the group could have been truly satisfied with any lasting reminder of their final concerts. No less than when the tapes rolled at concerts, all three complained that the farewell performances were nowhere near the best that Cream had ever played; all three agreed with *Rolling Stone*'s assessment of a certain 'poised quality . . . [a] detachment, the structure looked down upon from the stars – a self-begotten music whose brilliance seemed born of itself without labour. Cream have never played so formally.'

The set list, the same at both shows, disappointed, as well. Where they could have relaxed into a showcase of all that made Cream special, both on vinyl and in concert, the group reiterated the same barnstorming repertoire they'd dragged across the United States for much of the past nine months: 'White Room', 'Politician', 'I'm So Glad', 'Sitting on Top of the World', 'Crossroads', 'Toad', 'Spoonful', 'Sunshine of Your Love' and 'Stepping Out'.

But what were people really expecting? The weight of anticipation that built up before the show, among musicians and audience alike, was such that nothing short of perfection could have passed muster – and even that would probably have ruffled somebody's feathers. Besides, for all the concerts' faults, Bruce will still admit, 'We arrived at the Albert Hall feeling it would be good to get the whole thing finished with, but once we got on stage and started playing, it felt great. I remember looking at Eric onstage and I could see he was thinking the same thing as me: "Have we done the right thing?" If any one of us had said we hadn't, we might have stayed together.'

They didn't. Instead, 'We left the stage and just went our separate ways. There was no end-of-band party, we didn't even go for a farewell dinner. It was a case of coming off, going to our separate dressing rooms and then off into the night with our entourages and groupies and whatever. We didn't even shake hands.'

They thought it was all over . . . and it was.

EPILOGUE
BURIED BY THE MACHINE

The trio went their separate ways. Within weeks of saying farewell to Cream, Clapton was among the cast of itinerant minstrels performing at the Rolling Stones *Rock And Roll Circus* extravaganza, toying once more with the supergroup concept as he accompanied Keith Richard, Mitch Mitchell and John and Yoko Lennon in the Dirty Macs.

Weeks after that, while Jack Bruce launched the sessions that produced his landmark *Songs for a Tailor* solo album, Clapton and Baker were reunited in rehearsals for Blind Faith, the band that Cream could have become, as Steve Winwood (and, replacing Bruce, Family bassist Ric Grech) deserted Traffic for a new unit designed to steal back the thunder that the Band had battered the guitarist with.

Even as the earth was stamped down upon Cream's grave, however, so the mourning media's florid tributes gave way to more lasting vinyl memorials.

Of course there was some resentment over the way it had all gone belly-up; the *New Musical Express*'s Derek Johnson spoke for many when he slammed Cream for '[turning] its back on the fans who were directly responsible for its success'. But even he had to admit that the band's first posthumous UK single, a belated release for 'White Room', was destined for the chart; and, though 'Cream may be gone, it is certainly not forgotten – particularly when there are records like this to perpetuate its memory'.

In March 1969, the same month that Clapton and Bruce regrouped as part of Independent Television's *Superjam* extravaganza, blasting along beside Roland Kirk, Jon Hiseman and Dick Heckstall-Smith, Cream's final studio recordings were released as part of the pre-arranged *Goodbye* farewell album, nestling alongside three recordings from the LA Forum in October. The album topped the UK chart, while a single of 'Badge' at least made the Top Twenty, a lowly return for such a magnificent record, but further proof that Cream would not be swept beneath the carpet.

In June, as Blind Faith prepared for their much bally-hooed concert debut with a freebie in Hyde Park, the London *Evening Standard* previewed the show by describing the event as Cream's farewell performance. The following month, while Blind Faith toured the United States, Tony Palmer's *Farewell Cream* movie received its New York cinema premiere, and the first *Best of Cream* compilation arrived, to immortalise the group's hit singles-and-such.

In 1970, while Clapton enjoyed solo success with a laid-back cover of JJ Cale's 'After Midnight', the succinctly titled *Live Cream* emerged to remind people of when it was volume, not vibes, that rocked Clapton's world; in 1972, as Derek and the Dominoes' two-year-old 'Layla' headed towards the American Top Ten, *Live Cream Volume Two* was in the stores awaiting it.

And so on. From the umpteenth reissue of the band's original albums, to the lowliest once-more-go-round of their greatest hits, from the visual chicanery of the *Strange Brew* video collection, to the epic extravagance of the 4CD *Those Were the Days* box set anthology, Cream's two-year, four-album legacy has taken on an afterlife that even its creators could scarcely have imagined. At the same time the three players' own careers have spiralled off on tracks so unique, and certainly so different that it sometimes seems difficult to believe that they ever shared a dressing room together, let alone a group of such single-minded brilliance that its shadow still overhangs the rock scene today.

For many modern observers, the immensity of that shadow was confirmed when Cream were inducted into the Rock and Roll Hall of Fame.

To cynics (and there are plenty), the Rock and Roll Hall of Fame is just one more in the ever-expanding roster of self-congratulatory enterprises with which the American entertainment industry has been obsessed, since baseball inducted its first Hall of Fame-r in 1939. Soon, every sport, every art, every field of human endeavour, it seemed, had its own Hall of Fame and, in 1983, popular music joined the list, with the foundation of the Rock and Roll Hall of Fame in Cleveland.

With membership of the hallowed halls restricted to artists whose careers spanned at least 25 years, the Hall of Fame held its first induction ceremony in 1986, welcoming the cream of the very first wave of rock'n'rollers into its midst: Chuck Berry, Elvis Presley, Jerry Lee Lewis and Buddy Holly. In 1987 it was the turn of the

doo-wop and early soul era; and 1988 brought the first acknowledgement of 'modern' rock, as the Beatles, the Beach Boys and Bob
Dylan were brought into the fold.

As individuals, all three members of Cream were eligible for
induction that same year; with Cream first mooted for inclusion in
1991. In the event, it was two more years before they were
honoured, by which time Clapton had already made his own
appearance in the Hall as a member of the Yardbirds, inducted in
1992. (As a solo artist, he received a third induction in 2000.)

Cream finally took the rostrum on 12 January 1993, alongside
the Doors, Van Morrison, Sly and the Family Stone, and
(somewhat belatedly) Etta James and Frankie Lymon and the
Teenagers. Then, before an audience who paid up to $1,000 a
head to attend, and taking the stage together for the first time in
a quarter of a century, Bruce, Baker and Clapton performed three
songs – 'Born Under a Bad Sign', 'Crossroads' and 'Sunshine of
Your Love', rehearsing them for an afternoon the day before the
show, then stepping out to play them as though mere weeks, not
decades, had passed since the last time they performed. 'The
magic was still there,' Baker agreed afterwards. 'It was as if we
had just been away on holiday.'

Of course, the event was a one-off. There was some vague
discussion of writing and recording together once again, and Bruce
and Baker did hook up again immediately afterwards, 'replacing'
Clapton with Gary Moore in a new trio, BBM. But the reality of the
music industry, and of the band members' own lives and careers,
dictated that anything more permanent was not forthcoming. 'We
have played together a few other times, at people's weddings,' Bruce
shrugged off-handedly a decade later. But, in terms of any serious
intention, it was eleven years more before Cream again considered
coming together once more.

The trio's reluctance to re-form was understandable. Within a
year of Cream's original demise, Bruce was acknowledging,
'whatever [we] do [in the future] will be compared with Cream',
and lamenting audiences' refusal to accept his own then-latest
project, the *ad-hoc* Jack Bruce & Friends, as anything beyond a
Cream surrogate. 'Audiences expected lots of Cream numbers,' he
reflected. 'In fact we only did three out of eighteen.' On another
occasion, during 1970, Bruce actually cancelled a concert because
he saw the incriminating legend 'ex-Cream' on the promotional
posters, in defiant contradiction of his own contractual stipulations.

Eric Clapton's entire solo career, too, has been conducted not necessarily in the shadow of Cream, but at least in clear view of it. Every
time a new Clapton compilation rolls out, a handful of Cream songs
are inevitably included, while his live show has little alternative but to
throw in a few Creamy crowd-pleasers alongside 'Layla', 'Wonderful
Tonight' and 'I Shot the Sheriff'. And, though Ginger Baker has

shaken off many of the old ghosts, he has done so only by refusing to indulge in any musical activity that was even remotely capable of raising them. It was only once he was on stage with the other pair at the Rock and Roll Hall of Fame, reliving the pure musical synchronicity that Cream had once enjoyed, that his face opened up into that trademark goofy grin of his; and, watching the film footage of the event, it was hard to shake one thought from your mind – he looked like he'd just come home for the first time in a long while.

For many people, of course, it remains difficult to understand why any of the musicians left home in the first place. Cream were not the first band, by a long chalk, to exist on a diet of mutual antipathy – the four members of the Who, and the Kinks' founding Davies brothers, famously battled for as long as their bands held together, a span that can be measured in decades, not mere months. More recently, Oasis' Gallagher siblings punched and kicked their way through a five-year reign that produced some of the 90s' most invigorating pop.

But the pressures that crushed Cream were not merely personal; for, if they were, the band might have survived. Pete Townshend once described the band as having been 'created by the machine', in that the principles that brought the musicians together were founded firmly on abilities that the media had raised and praised to unprecedented levels. But the band was also buried by it, crushed beneath the soulless repetition of thankless concerts and mindless TV, of guileless profiteering and guiltless greed. Cream, their supporters insisted, were 'special'. But they were not treated any differently to any other band of the age; they were, in fact, milked more mercilessly than acts of far more stability and structure, as though the machine itself realised that such a union was, by its very nature, fragile, and needed to be sucked bone-dry before it collapsed beneath the weight of its own expectations.

And so it proved. In years to come, all three members of the group offered up their own hypotheses on why Cream blazed so briefly; on why their legacy is so much less than it ought to be (and their reputation, perhaps, so much greater than it ought to be – for they never hit the heights they were aiming for, regardless of the standards they set for everyone else).

Their workload, their temperament, the world in which they flourished, have all been lined up as the villains who robbed us of Cream's presence, but it was Eric Clapton, speaking just a couple of years after Cream imploded, who perhaps hit the nail the hardest on the head:

> The Cream were a source of great confusion to me. It had to end, and I don't think I could be a part of something like that now. Musically, its significance was rather like Pete Townshend said – 'a product of that time', symbolic of an era. It became a very heavy virtuoso thing without anyone really contributing

to a whole. I don't think there will ever be another group to take its place for success, you know, unless it invents a new formula, because we were the first trio, and the first kind of virtuoso people to do it.

For his part:

The virtuoso thing was a substitute for the fact that I wasn't singing myself, that I wasn't expressing myself through my words and my music and so I had to force it through a guitar.

For his bandmates, that same lack of the most personal control was expressed in their own brand of overachievement. Only once they had placed Cream behind them were they able to even begin to consider what they'd accomplished, and then bring the weight of that experience to bear upon the music they've been making ever since; and only then were they able to show, as individuals, all that Cream could, should, maybe even would, have achieved as a unit.

Were Cream to form for the first time today, with all the experience and expertise that its members could now bring to the table, they truly would be the greatest band the world has ever seen. Instead, we can only await their re-formation, sometime in 2005 says Jack Bruce, and hope that nostalgia is not the band's only driving force.

For the spirit of Cream does live on, in every band that tears itself away from its records and allows the live environment to shape what they play; in every performer who looks to the future when he steps into the studio, because what's done is done and you cannot remake the past hits forever; and in every musician who knows he's already taken his instrument as far as he can, but pushes on into its possibilities regardless.

Those were the attributes that first flavoured Cream; those, in crystallised nuggets across each of their studio albums, and in tanta-lising glimpses on the live tapes and records, were those that they strived to achieve. And, if rock history has magnified those achieve-ments out of all proportion, until even the musicians barely recognise their accomplishments for all the banners and bunting that coat them, then that only serves to underline the tragedy of Cream's triumph.

But, for all their failings, their complaints and mismanagement, for all the criticism, hypocrisy and scorn, and for all the manifold other flaws that scarred their time together, Cream's ultimate killer was their audience's expectations, and the musicians' refusal to disappoint them. In other words, Cream were literally loved to death. And it was not a nice way to go.

APPENDIX
WHERE NEXT, YOUNG MAN?

GINGER BAKER

Ginger Baker commenced re-evaluating his musical career the moment Blind Faith conceded that the entire project was doomed. Within months of the group's June 1969 concert debut, at London's Hyde Park, within weeks of the release of a self-titled debut album, and within days of the last night of a massively oversubscribed American tour, Blind Faith was already a memory.

Baker bounced back almost immediately, retaining Steve Winwood and Ric Grech, reuniting with Graham Bond, and recruiting his old idol Phil Seaman in Ginger Baker's Airforce, a sprawling, percussion based outfit that ultimately pursued its founder's fascination with African rhythms to their logical conclusion. Originally formed to play just two live shows, the group's lifespan was ultimately extended across a full tour and a pair of albums, as promoters and Polydor alike somehow divined a commercial future for a ten-piece aggregation that espoused jazz, blues, folk and rock alongside its African heartbeat.

The group lasted a year; then, in 1971 Baker, keen to continue his African education, and together with filmmaker Tony Palmer, travelled across the Sahara to Lagos, Nigeria, where Baker's stunning union with local musician Fela Kuti was captured on the album *Fela Ransome Kuti & Ginger Baker Live*. Baker subsequently formed his own troupe of Nigerian musicians, Salt; he also helped Kuti establish the country's first sixteen-track recording studio. It opened in 1973; Africa 70's *He Miss Road*, produced by

Kuti and Baker, was one of the studio's first recordings; Paul McCartney and Wings' *Band on the Run* one of the best known. Baker himself recorded his solo album *Stratavarious* there, before unpaid bills (including, he has claimed, McCartney's) saw him lose both the studio and most of his own money.

Baker returned to Britain in 1974, linking with the brothers Paul and Adrian Gurvitz, plus former Sharks vocalist Steve 'Snips' Parsons, in the jazz-fusion Baker–Gurvitz Army; that project collapsed during the late 1970s, having rarely achieved even a fraction of its original promise, and Baker's career thereafter paid more attention to his non-musical activities – playing polo, operating an olive farm, raising horses and, after 21 years, finally kicking his heroin habit.

The occasions when he has drifted back into the public view, however, have unquestionably and, understandably, raised eyebrows, both within his own coterie of supporters and among his foes.

The early 1980s found him briefly a member of Hawkwind, the long-serving space rockers formed in 1968 by Eric Clapton's old busking buddy, Dave Brock; the mid-decade saw him drafted into punk icon Johnny 'Rotten' Lydon's Public Image Ltd, at the behest of producer Bill Laswell; there was a pair of early 90s albums cut as a member of the metal band Masters Of Reality; and a 1994 reunion with Jack Bruce in BBM.

In 1986, Laswell oversaw a new Baker solo album, *Horses & Trees*, while Baker himself proved capable of upsetting every conception of how a drummer's solo record should sound with the 1991 release of *Unseen Rain*, a free-form instrumental album performed almost wholly on acoustic instruments. He returned, too, to his earliest jazz roots, forming the Ginger Baker Trio to cut 1994's aptly titled *Going Back Home*, and linking with jazz trumpeter Ron Miles for *Coward of the County*. Both in the studio and in conversation, Baker's days as a rock star – even as a rock *influence* – have been filed far behind him.

GRAHAM BOND

The Graham Bond Organisation never recovered from the departures of Jack Bruce and Ginger Baker, although the little evidence that survives of the band's next six months, a session recorded for Polydor in London during the summer of 1966 (featured on the *Solid Bond* compilation) suggests that the band continued to face the future bravely.

Sadly, Bond himself was no longer in any state to lead the band through the rigours of the British circuit and the Organisation finally collapsed when Dick Heckstall-Smith and Jon Hiseman were prised away by the Bluesbreakers. One of the group's final acts was to demo a handful of songs with Pete Brown, including one with the immortal title 'You Left Me with the Tattered Fragments of the A–Z of Hell'.

Bond remained at large around London through 1967–68, gigging occasionally, while becoming increasingly fascinated with the occult. His idiosyncrasies notwithstanding, however, Bond's talent remained unquestioned and, having become involved with the Fool clothing designers as they set about recording their debut album for Mercury, Bond and his partner, Diane, formed their own band, logically named the Magus (the Fool is the first card in the Tarot deck, the Magus is the second).

Mercury gladly flew the pair to California to assist on the Fool's album; there, Bond also played on sessions with Harvey Mandel and Screamin' Jay Hawkins, and famously jammed with the Airplane, the Dead and the Jimi Hendrix Experience. The two albums that Bond recorded in the US, however, *Love Is the Law* and the clumsily mistitled *Mighty Grahame Bond*, were released through the tiny Pulsar subsidiary and did next to nothing.

Bond returned to the UK in September 1969, full of plans for the future. The music press certainly welcomed him back with enthusiasm and, on 17 October, he debuted his new band, Initiation, with a massively publicised comeback concert at the Royal Albert Hall. Sadly, not even the presence of Pete Brown's newly formed Piblokto, nor an advertised appearance from Jack Bruce (who did not, in the end, show up) could draw more than a half-capacity audience to the event, but Bond was unperturbed. Initiation remained a vibrant concern on the London club circuit over the next few months, and were even among the headliners when Madame Tussaud's hosted a benefit for victims of the Biafran War in December.

There was a return to the Albert Hall when Initiation joined Family at a charity show for the homeless organisation Shelter; another benefit at the Roundhouse found Initiation raising funds for the Chicago Seven, on a bill that also starred David Bowie (himself still bathing in the starlight of his first-ever hit, 'Space Oddity'); and there was a spectacular reunion with some old friends and associates, again at the Roundhouse, when Jack Bruce, Brian Auger, Mitch Mitchell and Ric Grech joined the band onstage for a closing jam.

The only recorded evidence of Initiation lies in a session taped for John Peel's *Top Gear* in January 1970, cutting versions of 'Love Is the Law' and the Organisation favourites 'Wade in the Water' and 'Walking in the Park' (itself recently granted a new lease on life, after Colosseum covered it for their own debut single). The band also contributed a pair of live recordings to the soundtrack of the movie *The Breaking of Brumbo*. Hopes that Initiation might cut an album, however, were dashed in summer 1970 when the band split up, by which time, Bond and Diane had found other interests anyway, first as they linked up with Ginger Baker in Airforce and then, as they launched their own new band, Holy Magick.

Over the course of a little over a year, Bond was intimately involved in no less than four albums, Airforce's *I* and *II* sets, and Holy Magick's *Holy Magick* and *We Put Our Magick on You*. By the end of 1971, however, both projects had collapsed, while an attempt to reunite with Jack Bruce in the so-adventurous *Jack Bruce and Friends* (alongside Chris Spedding, Larry Coryell and, briefly, Mitch Mitchell) ended with Bruce sacking his old band leader, unable to deal with what Bond biographer Harry Shapiro described as his 'blustering effervescence' and 'magical ramblings'.

Another partnership paired Bond with Pete Brown as, logically, Bond and Brown; they cut an astonishing album, *Two Heads Are Better Than One*, and an equally superb EP but, by the end of 1972, the partnership had fizzled out and Bond lurched into a lost wilderness of half-formed bands, occasional gigs, and increasingly disturbing dalliances with both the drug and occult scenes. When his lifeless and badly mutilated corpse was pulled from beneath an underground train at Finsbury Park station on 8 May 1974, both suicide and the darker shadow of murder hung heavy over the speculation of what led up to his death.

PETE BROWN

Brown's earliest musical strivings, convened while Cream were still a going concern, revolved around his First Real Poetry Band, an anarchic jazz/poetry team that also featured John McLaughlin, bassist Binky McKenzie, drummer Laurie Allen and percussionist Pete Bailey. Augmented by Danny Thompson (double bass) and Dick Heckstall-Smith, among others, this outfit recorded several numbers that Brown composed with Graham Bond (he recalled 'The Week Looked Good on Paper' and 'Late Night Mental Tyre Service'), plus a lengthy version of 'Politician', some months before the lyric was handed on to Jack Bruce and Cream.

These sessions remain largely unreleased, as Brown tired of 'the musical heaviness of my accompanists; they were just much too good for my decidedly dodgy singing'; instead, he formed a new band, Battered Ornaments, around guitarist Chris Spedding and, by early 1969, the group had signed with Blackhill Management and Harvest Records, and was recording its debut album, *A Meal You Can Shake Hands with in the dark*. A second album, *Mantle-Piece*, was under way and the group was looking forward to an appearance at the Rolling Stones' Hyde Park free concert, when Brown himself was sacked from his own group (his vocals were replaced on the finished LP by Spedding).

Brown promptly resurfaced with a new band, Piblokto, sharing manager Gerry Bron with Dick Heckstall-Smith's Colosseum, and debuting with the single 'Living Life Backwards', a wicked number that Jeff Beck later covered. An album, *Things May Come and Things May Go, But the Art School Dance Goes on Forever*, followed and, over the next two years, Piblokto became a formidable presence on the college concert circuit, overcoming a string of personnel changes as they cut a second album, *Thousands on a Raft*, and several further singles.

By late 1971, however, the band had splintered, and Brown moved onto a new project, aligning with Graham Bond in Bond and Brown, and cutting the remarkable *Two Heads Are Better Than One*. Of course he also continued writing with Jack Bruce, turning in material for the albums *Harmony Row*, *Out of the Storm*, *How's Tricks* and 1978's unreleased *Jet Set Jewel*.

In 1973, Brown took a post as A&R man at Deram Records, for whom he recorded the poetry album *The Not Forgotten Association*; a single, 'Nights in Armour', featuring Jack Bruce and Jeff Beck, was also scheduled but ultimately went unreleased. Most of Brown's performing 70s, however, were spent fronting Back to the Front, a band formed with latter-day Piblokto keyboardist Ian Lynn. Frequently performing live between 1973 and their demise in 1977, the sound of the band was not captured on record until the very end of their lifespan – and, even then, the ensuing album, *Party in the Rain*, did not see release until 1984.

Though he continued working with other artists, another decade-plus elapsed before Brown resurfaced as a performer in his own right, recording a pair of albums for his own Interoceter label (*Ardours of the Lost Rake* and *Coals to Jerusalem*) with another Piblokto alumni, Phil Ryan, playing Graham Bond's old organ. A reunion with Jack Bruce, after some years apart, saw Brown collaborating on the 21st century albums *Shadows in the Air* and *More Jack Than God*, while Brown's own new band, the Interoceters, have been presenting a live show (captured on the 2004 album *Live at the Borderline*) whose contents span Brown's entire writing career so far.

JACK BRUCE

Jack Bruce once joked, with considerable pride, that the night Clapton, Baker and Blind Faith played their debut American concert at Madison Square Garden, 'I was playing in a club called Slugs in the East Village . . . a great experiential jazz club'; while the stream of albums, both solo and within a string of subsequent aggregations, that have sustained him over the decades since Cream, continue to mark him out as one of rock's most formidable talents, at the same time as deliberately body-swerving away from all that that band represented.

'Cream's success has been a double-edged sword for me. I still earn a lot of money from it and it's given me financial freedom and the opportunity to play whatever I've wanted to. But when I see an article about me and it says, "Jack Bruce of Cream", it kind of annoys me a little bit, because I've done so many other things. It's kind of like an actor being typecast.'

He has done his best to avoid that typecasting, of course. *Songs for a Tailor*, his first post-Cream solo album, was recorded just six months after the group's final concert, but it could have been another lifetime, as Bruce rebelled against every advisor who told him 'I should look out for a couple of young musicians and form another trio. Being me, I decided to do the exact opposite.'

He was dubious, too, about submitting to any future superstar combinations. Late in 1969, following the break-up of the Nice, Keith Emerson approached Bruce about forming a new organ-bass-and-drums fired combo, to fulfil both of their earlier bands' unfinished destinies. Bruce turned it down by agreeing under terms that he knew Emerson could never accept, that he, the bassist, be elected the group's leader. Emerson turned to Greg Lake and Carl Palmer; Bruce continued down his own path.

He did succumb to temptation once. Summer 1970, Bruce revealed, saw the hatching of 'plans for Tony Williams and myself to form a band with Jimi Hendrix . . .' The trio were deadly serious, too, 'but it never happened because Jimi died, which kind of put the kibosh on it.' One-time Organisation guitarist John McLaughlin was ultimately recruited to what became the fusion heavyweights Lifetime.

Further three-pieces appeared in Bruce's future. But the West, Bruce and Laing trio that married him to the remnants of Mountain between 1972 and 1974 was worth far more than the 'Cream substitute' tags that its configuration endured; so were BLT, formed in the early 1980s around the wreckage of the Robin Trower band, with vocalist Bill Lordan completing the acronymic equation; and 1994's BBM reunion with Baker, with guitarist Gary Moore completing a triumvirate that, again, was quickly shrouded by unjust comparisons with the past.

Then there was his partnership with Carla Bley and guitarist Mick Taylor, forged in the first months after Taylor quit the Rolling Stones in 1974, and debuted far too quickly on TV's *Old Grey Whistle Test*. Each and every one of these projects can be said to have continued the quest that Cream ignited; and might even have completed it had the public only not leaped so hard onto the ghosts of past electricity and demanded Bruce revel in the same nostalgia as they were.

Not for Bruce, then, a long retirement swinging from the laurels of some age-old classic; not for him a slow decline into autopilot senility. Even when he did step back into the past, to revisit a clutch of old Cream (and solo) songs on his first albums of the 21st century, *Shadows in the Air* and *More Jack Than God*, the resultant hybrids were as likely to infuriate fans, as thrill them – an Afro-Caribbean 'I Feel Free' indeed.

Bruce explained, 'It was quite funny; when I had the idea to do [these] records, I'd been playing with a few of the guys in my band, and with co-producer Kip Hanrahan, for a number of years, and we'd done a lot of Latin music together, because that was their background. So I thought, I'm playing their music, now it's time they came and played mine.'

'He the Richmond' and 'Boston Ball Game, 1967' from *Songs for a Tailor*, 'Dancing on Air' from 1980's *I've Always Wanted to Do This* and 'Out in the Fields' from his West, Bruce & Laing days all fell into place, together with a slew of remarkable new material. 'Then I started thinking about what other material I wanted to do, and "Sunshine of Your Love" and "White Room" came to mind, partly to attract people who might not normally listen to my new music, but also to find out what they sounded like today, as opposed to the "classic" versions we all know.'

Working with the nine-piece combo which was now his regular band, 'We recorded them in New York and they sounded great. But then I thought I'd really like to have Eric [Clapton] singing, doing the double lead with me, with all those years in between, kind of progressive evolution. So that was how it came about, and I'm really pleased with the way they turned out. The version of "White Room", I'm thrilled by, I think the intro almost sounds African, a dusty village in Africa somewhere.'

A third album in the sequence was in the planning stages when Bruce was diagnosed with liver cancer during summer 2003. Three weeks of crushing uncertainty were spent in and out of hospital before the doctors agreed that he could be saved with a liver transplant; the operation was carried out at Addenbrookes hospital in Cambridge on 19 September, although it remained touch-and-go whether Bruce would pull through. As Bruce wrote on his Jackbruce.com website the following May, 'It is so wonderful to be able to write to you on this my 61st birthday. There were times in the last few months when quite a lot of my medical people didn't think I would see this day. They didn't know me very well I don't think, cos I never really had any doubts!

'I work in fits and starts these days, I like to take a lot of time to do that other thing called living. I do a tour every year, I did a couple of Ringo [Starr]'s All-Star tours and they were great fun, no pressure. But I don't want to do that any more, it's time for me to move on, have my own group, be the leader again. When you've got a very long career, you've got to wait until the time is right. I'm not in the position to put out records every year, I like to wait until I've really got a hunger and something to say.'

ERIC CLAPTON

Eric Clapton was just 23 years old when Cream broke up and, if uncertainty assailed him as he looked at Bruce and Baker for the very last time, onstage at the Royal Albert Hall, then it battered him round the head when he opened the door one morning, a few weeks after, to find Baker walking back into his life.

Later, Clapton acknowledged just how ironic it was, as he and Steve Winwood pieced together Blind Faith, that he was as reluctant to reunite with Baker as the drummer was to team again with Bruce in Cream. It was Winwood's suggestion that the partnership be resumed and, ultimately, it became his decision. Clapton, once again, swallowed his own convictions and just went with the flow.

And so he continued to do, as the 1960s faded into the 1970s, as Blind Faith fell apart following one so-underachieving album and Clapton found himself cast adrift through a string of further projects – a few months buried anonymously away within American troubadours Delaney and Bonnie's backing group; a few more helming Derek and the Dominoes around the near-career-defining peak of 'Layla'; and a lot more lost within the kind of personal hell that only a fallen God could experience.

There was a solo album in 1970, set adrift amid the rumours of self-destruction that now appeared to follow him everywhere, but it was indicative of just how far Clapton had fallen from his pedestal that, when Robert Stigwood announced his comeback in 1973, the news was greeted with as much morbid curiosity as it was genuine excitement.

The guitarist's long romance with heroin was common under-ground knowledge, and a nightmare for his friends; on one occasion, Clapton revealed, Ginger Baker – himself no angel in the drug-taking stakes – hatched a scheme to physically kidnap Clapton, 'and take me off to the Sahara. His way of curing it is to get in his Land Rover and drive across the Sahara. You can't score anything in the desert.'

Clapton's relationship with Beatle George's wife Patti was a widely discussed scandal; and the restless self-destructiveness that had catapulted him into a lifetime of mere superjam sidemanship was as worthy a subject of a killer blues song as any of those standards he had once made his own. Once, Eric Clapton was God. Now God was clapped out, and that became the guitarist's media-given nickname for years to come, Eric Clapped-out, the young man who'd had everything, then let it fall away.

The comeback concerts at London's Rainbow Theatre in early 1973 marked another false dawn. The gigs themselves were solidly excellent, but with Clapton flanked on every corner by a bevy of superstar crutches, few of the fans in attendance, and even fewer of those who bought the souvenir live album later that year, doubted that this was as good as it was going to get.

Nobody could have predicted that within little more than a year, Clapton would not only have resurfaced with a new style and attitude, he would also be embarking upon a musical voyage which would see him create the three most consistent, and controversial, albums in his entire catalogue, and fronting a group – for the first time in his life – which really was compatible with all that he wanted to achieve.

Even today, the sequence of albums and concerts which kept the Eric Clapton Band in action between 1974 and 1977 – that is, *461 Ocean Boulevard*, *There's One in Every Crowd* (a wry commentary on Clapton's own opinion of his fame: 'guitar heroes? There's one in etc.') and *No Reason to Cry* – stands among the undisputed peaks of the guitarist's career. It was a period during which every facet of his talent, from tentative vocalist to aspiring songwriter, from band member to band leader, and on indeed to gracious guitarist, would first be prised out of its shell, then encouraged to develop in its own direction.

In the past, after all, Clapton was surrounded by Faces that were Names: Yardbirds vocalist Keith Relf, Bluesbreakers frontman John Mayall, fellow Cream-ers Jack Bruce and Ginger Baker, Blind Faith's Steve Winwood; only Derek and the Dominoes had truly rejoiced in the fameless shadows in which Clapton believed he functioned best, but his own life was so out of control at the time that even that band's music was left stranded on the sidelines.

In early 1974, however, as he re-emerged from the private hell that consumed the first years of the decade, Clapton was determined not to make any of those old mistakes again.

Neither did he, ploughing determinedly through both the screams of betrayal that arose from the once-faithful, and the scorn of the nay-sayers who simply couldn't understand why Clapton should want to delegate lead guitar playing to another musician entirely (bandmate George Terry), forsake the blues for reggae, soul, pop and balladeering. And, as he did so, so he came to terms with the fact that, no matter what he himself might want to accomplish with his music, there is an entire world out there that demands he do what they want as well.

So he chipped away at both his own resolve and theirs, to reach the compromise that forces him to record umpteen live renditions of 'Sunshine of Your Love' and 'I Shot the Sheriff' on the one hand, but allows him to turn out an entire album's-worth of Robert Johnson covers on the other (2004's *Me and Mr Johnson*); that has seen him relegate some of the greatest stars in the world to mere sidemen in his shows (Phil Collins was his drummer for a while), then subsume his own fame behind his heroes at others – in 2003, Clapton was almost anonymous, but brilliant nevertheless, at John Mayall's seventieth birthday concert.

Few listeners who first encountered Clapton as a Yardbird, Bluesbreaker or a member of Cream have truly remained alongside him ever since, not only buying but actively enjoying every album he has issued in that time; few who saw him at the Ricky Tick in '63 could have felt the same excitement if they saw him forty years on. But no matter how many peaks and troughs his music has endured over that span, still Clapton's perseverance cannot help but arouse a sense of absolute wonder.

Because, for every politely soulless MOR collection, there is a genuine labour of love; for every crippling delve into maudlinness, there is a soul-scorching flash of purity and grace; and for every 'My Father's Eyes', there is a 'Wonderful Tonight'.

Gone is the restless searching for something that even he could not truly identify; gone, too, is the need to hide his emotions behind his abilities. He came through every firestorm, and he not only survived, he grew stronger, until he was able to embrace the role of Elder Statesman of the Blues that he rejected so fiercely in his 20s and 30s. And, finally, he arrived in the position where he is today, at peace both with himself and with his prodigious talent.

'If I have to be a hero, even to myself, it's worth it,' he told *Guitar Player* in 1989, 'because it's something to strive for. I quite like having my mettle tested in that way. [But] I didn't like it so long ago; I tried to avoid it, to play it down, and tried to destroy it. And that process nearly destroyed me, too.'

DICK HECKSTALL-SMITH

With the Graham Bond Organisation already close to their end, Dick Heckstall-Smith joined John Mayall's Bluesbreakers, in time for the country-scouring road work that resulted in 1968's dishevelled (but so crucial) *Diary of a Band* live album, the last will and testament of the Bluesbreakers as they finally broke away from the blues and plunged instead into jazz fusion.

That move was confirmed in March 1968, when Mayall and Heckstall-Smith dropped by Klook's Kleek to see Graham Bond's latest band, and instead caught a bizarre musical battle between Bond and Jon Hiseman, a fifty-minute drum solo that the latter clearly had not been expecting, but which he dove into regardless.

Mayall decided there and then that this phenomenally versatile, and unflappable drummer was the man he wanted for the Bluesbreakers, and a couple of weeks later, Hiseman returned home from a show to discover Mayall had spent three hours sitting outside in his car, waiting to ask him to join the band.

With Heckstall-Smith and New Jazz Orchestra bassist Tony Reeves already on board, Hiseman should not have taken too much persuasion. However, he did. 'Jon was really taken aback when I asked him into the band,' Mayall recalled. 'He told me he knew next to nothing about the blues, and that he couldn't care less about my music. I told him I wasn't too worried about that, I just admired his playing. And that was the basis on which we worked.'

Besides, Hiseman soon changed his mind about Mayall's music. 'I'd always considered his band to be rubbish,' he agreed, 'but as it turned out, it was very good, much better than I'd ever dreamed!' It certainly was – that autumn 1968, having recorded Mayall's mould-breaking *Bare Wires* album, Hiseman, Reeves and Heckstall-Smith departed en masse to form Colosseum with Dave Greenslade (organ, piano, vibes) and James Litherland (guitar and vocals).

A single, covering the Graham Bond Organisation's 'Walking in the Park', and a dramatic debut album, the monumental *Morituri Te Salutant – Those Who Are About to Die Salute You*, quickly followed; Colosseum then became one of the first bands to sign to the newly launched, but soon-to-be-legendary Vertigo label (Bron Management stablemates Juicy Lucy were the other); their second album, *Valentyne Suite*, was the label's first-ever release in late 1969.

Widely feted both at home and abroad, Colosseum's magnificent jazz-rock fusion was never going to 'crack the big time'; nevertheless, the group became a much-loved addition to the US concert circuit, all the more so after Litherland was replaced by guitarist Clem Clempson and former Atomic Rooster vocalist Chris Farlowe. The band also achieved major notice as a star attraction in the rock movie *Super Session*, playing alongside Buddy Miles, Stephen Stills, Eric Clapton, Buddy Guy, Glen Campbell and Roland Kirk.

Sadly, the band's workload was such that, as Heckstall-Smith put it, 'We never sold enough records to take time off from gigs to compose, rehearse and record in peace ... and so we ran out of music!' A third album, *Daughter of Time*, was a rushed, patchwork affair and, though *Colosseum Live* should have bought the group some time, it didn't. Colosseum broke up in 1971, following a farewell performance at the Royal Albert Hall.

Heckstall-Smith moved into session work (he had already moonlighted alongside Jack Bruce, Pete Brown and Neil Ardley), before all-but reuniting Colosseum to help record his solo debut album, 1972's *A Story Ended* – Pete Brown, Caleb Quaye, Chris Spedding and Graham Bond also appeared on a remarkable album, while James Litherland returned to front the touring band that followed.

Crossing America alongside Fleetwood Mac and Deep Purple, the Dick Heckstall-Smith Band was preparing to record its own debut album when Heckstall-Smith himself was laid low by spinal injuries that dated back to his teens. He remained out of action for much of the remainder of the decade, his recovery then being followed by a return to college, where he took a degree in Social Sciences. By 1978, however, he was back in action, a welcome guest on Alexis Korner's 50th birthday *Party Album*, and an occasional member of the casual jazz and blues assemblages Big Chief, the Tough Tenors and the Famous Blues Blasters, who recorded three superb albums as Mainsqueeze.

New Heckstall-Smith bands 3-Space and DHSS followed, but he found himself increasingly drawn back to the freelance freedoms he had enjoyed in the 1950s; it was 1991 before Heckstall-Smith recorded a follow-up to *A Story Ended*, *Where One Is*, but the following year again brought a halt to his activities when he entered hospital for a heart by-pass operation, and suffered two strokes while the surgeons worked. He spent six days in intensive care, after which he found himself needing to learn to talk again.

Amazingly, Heckstall-Smith was back in action in 1993, forming a sax and drums duo, Free Jazz, with John Stevens (ex-Dando Shaft, and the drummer on Jack Bruce's first-ever solo single, in 1965). An album documenting his painful recovery, *Bird in Widness*, followed. Heckstall-Smith also guested on Jack Bruce's 1993 *Somethin' Else* album, and appeared at the bassist's own fiftieth birthday bash, alongside Ginger Baker, Gary Moore and Clem Clempson.

Bruce joined Heckstall-Smith and Stevens on their next Free Jazz album, *This That*; 1994 also brought a Colosseum reunion, as the Farlowe–Clempson line-up resurfaced for shows (and a live album) in Germany in late 1994, with a full European tour following in 1995. A studio album, *Bread and Circuses*, appeared in 1997, while Heckstall-Smith continued working outside of the band, as a sessioneer and on his own three-movement jazz suite, *Celtic Steppes*, commissioned by the Arts Council to trace 3,500 years of musical history, and produced by Pete Brown.

For fans of his own ancient history, meanwhile, Heckstall-Smith also teamed up with the Graham Bond Organisation's one-time partner, Duffy Power, to record the (still unreleased) *Dick & Duffy* album. He recently recorded a new solo album, *Blues and Beyond*, featuring contributions from Jack Bruce, Mick Taylor, Peter Green, Paul Jones, Clem Clempson and John Mayall.

Dick Heckstall-Smith passed away, aged seventy, on 17 December 2004.

ALEXIS KORNER

'If only for helping bring the Rolling Stones together,' Pete Townshend once proclaimed, 'Alexis Korner should be carried around London in a sedan chair for the rest of his life.'

That Korner's own musical importance was largely seen to diminish following the demise of the 'classic' Bruce–Baker–Bond era of Blues Incorporated was simply a consequence of the same restless curiosity and refusal to compromise that had allowed him to lay claim to such honours in the first place; the further the music scene leaned towards embracing his own original, incandescent fusion, the further Korner moved away from it, with a string of generally fine future albums constantly being overlooked in favour of the latest offerings from his own early acolytes.

Nevertheless, Korner remained a prepossessing presence on the music scene, as a broadcaster and journalist, as well as a performer, and evidence of his single-mindedness can be gauged as much from the records he did release, as those projects he abandoned – an album cut with future Led Zeppelin vocalist Robert Plant in 1968, and the chance to link up with the newly ex-Stones Brian Jones in 1969. Jones was, apparently, desperate to join Korner's newly formed New Church band, but Korner rejected his overtures, largely because of Jones's then well-publicised chemical and mental state.

In 1970, Korner launched his most commercially successful band yet, when the 25-member big band CCS signed with Micky Most's RAK label and, having debuted with a phenomenal version of Led Zeppelin's 'Whole Lotta Love', mustered no less than five UK Top Forty hits over the next three years: 'Walking' and 'Tap Turns on the Water' even crashed the Top Ten, while 'Whole Lotta Love' was quickly adopted as the theme to TV's *Top of the Pops*.

1972's *Bootleg Him* retrospective, and a new solo album, 1974's *Get Off My Cloud*, both brought Korner further recognition among the general public, the latter a truly star-studded affair of former bandmates and admirers: Peter Frampton, Steve Marriott and Keith Richard all contributed lead guitar to the proceedings and when, also in 1974, Mick Taylor left the Stones, Korner was one of the first names mentioned as a possible replacement. (Of course, the position was eventually filled by Ron Wood.)

In 1978 Korner celebrated his fiftieth birthday with a new LP, *The Party Album*, and a star-studded concert – Zoot Money, Paul Jones, Eric Clapton, Dick Heckstall-Smith, Chris Farlowe and Duffy Power all appeared, while 1981 saw Korner convene his final super-group, as he teamed with Jack Bruce, Ian Stewart and Charlie Watts, among others, as Rocket 88. However, his health was failing. Throughout 1982–83, a snowballing litany of ailments saw him in and out of hospital for tests, scans and X-rays; he was finally diagnosed with an inoperable combination of lung cancer and a brain tumour, and died on New Year's Day, 1984.

JOHN MAYALL

The departures of Jon Hiseman, Tony Reeves and Dick Heckstall-Smith in autumn 1968 marked the end of John Mayall's Bluesbreaking days. Although two months of touring followed before Mayall officially broke up the group, a three-week vacation in Los Angeles had already seen Mayall plot out an entire new course for both his career and his life.

'I really felt that I had to re-evaluate the whole thing. I felt that I had exhausted all the possibilities. Even though I had added horns, it really was [only] an embellishment of the same music.' Increasingly, he was convinced that it was time to 'do something different'.

Midway through a tour of Germany in spring 1969, Mayall figured out what that 'something different' was. 'I decided to ... drop the electric kind of feel and go acoustic, without the drums. Halfway through, without any days off in between. One show would be that band and the next night they'd be gone.'

It was a major step, not least of all because it involved completely restructuring the group, dismissing both drummer Steve Allen (he went on to form Stone the Crows) and guitarist Mick Taylor, who was promptly swallowed up by the Rolling Stones.

Audiences took to the new-look act immediately; it was, Mayall recalled, 'the promoter who was freaked out, trying to persuade me every way he could that I should not do it, or maybe have the band open the show, then sneak the acoustic in later. But the audiences went for it straight away, and that was very gratifying.'

The German tour over, Mayall brought the same show to Britain for a few dates, then it was back to the United States for the tour that literally changed his life. 'I was in LA, and suddenly I just got everything together to move there. I bought a house and I moved over. And that's when we recorded *Turning Point*.' By the end of the decade he had done so much to shape, Mayall had put much of his past behind him. He has remained a California resident ever since.

Gone, but not forgotten – although Mayall's subsequent output was to make little impression on British audiences (even as he became a US chart regular, with no less than fifteen Top Two Hundred albums between 1969 and 1975), the same sense of restless crusading that characterised his Bluesbreakers days remained the guiding spirit behind his music.

Albums such as *Empty Rooms* (1970), *Ten Years Are Gone* (1973) and *New Year, New Band, New Company* (1975) all advanced his musical reputation in a manner which few of his generation's other survivors ever dreamed possible; and while there were certainly a few wrong turns along the way (even fans prefer to gloss over his late 1970s output), by the time Mayall put a new generation of Bluesbreakers together in the early 1980s, even his biggest mistakes were forgotten.

Similarly, those occasions when he did appear to be indulging in sheer nostalgia – 1972's *Back to the Roots*, for example, with its hectic schedule of reunions with sundry past collaborators, and 1982's Twentieth Anniversary tour – at least allowed him to take stock of all he had accomplished so far, and plan what he wanted to do next.

Certainly age has not slowed him down; 2003 saw Mayall celebrate his seventieth birthday with a massive concert in Liverpool, recorded for CD and filmed for DVD release – and issued, coincidentally, within a few months of a reissue for the 1969 documentary *The Turning Point*. Two very different bands are at play across the two films, projecting two very different mind-sets, one thrusting fearlessly forwards, the other looking nostalgically backwards. But the man in the middle remained much the same, just as powerful a performer, just as wholehearted an entertainer, and just as true towards his own musical intentions as he ever was.

FELIX PAPPALARDI

Recorded in just two weeks before Pappalardi flew to London to complete Cream's *Goodbye* album, guitarist Leslie West's *Mountain* album became the foundation for one of the most impressive rock trios in American history, as producer/bassist Pappalardi and drummer Corky Laing teamed with West to form Mountain, purveyors of such instant metal classics as 'Mississippi Queen' and the breathtaking 'Nantucket Sleighride'.

Despite rapidly ascending to the peaks of American concert circuit success, Mountain broke up in 1972, at which point Laing and West linked with Jack Bruce in the short-lived West, Bruce & Laing; the original band reformed in 1974, but parted the following year due to Pappalardi's hearing problems, brought on by Mountain's own penchant of excruciating volume. He did return to production briefly the following year, overseeing an album by Creation, a Japanese band that had previously toured with Mountain; his own first solo album, *Don't Worry Ma*, then emerged in 1979, an endearing combination of jazz, funk and reggae.

Pappalardi seemed content, however, to remain a shadowy legend; it took tragedy to restore him to the headlines, on 17 April 1983, when he was shot and killed by Gail Collins, the wife with whom he wrote 'Strange Brew' for Cream. While the jury believed her claim that the shooting was an accident, occurring while Pappalardi was showing her how to use the gun, Collins was convicted of criminally negligent homicide and sentenced to four years' imprisonment.

Laing and West continue touring and recording as Mountain; the pair published a joint autobiography, *Nantucket Sleighride*, in 2003.

MARTIN SHARP

With his groundbreaking collages pioneering what the art world would come to regard as Appropriation Art, *Disraeli Gears/Wheels of Fire* sleeve designer Martin Sharp went on to create the cover for

Mighty Baby's 1969 debut album, then returned to his Australian homeland, where he took over the Clune Galleries for a series of highly acclaimed conceptual art exhibitions, *The Incredible Shrinking Exhibition* and *Yellow House*, a visualisation of a dream that Vincent van Gogh described in a letter to his brother Theo.

In 1972, Sharp published *Art Book*, a collection of 36 colour collages that he scissored from the pages of other publications, combining the works of a host of classical painters. 'I have never been shy about cutting things up if I had a good idea. To me it was worth the price of a book for the idea it expressed, the interconnecting of different worlds. I could put a Gauguin figure in a Van Gogh landscape, make the composition work, and also say something about their relationship.'

Sharp combined with Australia's Nimrod Theatre, for whom he produced the now widely praised (and much-collected) Nimrod posters; he was also heavily involved in the restoration of Sydney's Luna Park amusement park; tragically, the work had barely been completed and the park reopened when fire swept the Ghost Train attraction, killing seven people. For some time, the park was threatened with closure; that it did not eventually fold was down to the Friends of Luna Park, an organisation that Sharp co-founded in the belief that the fire was deliberately set by forces bent on redeveloping the grounds for other purposes.

Remaining active in the world of art, particularly in Australia, Sharp has only occasionally returned to the world of rock sleeve design in the decades since *Disraeli Gears* and *Wheels of Fire*. But his distinctive style leaped out of Tiny Tim's 1996 *Christmas Album*, while *Disraeli Gears*' sleeve was itself replicated for Cream's 1997 *Those Were the Days* box set.

ROBERT STIGWOOD

Cream's break-up coincided with Robert Stigwood's move into the world of London theatre, as producer of the London stage version of the American hippy hit *Hair*. An immediate success, *Hair* remained in the West End for five years, to be followed by the original production of Tim Rice and Andrew Lloyd Webber's *Jesus Christ, Superstar*, the super-controversial *Oh Calcutta!* (the first nude musical ever to play Broadway), *The Dirtiest Show in Town*, *Sweeney Todd*, the Beatles tribute *John, Paul, Ringo and Burt* and another Rice/Lloyd Webber production, *Evita*.

Throughout the first years of this new era, Stigwood distanced himself somewhat from the musical arena, although he retained catalogue rights over Cream's past recordings, and continued managing Baker, Bruce and Clapton for several years – it was 1978 before he and Clapton finally parted ways, with the guitarist's 1974 comeback album *461 Ocean Boulevard* and the attendant 'I Shot the Sheriff' hit single, the first major hits enjoyed by Stigwood's then year-old RSO label.

The re-emergence of the Bee Gees in 1975 cemented the label's fortune and, by the end of the decade, the brothers Gibb could quite feasibly claim to be the biggest band in the world, with a string of chart-toppers under both their own names, and a host of associated artistes – younger brother Andy and former Clapton Band singer Yvonne Elliman among them.

Their pre-eminence was assisted by another arm of Stigwood's manifold enterprises. RSO moved into movies in 1973, when Stigwood became co-producer of Norman Jewison's film version of *Jesus Christ, Superstar*. Two years later, Stigwood oversaw Ken Russell's hyperactive vision of the Who's rock opera, *Tommy*, before 1976 brought *Saturday Night Fever*, the movie that confirmed disco as *the* premier musical force of the late 1970s, and topped LP charts worldwide with a largely Bee Gee-fied soundtrack. *Grease*, likewise featuring *Fever* star John Travolta (and a Gibb-composed theme song), followed.

Considerably less successful were a third Travolta vehicle, *Moment by Moment*, and a movie adaptation of the Beatles' *Sgt Pepper* album, which remains one of history's most critically and commercially maligned ventures – twenty years on, Peter Frampton, the movie's star, shivered, 'It seems every time I put a new record out, Stigwood puts it out on TV somewhere. "You want to try a new record? Hold on while we put this out. We'll destroy you again."'

The failure of *Sgt Pepper* did, in fact, do a lot of damage to everyone concerned. RSO closed down very shortly after the movie and its attendant soundtrack made their public debut. According to Fred Gershon, Robert Stigwood's partner, the album shipped an unheard of triple platinum – three million copies. Almost every one came back as an unsold return, 'together with maybe another million in bootleg copies!'

Stigwood remained a power in Hollywood, however, as testified by such subsequent successes as *The Fan*, *Times Square*, and *Gallipoli*, follow-ups to both *Grease* and *Saturday Night Fever* and 1997's Golden Globe-winning movie version of *Evita*.

MIKE TAYLOR

Jazz pianist Mike Taylor, Baker's co-writer for three songs across the *Wheels of Fire* album, committed suicide in 1969.

DISCOGRAPHY

This discography is designed to reflect the contents of this book only – that is, the careers of Eric Clapton, Jack Bruce and Ginger Baker between their recorded debuts, and the demise of Cream in 1968, and is arranged in chronological order, to allow readers and collectors to trace the development of those careers.

JB – recording features Jack Bruce; GB – Ginger Baker; EC – Eric Clapton.

PART ONE – PRE-CREAM DISCOGRAPHY
Pre-1962
Several discographies vaguely note Baker as an accompanist on albums by Bob Wallis, Acker Bilk and others. Fully detailed confirmation of the existence of these releases has, unfortunately, proven impossible to find.

1962
12 July: **ALEXIS KORNER'S BLUES INCORPORATED (JB)**
Jazz Club (BBC radio) (included on *Bootleg Him* RAK SRAK 511-512)
includes 'Hoochie Coochie Man'

December: **NANCY SPAIN WITH ALEXIS KORNER AND HIS BAND (JB, GB)**
SINGLE 'Blaydon Races', 'Uptown' (flexidisc Lyntone LYN 298/299)

1963
January: **BLUES INCORPORATED (JB, GB)**
LP *Rhythm & Blues* various artists compilation (Decca LK 4616 – released 1964)
includes 'Night Time Is the Right Time', 'Early in the Morning'

24 January: **ALEXIS KORNER'S BLUES INCORPORATED (JB, GB)**
Jazz Club (BBC radio) (included on *Bootleg Him* RAK SRAK 511-512)
includes 'Rockin''

May: **DUFFY POWER & THE GRAHAM BOND QUARTET (JB, GB)**
SINGLE 'I Saw Her Standing There', 'Farewell Baby' (Parlophone R 5024)

June: **GRAHAM BOND QUARTET (JB, GB)**
live at Klook's Kleek (released on LP *Solid Bond* Warner Brothers 2LS 2555, 1970)
includes 'The Grass Is Greener', 'Doxy', 'Ho Ho Country Kicking Blues'

July: **DUFFY POWER & THE GRAHAM BOND QUARTET (JB, GB)**
Pop Go the Beatles BBC radio (unreleased)
includes 'I Got a Woman', 'Cabbage Greens', 'I Saw Her Standing There', 'Spanish Blues'

7–8 December: **SONNY BOY WILLIAMSON & THE YARDBIRDS (EC)**
LP *Sonny Boy Williamson & the Yardbirds* (released Jan 1966 – Fontana TL 5277)
includes 'Bye Bye Bird', 'Mr Downchild', 'The River Rhine', '23 Hours Too Long', 'Out of the Water Coast', 'Baby Don't Worry', 'Pontiac Blues', 'Take It Easy Baby', 'I Don't Care No More', 'Western Arizona' & 'Smokestack Lightning', 'Let It Rock', 'Honey in Your Hips', 'I Wish You Would', 'You Can't Judge a Book by Its Cover', 'Who Do You Love' (included on *Shapes of Things* box set)

1964
— ERNEST RANGLIN & THE GBS (JB, GB)
EP *Swing-a-Ling* (Black Swan 1EP 704)
includes 'Swing-a-Ling Parts 1 and 2', 'Soho'

— GRAHAM BOND ORGANISATION (JB, GB)
SINGLE 'Long Tall Shorty', 'Long-Legged Baby' (Decca F 11909)

— GRAHAM BOND ORGANISATION (JB, GB)
EP *Graham Bond Organisation* (Decca DFE 4616)
includes 'Hoochie Coochie Man', 'Little Girl', 'High-Heeled Sneakers', 'Strut Around'

— GRAHAM BOND ORGANISATION (JB, GB)
original soundtrack: *Gonks Go Beat* (Decca LK 4673)
includes 'Harmonica'

— THE YARDBIRDS (EC)
Go Tell It on the Mountain (TV) (1 included on *Cream of Eric Clapton* VHS/DVD, 2 included on *Yardbirds* VHS/DVD)
includes 'Louise', 'I Wish You Would'

— THE YARDBIRDS (EC)
Alexis Korner (BBC World Service)
Tracks unknown. According to Jim McCarty, 'I think he ... played on the Alexis Korner [session], the first one we did, but ... we wouldn't have done any more BBC until we'd had a hit.' The group's next session on 20 March 1965, the opening tracks on the Yardbirds' *Where the Action Is* BBC sessions collection, featured Jeff Beck.

February: **THE YARDBIRDS (EC)**
Session (included on *Shapes of Things* box set)
includes 'Boom Boom', 'Honey in Your Hips', 'Baby What's Wrong', 'I'm Talking About You' + 'I Wish You Would' (included on *Remember The Yardbirds* compilation)

May: **OTIS SPANN (EC)**
Session (included on *Cracked Spanner Head* LP – Deram DML 1036, 1969)
includes 'Pretty Girls Everywhere'

June: **THE YARDBIRDS (EC)**
SINGLE 'I Wish You Would', 'A Certain Girl' (Columbia DB 7283)

June: **THE YARDBIRDS (EC)**
TV performances untraced

July: **THE YARDBIRDS (EC)**
LP *Live! Blueswailing 1964* (Castle 81331-2, 2003)
includes 'Someone to Love Me', 'Too Much Monkey Business', 'Got Love If You Want It', 'Smokestack Lightning', 'Good Morning Little Schoolgirl', 'She Is So Respectable', 'Humpty Dumpty', 'The Sky Is Crying'

October: **GRAHAM BOND ORGANISATION (JB, GB)**
Live at Klook's Kleek (originally released within the French, Giorgio Gomelsky-designed *Rock Generation* series, spread across two separate LPs. The Yardbirds' *Five Live Yardbirds* was featured across the same two LPs. The full show was then reissued as *The Beginnings of Jazz Rock* (Charly CR 30017, 1977).
includes 'Wade in the Water', 'Big Boss Man', 'Early in the Morning', 'Person to Person Blues', 'Spanish Blues', 'Introduction by Dick Jordan', 'The First Time I Met the Blues', 'Stormy Monday', 'Train Time', 'What'd I Say'

October: **THE YARDBIRDS (EC)**

SINGLE 'Good Morning Little Schoolgirl', 'I Ain't Got You' (Columbia DB 7391 – alternative versions of A-side included in *Shapes of Things* box set)

1965
— **GRAHAM BOND ORGANISATION (JB, GB)**
LP *Blues Now* various artists compilation (Decca LK 4681)
includes 'Wade in the Water'

January: **GRAHAM BOND ORGANISATION (JB, GB)**
SINGLE 'Tammy', 'Wade in the Water' (Columbia DB 7471)

February: **THE YARDBIRDS (EC)**
LP *Five Live Yardbirds* (Columbia 33SX 1677)
includes 'Too Much Monkey Business', 'Got Love If You Want It', 'Smokestack Lightning', 'She Is So Respectable', 'Five Long Years', 'Pretty Girl', 'Louie', 'I'm A Man', 'Here 'Tis'

February: **THE GRAHAM BOND ORGANISATION (JB, GB)**
LP *The Sound of '65* (Columbia SX 1711)
includes 'Hoochie Coochie', 'Baby Make Love to Me', ' Neighbour, Neighbour', 'Early in the Morning', 'Spanish Blues', 'Oh Baby', 'Little Girl', 'I Want You', 'Wade in the Water', 'Got My Mojo Working', 'Train Time', 'Baby Be Good to Me', 'Half a Man', 'Tammy'

March: **THE YARDBIRDS (EC)**
SINGLE 'For Your Love', 'Got to Hurry' (Columbia DB 7499 – alternative versions of B-side included in *Shapes of Things* box set)

March: **GRAHAM BOND ORGANISATION (JB, GB)**
SINGLE 'Tell Me', 'Love Came Shining Through' (Columbia 7528)

April: **JOHN MAYALL'S BLUESBREAKERS (EC)**
Saturday Club (BBC radio – unreleased)
includes 'Crawling Up a Hill', 'Crocodile Walk', 'Bye Bye Bird'

June: **ERIC CLAPTON + JIMMY PAGE (EC)**
Sessions (included on *Blues Anytime* vols 1–3 compilations)
includes 'Miles Road', 'Tribute to Elmore', 'Freight Loader', 'Snake Drive', 'West Coast Idea', 'Draggin' My Tail', 'Chocker'

July: **GRAHAM BOND ORGANISATION (JB, GB)**
SINGLE 'Lease on Love', 'My Heart's in Little Pieces' (Columbia DB 7647)

July: **THE YARDBIRDS (EC)**
LP *For Your Love* USA (Epic LN 24167)
includes 'For Your Love', 'I'm Not Talking', 'Putty', 'I Ain't Got You', 'Got to Hurry', 'I Ain't Done Wrong', 'I Wish You Would', 'A Certain Girl', 'Sweet Music', 'Good Morning Little Schoolgirl', 'My Girl Sloopy'

October: **YARDBIRDS (EC)**
EP *Yardbirds* (Columbia SEG 8421)
includes 'My Girl Sloopy', 'I'm Not Talking', 'I Ain't Done Wrong'

October: **GRAHAM BOND ORGANISATION (JB, GB)**
LP *There's a Bond Between Us* (Columbia SX 1750)
includes 'Who's Afraid of Virginia Woolf?', ' Hear Me Calling Your Name', 'The Night Time Is the Right Time', 'Walkin' in the Park', 'Last Night', 'Baby Can It Be True', 'What'd I Say', 'Dick's Instrumental', 'Don't Let Go', 'Keep a Drivin'', 'Have You Ever Loved a Woman', 'Camels and Elephants'

October: **DUFFY POWER (JB, GB)**
Sessions featuring Bruce (all four tracks) and Baker (tracks 2–4), plus John McLaughlin and Phil Seaman. 'Mary Open the Door' was issued as the B-side to Duffy's Nucleus single 'Hound Dog' (Decca F 22547, UK, 1967). The remainder were unissued until appearing on the Duffy Power CD *Just Stay Blue* (RPM 802).
includes 'Dollar Mamie', 'Little Boy Blue', 'Little Girl', 'Mary Open the Door'

October: **JOHN MAYALL & ERIC CLAPTON (EC)**
SINGLE 'I'm Your Witchdoctor', 'Telephone Blues' (Immediate IM 012: 'On Top of the World' from subsequent session included on *Anthology of British Blues* compilation)

December: **GRAHAM BOND ORGANISATION (GB)**
SINGLE 'St James Infirmary', 'Soul Tango' (Columbia DB 7838)

December: **JACK BRUCE (JB)**
SINGLE 'I'm Getting Tired (of Drinking and Gambling)', 'Rootin' Tootin" (Polydor BM 56036)

December: **MANFRED MANN (JB)**
BBC session (track 1 issued on *BBC Sessions* CD)
includes 'When Will I Be Loved', 'It Took a Little While', 'There's No Living Without Your Loving', 'Spirit Feel', 'Tired of Trying, Bored with Lying, Scared of Dying'

December: **MANFRED MANN (JB)**
Session. Track 1 included on *As Was* EP (HMV 7EG8962 – October 1966); tracks 2–3 on *Soul Of Mann* LP (Capitol 6199 – 1967)
includes 'That's All I Ever Want From You Baby', 'Spirit Feel', 'Tengo Tengo'

1966
February–March: **MANFRED MANN (JB)**
Session. Track 1 included on *Mann Made* (Canadian LP T-6187); tracks 2, 3 on *Pretty Flamingo* (US LP United Artists UAL 3549)
includes 'She Needs Company (alternative version)', 'Driva Mann', 'It's Getting Late'

February **CHAMPION JACK DUPREE (EC)**
LP *From New Orleans to Chicago* (Decca LK 4747 – 1966)
includes 'Third Degree', 'Shim Sham Shimmy' + 'Calcutta Blues' included on *Raw Blues* LP

February: **MANFRED MANN (JB)**
SINGLE 'She Needs Company', 'Hi Lili Hi Lo' (Ascot AS 2210 – US)

March: **THE WHO ORCHESTRA (GRAHAM BOND ORGANI-SATION) (GB)**
SINGLE 'Waltz for a Pig' (Reaction 591 001 – B-side of 'Substitute')

March: **THE POWERHOUSE (EC, JB)**
LP *Good Time Music* aka *What's Shakin'* (Elektra EUK 260)
includes 'I Want to Know', 'Crossroads', 'Steppin' Out'

17 March: **JOHN MAYALL'S BLUESBREAKERS (EC, JB)**
Live at the Flamingo tracks 1–5 issued on *Primal Solos* (London, US
LP 1983); 6 on *Looking Back* (Decca SKL 5010, UK, 1969)
includes 'Intro-Maudie', 'It Hurts to Be in Love', 'Have You Ever
Loved a Woman', 'Bye Bye Bird', 'Hoochie Coochie Man', 'They
Call It Stormy Monday'
NOTE: John Mayall's liner notes date these recordings to 17 March
1966, following Bruce's departure for Manfred Mann, suggesting
they were recorded at one of several subsequent gigs where Bruce
stood in for regular bassist John McVie.

19 March: **JOHN MAYALL'S BLUESBREAKERS (EC, JB)**
Saturday Club (BBC session – unreleased)
includes 'Little Girl', 'Hideaway', 'Steppin' Out', 'On Top of the
World', 'Key to Love'
NOTE: Recorded two days after the Flamingo recording date (see
above), Marc Roberty's *Eric Clapton – The Complete Recording
Sessions* confirms Jack Bruce as bassist on this session.

April: **MANFRED MANN (JB)**
SINGLE 'Pretty Flamingo', 'You're Standing By' (HMV POP 1523, UK)

April: **MANFRED MANN (JB)**
EP *Machines* (HMV 7EG 8942)
includes 'Machines', 'She Needs Company', 'Tennessee Waltz', 'When
Will I Be Loved'

April: **MANFRED MANN (JB)**
BBC session
includes 'Longhair, Unsquare Dude Called Jack', 'When Will I Be
Loved', 'You Better Be Sure', 'Still I'm Sad', 'Machines'

May: **THE HOLLIES (JB)**
SINGLE 'After the Fox' (United Artists UP 1152)

June: **MANFRED MANN (JB)**
EP *Instrumental Asylum* EP (HMV 7EG 8949)
includes 'Still I'm Sad', 'My Generation', '(I Can't Get No)
Satisfaction', 'I Got You Babe'

August: **JOHN MAYALL AND ERIC CLAPTON (EC)**
SINGLE 'Lonely Hearts', 'Bernard Jenkins' (Purdah 45-3502)

September: **JOHN MAYALL'S BLUESBREAKERS WITH ERIC
CLAPTON (EC)**
LP *John Mayall's Bluesbreakers with Eric Clapton* (Decca LK 4804)
includes 'All Your Love', 'Hideaway', 'Little Girl', 'Another Man',

'Double Crossin' Time', 'What'd I Say', 'Key to Love', 'Parchman Farm', 'Have You Heard', 'Ramblin' on My Mind', 'Steppin' Out', 'It Ain't Right'

September: **JOHN MAYALL'S BLUESBREAKERS WITH ERIC CLAPTON (EC)**
SINGLE 'Parchman Farm', 'Key to Love' (Decca F12490)

1967
— DONOVAN (JB)
session (included on *A Gift From a Flower to a Garden* Pye NPL 20000 – April 1968)
includes 'Someone Singing'

January: **PAUL JONES (JB)**
SINGLE 'Sonny Boy Williamson' (HMV POP 1576 – B-side to 'I've Been A Bad Bad Boy')

December: **GEORGE HARRISON (EC)**
Original soundtrack *Wonderwall* (Apple APCOR 1 – 1968)
includes 'Ski-ing'

1968
— ROGER MCGOUGH & MIKE MCGEAR (JB)
LP *McGough & McGear* (Parlophone PMC 7047)
Unknown tracks

June: **JACKIE LOMAX (EC)**
LP *Is This What You Want?* (Apple APCOR 6 – 1969)
includes 'Sour Milk Sea', 'The Eagle Laughs at You', 'You've Got Me Thinking' + 'New Day' (single Apple 11)

July: **MARTHA VELEZ (EC, JB)**
LP *Fiends and Angels* (London HA-K 8395)
includes 'It Takes a Lot to Laugh', 'I'm Gonna Leave You', 'Feel So Bad', 'In My Girlish Days'

August: **JACK BRUCE (JB)**
LP *Things We Like* (released January 1971 Polydor 2343 033)
includes 'Over the Cliff', 'Statues', 'Sam Enchanted Dick', 'Born to Be Blue', 'HCKHH Blues', 'Ballad for Arthur', 'Things We Like' + 'Ageing Jack Bruce, Three, from Scotland, England' (CD bonus track)

September: **THE BEATLES (EC)**
LP *The Beatles* (PMC 7067 – November 1968)
includes 'While My Guitar Gently Weeps'

PART TWO – CREAM DISCOGRAPHY

SINGLES

October 1966: 'Wrapping Paper', 'Cat's Squirrel' (Reaction 591 007)

December 1966: 'I Feel Free', 'NSU' (Reaction 591 011)

May 1967: 'Strange Brew', 'Tales of Brave Ulysses' (Reaction 591 015)

October 1967: 'Spoonful' parts 1 & 2 (Atco 6522 – US)

February 1968: 'Sunshine of Your Love', 'SWLABR' (Atco 6544 – US)

May 1968: 'Anyone for Tennis', 'Pressed Rat and Warthog' (Polydor 56258)

September 1968: 'Sunshine of Your Love', 'SWLABR' (Polydor 56286)

January 1969: 'White Room', 'Those Were the Days' (Polydor 65300)

January 1969: 'Crossroads', 'Passing the Time' (Atco 6646 – US single)

April 1969: 'Badge', 'What a Bringdown' (Polydor 56315)

ALBUMS

December 1966: *Fresh Cream* LP: 'NSU', 'Sleepy Time Time', 'Dreaming', 'Sweet Wine', 'Spoonful', 'Cat's Squirrel', 'Four Until Late', 'Rollin' and Tumblin'', 'I'm So Glad', 'Toad' (Reaction 593 001)

March 1967: *Fresh Cream* US LP: 'NSU', 'Sleepy Time Time', 'Dreaming', 'Sweet Wine', 'I Feel Free', 'Cat's Squirrel', 'Four Until Late', 'Rollin' and Tumblin'', 'I'm So Glad', 'Toad' (Atco 33206)

November 1967: *Disraeli Gears* LP: 'Strange Brew', 'Sunshine of Your Love', 'World of Pain', 'Dance the Night Away', 'Blue Condition', 'Tales of Brave Ulysses', 'SWLABR', 'We're Going Wrong', 'Outside Woman Blues', 'Take It Back', 'Mother's Lament' (Reaction 593 003)

August 1968: *Wheels of Fire* LP: 'White Room', 'Sitting on Top of the World', 'Passing the Time', 'As You Said', 'Pressed Rat and Warthog', 'Politician', 'Those Were the Days', 'Born Under a Bad Sign', 'Deserted Cities of the Heart', 'Crossroads', 'Spoonful', 'Train Time', 'Toad' (Polydor 582 031/2)

August 1968: *Wheels of Fire – in the Studio* LP: 'White Room', 'Sitting on Top of the World', 'Passing the Time', 'As You Said', 'Pressed Rat and Warthog', 'Politician', 'Those Were the Days', 'Born Under A Bad Sign', 'Deserted Cities of the Heart' (Polydor 582 033)

December 1969: *Wheels of Fire – Live at the Fillmore* LP: 'Crossroads', 'Spoonful', 'Train Time', 'Toad' (Polydor 582 040)

March 1969: *Goodbye* LP: 'I'm So Glad', 'Politician', 'Sitting on Top of the World', 'Badge', 'Doing That Scrapyard Thing', 'What a Bringdown' (Polydor 583 053)

July 1969: *Best of Cream*: 'Sunshine of Your Love', 'Badge', 'Crossroads', 'White Room', 'SWLABR', 'Born Under a Bad Sign', 'Spoonful', 'Tales of Brave Ulysses', 'Strange Brew', 'I Feel Free' (Polydor 583 060)

POSTHUMOUS RELEASES FEATURING PREVIOUSLY UNRELEASED MATERIAL
April 1970: *Live Cream*: 'NSU', 'Sleepy Time Time', 'Sweet Wine', 'Rollin' and Tumblin'', 'Lawdy Mama' (studio outtake) (Polydor 2383 016)

June 1972: *Live Cream 2*: 'Deserted Cities of the Heart', 'White Room', 'Politician', 'Tales of Brave Ulysses', 'Sunshine of Your Love', 'Stepping Out' (Polydor 2383 119)

1975: *Cream Flashback*: includes 'The Coffee Song' (2384 067)

September 1997: *Those Were the Days* 4CD box set includes 'You Make Me Feel', 'We're Going Wrong', 'Hey Now Princess', 'SWLABR' (demo), 'Weird of Hermiston', 'The Clear-out', 'Falstaff Beer Commercial', 'NSU' (live), 'Toad' (live), 'Sunshine of Your Love' (TV) (Polydor 31453 9000-2)

September 2003: *BBC Sessions*: 'Sweet Wine', 'interview', 'Wrapping Paper', 'Rollin' and Tumblin'', 'Steppin' Out', 'Crossroads', 'Cat's Squirrel', 'Train Time', 'I'm So Glad', 'Lawdy Mama', 'interview', 'I Feel Free', 'NSU', 'Four Until Late', 'Strange Brew', 'interview', 'Tales of Brave Ulysses', 'We're Going Wrong', 'interview', 'Born Under a Bad Sign', 'Outside Woman Blues', 'Take It Back', 'Sunshine of Your Love', 'Politician', 'SWLABR', 'Steppin' Out' (Polydor B0000069-02)

September 2004: *Disraeli Gears Deluxe Edition* 2CD includes 'Lawdy Mama' (alternative version) (Polydor B0002XDOBC)

RADIO AND TV APPEARANCES
October 1966: *Band Beat* (BBC radio) 'Spoonful', 'Sleepy Time Time', 'Rollin' and Tumblin'' (unreleased)

November 1966: *Saturday Club* (BBC radio) 'Sweet Wine', 'Wrapping Paper', 'Rollin' and Tumblin'', 'Steppin' Out' (included on *BBC Sessions* CD) + 'I'm So Glad', 'Sleepy Time Time' (unreleased)

November 1966: *Guitar Club* (BBC radio) 'Crossroads' (included on *BBC Sessions* CD) + 'Steppin' Out', 'Sitting on Top of the World' (unreleased)

November 1966: *Ready Steady Go* (ITV) 'Wrapping Paper' (unreleased)

November 1966: *Monday Monday* (BBC radio) – unknown (unreleased)

December 1966: *Rhythm & Blues* (BBC radio) 'Cat's Squirrel', 'Train Time', 'I'm So Glad', 'Lawdy Mama' (included on *BBC Sessions* CD)

January 1967: *Saturday Club* (BBC radio) 'I Feel Free', 'NSU', 'Four Until Late' (included on *BBC Sessions* CD) + 'Train Time', 'Toad' (unreleased)

January 1967: *Monday Monday, Parade of the Pops* (BBC radio) – unknown (unreleased)

January 1967: *Top of the Pops* (BBC TV) 'I Feel Free' (unreleased)

February 1967: *Beat Club* (German TV) 'I Feel Free' (*Cream of Eric Clapton* VHS/ DVD)

March 1967: *unknown* (Swedish radio) 'NSU', 'Steppin' Out', 'Train Time', 'Toad', 'I'm So Glad' (unreleased)

19 May 1967: *Beat Club* (German TV) 'Strange Brew' (*Cream of Eric Clapton* VHS/ DVD)

22 May 1967: *Dee Time* (BBC TV) 'Strange Brew' (unreleased)

30 May 1967: *Saturday Club* (BBC radio) 'Strange Brew', 'Tales of Brave Ulysses', 'We're Going Wrong' (included on *BBC Sessions* CD)

1 June 1967: *First Festival of Pop Music* (French TV) 'I Feel Free' (*Fresh Live Cream* VHS), 'We're Going Wrong' (unreleased)

14 July 1967: *Joe Loss Show* (BBC radio) 'Tales of Brave Ulysses', 'Take It Back' (unreleased)

24 October 1967: *Top Gear* (BBC radio): 'Born Under a Bad Sign', 'Outside Woman Blues', 'Take It Back', 'Sunshine of Your Love' (included on *BBC Sessions* CD) + 'Tales of Brave Ulysses' (unreleased)

11 November 1967: *Top Pop Show* (Denmark TV) 'NSU', 'Strange Brew', 'I'm So Glad' (unreleased)

21 November 1967: *unknown* (French TV) 'Tales of Brave Ulysses', 'Sunshine Of Your Love', 'Spoonful' (included on *Fresh Live Cream* VHS)

25 November 1967: *Twice a Fortnight* (BBC TV) 'We're Going Wrong' (included on *Fresh Live Cream* VHS)

9 January 1968: *Top Gear* (BBC radio) 'Politician', 'SWLABR', 'Steppin' Out' (included on *BBC Sessions* CD) + 'We're Going Wrong', 'Blue Condition' (unreleased)

7 February 1968: movie *Det Var En Lordag Aften*: 'We're Going Wrong', 'World of Pain' (VHS)

7 March 1968: *All My Loving* (BBC TV) 'I'm So Glad', 'Toad' (included on *Fresh Live Cream* VHS)

17 May 1968: *Summer Brothers Smothers Show* (US TV) 'Anyone for Tennis' (included on *Fresh Live Cream* VHS), 'Sunshine of Your Love' (*Those Were the Days*)

26 November 1968: *Farewell Cream* (BBC TV): 'White Room', 'Politician', 'I'm So Glad', 'Sitting on Top of the World', 'Crossroads', 'Toad', 'Spoonful', 'Sunshine of Your Love' (included on DVD *Farewell Cream*)

LIVE RECORDINGS

7 March 1968: Fillmore Auditorium: 'Rollin' and Tumblin'' (included on *Live Cream*), 'Sunshine of Your Love' (Eric Clapton B-side 1988), 'Toad' (*Wheels of Fire*)

8 March 1968: Winterland, San Francisco: 'Train Time' (included on *Wheels of Fire*), 'Toad' (excerpt included on *Those Were the Days*)

9 March 1968: Winterland, San Francisco: 'NSU' (included on *Those Were the Days*), 'Sleepy Time Time' (*Live Cream*), 'Sunshine of Your Love', 'Steppin' Out' (*Live Cream 2*)

10 March 1968: Winterland, San Francisco: 'Sweet Wine', 'NSU' (*Live Cream*), 'Tales of Brave Ulysses' (*Live Cream 2*), 'Spoonful', 'Crossroads' (*Wheels of Fire*)

4 October 1968: Oakland, CA: 'White Room', 'Politician', 'Deserted Cities of the Heart' (*Live Cream 2*)

19 October 1968: Forum, Los Angeles: 'Politician', 'I'm So Glad', 'Sitting on Top of The World' (included on *Goodbye*)

PART THREE – REACTION LABEL CATALOGUE

SINGLES

591 001 The Who: Substitute/Instant Party
591 001 The Who: Substitute/Waltz for a Pig (the Who Orchestra)
591 002 Paul Dean & The Thoughts: She Can Build a Mountain/ Day Gone By
591 003 Oscar: Club of Light/Waking Up
591 004 The Who: I'm a Boy/In the City
591 005 The Birds: Say Those Magic Words/Daddy Daddy
591 006 Oscar: Join My Gang/Day Gone By
591 007 Cream: Wrapping Paper/Cat's Squirrel
591 008 Lloyd Banks: We'll Meet Again/Look Out Girl
591 009 The Maze: Hello Stranger/Telephone
591 010 The Who: Happy Jack/I've Been Away
591 011 Cream: I Feel Free/NSU
591 012 Oscar: Over the Wall We Go/Every Day of My Life
591 014 Billy J Kramer & The Dakotas: Town of Tuxley Toy Maker/Chinese Girl
591 015 Cream: Strange Brew/Tales of Brave Ulysses
591 016 Oscar: Holiday/Give Her All She Wants
591 017 The Sands: Mrs Gillespie's Refrigerator/Listen to the Sky
591 018 Marian Montgomery: Love Makes Two People Sing/ Monday Thru Sunday

EPs
592 001 The Who: *Ready Steady Who*
592 002 Cream: untitled/unreleased

Mono LPs
593 001 Cream: *Fresh Cream*
593 002 The Who: *A Quick One While He's Away*
593 003 Cream: *Disraeli Gears*

Stereo LPs
594 001 Cream: *Fresh Cream*
594 003 Cream: *Disraeli Gears*

INDEX

Adler, Danny 97
Alan Brown Set 127, 128
Allison, Mose 51
All My Loving (Palmer) 234–5
Alpert, Herb 221
Altham, Keith 226–7
American Civil Rights movement 85–6, 203, 206
American Folk Blues Festival 1963 33, 37, 83
Angel, Jorgen 136
Animals, The 61, 100, 105, 108
'Anyone for Tennis' 160, 193, 194, 215–16, 224
Apple Records 225
'As You Said' 197, 220–1
Atco 130
Atlantic Records 4, 84, 130, 146, 150, 151, 152, 183, 185, 191, 199, 200, 203, 215, 233
Auger, Brian 21, 37, 44, 55, 109, 148, 170, 212, 217, 225, 244

Baez, Joan 61
'Badge' 6, 232, 238
Bag O'Nails 117, 162
Baker, Ginger 1, 109

Baker-Gurvitz Army 243; Blues Incorporated, member of 14, 19, 20, 47; Bob Wallis's Storyville Jazzmen, member of 17–18; Bruce, relationship with 19, 57–8, 73, 77–8, 80, 124, 125, 155, 161, 195; Clapton, relationship with 51–2, 76, 91, 97, 114, 124, 125, 155, 195, 212; *Coward of the County* 243; Cream compositions 93, 103, 104, 192, 193, 197, 218; Cream management, relationship with 132, 200; Cream sound, comments upon 92; Cream split, part in 210, 226; Cream studio and live sounds, on difference between 116; Cream, contribution to sound of 142, 153, 177, 178, 194, 207, 224; Cream, suffers exhaustion on tour with 190–1, 208; Cream, forms 76–80, 82, 86–7; Cream, sacked and reinstated from 125, 126; early life 15, 17–18; *Farewell Cream*, involvement in 235, 236; *Ginger Baker in Africa* 236; Ginger Baker's Airforce 242, 245; *Going Back Home*

243; Graham Bond Organisation, member of 18–19, 48, 51, 52, 55, 56–8, 72, 73, 76, 80; *Horses & Trees* 243; image 133, 142, 149; Ken Oldham Showband, member of 18; money, worries about 169, 206; musical talent 17, 19, 142, 147 *see also* Cream compositions; Pete Brown, relationship with 100, 101, 102, 103, 192, 193; politics 205; post-Cream career 236, 242–3; solos 98, 99, 176; *Stratavarious* 243; *Unseen Rain* 243

Baldry, John 12, 13, 29–30, 34, 35, 50, 51, 54

Ball, Kenny 25

Balling, Erik 195

Band, The 5, 211–12, 213–14, 215, 218, 224, 237

Bandbeat 114–15

Banks, Pete 233

Barbecue 67 165–6, 174

Barber, Chris 25

Barrata, Paul 180

Barrett, Syd 117, 135, 159, 169

Barsalona, Frank 140

Barton, Cliff 76

Basement Tapes (Dylan) 212–13

BBC 12, 16, 17, 21, 28–9, 51, 71, 85, 87, 98, 103, 112–13, 114, 115, 123, 124, 129, 151, 157, 159, 169, 190, 198, 234

BBM 239, 243, 247

Beach Boys 86, 149, 166, 239

Beat Club 157–8

Beatles, The 3, 31, 39, 43–4, 56, 86, 89, 95, 117, 120, 124, 130, 131, 133, 135, 148, 152, 166–7, 169, 181, 183, 187–8, 189, 198–9, 217, 224–5, 226, 239, 258

Beck, Jeff 5, 32, 45, 70, 76–7, 88–9, 110–11, 120, 122, 134, 147, 170, 171, 186, 187, 190, 219–20, 221, 233, 246

Beck, Ronnie 44

Bee Gees 131–2, 133, 168, 258

Bell, Simon Napier 54, 74

Bernstein, Leonard 231

Berry, Chuck 29, 36, 39–40, 44, 54, 57, 73, 81

Best of Cream 238

Beuselinck, Oscar 90

Beuselinck, Paul 90

Big Brother 180

Blackmore, Ritchie 32, 229

Blackwell, Chris 50, 52–3

Blind Faith 237, 238, 242, 246, 249

Bloomfield Band 82

'Blue Condition' 155, 186, 198

Blue Horizon 65, 66, 170

Blues and Barrelhouse 12–13

Blues Incorporated 2, 13–14, 15, 16, 19–20, 21–2, 23, 30, 55, 67, 96–7, 260

Bluesbreakers 26–7, 38–44, 60–2, 63, 65, 67, 71, 77–8, 79, 87, 88, 105, 108, 111, 121, 125, 143, 149, 153, 167, 169–70, 171, 178, 180, 209, 214, 243, 251, 255

Bluesbreakers with Eric Clapton 67, 180, 218

Bolan, Marc 3, 134

Bond, Graham 18–19, 20, 47, 48, 50, 51, 56–7, 69, 70, 72, 82, 101, 124, 133, 143, 162, 242, 243–5, 246, 260

Bonzo Dog Doo Dah Band 102, 103, 134, 189

Booker T 152, 167–8

Bowie, David 6, 90, 159

Boyd, Eddie 67

Boyd, Joe 81, 159

Boyle, Mark 101

Brennan, Terry 31

Brian Auger Trinity 37, 212

Brock, Dave 30–1, 243

Bron, Gerry 102

Brown, Joe 48

Brown, Pete 57–8, 100–2, 103, 113, 116, 126, 135, 146, 149, 161, 174, 192, 197, 232, 244, 245–6, 252

Brown, Ricky 36

Bruce, Jack 1, 6, 99
Baker, relationship with 19, 57–8, 73, 77–8, 80, 124, 155, 161, 206, 208; Blind Faith, member of 246; Blues Incorporated, member of 14–15, 17–18, 19, 20, 22; Bluesbreakers, member of 63, 64–5, 69, 70–2, 73; Clapton, relationship with 51–2, 63, 64–5, 98, 114, 155, 156, 206; Clapton's perm, remembers reasons for 122; Cream live, thoughts on 3–4, 141, 151, 152, 201; Cream Saville Theatre debut, remembers 134; Cream sound,

comments on 92, 113, 176; Cream split, thoughts on 207–8, 210, 223; Cream, becomes lead singer 82–3, 87, 89; Cream, joins 78–9, 81, 87; Cream, thoughts on timing of break up 2–3; Cream, songwriting in 78, 93, 102, 103, 116, 125–6, 146, 156, 160, 167, 182, 193, 197; Cream's influence on others, remembers 179–80, 181; *Disraeli Gears*, defends 187; English live circuit, remembers sixties 95; exhaustion, suffers during Cream tours 207–8; Experience and Cream rivalry, denies 121; *Farewell Cream*, involvement in 235–6; Graham Bond Organisation, member of 47, 50, 51–2, 54, 56, 57, 58–9, 78; Hendrix, on first hearing of 109, 111, 113; image 133, 149; Jack Bruce & Friends 239; jailed 229, 230; Jim McHarg Scotsville Jazz Band, member of 16–17; LSD experience 145; Manfred Mann, member of 69–72; Murray Campbell Big Band, member of 15–16; musical talent *see also* Cream compositions 50, 55, 57–8, 63, 64–5, 97, 98, 102; nervousness, remembers 97; Pete Brown, relationship with 102, 103; politics 205; post–Cream career 156, 182, 228, 232, 237, 246–8; *Rope Ladder to the Moon* 236; *Songs For a Tailor* 156, 182, 228, 232, 237, 247; *Things We Like* 227–8

Brunswick Records 75
Buffalo Springfield 204–5
Burch, Johnny 19, 20
Burdon, Eric 13, 61, 71–2, 88, 108
Burford, Pete 70

Café Au Go Go 182
Calder, Tony 61, 62
Capitol Theatre, Ottawa 208
'Cats Squirrel' 6, 79–80, 112, 116
Cellar Club 99
Chamberlain, Harry 56
Chandler, Chas 105, 108, 109–10, 119–20, 121, 122, 168

Charles, Ray 52, 57
Chess Studios 33, 93
Chicken Shack 126, 171
Clapton, Eric 1
    arrested in America 204–5; Baker and Bruce, first meets 51–2; Baker, relationship with 51–2, 78, 80, 124–6, 159, 195, 206; *Blues Anytime* 61–2, 76; blues, love of 30–1, 57, 91, 114, 136, 178, 218; Bluesbreakers, member of 45, 59–65, 66–8, 87, 88, 89; Bruce, relationship with 51–2, 62–3, 65, 78, 80, 124–6, 157, 159, 195, 206; Bruce's gig nerves, remembers 97; Cream gigs, first 83, 96; Cream management, relationship with 162, 200; Cream sound, comments on 98, 113; Cream sound, influence upon 91–2, 146, 149, 150, 151, 152, 153, 154–5, 207; Cream split, involvement in 210, 223–4, 240–1; Cream, ambitions for 80–1; Cream, comes up with name 89; Cream, joins 78, 79, 82; Cream, on American popularity of 180; *Disraeli Gears*, opinion of 186, 187; Dylan and The Band, influence upon 212–15, 217, 218–19; early influences 28–30; early life 28–30; fame 27, 99, 105, 113, 231; *Farewell Cream*, disgusted with 235; Fillmore, on first gig at 175, 177; *461 Ocean Boulevard* 60, 250, 257–8; George Harrison, friendship with 224–6, 232; Grateful Dead, dislikes 179; groupies, comments on the pleasure of 144; guitar genius 3, 27, 83, 84, 114–15, 169, 171, 175–6, 178, 197, 218 *see also* Hendrix, relationship with; Hendrix, relationship with 4, 108–12, 120, 121–2, 129, 133, 134, 219–20; image 202, 204–5; Kingston Art College 29; LSD experiences 179; *Pet Sounds*, compliments 166–7; Pink Floyd fan 135; politics 205; post–Cream career 60, 237, 238, 239, 249–51; Rhode Island Red and the Roosters 31, 70, 77; singles, loses

enthusiasm for format of 189–90;
Slowhand 28, 35; songwriting 153,
192, 193, 198; *There's One in Every
Crowd* 51; 'While My Guitar Gently
Weeps', involvement in 225–6;
Yardbirds, member of 27, 31–2, 33,
34, 37, 38, 43, 44, 45
Clapton, Patricia 28
Clapton, Rose 28
Coleman, Cy 52
Coleman, James 52
Collins, Gail 151
Columbia Records 39, 43, 54, 74
Connover, Willis 24
Cooks Ferry Inn, Edmonton 98–9
Cornyn, Stan 84
Coryell, Larry 180
Crawdaddy 186, 191, 218
Crawdaddy Club 31, 32, 33, 34, 36, 37, 44
Crazy Blue 170–1
Crazy World of Arthur Brown 126, 134, 157,
171, 216–17, 227
Cream: The Legendary Sixties Super–group
215
'Crossroads' 115, 141, 228, 236
Crosstown Bus Club 181–2

D'Abo, Mike 89
Daltrey, Roger 77, 86, 163, 226
'Dance The Night Away' 186
Danko, Rick 213
David, Clifford 170
Davies, Cyril 12–13, 16, 17, 19–20, 23, 24, 25,
32, 36, 38, 49, 51, 56, 76, 82
Davis, Billie 53–4
Davis, Miles 6
Dean, Jenny 154
Dean, Roger 41, 45, 59
Decca 13, 21, 22, 39, 40, 42, 43, 47, 48, 49,
50, 61, 65, 66–7, 115, 225
Decca Rhythm & Blues 49
Dee Time 157–8
Deep Purple 136, 229, 252
Derek and the Dominos 249
'Deserted Cities of the Heart' 197, 221
Disley, Dis 18
Disraeli Gears 167, 169, 185, 186, 187–8, 191,
195, 199, 206, 221, 256
Dixon, Willie 33, 34, 81, 116

Dobbs, Baby 18
Dobson, Lyn 70
'Doing That Scrapyard Thing' 232
Don Rendell Jazz Band 19
Don't Look Back 61
Donovan 61, 133, 162, 171, 229–30
Donovan, John 207
Doors, The 179, 221, 228, 239
Double Giant Freak–Out Ball 126–7
Dowd, Tom 150–3, 154, 183, 191, 200, 201,
220, 222
Down Beat 30
Downliner Sect, The 32
Dreja, Chris 27, 31, 32, 44
Driscoll, Julie 212, 217
Dudgeon, Gus 68
Dunbar, Aynsley 108, 170, 171
Dupree, Jack 67
Dylan, Bob 3, 5, 60–1, 69, 80, 86, 122, 137,
173, 187, 202, 211–14, 215, 225, 230, 239

Ealing R&B Club 13, 15
Eel Pie Island 26, 32
Electric Flag 82, 177, 180, 181
Elektra Records 81
EMI 48, 52, 53, 54, 73–4, 188
Entwistle, John 76, 77, 141, 143, 162
Epstein, Brian 43, 131, 133
Ertegun, Ahmet 84, 130, 136–8, 146, 150,
152, 153–4, 167, 169, 233
Etchingham, Kathy 110, 121

Fabulous Publishing 90
Fairport Convention 212
Faithfull, Marianne 61, 133
Falana, Mike 72
Fame, Georgie 21, 48, 51, 55, 73, 92, 96, 114
Farewell Cream 234, 235–6, 238
Farlowe, Chris 61
Farr, Gary 35, 92
Fela Ransome Kuti & Ginger Baker Live 242
Fiddler, John 129–30
Fillmore Auditorium 173–7, 183, 194, 199,
234
Finch, Barry 133
First Festival of Pop Music 166
First Real Poetry Band 161, 198, 245
Five Live Yardbirds 40, 43, 45, 51
Flamingo 21, 22, 64, 87, 99, 100, 198, 209

Fleetwood Mac 26, 36, 170, 171, 252
Flint, Hughie 25, 41, 42, 59, 68, 87, 88
Fontana Records 81
Fool, The 132–3, 168, 244
'For Your Love' (Gouldman) 43–5
14-Hour Technicolor Dream 127, 159
Frampton, Peter 105, 226, 254, 258
Franklin, Aretha 150, 183
Fresh Cream 111–12, 116–17, 124, 125, 130, 136–8, 142, 155, 167–8, 185, 186, 188, 199, 218
Fryer, Edward 28
Furay, Ritchie 204

Gallagher, Rory 6, 233
Gary Burton Band 180–1
Gaye, Marvin 50
Gee, John 226
Geno Washington 127, 149, 165
Gibson, Brian 226
Gilbey, John 63
Gillan, Ian 32
Godfrey, Janet 73, 103–4, 114
Gomelsky, Giorgio 32, 34, 35, 37, 38, 39, 44, 66, 74, 212
Gonks Go Beat 50, 56
Goodbye 232, 238
Good Good Band 35
Good Time Music 81–2
Gouldman, Graham 43, 44, 86
Graham Bond Organisation 18–19, 49–52, 54–6, 57, 58, 63, 65, 58–9, 63, 69, 71, 72, 73, 75–6, 78, 83, 87, 93, 96, 100, 125, 152, 156, 243, 251
Graham Bond Trio 20, 21, 22, 23, 47, 48
Graham, Bill 173, 174, 178, 199–200
Graham, Davy 26
Grand Funk Railroad 219
Grateful Dead 137, 177, 178, 179, 180, 221
Green, Peter 63–4, 87, 88–9, 111, 148, 167, 169, 170, 171
Gunnell, John 21, 25, 99–100, 170
Gunnell, Rik 21, 25, 26, 61, 77, 99–100, 170
Gurvitz, Adrian 243
Gurvitz, Paul 243
Guy, Buddy 83, 93, 135, 170

Halverson, Bill 200, 201, 228
Harpo, Slim 36

Harrison, George 86, 224, 225–6, 232–3, 249
Harrison, Patti 249
Havens, Richie 197
Hawkins, Ronnie 211
Hawks, The 211–12
Hawkwind 243
He Miss Road 242–3
Heatley, Spike 13
Heckstall–Smith, Dick 13–15, 16, 17, 18, 19, 20, 21, 49, 50, 57, 58, 72, 101, 125, 209, 227, 228, 232, 238, 243, 245, 246, 251–3, 254
Hell's Angels 179, 193
Hendrix, Jimi 3, 5, 107–9, 110, 111–12, 114, 119–22, 123–4, 126–7, 129, 134, 149, 153, 155, 157, 159, 162, 163, 165–6, 168, 169, 175, 187, 202, 214, 217, 218–19, 228, 247
Herd, The 105, 154
'Hey Now Princess' 146, 156
Hiseman, Jon 125, 192–3, 227, 238, 243, 251–2, 254
Hollies, The 112, 133
Hoogenboom, Andy 13
Hooker, John Lee 11, 33, 39, 148
Hopkins, Nicky 76
Horowitz, Michael 101
Hyde, David 70

'I Feel Free' 6, 116–17, 122, 123–4, 130, 135, 142, 149, 157, 159, 160–1, 166, 167, 168, 175, 186, 218
'I'm So Glad' 6, 141, 148, 167, 175, 234–5, 236
Immediate Records 61, 62, 90
Innes, Neil 102
International Times 126, 174
In the Studio 221
Island Records 50

Jagger, Mick 11, 12, 13, 16, 17, 30, 34, 35, 38, 61, 108, 120, 187, 214
James, Etta 52, 239
James, Skip 91, 93, 116, 175
Jazz Club 21
Jazz Gehört und Gehesen (Jazz Heard and Seen) 33
Jeff Beck Group 5, 148, 149, 167, 170, 188, 219
Jefferson Airplane 3, 137, 163, 173, 177, 178–9, 182, 221, 244

Jeffrey, Mike 108, 123
Jimi Hendrix Experience 5, 111, 119, 121, 126–7, 153, 244
John Mayall Plays John Mayall 42
Johnny Burch Octet 20, 21, 72
Johnson, Lonnie 34
Johnson, Robert 30, 81, 91, 92, 116, 125, 128, 250
Jones Brian 13, 27, 34, 64, 214, 254
Jones, Nick 186, 202
Jones, Paul 13, 70, 76, 81, 89, 254
Jones, RG 39
Jones, Ronnie 35
Joplin, Janis 163

Kaufman, Murray 'the K' 139, 140, 141, 142, 143, 144, 145, 149, 162, 163
Kaukonen, Jorma 178
Keene, John 'Speedy' 90
Keith, Linda 108, 109
King, Albert 135, 158, 168
King, BB 135, 144
King, Dr Martin Luther 203, 206
Kinks, The 72, 74, 86, 123, 130, 188, 190, 240
Kirk, Roland 25
Klook's Kleek 19, 26, 42, 43, 48, 49, 67, 96, 115, 189, 251
Kogel, Holm 160–1
Komlosy, Stephen 52
Kooper, Al 81, 141, 144, 154
Korner, Alexis 2, 12–13, 14, 16, 17, 19, 20, 21, 22, 23, 24, 25–6, 31, 42–3, 49, 114, 190–1, 252–4, 259–60
Kral, Ivan 142, 145
Kramer, Billy J 131
Kuti, Fela Ransome 236, 242

La Locomotive Club 124
Laing, Corky 144, 206, 231, 247, 256
Lambert, Kit 74–5, 76, 120, 122, 157, 162
Landau, Jon 217, 218
'Lawdy Mama' 93, 115, 146, 147, 151
Led Zeppelin 4, 6, 197, 219, 254
Lennon, John 167, 237
Lewisohn, Mark 226
Leyton, John 52–3
Lightfoot, Terry 18
Lipenhoff, David 212

Lippman, Horst 33–4, 37
Lisburg, Harvey 43–4
Little Richard 105
Little, Carlo 76
Live at the Fillmore 221
Live Cream 238
Lloyd, Richard 49
Lomax, Alan 55
Lord, Jon 229
Lowther, Henry 70
LSD 145, 157, 179

Manfred Mann 12, 31, 35, 39, 51, 64, 69, 70–1, 72, 78–9, 81, 87, 89, 92, 102, 112, 212
Mardin, Arif 151
Marquee Club 13–14, 19, 20, 25, 35, 40, 48, 51, 57, 71–2, 79, 99, 101, 105, 117, 126, 159, 165, 190, 200
Martin, Charlotte 154
Mason, Nick 135
Mason, Robin 31
Masters of Reality 243
Masters, Robert 96
Matthews, Brian 113
May, Phil 11, 12
Mayall, John 23, 24–7, 31, 34, 38, 40, 41–3, 45, 47, 48, 59–63, 64–5, 66–7, 68, 70, 71, 77, 81, 82, 87, 88, 89, 92, 96, 114, 137, 148–9, 167, 170, 171, 177, 180, 209, 250, 251, 252, 254–6
Mayall, Pamela 23
Mayfair 133
MC5 194
McCartney, Linda 154
McCartney, Paul 131, 137, 154, 163, 167, 226, 230, 243
McCarty, Jim 27, 34, 36
McCulloch, Derek 'Uncle Mac' 28–9
McGhee, Brownie 29, 33, 93
McGuinn, Roger 142
McGuinness, Tom 11, 12, 31, 70, 71
McLaughlin, John 13, 47, 48, 49, 161, 227, 245, 247
McPhee, Tony 67
McVie, John 26, 59, 62–3, 64, 87, 88, 170
Meek, Joe 52–3
'Meet Me in the Bottom' 115
Mellotron 56–7

Melody Maker 15, 25, 30, 49, 51, 57, 67–8, 70, 76, 78, 82, 86, 87, 89, 99, 127, 128, 132, 156, 159, 166, 167, 169, 171, 174, 180, 186, 189, 202, 214, 215, 222, 223, 225, 228
Memphis Slim 33, 34, 51, 81
Messina, Jim 204–5
Michaels, Kevin 99
Miles, Buddy 144
Miller, Aleck 'Rice' 36
Million Dollar Quartet 2
Mitchell, Adrian 101
Mitchell, Mitch 108, 111, 225, 237, 244
Mockingbirds 43, 44
Moist Hoist 13
Mojo 67
Monkees, The 163, 167
Monterey Pop Festival 5, 162–3, 169, 178
Moody Blues, The 126
Moon, Keith 76, 77, 94, 143, 161
Moore, Gary 239, 247
Morrison, Van 239
'Mother's Lament' 156
Mothers of Invention 144
Move, The 92, 105, 117, 126, 127, 128, 157, 162, 171
MTV 234
Muddy Waters 12, 20, 26, 30, 34, 55, 60, 114, 116, 128, 139, 148
Music from the Big Pink (Dylan and the Band) 213, 218–19

National Jazz and Blues Festival, Windsor 1966 34, 57, 89, 92, 95, 171, 226
NEMS 43, 131, 132–4
Neville, Richard 154, 159, 220
New Departures 101
New Musical Express 44, 55, 57, 95, 113, 149, 160, 168, 209, 222, 226, 237
Pollwinners Concert 149
Nice 20, 247
Nicholas, Paul 90
Nolan, Kevin 37–8
'NSU' 92, 115, 116, 167, 218

O'Neill, Mike 108
O'Rahilly, Ronan 47, 52
Oldham, Andrew Loog 32, 38–9, 61, 65, 74, 163
100 Club 159, 228

Omnibus 235–6
Outa-Site 65–6
'Outside Woman Blues' 155
Oz 154, 187

Page One 74
Page, Jimmy 2, 32, 34, 61, 62, 76, 90, 111
Page, Larry 74
Paige, Brian 219
Palmer, Ben 31, 77, 81, 92, 97, 99, 110, 140, 145, 235–6, 238, 242
Palmer, Tony 98, 190, 233–4
Pappalardi, Felix 150, 151, 152, 153, 155, 167–8, 186, 191, 194, 228, 231, 256
Parlophone 48, 49, 74
Parsons, Steve 'Snips' 243
'Passing Time' 220
Paul Butterfield Blues Band 81, 93, 137, 163, 177, 180
Peel, John 159, 190, 244
Pendleton, Harold 34
Pennebaker, DA 61, 178
Perfumed Garden 158
Pet Sounds (Beach Boys) 166
Pickett, Wilson 84
Pink Floyd 117, 127, 128, 130, 134–5, 153, 157, 159, 165, 188, 234
Plant, Robert 4, 130, 254
'Plastic Eye' 182
'Politician' 197, 198, 221, 236
Polydor 71, 73–4, 75, 123, 125, 131, 132, 216, 221, 228, 243
Pool, Malcolm 67
Porteus, Brice 98
Power, Duffy 48, 49, 50, 254, 260
Powerhouse Four 24, 81–2
Prager, Bud 151
Presley, Elvis 2
'Pressed Rat and Warthog' 192, 193, 221
Pretty Things 12, 148, 188
Primal Solos 87
Procol Harum 133, 175
Psychedelic Supermarket 181
Public Image Limited 243
Purdah 65, 66, 98

Q Magazine 94

R&B Monthly 35, 65

Radio Caroline 52, 86, 123, 157
Radio London 112–13, 123, 159
Radio One 190
Ram Jam Band 127, 149
Ram Jam Club 99–100, 166
Ranglin, Ernest 50
Rau, Fritz 33
Reaction 74, 77, 89, 90, 104–5, 112–13, 123, 132, 134, 216, 229
Reading Rock Festival 51
Ready Steady Go 39, 57, 112, 120–1, 130
Record Mirror 57, 88, 115–16
Record Star Show 149
Redding, Noel 108, 111, 159, 217
Redding, Otis 148, 150, 152, 163
Reece, Red 73
Regan, John 226
Relf, Keith 27, 31, 35, 38, 39, 250
Rennie, Roland 74
Revolution Club 190
Reynolds, Blind Willie 30
Richard, Keith 11, 12, 34, 64, 214–15, 237, 254
Ricky Tick Club 25–6, 35, 88, 100, 147, 198, 251
Rifbjerg, Klaus 195
RKO Theatre 139–42
Roach, Max 18
Robert Stigwood Organisation (RSO) 73–4, 90, 159, 162, 258
Robertson, Robbie 211, 213
Rock and Roll Hall of Fame 238, 239
'Rollin' and Tumblin' 114
Rolling Stone 37, 110, 135, 151, 177, 179, 180, 186, 187, 191–2, 202, 206, 217, 218, 221, 236
Rolling Stones, The 11, 12, 13, 16, 27, 31, 32, 38, 44, 48, 51, 61, 86, 90, 95, 117, 125, 137, 169, 183, 189, 214, 215, 217, 237, 247, 254, 255
Rollins, Sonny 48
Ronnie Scott's 21, 117
Ronson, Mick 6
Ross, Doctor 79
Rowlands, Steve 105
Rundgren, Todd 186
Ryder, Mitch 140, 141, 144
Ryemuse Studios 104, 146, 152

Sabina, Mariá 229–30

Samwell-Smith, Paul 27, 36, 44
Santa Monica Civic Auditorium 198
Sarne, Mike 53–4
Sarns, Chris 205
Saturday Club 103, 124, 129, 157, 198
Savage Seven, The 193–5
Saville Theatre 134, 189–90
Savoy Brown Blues Band 98–9, 126
Scene 51 47
Scotch of St James 117, 120, 162
Scott, Keith 13
Scott, Simon 53
Screaming Lord Sutch 26, 41, 90, 229
Seaman, Phil 18–19, 99, 226, 242
Secunda, Tony 54, 117, 126, 127, 162
Sgt Pepper (Beatles) 166–7, 188
Shankar, Ravi 86, 163
Shapiro, Harry 22, 49, 57, 73
Sharp, Martin 153–4, 182, 187, 193, 220, 256–7
'She Walks Like a Bearded Rainbow' 146, 155, 167, 198
Shippen, Ian 147
Simmons, Kim 98
Simper, Nick 32
'Sitting on Top of the World' 147, 192, 222, 236
Skaggs, Joey 144
Slaven, Neil 35
'Sleepy Time Time' 103–4, 114, 115, 116
Small Faces 90, 92, 117, 157, 171, 190
Smart, Harold 20
Smith, Bessie 30, 54
Smith, Legs Larry 102–3
Son House 92
Spector, Phil 86, 151, 193
Spencer Davis Group 55, 81, 86, 92, 114, 126
Spivey, Victoria 34
'Spoonful' 6, 114, 115, 117, 130, 141, 148, 185, 236
Spot 104
Springer, Axel 217
Stamp, Chris 74–5, 76, 120, 145, 157, 162
Stanley III, Augustus Owsley 179
Stanshall, Viv 102
Starr, Ringo 225, 248
Stax Records 148
'Steppin' Out' 198, 236
Stevens, Dave 17

Stevens, John 71
Stevens, Linda 204
Stewart, Ian 62
Stewart, Rod 35, 148, 153, 170
Stigwood, Robert 52, 53, 54, 55, 71, 73–5, 76,
    82–3, 84, 89, 96, 104, 117, 130–1, 132,
    133, 136, 138, 140, 145–6, 157, 160, 161,
    162, 163, 167, 168, 174, 180, 191, 192, 199,
    200, 208, 209, 214, 216, 222, 223, 227,
    229, 233, 249, 257–8
Stills, Stephen 204
Strange Brew 238
'Strange Brew' 151, 157, 159, 163, 175, 256
Studio 51 34
Sullivan, Big Jim 13
Sumlin, Hubert 65
Summer Brothers Smother Show, The 216
Sun Records 79
'Sunshine of Your Love' 6, 147, 152–3, 155,
    185, 198, 199, 216, 221, 236, 250
Swallow, Steve 180–1
'Sweet Wine' 103, 112, 114, 115, 116, 218

Talmy, Shel 74–5, 89
'Take It Back' 154, 160
'Tales of Brave Ulysees' 153–5, 157, 159–60
Taylor, Mick 167, 214, 254, 255
Taylor, Mike 73, 192–3, 258, 247, 258
Terry, Sonny 29, 33
Tex, Joe 92
'The Clear-Out' 155, 156
'Theme From an Imaginary Western' 6,
    156
Those Were the Days 238
'Those Were the Days' 197
Timperley, John 104, 152
'Toad' 93, 116, 176, 218, 221, 228, 234–5, 236
Top Gear 198, 244
Top of the Pops 129, 234
Top Rank 53, 190
Topham, Tony 'Top' 31–2, 33
Tormé, Bernie 83, 129
Townshend, Pete 75, 77, 90, 111, 120, 128,
    129, 134, 137, 143, 159, 179, 189, 230,
    240–1
Track Records 120, 122–3, 157
Traffic 133–4, 237
'Train Time' 141, 228
Triumph Records 52, 53

Trynka, Paul 67
Turner, Mick 92
Twice a Fortnight 191
Twisted Wheel 92–3, 231

UFO Club 126–7
Uncut 179, 214
USA 139–46, 173–83, 197–210, 215, 223–31

Valentine, Elmer 180, 181
Vanilla Fudge 168, 199, 221
Velvet Underground 207
Vernon, Mike 35, 38, 39, 40, 42, 47, 49, 51,
    65–6, 88, 98, 170, 225
Vernon, Richard 35
Vickers, Mike 70
Vietnam 85–6, 160, 202–3, 217
Village Theatre 182
Voorman, Klaus 89

Walker, Dave 36–7, 126
Walker, T Bone 33
Waller, Micky 32
Walter, Little 60
Ward, Peter 24, 25, 26, 41
Warner Brothers 84
Waters, Roger 135
Watson, Bernie 26, 40–1
Watts, Charlie 13, 17, 19, 254
'We're Going Wrong' 155, 166, 186, 190,
    195, 198
'Weird of Hermiston' 146, 156
Welch, Chris 86–7, 92, 116, 215, 222
Wenner, Jan 180, 217
West, Leslie 231
'What a Bringdown' 232
What's Shakin' 93
Wheels of Fire 219–21, 224, 228, 231, 256–7,
    258
Whiskey A Go Go 180, 181
'White Room' 6, 135, 167, 169, 192, 221–2,
    228, 236, 237
Whittaker, Bob 187
Who, The 5, 74, 75–6, 77, 86, 92, 104, 105,
    113, 116, 123, 128, 130, 133, 139, 140, 141,
    143, 145, 148, 149, 161, 162, 163, 175, 181,
    188, 189, 190, 199, 228, 240
Wilde, Marty 48
Williams, Dave 34

Williams, Larry 35, 66
Williamson II, Sonny Boy 34, 36–8, 39, 40,
    51, 65, 81, 139, 260
Wilson, Tom 61
Wings 243
Winston G 54, 57
Winterland 199–200, 234
Winwood, Steve 55, 81, 82, 83, 86, 100,
    133–4, 214, 237, 242, 249
Witherspoon, Jimmy 51
Wolf, 'Howlin' 30, 36, 65, 93, 109–10, 139
Wood, Art 13, 16
Wood, Philip 'the Spaniel' 40
'World of Pain' 155, 195
'Wrapping Paper' 104–5, 112–14, 149, 175

Wyman, Bill 62, 214

Yardbirds 11, 27, 31–2, 34–40, 42–5, 48, 51,
    54, 59–60, 62, 66, 70, 74, 76, 88–9, 98,
    100, 110, 111, 113, 114, 117, 121, 143, 153,
    168, 189, 195, 200, 220, 224, 229, 239,
    250, 260
Yes 233
York, Pete 81
'You Make Me Feel Like a Hat Stand' 100
Young, Neil 204
Yule, Doug 207

Zappa, Frank 144, 172, 183, 234
Zoot Money 114, 165, 171, 254